ORTHODOX IDENTITIES IN WESTERN EUROPE

Orthodox Identities in Western Europe

Migration, Settlement and Innovation

Edited by

MARIA HÄMMERLI
University of Fribourg, Switzerland

JEAN-FRANÇOIS MAYER
Institut Religioscope, Switzerland

LONDON AND NEW YORK

First published 2014 by Ashgate Publishing

Published 2016 by Routledge
2 Park Square, Milton Park, Abingdon, Oxon OX14 4RN
711 Third Avenue, New York, NY 10017, USA

Routledge is an imprint of the Taylor & Francis Group, an informa business

Copyright © 2014 Maria Hämmerli and Jean-François Mayer

Maria Hämmerli and Jean-François Mayer have asserted their right under the Copyright, Designs and Patents Act, 1988, to be identified as the editors of this work.

All rights reserved. No part of this book may be reprinted or reproduced or utilised in any form or by any electronic, mechanical, or other means, now known or hereafter invented, including photocopying and recording, or in any information storage or retrieval system, without permission in writing from the publishers.

Notice:

Product or corporate names may be trademarks or registered trademarks, and are used only for identification and explanation without intent to infringe.

British Library Cataloguing in Publication Data
A catalogue record for this book is available from the British Library

The Library of Congress has cataloged the printed edition as follows:
Orthodox Identities in Western Europe: Migration, Settlement, and Innovation / edited by
    Maria Hämmerli and Jean-François Mayer.
        pages   cm
    Includes bibliographical references and index.
    1. Orthodox Eastern Church members – Europe, Western. 2. Identity (Religion)
    3. Group identity. I. Hämmerli, Maria, editor of compilation. II. Mayer, Jean-François,
    editor of compilation.
    BX250.O65 2014
    281.9'4–dc23   2014000529

ISBN 9781409467540 (hbk)

Contents

List of Figures	*vii*
List of Tables	*ix*
List of Contributors	*xi*

Introduction   1
Maria Hämmerli and Jean-François Mayer

PART I: MIGRATION AND SETTLEMENT

1   Romanian Orthodox Churches in Italy: The Construction of the
Romanian–Italian Transnational Orthodox Space   29
Suna Gülfer Ihlamur-Öner

2   The Myth of an Ideal Leader: The Case of the Syriac Orthodox
Community in Europe   51
Naures Atto

3   The Transformation of Social Capital among Assyrians in the
Migration Context   67
Soner Onder Barthoma

4   Orthodox Churches in Germany: From Migrant Groups to
Permanent Homeland   89
Reinhard Thöle

5   The Ambivalent Ecumenical Relations among Russian Orthodox
Faithful in Germany   99
Sebastian Rimestad and Ernest Kadotschnikow

6   How do Orthodox Integrate in their Host Countries? Examples
from Switzerland   115
Maria Hämmerli

7   The Orthodox Churches in the United Kingdom   133
Hugh Wybrew

8	Population Movements and Orthodox Christianity in Finland: Dislocations, Resettlements, Migrations and Identities *Tuomas Martikainen and Teuvo Laitila*	151
9	Orthodox Parishes in Strasbourg: Between Migration and Integration *Guillaume Keller*	179
10	Orthodox Priests in Norway: Serving or Ruling? *Berit Thorbjørnsrud*	191

PART II: INNOVATION

11	Not Just Caviar and Balalaikas: Unity and Division in Russian Orthodox Congregations in Denmark *Annika Hvithamar*	213
12	Mediating Orthodoxy: Convert Agency and Discursive Autochthonism in Ireland *James A. Kapaló*	229
13	The Great Athonite Tradition in France: Circulation of Athonite Imaginaries and the Emergence of a French Style of Orthodoxy *Laurent Denizeau*	251
14	'We are Westerners and Must Remain Westerners': Orthodoxy and Western Rites in Western Europe *Jean-François Mayer*	267
15	Innovation in the Russian Orthodox Church: The Crisis in the Diocese of Sourozh in Britain *Maria Hämmerli and Edmund Mucha*	291

Index	*303*

List of Figures

3.1	Relationships between different forms of social capital	69
3.2	Membership	73
3.3	Participation in national elections	76
3.4	Participation in national elections and educational level	77
3.5	Voting attitudes and membership of an organisation	77
3.6	I can trust a community member	78
3.7	Individualist and collectivist attitudes	81
3.8	Frequency of going to church	84
8.1	Membership in the Orthodox Church of Finland 1945–2012	163

List of Tables

8.1	Russian and Karelian refugees in Finland 1918–1938	158
8.2	Registered members and the share of foreign-born members in the Orthodox Church of Finland and the Russian Orthodox Church parishes from 1990 to 2009	166
8.3	Members by registered language in the Orthodox Church of Finland and the Russian Orthodox Church parishes in Finland in 2008	167
8.4	Registered members in the Orthodox Church of Finland and the Russian Orthodox Church parishes by country of birth in Finland in 2009, as a percentage	168

List of Contributors

Naures Atto is a Mellon Postdoctoral Fellow in World Christianities at the Faculty of Divinity, University of Cambridge. She is a College Research Associate at Wolfson College and affiliated with the Department of Social Anthropology. Atto is author of *Hostages in the Homeland, Orphans in the Diaspora: Identity Discourses of Assyrian/Syriac Elites in the European Diaspora* (Leiden, 2011).

Laurent Denizeau is an anthropologist and teaches at the Catholic University of Lyon, France. His main research areas deal with religion (Orthodox monastic life, experience of belief) and body (pain, quest of healing).

Maria Hämmerli is a PhD candidate at the University of Fribourg, Switzerland. Her main research interest is the migration and integration of Orthodox communities in Western Europe (with a special focus on Switzerland). Her publications discuss Orthodoxy in a migration context related to issues such as secularisation, ethnicity and culture, diaspora, and monasticism.

Annika Hvithamar is Associate Professor at the Department of Cross-Cultural and Regional Studies, University of Copenhagen. She has published in the areas of Russian Orthodoxy, contemporary Christianity and contemporary Christian minorities.

Dr Suna Gülfer Ihlamur-Öner is a lecturer in the Department of Political Science and International Relations at Marmara University, Istanbul. She completed her PhD in Sociology and Social Research at the University of Trento in 2009. Her research interests include transnational migration, European integration and religious studies, and she has several publications in these fields. Her most recent publications include, as co-editor, *Küreselleşme Çağında Göç: Kavramlar, Tartışmalar* [*Migration in the Global Age: Concepts and Debates*] (2012) and 'The Orthodox Tradition in a Globalizing World: The Case of the Romanian Orthodox Church' in *Religions in Movement: The Local and the Global in Contemporary Faith Traditions* (New York, 2013).

Ernest Kadotschnikow studied Religious Studies in Erfurt after completing an Orthodox theological seminary in Ukraine. His research interests include the inter-religious dialogue and current developments in the Russian Orthodox Church, as well as Orthodox liturgy and canon law.

James A. Kapaló is a lecturer in the Study of Religions at University College Cork, Ireland. His research focuses on religious and ethnic minorities in Eastern Europe in the twentieth century, folk religious practices and, more recently, Orthodox Christianity in Western Europe. Recent publications include: *Text, Context and Performance: Gagauz Folk Religion in Discourse and Practice* (Leiden, 2011), an ethnographic study of lived religion and identity amongst Moldova's Turkish-speaking Orthodox Christian minority, and the co-edited volume (with Éva Pócs and Will Ryan) *The Power of Words: Studies on Charms and Charming in Europe* (Budapest, 2013).

Guillaume Keller holds an MA in History of Religions from the University of Strasbourg. He specialised in twentieth-century Orthodox Christianity, with a particular focus on the relationship of the Orthodox diasporas with their Mother Churches.

Teuvo Laitila, PhD, is Associate Professor of Orthodox Church History and Comparative Religion at the University of Eastern Finland (Joensuu Campus). His research interests include Orthodox Christianity, Islam and religion in Karelia and the Balkans. His publications include *The Finnish Guard in the Balkans* (Helsinki, 2003), *Nationalism and Orthodoxy* (Helsinki, 2004), *Abrahamin vieraanvaraisuus: Näkökohtia kristityn ja muslimin dialogiin* [*Abrahamic Hospitality: Aspects of Christian–Muslim Dialogue*] (Joensuu, 2009), and numerous articles in books and journals.

Tuomas Martikainen is Professor in Ethnic Relations at the Swedish School of Social Science, University of Helsinki. His areas of interest include contemporary religious and ethnic diversity, the governance of religion, religion in the consumer society and the incorporation of immigrant religions in Europe. His publications include *Religion, Migration, Settlement: Reflections on Post-1990 Immigration to Finland* (Leiden, 2013), *Immigrant Religions in Local Society: Historical and Contemporary Perspectives in the City of Turku* (Turku, 2004), several edited volumes and numerous articles in books and journals.

Jean-François Mayer received his PhD in History in 1984 at the University of Lyon, France. His research has focused on contemporary religious movements. He is the author of ten books, some of them translated into several languages, and numerous articles in academic journals. Since 2008, he has been Director of the Religioscope Institute (Fribourg, Switzerland) and the editor of the website www.religion.info. For additional details and a full list of publications, go to www.mayer.info.

List of Contributors

Edmund Mucha is an Orthodox deacon at St John's Orthodox Mission in Toronto, Canada and teacher at the Lived Theology School. He has a special interest in the inculturation of Orthodoxy in non-Orthodox contexts.

Soner Onder Barthoma is a PhD candidate at the Amsterdam School for Social Science Research (ASSR) at the University of Amsterdam. His PhD research is about the contemporary changes in Turkish foreign policy discourses towards the Middle East. He has recently published the book chapter 'Minority Rights in Turkey: Quo Vadis, Assyrians?' in P.H. Omtzigt et al. (eds) *The Slow Disappearance of the Syriacs from Turkey and of the Grounds of the Mor Gabriel Monastery* (Münster, 2012).

Sebastian Rimestad studied Political Science and Religious Studies in Aberdeen, Tartu and Erfurt. In 2011, he finished a PhD project concerning the Orthodox Churches of Estonia and Latvia in the Inter-War period at the University of Erfurt. Since then, he has been engaged in research on the Orthodox Church in minority contexts, also in Erfurt.

Prof. Dr. theol. habil. Reinhard Thöle D.D. teaches on Eastern and Oriental Orthodox Christian Denominations at the Faculty of Theology, Martin Luther University of Halle-Wittenberg, Germany, and is Professor *honoris causa* for Ecumenical Theology at the Patriarch Justinian Faculty of Theology, Bucharest, Romania. He is a consultant for the Evangelical Church in Germany regarding dialogues with the Orthodox Churches. As a minister of the Lutheran Church, he is connected with the Byzantine rite tradition of the Ukrainian Lutheran Church, and he has edited liturgical services for German language use.

Berit Thorbjørnsrud is Associate Professor at the Department of Cultural Studies and Oriental Languages, University of Oslo. For many years she has done research on various topics related to the revival of the Coptic Orthodox Church in Egypt. Presently, Thorbjørnsrud is involved in research on the Orthodox Church in Norway. Her main interests are religious minorities in the Middle East and in Norway, the relationship between civil and religious laws, gender and body rituals.

The Revd Canon Hugh Wybrew is a retired priest of the Church of England living in Oxford. He has spent most of his ministry in parishes in London and Oxford. He was Chaplain at the Church of the Resurrection in Bucharest from 1971 to 1973, and served congregations in Romania, Bulgaria and Yugoslavia. From 1986 to 1989 he was Dean of St George's Anglican Cathedral in Jerusalem. From 1974 to 2007 he was a member of the Anglican–Orthodox international theological dialogue.

Introduction[1]

Maria Hämmerli and Jean-François Mayer

The impetus for this book stems from a shared conviction among its contributors that Orthodox migration in Western Europe matters, despite its discreet presence.[2] And it matters in a way that has not yet been explored in social and religious studies: in terms of size, geographical scope, social impact and theological input.

This book is a follow-up to an international conference organised by the editors at the University of Neuchâtel, Switzerland in December 2010. The group of scholars gathered there agreed that the migration and settlement of Orthodox people and their churches in the West has occasioned significant negotiations and reinterpretations of their religious identity, which need further scrutiny. Yet, despite unprecedented migration from Eastern Europe and Asia Minor over the last decades, the mushrooming literature on migration and religion has overlooked the Orthodox component. Research still being scanty, we can only offer *glimpses* on the Orthodox presence in Western Europe: we do not claim to provide an exhaustive picture on all European countries or to cover adequately each ethnic community. Notwithstanding such limitations, this volume offers fresh and original insights in the field of religion and migration literature.[3]

Why such a scarce interest in Orthodox migrations? First, much scholarly attention focuses on Islam and the 'religious other' (e.g. Buddhist and Hindu migrations) in Europe, although almost half of the immigrants to the continent are Christians (Martikainen 2013). Second, the Orthodox communities are under-researched because, as a religious group, they are socially invisible and unproblematic in the receiving countries, owing to religious similarities with the host Christian environment. Though different ethnic groups who are Orthodox may be noticeable, their religious background rarely comes into discussion.

---

[1] The editors would like to thank Suna Gülfer Ihlamur-Öner for her input to this introduction on the topic of transnationalism.

[2] Several years ago, a useful overview of the Orthodox presence of European countries (the only existing work of its kind), with chapters on single countries written by Orthodox authors, was published by Christine Chaillot (2005), an Orthodox lady otherwise well known for her efforts toward dialogue between Eastern and Oriental Orthodox Churches.

[3] The contributors to this book come from various disciplinary backgrounds. While most are anchored in social sciences in the broad sense, a few chapters have been written by theologians with a special interest in the life of Orthodox communities.

For instance, while Romanians receive media coverage, public and political attention in Italy, the Orthodox as a religious group do not. Conversely, Muslims are visible in the Italian public sphere, appear in political agendas and are subject to academic scrutiny, but not primarily as Algerians or Somalis.[4] The third reason why Orthodox capture little attention is their own internal pluralism and presently complicated jurisdictional system, organised along ethnic criteria, which gives the mistaken impression that there are several denominations (Greek Orthodox, Russian Orthodox, Romanian Orthodox, etc.). Moreover, there are two different families of Churches labelled as 'Orthodox': Eastern and Oriental. 'Eastern' describes Churches with a mostly Byzantine liturgical legacy, accepting the Seven Ecumenical Councils of the first millennium and in communion with the Western Church until the 1054 break. 'Oriental' is used for non-Chalcedonian Churches, which did not recognise the Fourth Ecumenical Council (Chalcedon, 451 CE); they have their roots in the Armenian, Coptic (and Ethiopian) or West Syriac liturgical traditions. Another, separate case is the Church of the East (sometimes called the 'Assyrian' or 'Ancient' Church of the East, commonly known as 'Nestorian', though not a name used by the church itself), which belongs to the East Syriac liturgical tradition and which did not accept the Council of Ephesus (Third Ecumenical Council according to the other churches, 431 CE).

Orthodoxy as a Category of Analysis

The internal pluralism of the Orthodox Churches in the West in terms of ethnicity, language and ecclesiastical organisation elicits an important methodological question: given this diversity, is it not more legitimate to speak about Russian Orthodox or Greek Orthodox or simply Romanians or Serbians in Western Europe, instead of 'the Orthodox'? And can we bring together Eastern Orthodox and Oriental Orthodox, who may be religious 'cousins', but are not in communion and do not often interact with one another? From the perspective of research on migrant congregations, both decisions can be easily justified. The similarities between the churches of these two communions are obvious: a strong liturgical emphasis, the same fundamental organisational structures (episcopal), a stress upon tradition and a theology appealing to the ancient Fathers of the Christian East, a spirituality marked with a distinct monastic influence, and usually a close link between religious faith and ethnic origins. Sociologically, the family air is significant enough for producing fruitful

---

[4] This observation stems from an informal discussion between Maria Hämmerli and Giuseppe Giordan about Orthodox Churches in Italy.

Introduction

comparative analysis: only the contested theological differences could justify keeping them separate.

Is it then appropriate to speak about 'Orthodoxy' as a category of analysis? We believe it is. Though migrants from Orthodox countries do not coalesce around the religious reference nor form one single religious community, one has to acknowledge the strong continuity and consistency in Orthodox liturgy, religious practice and doctrine, even if distinctions between Eastern and Oriental Orthodox, on the one hand, and among Oriental Orthodox themselves, with their different liturgical traditions, on the other hand, should not be forgotten. Moreover, as James Kapaló argues, there is 'a common Orthodox discursive space' (Chapter 12 in this volume): 'Orthodox Churches and their members address one another in a "common language of Orthodoxy" and ... are affiliated to an Orthodox network' (232).

Some of the chapters in the present volume (Thöle, Keller, Kapaló, Hämmerli, Wybrew, Martikainen and Laitila, Thørbjornsrud) do favour the category 'Orthodoxy' and look at ethnic origins, migration waves, process of settlement and institutional organisation in precise national contexts and relations with the new social and religious environment in Germany, France, Ireland, Switzerland, Great Britain, Finland and Norway. Other chapters, however, focus on one specific ethnic group, mainly Russian (Rimestad and Kadotschnikow, Hämmerli and Mucha, Hvithamar), but also Romanian (Ihlamur-Öner) and Assyrians of both West and East Syriac traditions (Onder Barthoma, Atto).

All the authors reported challenges of insufficient sources available at the national level, which made it difficult to draw a comprehensive picture of the Orthodox communities in the respective national settings in terms of their history, geographical spread, social composition and internal organisation of parishes. This practical difficulty arises particularly when attempting to gather statistical information about the category 'Orthodox': on the one hand, there is natural tendency to conflate ethnicity and religion, i.e. to consider that the cumulative number of Greeks, Romanians, Russians and Serbs coincides with the number of Orthodox people in a given country, while this is only a pool from which one can identify potential Orthodox. Most ethnic parishes and dioceses use this method in order to count their members, although the numbers of those attending religious services regularly or at least occasionally are much smaller. Not only does this give a distorted picture of the size of the Orthodox community, but it also fails to include the local converts or those long-term migrants and their descent who have maintained their religious identity but hold local citizenship and are assimilated in the local cultural ethos: for example, among Russian Orthodox linked to the first wave of immigration after the 1917 Bolshevik revolution, there are families who have managed to become successful citizens of the adopted countries of their great-grandparents while remaining faithful to their ancestors' legacy.

4   *Orthodox Identities in Western Europe*

Alexei Krindatch tried to avoid this pitfall when he conducted his survey in the USA, and proceeded to obtain data on Church membership 'directly from the local Orthodox parishes by asking parish clergy: "Approximately how many individual persons in total are associated in any way with the life of your parish: counting adults and children, regular and occasional attendees, paid stewards and persons who do not contribute financially?"'.[5] Yet this approach has the limitation that it defines religious identity on the basis of practice and leaves out those self-identified Orthodox who are not related to a particular parish and who may have a more privatised way of living their faith. In Orthodox countries themselves, religious practice is more diffuse and the faith is often absorbed by mere socialisation in a culture marked by Orthodoxy.

The chapters in this volume used existing statistics produced either by estimates of ethnic dioceses and parishes (figures published online or obtained directly from clergy) or by official national statistics; none of the authors took the task of developing a method of counting the Orthodox population or conducting a quantitative survey nation-wide. Yet they are all aware that the simple act of counting the Orthodox implies a delineation of this religious category; hence, the issue of identity becomes particularly acute here.

The Issue of Orthodox Identities

What does it mean to be Orthodox (Romanian, Greek, Russian, etc.) in France, in Great Britain or in Denmark today? And what does it mean to be French, British or Danish and be Orthodox? The contributions to this book illustrate through specific case studies that there is no one single, homogeneous and coherent answer to these very simple questions. On the contrary, the intricate arguments that help formulate a reply indicate that we are entitled to speak about multiple Orthodox identities.

Despite challenges brought by attempts of non-Orthodox, missionary-minded groups to proselytise (Mayer 2009), the question of religious identity is not a pressing one in the Orthodox heartland, where religious identity is something people take for granted because the great majority of the country identifies at least nominally with the Orthodox faith (85.9 per cent in

---

[5]   Krindatch, A. 2010. Highlights from the Census 'Religious Congregations and Membership Study 2010'. Available at: http://www.hartfordinstitute.org/research/2010-USOrthodox-Census.pdf [accessed December 2012].

Introduction   5

Romania;[6] 90 per cent in Greece; 53.1 per cent in Russia).[7] It is perhaps when one faces religious otherness and a minority status in a migration context that this question arises, prompting people and churches to reflect on it.[8] Hence, this book is centred round the issue of *Orthodox identities in a migration context*. The contributions cover this central subject with a variety of empirical situations relevant for different aspects of immigrant identity construction. Some of the deriving sub-themes are as follows: identity adaptations entailed by the integration in the host countries (Onder Barthoma, Atto, Hämmerli); the innovations needed for Orthodox to enter dialogue with modernity (Onder Barthoma, Atto, Hämmerli and Mucha); the role of transnational relations between migrant Orthodox communities and their respective homelands in religious identity preservation (Ihlamur-Öner); the enlargement or widening of Orthodox identity through outreach to the local people (Kapaló, Hvithamar); the emergence of local Western Orthodox identities (Denizeau, Mayer); the consequences for inter-Orthodox relations of the overlapping jurisdictions of the Mother Churches in the West (Thørbjornsrud, Thöle, Keller); and the impact of Orthodox ethnocentrism for ecumenical dialogue with local Christian denominations (Rimestad and Kadotschnikow, Wybrew).

These case studies confirm that migration and settlement generate a process of identity reconstruction because Orthodox migrants need to deal with the transition from majority status and social and cultural embeddedness in the homeland, to the more secular, religiously pluralistic society of Western Europe, where they are a minority. Thus the unquestioned, assumed interplay between ethnicity and religion is a crucial locus of debate on Orthodox identity, both for individuals and churches. Additionally, churches are no longer in a privileged position politically, but are confined to the status of regular, civil organisations. The practical consequences of this situation will be discussed later in this chapter. For the time being, we will look at some current theoretical developments which discuss the impact of migration and settlement on religion, and try to situate the Orthodox case in this body of literature.

---

6   Ministry of Administration and Interior. 2012. Tab. 8: Populatia Stabila Dupa Principalele Religii la Recensamantul Din Anul 2011 – Rezultate Preliminare. Available at: http://www.recensamantromania.ro/wp-content/uploads/2012/08/TS8.pdf [accessed 30 July 2013].

7   Encyclopaedia Britannica. 2013. *2013 Britannica Book of the Year*. In the case of Russia, variations can be very strong, according to other sources that suggest as much as 75 per cent: Eurel. 2010. Religious Affiliation in 2010. Available at: http://www.eurel.info/spip.php?rubrique495 [accessed 30 July 2013].

8   The situation is very different with Oriental Orthodox, who emigrate from territories where they are already a religious minority and where their religious identity has a negative impact on their social status. The chapter by Onder Barthoma points out the fact that Assyrians have developed in the course of their history a very strong identification between their ethnic minority status and their religion.

Migration and Settlement

The content of this book obviously includes a section accounting for the history of Orthodox migrations to some of the countries covered. If we were to summarise this, we could say that there are two key events that produced a significant exodus of the Orthodox population to the West: the advent and the fall of communism in Eastern Europe. 1917 and 1990 were turning points for the European religious landscape: while the former brought into power a political regime that was highly hostile to religion and imposed radical secularisation in Eastern Europe, the latter marked the reinstatement of religious freedom and an unprecedented comeback of religion in those societies. While 1917 was the beginning of several waves of political migration, 1990 led to a diversification of migration causes, though economic precariousness in the sending countries remains a key issue.

Other events that are at the origin of Orthodox presence in the West are military conflicts in the Mediterranean (for instance the 1919–1922 Greco-Turkish war) and in the former Yugoslavia (end of the 1990s). Apart from a series of unhappy incidents in the Orthodox heartland (so-called 'push factors' of migration located in the sending countries), we have to consider also the 'pull factors' (Lee 1966) specific to the receiving contexts: during the post-war reconstruction period, Western Europe went through rapid development and economic growth and needed labour force in various industrial sectors. Among other guest workers who took this opportunity, Greeks and former Yugoslavs started to arrive in the 1950s, continuing all the way through to the 1980s.

There are many sets of differences between the political and the economic-driven migrations, in terms of migrants' cultural and social features (class, education, marital status, human and social capital), reasons for migration (voluntary or forced), and the post-migratory representations of the place of origin (Martikainen 2013). In Belgium in the late 1950s, earlier middle-class Greek expatriates were not so pleased with the arrival of young males who had little education and had been recruited as coal miners; the older generation sometimes complained that 'the church has become full of coal dust' (Venturas 2002: 51). For Orthodox people and churches these categories have proved crucial for their further settlement and organisation in the host country (see chapters by Hämmerli, Thöle, and Keller). Political migration may set on the road political, military or intellectual elites and dissidents opposing a given regime, as happened with Russian intelligentsia or with the Romanian cultural elites who found refuge in France and the USA, as well as in Great Britain and Germany. These elites played a crucial role in developing an Orthodox identity in the West through theological renewal wrought in seminaries (Saint-Serge in Paris and St Vladimir's in New York) and efforts to enculturate Orthodoxy in the West. However, other political migrants developed imaginaries about

Introduction   7

the country of origin that idealised it and maintained it as the main point of identification. This happened with the Russian Orthodox Church Outside of Russia (ROCOR) and also Romanian parishes at some point in their history in Western Europe. In any case, religion becomes an important element in preserving the ethnic and national identity and of increasing group self-awareness (Vertovec 2009; Baumann 2002). This can be deliberately encouraged by both mother churches and states: an increasing number of countries – not only Orthodox ones – have become aware of the interest of mobilising 'compatriots' abroad (Koser 2007).

Labour migration, low and highly skilled, tends to happen among young people at the beginning of their working lives. Though usually voluntary migrants have strong motivations to improve their economic status and social welfare, it may happen that their migration project has to change or be interrupted, involving return to the homeland or moving further to another destination, closely following the evolution of global markets and economies. The movement of Orthodox populations mirrors this trend, as illustrated by the case of Greek and Serbian guest workers in Germany and Switzerland in the late 1990s and early 2000s; more recently, Romanians, have been departing from Italy and Spain because of the economic crisis and the high unemployment rates affecting these countries. Such situations impact religious organisation and the way migrants participate in parish life, which is the space where the various waves of migrants meet and negotiate their religious identity, pastoral needs and representations about the vocation and mission of the Church. As illustrated in Chapter 15, on the Sourozh diocese crisis, this diversity is not easy to cope with in an Orthodox parish.

Apart from the reasons for migration, which differentiate how religion is organised in the receiving countries, literature highlights that post-1990 migrations present specific characteristics. In her discussion of this matter, Peggy Levitt (2001b) identifies several differences between old and new migrations. First, she argues that

> New communication and transportation technologies permit more frequent and intimate connections between those who move and those who remain behind. The airplane and the telephone make it easier and cheaper to remain in touch. New technologies heighten the immediacy and intensity of migrants' contact with their sending communities, allowing them to be actively involved in everyday life in fundamentally different ways than in the past (Levitt 2001b: 10).

This easier way of staying in touch with the homeland contributes to the continuation of the strong bond between ethnicity, culture and Orthodoxy, but also to the creation of what Ihlamur-Öner describes as 'a transnational Orthodox space', in which circulate religious objects, spiritual charismatic figures, religious literature, etc. On the one hand, this circulation of Orthodox goods and imaginaries can be interpreted as an obstacle to faster integration in the host country's cultural and religious landscape and a hindrance to the formation of local Orthodox Churches, independent of the mother churches back home (Hämmerli and Mucha). On the other hand, it is viewed as an asset for maintaining an 'authentic' Orthodox identity, close to the 'roots' and to the Orthodox *habitus*, which the West has lost (Denizeau in this volume).

The second characteristic of new migrations that differentiates them from previous experiences is the fact that the present receiving contexts are usually more tolerant to ethnic and religious pluralism. This provides a social and political environment that encourages the maintenance of migrants' religious, cultural and ethnic traditions. Tuomas Martikainen argues that 'contemporary migrant populations are more diverse than they have been previously and they have more resources available to them to sustain this diversity in the new local context' (Martikainen 2013: 3). In the case of Orthodox Churches this translates into simpler procedures for establishing religious organisations (Denizeau, Kapaló, Thørbjornsrud, Hvithamar), help from local Christian denominations in finding worship places (Rimestad and Kadotschnikow, Keller, Thöle, Wybrew), or in some cases politically facilitated recognition (Italy and Switzerland[9]).

The ties migrants maintain with their homeland and the relationships they develop with the host society have been theorised under two models: diaspora and transnationalism. Steven Vertovec (2009) has drawn attention to the fact that these concepts are often used interchangeably and that the prolific literature on these topics conflates minority status in a migration context with diaspora and transnationalism, undermining the heuristic values of the concepts. Vertovec further states the importance of a clear definition and delineation of these concepts because 'religious and other socio-cultural dynamics develop distinctively within the realms of (a) migration and minority status ..., (b) diaspora, and (c) transnationalism' (Vertovec 2009: 136). Migration studies seem to take these categories as three steps of an evolutionary process: after migration, the organisation of the respective minority develops into a diaspora, which further intensifies connections with the place of origin and other co-ethnic or co-religionist communities in the world, thus becoming transnational. We believe these concepts cover different realities and entail different patterns of adaptations and transformations of migrants' religion and of reconstruction of religious identity during the process of settlement.

---

[9] The attempt to pave the way for public recognition of Orthodox churches in the canton of Vaud failed, but because of complications on the Orthodox side (see Chapter 6).

(a) Migration and Minority Status

Migration refers to state border-crossing, followed by a process of reconstitution of cultural patterns and social relations in the new setting. Migrants are usually set apart from the host society by language, cultural traditions, and religion, and as such they constitute minorities. Fenggang Yang and Helen Rose Ebaugh (2001) looked at what happens when 'an immigrant group moves from a majority status in the home country to a minority status in the United States (Chinese Buddhists) and a minority group (Chinese Christians in China) becomes part of the Christian majority in the United States' (Yang and Ebaugh 2001: 367). Their findings show that, although Chinese Buddhists retain a secure Chinese identity because of Buddhism being strongly rooted in the Chinese culture and society, they try hard to indigenise their religion and successfully reach out to the American society. Chinese Christians, despite being part of the mainstream American religious landscape, focus on emphasising the ethnic element and 'Sinicise' the church in their effort to convert fellow Chinese. This is because for Chinese to become Christians means betraying their ethnic identity. The research concluded that 'majority/minority religious status in the home and host countries is an important factor that impacts the internal dynamics and overall changes in immigrant religious institutions ... and is predictive of variations of patterns of adaptation' (Yang and Ebough 2001: 376).

This is very instructive for the situation of Orthodox migrants in Western Europe: while Eastern Orthodox churches experience a hard and often troublesome transition from majority to minority status, for the Oriental Orthodox the minority consciousness is very deeply rooted already in the place of origin. We can assume that, in the latter case, migration enhances the status of the religious community because the receiving context is more tolerant with religious and ethnic minorities than the one in the homeland. Further comparative research is needed to substantiate this particular point. The chapters of the present volume allow, however, for a few observations.

First, for Eastern Orthodox churches migration means de-territorialisation from a social, cultural, and political context which backs religious identity, and settlement in culturally and religiously alien contexts, where Orthodoxy takes on new meanings. In the face of religious otherness, Orthodox people become more aware of their religious identity and start questioning the content of their faith and thus increase their theological literacy. What was self-evident, taken for granted and culturally transmitted in the homeland, needs to be rationalised in the minority context:[10] the meaning of sacraments (most frequent are

---

[10] By 'rationalise', we do not mean that the content of the Orthodox faith is irrational and needs to be brought into accord with reason; rather, we suggest that it becomes subject to explanation and categorisation, borrowing from theology and tradition.

baptism, marriage, Eucharistic communion and confession), the meaning and practice of fasting, iconography, the structure of the sacred space, the importance of monasticism, etc. Also, the question of differentiating between what is religious and what is merely cultural arises very acutely. This effort of discriminating between religion and theology on the one hand and ethnicity and culture on the other hand is visible in the work of outstanding theologians of Russian origin who lived and published in France and the USA (e.g. Georges Florovsky, Nicolai Afanasiev, Alexander Schmemann, and John Meyendorff). These figures marked not only the way Orthodoxy was practiced in the West, but had an important impact on the twentieth-century Orthodox theology also in Eastern Europe. This topic represents an entire field of research in itself; therefore we will not dwell on it here. The chapters by Hämmerli and Denizeau touch on this point and give some examples in this sense. Yet this point needs deeper empirical inspection as well as theoretical substance.

Second, living as a minority outside an Orthodox society affects Orthodox identity in a more subtle and intimate way, because it means living outside an Orthodox *habitus,* a time and space shaped by the Church:

> the week with the recurrence of Sunday, the day of the Resurrection; the sequence of seasons revolving round Easter, the Feast of the resurrection, and Christmas, the Feast of Christ's birth – two sequences of feasts and fasts that nestle into each other, which are supplemented by a sequence of feasts commemorating the Virgin Mother of God; and the yearly sequence of commemoration of the Saints (Louth 2012: 99).

Thus, migration often involves for Orthodox migrants the requirement of resituating themselves in a more secular way of organising time: no more (or only to a very small extent) in the rhythm of religious feasts, but more in line with work and school schedules, hobbies and leisure activities, social events, etc.

Third, with regard to religious practice, in traditionally Orthodox countries it is more diffuse: only a small fraction of believers attends services regularly, but great numbers of people enter churches any time of the day and pray, venerate the icons, light candles and even have a short talk with the priest or confess. In a minority context, though practice may become more substantiated with theological knowledge, it takes a rather Protestant model of Sunday service attendance only. This is because the Orthodox in Western Europe seldom have their own worship spaces with full-time priests and even if they do, there is rarely the critical mass of believers available during working hours to perform regular religious services during the week. Also, people are geographically very dispersed in relation to the physical location of their parish, which adds to the difficulties of gathering the community more frequently.

Introduction   11

Fourth, a minority context brings about the issue of clergy education, recruitment and remuneration, as well as clergy–laity relations. In Orthodox countries priests can wear the cassock or *riassa*[11] in public spaces and are thereby recognised as priests, in a social environment in which they can have substantial authority. In Greece and in Romania, priests receive a certain part of their salary from the state. Also, they can be educated in state-run confessional theological seminaries. In a migration context, priests are no more recognisable in the public space, as their habit is not socially meaningful; on the contrary, it can be confused with Islamic male dress. Therefore their sphere of authority shrinks dramatically and becomes limited to the level of the parish. And even there, this authority is being undermined by the fact that priests are employees of their parish, on a contractual basis, involving also public authorities from the host country in case of a misunderstanding. The chapter by Thørbjornsrud excellently illustrates this tremendous change in status for priests who serve in a minority context.

Fifth, emerging migrant religious organisations help Orthodox people to adapt to the new setting while themselves having to adjust their own practices. Such adjustments include organisational changes, taking on new responsibilities, turning into community centres, acting as a social space for information sharing, providing access to networks vital for migrants' survival and adaptation, and performing new activities different from the original setting. The chapters by Onder Barthoma and Hämmerli indicate how Orthodox parishes may extend their role from mere religious service providers to community centres.

Sixth, we are reminded by Denizeau's chapter that when Orthodox establish religious organisations in the West, they fall under a legislation that was not conceived for an Orthodox type of institution, and which may place immigrant religious associations under the legal category as secular associations, similar to sports, youth or leisure groups. According to the civil statutes, an Orthodox parish has to function democratically, with decision-making based on voting and with election of the leader. This mode of functioning is alien to the Orthodox parish administration, which has the priest as its leader by default and also involves the external authority of the bishop.[12] In the case of monasteries, this is all the more contrary to the Orthodox leadership, entrusted to the abbot, in principle on a lifetime basis. How Orthodox parishes enter the legal framework of their host country is a particularly interesting point, on which we lack empirical evidence, therefore further research could bring more clarification, especially in a comparative perspective. Let us also note that Chapter 1, on Romanian Orthodox Churches in Italy, shows that there are exceptions to the rule: the

---

[11]   A black, ankle-length clerical garment.

[12]   Solutions can be found in practice through the use of internal regulations. Similar challenges are met in some places by the Roman Catholic Church, with its similar episcopal structure.

12　　　　　　　　*Orthodox Identities in Western Europe*

Romanian Orthodox Church enjoys a special status and state recognition in Italy.[13]

Apart from rediscovering the content of their faith, changes in religious practice and a repositioning of the Orthodox churches within the political and legal framework of the receiving contexts, new issues arise in a minority context: preservation and transmission of the faith, children's religious education, intermarriage, etc. For space reasons, we cannot deal with these aspects in this introduction.

In light of all these observations, we would like to note the very peculiar character of the Orthodox migration to Finland, where the Orthodox Church is 'both an "indigenous" as well as an "immigrant" religion' (Martikainen 2013: 100). In this case, migrants join existing parishes and a religious minority with social and political recognition and historically and culturally embedded in the host country. Orthodox migrants do not need to set up structures from scratch, but only ensure parish activities in their language (Martikainen 2004).

While all the previous remarks apply also to the Oriental Orthodox, they have nonetheless some specificities: difficulty in finding proper leadership for the community (Atto in this volume), and the Church losing its authority in organising the community while authority is drifting toward more lay, secular ethnic organisations (see chapter by Onder Barthoma). Maybe the background of those communities as minorities in their home countries, and the fact that there is no state power closely associated with the mother churches in such a way that it could co-opt them as privileged partners, leaves the ground more open for other political forces to emerge as additional or alternative community representatives; in addition, quite naturally, in more secular environments, religious and ethnic identities are no longer necessarily overlapping and the church is no longer seen as the natural expression of the group's identity, thus opening opportunities for non-religious competitors to emphasise their role.[14]

Coming back to the theoretical framework regarding migration and settlement of religious communities, let us note that migrants' *de facto* minority status, their awareness of it, and their organisation as a minority community is

---

[13]　There is no chapter in this book on Belgium, but it should be mentioned that 'a ministerial act of 1985 recognised the Orthodox doctrine and the metropolitan appointed by the Ecumenical Patriarchate of Constantinople as its representative. Since 1988, Orthodox priests have been paid their wages by the Belgian state, while pupils in Belgian schools are entitled, at least in theory, to be taught the Orthodox religion' (Venturas 2002: 49). This applies not only to Orthodox of Greek affiliation, but to all Orthodox jurisdictions. The same legal recognition was granted to Orthodox parishes in Luxembourg in 1998. In Austria, both Eastern Orthodox (1967) and Oriental Orthodox Churches (2003) received public law recognition. Regarding Denmark, see Hvithamar (Chapter 11 in this volume).

[14]　Under the Ottoman *millet* system, the Church had been made into the representative of the community, not only for purely religious matters.

Introduction 13

misleadingly interpreted as a 'diasporic' type of organisation. James Clifford notes that 'Diasporic language ... appears to be replacing, or at least supplementing, minority discourse' (Clifford in Vertovec 1999). The following section will look into diaspora theories and their possible application to the Orthodox migration.

(b) Orthodox Diaspora?[15]

Restricted to the theological sphere until the twentieth century, 'diaspora' was adopted in the field of social sciences only during the 1950s, in order to describe Jewish, Armenian or Greek migrations. This conceptual tool met such a success that it extended to more than 36 communities[16] and is 'often used today to describe practically any population which is considered "deterritorialised" or "transnational" – that is, which has originated in a land other than which it currently resides, and whose social, economic and political networks cross the borders of nation-states or, indeed, span the globe' (Vertovec 1999).[17]

Broadening the scope of 'diaspora' to include recent forms of migrant community organisation is a natural development of the concept (Schnapper 2001); yet this unexpected proliferation imperils the heuristic value of the concept (Dufoix 2003, Baumann 2000). We believe one way of keeping 'diaspora' a convenient conceptual tool is to remain close to its origin, the Jewish model. Robin Cohen is one of the authors who theorised diaspora in this sense, highlighting a number of features that can be summed up as follows: dispersal from an original 'centre'; a collective memory and an idealisation of their original homeland; the development of a return movement; a strong ethnic group consciousness sustained over a long time and based on a sense of distinctiveness; a troubled relationship with host societies.[18] Very significantly, Cohen, in line with Marienstras, insists on the historical dimension of diaspora formation. 'Time has to pass' before we can announce that an expatriate community has become a diaspora (Marienstras 1989).

Ironically, sociologists imported the concept of *diaspora* from theology, but they used it little in relation to faith communities. Moreover, some (Baumann,

---

[15] This section is based on a previous publication by Maria Hämmerli, in which she analysed sociological and theological arguments testing the validity of the phrase 'Orthodox diaspora' (Hämmerli 2010).

[16] Vertovec, S. 2000. Religion and Diaspora. Paper presented at the conference *New Landscapes on Religion in the West*, School of Geography and the Environment, University of Oxford, 27–29 September 2000.

[17] Vertovec, S. 1999. Three Meanings of 'Diaspora', Exemplified among South Asian Religions, in *Diaspora* 7(2). Available at: http://www.transcomm.ox.ac.uk/working%20 papers/diaspora.pdf [accessed December 2009].

[18] 'Nearly every conception of diaspora features the idea of return to a homeland in some form' (see also Kenny 2013: 61).

Cohen) are sceptical about the possibility of applying this concept to religious groups. Cohen substantiates his position with two arguments: first, religions involve various ethnic communities; second, they tend to spread universally and not to recreate a homeland to which they would seek to return. For Cohen religions are rather providers of 'additional cement' in ethnic/national diaspora consciousness formation (Cohen 1997: 189).

A closer look at the Eastern and Oriental Orthodox migrant communities reveals diaspora-like features: first, some of these ethnic populations were delocalised because of unpleasant contexts, as shown in the section 'Migration and Settlement'. Second, the structural unity of the ethnic communities (Russian, Romanian, Greek, etc.) derives from the creation of religious institutions, cultural centres, schools in original language, and charity organisations (Bruneau 1993). Orthodox Churches are both the expression of the existence of a collective memory about the homeland and the venue for its reinforcement and refreshment, as they constantly reinvent ethnic identity. Third, in early stages of migration, the homeland remains the central reference, yet there is no collective aspiration to return to the original land – although nuances should be introduced here, since there was definitely a dream to return to the home country among those who had been suddenly uprooted by political upheavals.[19] Neither Eastern nor Oriental Orthodox have developed a tense relation with the host country into which they migrated: on the contrary, they try to build sustainable relations with the local environment and make it a new home. All chapters in this volume illustrate this observation. The ethnic groups that form Eastern Orthodox communities in the West could be therefore characterised as 'diaspora-minded', but they do not constitute diasporas in the sense we use this concept. In the case of the Oriental Orthodox, there is one group which constitutes a diaspora: the Armenians. Considering some serious developments in the Middle East over the last decades, and currently intensifying, maybe a similar fate is awaiting some other Oriental Orthodox in the coming decades, with more people in exile than in the original countries, although it is unlikely that it will lead to a lasting longing for return, due to the likely acceptance in host societies and irreversible changes in the original home countries. Only the future will tell how Syriac or Coptic identities will evolve, and this depends to a significant extent on external factors in regional politics.

Whether these ethnic communities constitute national/ethnic diasporas or not, can we say that, because they share the same religious affiliation – Orthodoxy – they form an Orthodox diaspora? This would imply that Orthodoxy would federate these communities in a unique diaspora, coalesced around

---

[19] There were Russians of the first emigration in the 1920s who spent years sitting on their suitcases, waiting for the first signal to return; under various guises, such expectations partly continued for decades.

Introduction   15

shared faith. But it rather looks like a co-habitation of national/ethnic diaspora-minded communities with their respective churches, who are nevertheless aware of their religious affinity. Moreover, their collaboration in the religious field is still scanty. It is hindered, among other things, by the following various factors: (1) the linguistic and cultural variety of these communities, which prefer to celebrate in their mother tongue and according to home traditions;[20] (2) the strong ecclesiastical dependence on the mother churches, which leads to a concentration of resources and agency at the level of national diocese; and (3) the fact that the Orthodox Church has been historically linked to the preservation of ethnic identity in the homelands, and therefore continues to play this role also within the expatriate communities. Paradoxically, what unites these communities, their belonging to the Orthodox Church, is also a point of separation, because the Church reproduces ethnic identities.

The two arguments that Cohen takes into account when rejecting the very idea of religious diasporas (i.e. their social composition and the relationship of the expatriate religious group with the homeland) apply also to the Orthodox communities. First, 'Orthodox diaspora' covers several ethnic migrant communities, as illustrated above. The diasporic consciousness, if there is one, is usually strongest among the first and second generations and diminishes with the subsequent descendants.[21] Moreover, apart from members of migrant origin, what is called 'Orthodox diaspora' encompasses an increasing number of local Western converts.[22] How can these natives of historically non-Orthodox countries, as wholly members of the Orthodox Church as the migrants from traditionally Orthodox lands, be part and parcel of a *diaspora*? While so far not welcomed by all Orthodox, attempts to make a space for the use of Western rites in the Orthodox Church, as described in Mayer's chapter, emphasise even more a claim of universality for Orthodoxy, not confined to 'Eastern Christianity'.

---

[20]   Many parishes are reluctant to introduce the local language into liturgical life, even though the latter is more accessible to youth, converts or non-Orthodox spouses attending services. This is due not only to alleged ethnocentrism, but also to the fact that Orthodox theological terminology is sometimes difficult to translate in languages that did not develop in an Orthodox environment. This is obvious when one looks at French and English Orthodox prayer books and service translations, which reproduce untranslatable Greek or Slavonic words.

[21]   There are some exceptions, however: for example, some descendants of Armenian and Russian émigrés maintain a strong cultural identification with their ancestors.

[22]   Unfortunately, reliable quantitative and qualitative data about their presence in the Church is not available. According to estimates by Serge Model, converts do not make up more than 1 per cent of Orthodox population in countries such as France, the United Kingdom or Belgium (Model 2008). In some countries, converts are over-represented among clergy: in the mid-2000s they made up more than 40 per cent of Orthodox clergy in the United Kingdom (Ware 2005: 52).

16   *Orthodox Identities in Western Europe*

Second, the relationship between dioceses in the West and their respective patriarchates back home is best described by the term 'mother churches'. It means that the ethnically various Orthodox in the West pledge ecclesiastical allegiance to their national patriarchates in the homeland, while enjoying administrative and financial self-governance.[23] Despite this solid umbilical cord, the Orthodox Churches in the West do not dream of some return to the breast of the 'mother churches'. On the contrary, they tend to rediscover Orthodoxy's universal dimensions and develop strategies of implantation in the host countries, although simultaneously they are committed to ethnic identity preservation. These strategies are deployed by each national church separately, depending on factors such as: the social composition and size of the ethnic diasporas they serve (the migration waves that fostered them); the relationship the expatriate population has with the homeland; the personality of bishops that are in charge of the national diasporas; the religious landscape; and the church–state relationship specific to the host country.

If, for all the reasons exposed above, one cannot speak of an 'Orthodox diaspora', one cannot deny that there is a particular way in which Orthodoxy is practised within the migrant communities with a diaspora-type organisation and functioning. Hinnells suggests that one meaningful association between religion and diaspora is the idea of a 'diaspora religion'. He defines it as 'the religion of any people who have a sense of living away from the land of the religion or away from the old country' (Hinnels 1997: 686). Can we perhaps speak of a 'diaspora Orthodoxy'? His formulation limits the religious phenomenon to the existence of a centre and to the relationship the faithful have with this centre. This implies asserting the centrality of the mother churches and reducing the practice of Orthodoxy in the West to the condition of a periphery, which contradicts Orthodoxy's claim for universality. One possible interpretation of 'diaspora Orthodoxy' is 'Orthodoxy practised outside traditional territories', in which case we reopen the meaning of 'diaspora' and extrapolate it to any form of migration.

'Orthodox diaspora' is problematic also at the theological level. The concept of diaspora, as inherited from Judaism, presupposes a unique and exclusive centre (the Temple). This concept cannot be applied to Orthodox ecclesiology, based on the concept of 'local Church' which allows for a plurality of locations, each equally and fully epitomising the *Una Sancta*, the Universal Church. For Christians, the Temple is the Body of Christ (cf. John 2:20) and the Church exists everywhere where the Eucharist is celebrated. 'Diaspora is the means through which the national identity is preserved, it is not an ecclesiological category… A State can grant a nationality and issue a passport, but Church cannot grant

---

[23]   Nikolaos Daldas (1995) calls this 'political orthodoxies'.

Introduction 17

"ecclesial nationality" and provide an "ecclesial passport" to its faithful when they are outside its bounds' (Papathomas 2005).

'Diaspora' is thus used rather as a catchall term in order to express the idea of migration of populations who share Orthodoxy, but it fails to define the Orthodox presence in the West. The use of 'Orthodox diaspora' is not consistent in this volume. Some contributors consider it as inappropriate and avoid it, while others use it indistinctively, without really questioning the concept, meaning simply Orthodox people who migrated and settled in territories other than those historically Orthodox.

(c) Transnationalism

Like 'diaspora', 'transnationalism' is also one of the concepts *en vogue* in migration studies, used for different types and forms of persistent border-crossing. Steven Vertovec, in his attempt to provide theoretical clarification of this concept, defined it as 'sustained linkages and ongoing exchanges among non-state actors based across national borders ... The collective attributes of such connections, their processes of formation and maintenance, and their wider implications are referred to broadly as "transnationalism"' (Vertovec 2009: 3).

Apart from the circulation of goods, remittances, ideas or capital, people bring with them their religious beliefs. Religions are among the oldest transnational players, since the very spread of Christianity and Islam happened through border-crossing of traders, missionaries or colonial administrators. Victor Roudometof (2000: 386) argues for 'the necessity of a world historical conceptualisation of transnationalism', which connects the latter with the emergence of nation-states in the world and which makes meaningful the idea of *trans*-national border crossing, exchange and circulation. This approach is necessary all the more for Orthodox Churches, whose history shows a tightly knit connection between their ecclesiology and national reference.

Literature on religion and transnationalism usually analyses the transformations of religion and religious institutions occasioned by migration and settlement, in the course of exchange between migrants across national borders, between the sending and receiving country. The bulk of literature erroneously describes these transformations as the result of interconnectedness, when in reality they happen mainly because migrants and their religion are in minority situation in the host country and need to recreate and reinvent their religious identity in a context that has not been shaped by the respective religious tradition (or, it has, but with different historical developments, like in the case of the Roman Catholic Church). This observation is supported by Vertovec (2009). For the sake of theoretical consistency, we would like to stick to transnationalism as inherently composed of networks of individuals and institutions that act across nation-state borders. We will look at *what* circulates and how this circulation affects religious identity and religious institutions, resulting into a transnational religious space.

The 'original metaphor' of transnational religion has often been Roman Catholicism, with its multi-layered structures around a world centre down to local congregations – something close to a 'religious international' (Hervieu-Léger 1997: 104), despite the reality of competing strategies among subgroups. However, researchers on transnationalism warn against overdependence on such a paradigm and insist on the variety of expressions of transnational religion (Hoeber Rudolph 1997: 248–9). 'Orthodox Christianity is rarely mentioned as an example of transnational religion' (Roudometof 2013: 1). This is because throughout the history of the Orthodox Church, the principle of congruence between ecclesiastical and political authority has provided a foundation for church organisation. Recent massive migrations from the Orthodox heartlands into the West have occasioned the extension of the jurisdiction of 'mother Churches' outside their national and canonical territories, generating what Roudometof calls 'transnational national communities': 'in several of the host states, these communities employ religion as a major marker of inclusion of their members into a specific ethnic or national group and an important means of maintaining ties with the home country' (Roudometof 2013b: 1). Thus it is safe to say that Orthodox Churches operate as transnational institutions, while maintaining their national focus. To give some examples, let us mention the Russian Orthodox Church's strategy of keeping its jurisdiction over the newly formed post-Soviet Orthodox states, such as Belarus, Ukraine and Moldova, granting autonomy to those national Churches, but not autocephaly. While it has been the practice in Orthodox history that new independent nation-states are granted autocephaly by the previous 'mother Church' (admittedly with more or less reluctance, and sometimes decades of waiting), the Russian Orthodox Church stuck to the idea of a 'Russian world' whose unity should be maintained and thus did not retreat from these territories: a 'spiritual citizenship' was thus supposed to survive the border changes (Rousselet 2001: 194). The Russian Orthodox Church operated also with the same concept at the beginning of the millennium, when the Moscow Patriarchate launched the idea of an all-Western European Russian Metropolia, which would federate all parishes and dioceses of Russian tradition. Another example is the appeal the Romanian Patriarch Daniel made in 2009 to those Romanian parishes in the West which for various reasons had asked for canonical reception in other jurisdictions (e.g. Ecumenical Patriarchate of Constantinople) to return back to the 'mother Church'.

This close relation that the Orthodox parishes in the West maintain with the Churches back home has numerous consequences. One of them is that the political, social and religious transformations in the sending countries have affected the Churches established in the West. For example, the Bolshevik revolution in 1917 has caused divisions in the expatriate Russian Orthodox

Churches, resulting into three jurisdictions in a country such as France: the Russian Orthodox Church Outside of Russia (ROCOR), the Exarchate of the Moscow Patriarchate and the Exarchate of Orthodox Parishes of Russian Tradition in Western Europe (under the Ecumenical Patriarchate). During the Communist period, parishes chose to ask for 'canonical asylum' in other jurisdictions in order to escape the long arm of inimical States through Churches they kept under control: a Romanian parish in the centre of Paris thus came under ROCOR; the Georgian parish founded in the French capital in 1929 placed itself under the Ecumenical Patriarchate. Emigration communities were also able to keep alive a legacy extinct in the home countries: while Ukrainian autocephalist groups had been completely suppressed in Ukraine under Communist rule, they continued in exile, either under the Ecumenical Patriarchate or as independent (non-canonical) bodies, in connection with Ukrainian nationalist aspirations.

It is also noteworthy that most transnational studies focus on transformations taking place in the migrants' religion in host societies as compared to the homeland, but few investigate the further impact these changes have on religion back in the homeland. Example of such reverse influences are found in the field of theology: theological developments in Orthodox theological schools in Paris and New York are now very popular in the Orthodox heartlands and even provide a basis for theological renewal, through the works of Alexander Schmemann, John Meyendorff, Nicolai Afanasiev, Georges Florovsky, Sergii Bulgakov, Olivier Clément, Kallistos Ware, etc. Though the works of these authors may also encounter some opposition (books by Schmemann and Meyendorff – as well as works by Russian priest Alexander Men – were publicly burned as 'heretical' in Yekaterinburg, Russia, upon the instructions of the local bishop in 1998), their writings are now widely spread and read.

Despite this predominantly ethnic character of the Orthodox transnational ties, there are also signs of an emergence of a pan-Orthodox consciousness due to the rediscovery of the universal vocation of Orthodoxy in a migration context.[24] Transnational inter-ethnic Orthodox networks support this type of consciousness. Let us quote the Fraternité Orthodoxe in France, the Orthodox Fellowship of Saint John the Baptist in the UK, Association Saint Silouane, the pan-Orthodox youth movement Syndesmos and other ethnic ones with pan-Orthodox vocation (ACER, Nepsis). These different forums organise annual conferences, spiritual retreats and youth camps; in addition, there are some pan-Orthodox websites (www.orthodoxie.com, www.orthodoxie. ch, www.orthodoxie.be, www.orthodoxie-in-deutschland.de). All these means empower Orthodox in the West (especially converts and Western-born and

---

[24]   Orthodox missionary work outside of the 'Western world', which often comes as a surprise to non-Orthodox, also contributes to such an understanding of the universal call of Orthodoxy. It would make an interesting topic in itself.

-raised Orthodox) with the necessary social capital for maintaining their religious identity.

If we shift the focus to the individual or parish level, we find out that transnational ties help build and strengthen religious identity, which is viewed as endangered by living in a non-Orthodox environment. Thus people and parishes organise pilgrimages and youth camps in Orthodox monasteries back in the homeland, invite spiritual charismatic figures for regular conferences, maintain close connections to a spiritual father in the home country, etc. This transnational circulation of Orthodox ideas, people, spiritual and material goods (books, icons, religious objects) creates what Ihlamur-Öner calls 'the transnational Orthodox space', which, however, often operates on an ethnic basis. This has not only an impact on the migrants, helping them sustain and reaffirm their religious identity, but also on those actors which are not migrants, back in the sending context, by way of making them familiar with challenges their co-religionists face in the West: conversion, intermarriage, recomposed families and other personal issues. For spiritual fathers located in remote monasteries who listen to emigrants' confessions, this entails a broadening of their vision of the Orthodox world and of social and spiritual issues Orthodox face in the West.

Orthodoxy and 'Glocalization'

The relationship between religion and globalisation can be reformulated in terms of 'glocalization' (Robertson, cited in Martikainen 2013), which describes the interplay between local cultures and world religions. In discussing glocalizations of Eastern Orthodox Christianity, Victor Roudometof (2012) broadened the picture with a historical perspective, producing a list of four forms of blending universal religion with local particularism: vernacularisation (Orthodoxy expressed in a particular language), indigenisation (Orthodoxy related to a particular ethnic identity), nationalisation (Orthodoxy as a source for nation formation) and transnationalisation (the extension of the jurisdiction of 'mother churches' to other territories than the traditional national ones). Though it is not clear how transnationalisation can be a form of glocalization, since the former implies multiple locations and multiple cultural references, this theorisation is a valuable one. We would like to expand Roudometof's list with the idea of 'autochthonism', brought by James Kapaló in his contribution to this volume: 'The arrival of Orthodoxy and Orthodox migrants in the West has given rise to a process of reinterpretation of the West's religious past as prototypically Orthodox. This discourse, and the practices that flow from it, can serve to strengthen a sense of belonging amongst migrant Orthodox, who have a means of conceptualising themselves as representatives of the ancient past of their new homeland, tapping into a local "Orthodox memory" and "imaginary",

Introduction 21

and at the same time can also operate to legitimise the religious choices and identities of local Western converts to Orthodoxy' (243).

Innovation

The Orthodox Church is rarely associated with the idea of innovation, but rather with its apparent opposite: conservatism. That might stem from a hasty interpretation of Orthodoxy's commitment to tradition (patristics, past practices, Ecumenical Councils, experience of the saints) as something immutable and rigid. This impression is further reinforced by the fact that the Orthodox Church ascribes to tradition a normative and authoritative value. Orthodox theology considers patristics and the experience and the teachings of the saints as permanent expressions of eternal truth (Lossky 1974). Though these teachings are admittedly shaped in precise cultural and historical contexts, their spirit bears a universal dimension which transcends culture and history and thus makes them operable in other societies and times (Meyendorff 1978). Therefore, the Orthodox Church does not hesitate to draw inspiration from the past for solutions to contemporary issues.

This has attracted a great deal of criticism against the Orthodox Church, often depicted as a monolithic institution which rejects change and is unable to adapt. Yet, recent research (Denizeau 2007, Makrides and Roudometof 2010, Willert and Molokotos-Liederman 2012) proves that, despite a strong attachment to the past and to tradition, the Orthodox Church does innovate. However, innovation is not to be understood from a modern and Western perspective, as originality and radical change breaking with the past, but rather as a modality of interpreting tradition. Makrides shows that

> since the beginning of the modern age until today people are more used to connecting innovation with novelty and originality, which is perhaps understandable in the context of a linear perspective on history and the concomitant idea of continuing progress. Yet, this was not necessarily the case with previous historical eras. For example, in Byzantium there were aesthetic preoccupations that differed from the modern sense of originality [in that] it was not coterminous with innovation and the constant look for novelties everywhere, but with an imitation (μίμησις) of the ancient originals and the copying of the prototypes. (Makrides 2012: 33)

Therefore, innovation in the Orthodox Church consists in a creative interpretation of tradition, in adaptations that maintain the spirit of tradition while allowing for a 'normal' functioning in a modern world. Denizeau's chapter in this volume illustrates the fact that tradition is not a 'copy-and-paste' of the past into the present, but is highly adaptive and plastic and therefore permanently allowing for innovation: 'tradition consists in a process of translation, an accurate one, despite the need to innovate – or rather precisely because of this need. Far from being a mere literal repetition, the spirit of tradition allows for creativity. Its adaptability is incompatible with a literal transmission' (256).

Yet, there is no one general Orthodox way in which to implement tradition in a new cultural setting. Migration has occasioned the need to innovate and adapt to such new environments, but not all Orthodox Churches have deployed the same strategies: while some bishops encourage their dioceses in Western Europe to maintain Orthodoxy through the perpetuation of their ethnic and national identity and their ancestral customs, others assert the need to enculturate Orthodoxy in the host countries and shift the focus from the ethnic character of their faith in order to leave more space for its universal dimension.

Another important point about innovation in the Orthodox Church is the fact that novelties are introduced not for the sake of change, but as a way of getting back to the authentic tradition. Drawing on conclusions from Willert and Molokotos-Liederman (2012), we can say that 'innovative attempts or achievements have often occurred under the cover of traditionalist and conservative discourses' and that 'advocates of innovation in orthodoxy have often presented their arguments in a traditionalist rhetoric'. Paraphrasing Halbwachs, Anastassiadis has noted that 'a successful innovation has to appear as non-innovative as possible' (Anastassiadis, cited in Willert and Molokotos-Liederman 2012: 4). This is illustrated in the chapters by Mayer, and Hämmerli and Mucha.

We would like to note that innovation is context-bound and that it may appear as a novelty or as a continuity, depending on the perspective taken on it (insiders versus outsiders, conservatives versus progressives, etc.). Thus, in the Sourozh case, discussed by Hämmerli and Mucha in this volume, what appeared as 'Westernisation' to some members was just 'normalisation' and return to the sources to others. And later, when massive influx of Russians arrived in the diocese, these innovations introduced for the sake of being more authentically traditional, were challenged because they seemed too remote from tradition.

To summarise, innovation is 'an inherent modality' of the Orthodox Church (Willert and Molokotos-Liederman 2012), but it operates in the framework of tradition and not as a break from it. Renewal and adaptations are often justified in the name of deepening the meaning of tradition and not as departing from the past. Innovation does not involve sustainable change, but is highly relative and context-bound.

Conclusion

In conclusion, we would like to note that it is highly important that we begin to reflect on the theoretical tools available in the migration and religion field and test their validity for the Orthodox realities. This is an urgent matter for future developments in the study of Orthodox Churches and migration, as evidenced by the fact that concepts are often used randomly and inconsistently: most authors seem to be rarely aware of their complexity or of their questionable application to their field of research. This introduction has attempted to make such an effort of systematisation of the most recent theories on migration, minority, diaspora, transnationalism, globalisation with respect to Orthodox migrations. We are aware of the weaknesses inherent in such a first attempt, but we intend it as a starting point for further research and reflection. We are confident that this volume offers informative material, despite the many remaining black holes, and we hope that reading it will challenge more scholars and students to engage into a field where much remains to be done.

The editors of this book would like to thank those who have made it possible, starting with the staff of Ashgate, especially Sarah Lloyd, who showed interest in the project from the beginning, and Kirsten Weissenberg, who supervised the production of this book step by step. We would also like to thank Professor François Hainard (Sociological Institute of the University of Neuchâtel), who welcomed the December 2010 conference that gave the impetus for this volume. We feel a special gratitude toward Matthew Baker (PhD candidate, Fordham University) who helped with language editing and made many other useful suggestions. We are also grateful to Henry Bertram for his careful final editing of the book. Finally, we thank the Religioscope Institute (Fribourg) for having provided some of the funding for this volume, as well as the Swiss National Foundation for Scientific Research (Bern) for having funded part of the 2010 conference.

Bibliography

Baumann, M. 2000. Diaspora: Genealogies of Semantics and Transcultural Comparison. *Numen*, 47(3): 313–37.

Baumann, M. 2002. Migrant Settlement, Religion and Phases of Diaspora. *Migration: A European Journal of International Migration and Ethnic Relations*, 33–5: 93–117.

Bruneau, M. 1993. L'Église orthodoxe et la diaspora hellénique. *Social Compass*, 40(2): 199–216.

Chaillot, C. (ed.) 2005. *Histoire de l'Église orthodoxe en Europe occidentale au 20e siècle*. Paris: Dialogue entre Orthodoxes.

Cohen, R. 1997. *Global Diasporas*. Seattle: University of Washington Press.

Daldas, N. 1995. Le statut de la diaspora orthodoxe. *Istina*, 40(4): 386–404.

Denizeau, L. 2007. Le reste et la promesse: Étude ethnographique d'une tradition monastique orthodoxe en France. Doctoral Thesis, defended 30 November 2007, Université Lumière Lyon II.

Dufoix, S. 2003. *Les diasporas*. Paris: PUF.

Encyclopaedia Britannica. 2013. *2013 Britannica Book of the Year*. Chicago: Encyclopaedia Britannica, Inc.

Eurel. 2010. Religious Affiliation in 2010. Available at: http://www.eurel.info/spip.php?rubrique495 [accessed 30 July 2013].

Hämmerli, M. 2010. 'Orthodox *Diaspora*?': A Sociological and Theological Problematisation of a Stock Phrase. *International Journal for the Study of the Christian Church*, 10(2): 97–115.

Hervieu-Léger, D. 1997. Faces of Catholic Transnationalism: In and Beyond France, in *Transnational Religion and Fading States*, edited by S. Hoeber Rudolph and J. Piscatori. Boulder: Westview Press, 104–118.

Hinnells, J.R. 1997. The Study of Diaspora Religion, in *A New Handbook of Living Religions*, edited by J.R. Hinnells. Oxford: Blackwell, 682–90.

Hoeber Rudolph, S. 1997. Dehomogenizing Religious Formations, in *Transnational Religion and Fading States*, edited by S. Hoeber Rudolph and J. Piscatori. Boulder: Westview Press, 243–61.

Kenny, K. 2013. *Diaspora*. Oxford: Oxford University Press.

Koser, K. 2007. *International Migration*. Oxford: Oxford University Press.

Krindatch, A. 2010. Highlights from the Census 'Religious Congregations and Membership Study 2010'. Available at: http://www.hartfordinstitute.org/research/2010-USOrthodox-Census.pdf [accessed December 2012].

Lee, E.S. 1966. A Theory of Migration. *Demography*, 3: 47–57.

Levitt, P. 2001a. *The Transnational Villagers*. Berkeley: University of California Press.

Levitt, P. 2001b. Between God, Ethnicity, and Country: An Approach to the Study of Transnational Religion. Paper presented at the Workshop *Transnational Migration: Comparative Perspectives*, 30 June–1 July 2001, Princeton University.

Lossky, V. 1974. *In the Image and Likeness of God*. Crestwood, NY: St Vladimir's Seminary Press.

Louth, A. 2012. Orthodoxy and the Problem of Identity. *International Journal for the Study of the Christian Church*, 12(2): 96–104.

Makrides, V. and Roudometof, V. 2010. *Orthodox Christianity in 21st Century Greece. The Role of Religion in Culture, Ethnicity and Politics*. Farnham: Ashgate.

Makrides, V. 2012. Orthodox Christianity, Change, Innovation: A Contradiction in Terms?, in *Innovation in the Orthodox Christian Tradition? The Question of Change in Greek Orthodox Thought and Practice*, edited by T.S. Willert and L. Molokotos-Liederman. Farnham: Ashgate, 19–52.

Marienstras, R. 1989. On the Notion of Diaspora, in *Minority Peoples in the Age of Nation States*, edited by G. Chaliand. London: Pluto Press, 119–25.

Martikainen, T. 2004. *Immigrant Religions in Local Society: Historical and Contemporary Perspectives in the City of Turku*. Turku: Åbo Akademi University Press.

Martikainen, T. 2013. *Religion, Migration, Settlement: Reflections on Post-1990 Immigration to Finland*. Leiden and Boston: Brill.

Mayer, J.-F. 2009. A Field Ripe for Harvest: Missionaries and New Religious Movements in Eastern Europe, in *Quo Vadis Eastern Europe? Religion, State and Society after Communism*, edited by Ines Angeli Murzaku. Ravenna: Longo Editore, 75–88.

Meyendorff, J. 1978. *Living Tradition: Orthodox Witness to the Contemporary World*. Crestwood, NY: St Vladimir's Seminary Press.

Ministry of Administration and Interior. 2012. Tab. 8: Populatia Stabila Dupa Principalele Religii la Recensamantul Din Anul 2011 – Rezultate Preliminare. Available at: http://www.recensamantromania.ro/wp-content/uploads/2012/08/TS8.pdf [accessed 30 July 2013].

Model, S. 2008. Une page méconnue de l'histoire de l'orthodoxie en Occident: La mission orthodoxe belge (1963–1987). *Irénikon*, 81(1): 24–49.

Papathomas, G. 2005. La relation d'opposition entre 'Église localement établie' et 'Diaspora Ecclésiale'. *Contacts*, 210: 96–132.

Roudometof, V. 2000. Transnationalism and Globalization: The Greek Orthodox Diaspora between Orthodox Universalism and Transnational Nationalism. *Diaspora*, 9: 361–98.

Roudometof, V. 2012. The Glocalisations of Eastern Orthodox Christianity. *European Journal of Social Theory*. Available at: http://est.sagepub.com/content/early/2012/10/16/1368431012459694 [accessed July 2013].

Roudometof, V. 2013a. The Glocalizations of Eastern Orthodox Christianity. *European Journal of Social Theory*, 16(2): 226–45.

Roudometof, V. 2013b. Orthodox Christianity as a Transnational Religion: Theoretical, Historical and Comparative Considerations. Paper prepared for presentation at the International Society for Sociology of Religion Conference *Rethinking Community: Religious Continuities and Mutations in Late Modernity*, Turku, Finland, 27–30 June 2013.

Rousselet, K. 2001. Globalisation et territoire religieux en Russie, in *La Globalisation du Religieux*, edited by J.-P. Bastian, F. Champion and K. Rousselet. Paris: L'Harmattan, 183–96.

Schnapper, D. 2001. De l'État-nation au monde transnational: Du sens et de l'utilité du concept de Diaspora. *REMI*, 17(2): 9–36.

Venturas, L. 2002. Greek Immigrants in Postwar Belgium: Community and Identity Formation Processes. *Journal of the Hellenic Diaspora*, 28(1): 33–72.

Vertovec, S. 1999. Three Meanings of 'Diaspora', Exemplified among South Asian Religions. *Diaspora*, 7(2). Available at: http://www.transcomm.ox.ac.uk/working%20papers/diaspora.pdf [accessed December 2009].

Vertovec, S. 2000. Religion and Diaspora. Paper presented at the conference *New Landscapes on Religion in the West*, School of Geography and the Environment, University of Oxford, 27–29 September 2000.

Vertovec, S. 2009. *Transnationalism*. London and New York: Routledge.

Ware, K. 2005. L'Église orthodoxe dans les Iles britanniques, in *Histoire de l'Église orthodoxe en Europe occidentale au 20e siècle*, edited by C. Chaillot. Paris: Dialogue entre Orthodoxes, 37–56.

Willert, T.S. and Molokotos-Liederman, L. 2012. *Innovation in the Orthodox Christian Tradition? The Question of Change in Greek Orthodox Thought and Practice*. Farnham: Ashgate.

Yang, F. and Ebaugh, H.R. 2001. Religion and Ethnicity among New Immigrants: The Impact of Majority/Minority Status in the Home and Host Countries. *Journal for the Scientific Study of Religion*, 40(3), 367–78.

PART I
Migration and Settlement

Chapter 1

Romanian Orthodox Churches in Italy: The Construction of the Romanian–Italian Transnational Orthodox Space

Suna Gülfer Ihlamur-Öner

The growing presence of migrants has become an important structural characteristic of Italian society, the labour market, organisation of private and urban space, and the functioning of the welfare state (Sciortino and Colombo, 2003: 7). Italy, as a receiving country of immigration since the late 1970s, is becoming more religiously pluralistic due to the arrival and settlement of migrants belonging to different faiths and religious organisations. The Italian population is predominantly Catholic. Despite the revision of the state's relations with the Catholic Church in 1984 (Spini 2003: 420), the Catholic Church is a privileged actor in the Italian religious landscape and in migration management. The transplantation of migrant religious institutions in Italy enhances the encounters of the Catholic Church and Italian society with different religions, while rendering the Italian religious landscape diverse and competitive.

The majority of immigrants that arrive in Italy today belong to the Christian faith, particularly Orthodox Christianity. Recent East-to-West migration makes Orthodoxy a Western European religion as much as an Eastern European one. However, the growing presence and visibility of the Orthodox churches and communities in the Italian religious landscape reflects and reproduces the fragmented nature of the Orthodox world and the complex divisions and rivalries among different Orthodox Churches. Among all the Orthodox Churches present in Italian territory, the Romanian Orthodox parish churches are the most numerous, and could construct a well-structured and functioning network extending beyond Italy to Romania and other parts of Europe. This chapter analyses the way in which the Romanian Orthodox Church (BOR, Biserica Ortodoxă Română) acts, organises and positions itself within the religious landscape of Italy following the mass immigration of Romanians, its adaptive practices and socio-religious role within the receiving context, and the extent of its agency within the Romanian–Italian transnational migration space. After touching upon the migratory processes that led to the emergence

30 *Orthodox Identities in Western Europe*

of Romanian Orthodox communities within the Italian religious landscape, the establishment of the BOR parishes within Italy and the organisational and structural adaptation processes that the BOR parishes go through in a new setting are elaborated upon. The concluding section discusses the future prospects for the BOR parishes and Romanian Orthodox communities in Italy.

Transnational Romanian Migration to Italy and the Romanian Orthodox Church

It was the abrupt collapse of the communist regime with a violent uprising as well as delayed reforms (Phinnemore and Light 2001: 1) that paved the way for labour migration from Romania to Europe, which evolved mainly in three phases.[1] The first phase, from 1990 to 1994, consisted of trans-frontier movements and shuttle trade. The second phase, from 1994 to 2000, consisted of migratory waves with or without visas, which were first directed towards Germany and then changed direction towards Italy and Spain, while the last phase, from 2002 onwards, involves different forms of mobility and circuits (Diminescu, cited in Perrotta 2007: 96).

However, it was the decision of the EU to abolish visa requirements for the Romanians in the Schengen area in 2002 that transformed the Romanian migration patterns to Italy (Anghel 2008a: 39). The Bossi-Fini law, which regularised many immigrants including Romanians, was also passed in 2002 and had a crucial impact on the mobility of the Romanians in Italy and Europe.[2] A policy change from above (at the EU and Italian level) has led to change in patterns, relations and transnational practices from below, 'opened up a space for multiple forms of mobility' (Anghel 2008b: 795) and imposed a circular character on the Romanian migration (Ciobanu 2008: 22). With the abolition of visa requirements Romanian migration to Italy turned into mass migration (Anghel 2008a: 46), and with the accession of Romania into the EU in January 2007 the Romanians became EU citizens and Romanian migration gained the character of 'mobility within the European Union', rather than

---

[1] Baldwin-Edwards defines four phases of Romanian migration into Europe: 1990–1993 – mass permanent emigration of ethnic Germans and Hungarians and emigration of ethnic Romanians seeking political asylum in Western Europe; 1994–1996 – Romanian economic irregular migration to Western Europe at a limited scale; 1996–2001 – emergence of different types of migratory waves; 2002 to present – following the abolition of visa requirement for the Schengen area, an increase in circular migration (2008: 260).

[2] On 30 July 2002, law no. 189 (the Bossi-Fini law) was passed and 702,156 irregular immigrants applied for regularisation (Colombo and Sciortino 2003: 195). 143,000 Romanians without a stay permit applied for regularisation in 2002 (Baldwin-Edwards 2008: 262). The Bossi-Fini law regularised 141,673 Romanians (Perrotta 2007: 97).

migration (Silaşi and Simina 2008: 320). Commuting ('pendolarism') between Romanian villages and Italy for seasonal work comprises an important part of the Romanian migration to Italy (Cionchin 2006: 170). Circular migration has become a 'life strategy' for many Romanian migrants (Sandu 2000) who are embedded in two contexts and establish networks linking different localities (Cingolani 2009: 14, 201; Perrotta 2007: 104) through which goods, resources, ideas, experiences and symbols flow. Moreover, geographical, cultural and linguistic proximity of Romania to Italy as well as phone calls, internet, visits (from and to Romania), cheap airlines or buses, Romanian transport companies that carry gifts or food packs or money in between facilitate this flow. Today Romanians constitute the most numerous migrant group in Italy (21.2 per cent of all migrants). According to the Italian National Institute of Statistics (Istat) in its December 2010 figures, there are 968,576 Romanians resident in Italy among 4,570,317 foreign nationals.[3]

It was the transnational Romanian migration that brought the BOR parishes into Italy. The BOR was faced with new opportunities and challenges immediately after the fall of the communist regime, and was engaged in reconquering the Romanian landscape, public space and institutions. Mass migration and the spread of Romanian diaspora have radically changed the way the BOR perceives its jurisdiction.[4] Throughout the Cold War years, the jurisdiction of the BOR extended over Romania.[5] Soon after the fall of the Ceauşescu regime, however, the Romanian nation – both the Romanian Orthodox Christians in Romania and in diaspora[6] – became the main reference point for the BOR. The extension of its jurisdiction beyond its traditional homeland, while providing the BOR with the possibility of access to and agency within the transnational space, has put its abilities in an enlarged space with a bigger agenda to test.

---

[3] Italian National Institute of Statistics (Istat). 2010. Popolazione Straniera Residente in Italia. Available at http://demo.istat.it/str2010/index.html [accessed 25 October 2012]. However, this figure does not include seasonal and circular migrants. According to the Romanian authorities there are 1.5–2.5 million Romanians in Italy. The difference in figures stems from high level of circular migration between the two countries, which ranges around 600,000 to 1,000,000 (Simina, cited in Baldwin-Edwards 2008: 263).

[4] The term diaspora refers to 'the dispersion in time and space of the Orthodox communities, which settle in regions different from their mother churches are located, keeping with them the ultimate canonical dependence relation or spiritual ties, but progressively searching to organise themselves in an autonomous way' (Bobrinskoy 2003: 303).

[5] Ministry of Religious Affairs. 1949. Statut Pentru Organizarea si Functionarea Bisericii Ortodoxe Române. Available at: http://www.legex.ro/Statut-Nr.4593-din-17.02.1949-198. aspx [accessed 1 February 2012].

[6] Statutul Pentru Organizarea şi Funcţionarea Bisericii Ortodoxe Române 1989. 1990. *Biserica Ortodoxa Romana* [*Official Bulletin of the Romanian Orthodox Church*], 108(11–12): 222.

Organisational Adaptation of the Romanian Orthodox Churches in the Romanian–Italian Transnational Space

Human mobility leads to the transfer or transplantation of home country institutions in a new setting with a view to emulating the home country's social order. While a social order cannot be emulated to its full, transplantation of institutions always leads to a process of adaptation, which depends on the particularities of migration patterns and migrant community as well as the particularities of the receiving context and ties with the sending context. As Martikainen argues, migrant religious organisations go through organisational and structural adaptation processes as they try to organise themselves in a new setting. Organisational adaptation includes the relationship of the migrant parishes with the mother church in the country of origin, the decisions of which directly affect the migrant parishes, besides the decrees and acts of the local authorities and national legislation (2005: 125–6).

Berzano argues that the religious aspect remains dormant for new immigrants to be reawakened in latter phases of the migration cycle (2008: 1). Migrants start reactivating their religious values and spirituality, and in this reactivation basic needs come first. This paves the way for the transplantation of the religious organisations in the receiving context, followed by full integration with citizenship rights and then the emphasis shifts to cultural rights and identity (ibid.). It is the Romanian migrants that pulled the BOR parishes into Italian territory. In almost all cases, it is the Romanian community of an Italian city or town that took the initiative for the opening of a Romanian Orthodox parish church in their town, as the first generation of migrants grew in number. As one priest argues, the Romanians want to have their own churches, since away from home they feel 'without roots'. The priest brings some of the 'roots' and 'like a magnet' attracts and brings together the scattered members of the community (Pr. Milăşan,[7] personal communication, Bolzano, 18 January 2008). Religion within the migration context has the power of regrouping and reorganising people who have gone through a process of disorganisation or a process of 'decomposition and recomposition' (Chiaramonte 2008: 18). The migrant churches have a very important function in reorganising unorganised and atomised migrant communities (Berzano 2008: 2). The BOR reminds the faithful of their home, traditions, Romania. It provides a familiar space for reproduction of traditions and, by acting as a reference point for solution of problems, facilitates adaptation to the new setting. Therefore, resort to religion is an adaptive means (Pr. Roşu, personal communication, Turin, 19 March 2008).

---

[7] Pr. is an abbreviated form of the word *preot* in Romanian, which means 'priest' in English.

Even though the parishes are growing in number – today there are 193 BOR parishes all around Italy[8] – they are still under construction. While within their traditional homeland, the parish churches emerge and develop somewhat naturally in accordance with the canon law of the Orthodox Church formulated through the Ecumenical Councils and Byzantine legislative system, within the migration context the canon law is observed to the extent that it is possible depending on the resources and circumstances. Economy (*oikonomia*)[9] and *akribeia*[10] are two elements that guide the application of canon law and balance each other. The Rev. Prof. Alexandru I. Stan defines the BOR in diaspora as a 'honeycomb' type of organisation which, depending on the size and contributions of the migrant community, renders the church organisation very flexible and efficient, and facilitates adaptation to the new context (personal communication, Bucharest, 12 March 2007).

There are two main organs of the parishes in Italy: the parochial council, which takes care of the administrative issues, and the committee of women, which deals mainly with practical and socio-cultural aspects of the parish life. A parish council is composed of councillors in charge of church finances, social sphere and administrative issues; its organisational structure is similar to that of a diocese. The women's committee takes the responsibility to make necessary arrangements for preparation of the food packs distributed after the liturgy, cleaning of the church and charity work as well as the representation of the BOR in cultural festivals (parochial council member of the BOR in Trento, personal communication, Trento, 10 April 2008). Apart from the two principal organs, some BOR parishes have associations for teenagers. However, additional organs and activities depend very much on the limited available resources.

Up until very recently one of the main constraints on the ability of the BOR parishes to better organise religious life and church activities within the Italian context was the BOR's non-recognition by the Italian state. In Italy the Concordat system regulates the Italian state's relations with religious

---

[8] See the official website of the Romanian Orthodox Diocese of Italy. Available at: http://www.diocesiortodossa.it/index.php/ro/parohii-filii-si-paraclise [accessed 11 March 2014].

[9] The concept of economy (*oikonomia*) – adhering to the spirit rather than the letter of the law – refers not only to a canonical practice, but a principle that has shaped the religious outlook of the Orthodox clergy and that regulates the Orthodox Church's relations with the world (Morini 2002: 93). The principle of economy within the Italian context provides the parish priests and community with a certain level of autonomy and flexibility and discretionary power.

[10] In the Orthodox canonical tradition *akribeia* ('exactness') refers to 'strict adherence to the letter of the law' (Richardson and Bowden 1983: 171).

organisations.[11] Article 8 of the Italian Constitution guarantees the equality of all the religious confessions before the law and stipulates that religions other than Catholicism can organise under the Concordat they sign with the Italian state.[12] It is possible for religious communities to sign a Concordat with the Italian state only if there is a religious body representing it, recognised by the Italian state.[13] After lengthy negotiations the BOR was recognised by the Italian state on 12 September 2011 – a significant step towards the signing of a Concordat with the Italian government that would allow the BOR to benefit from *otto per mille*.[14]

Today, despite all the obstacles and lack of limited resources, it is possible to talk about a well-functioning network of the BOR parishes in Italy connected with continuous communication and flow of information. Other means of communication include a monthly journal published by the Metropolitan Church in Paris, regional meetings among the BOR parishes in Italy or

---

[11]   In 1984 the Italian state signed a new Concordat with the Catholic Church and stopped paying the salaries of the Catholic priests. It also introduced the *otto per mile* (0.08 per cent) tax system, which is a voluntary check-off on taxpayer returns. According to this tax system, the tax would be distributed between the Italian state and religious institutions that signed a Concordat with the state or the religious body taxpayers specified. A Concordat also allows the priests of a religious organisation to have access to military barracks, hospitals, schools and prisons to provide their faithful with spiritual support and assistance. A Concordat system also legally recognises the marriages performed by the priests of the religious organisation with the Concordat (Schmidt di Friedberg 2002: 144; Introvigne 2012).

[12]   See Constitution of the Italian Republic. Available at: http://www.senato.it/documenti/repository/istituzione/costituzione_inglese.pdf [accessed 5 March 2013].

[13]   Apart from the Concordat the Italian state signed with the Catholic Church, in 1984 it signed a Concordat with the Waldensian Protestant Church, which also represented the Methodists. Then the state signed Concordats with the Seventh-Day Adventists and Assemblies of God Pentecostals in 1986, the Union of Jewish Communities in 1987 and the Baptists and Lutherans in 1993 (Schmidt di Friedberg 2002: 144), the Mormon Church, the Italian Apostolic Church and Ecumenical Patriarchate of Istanbul in July 2012 and finally the Buddhist Union and the Italian Hindu Union (as the first non-Christian religious organisations) in December 2012 (Introvigne 2012). In 1998, Islamic organisations in Italy demanded to sign a Concordat with the Italian state. However, the government decided not to start negotiations with any of the Muslim groups or associations (Spini 2003: 423).

[14]   The Italian state legally recognised the Romanian Orthodox Diocese of Italy on 12 September 2011, two years after the Diocese's application. Now having the legal personality, the Diocese can buy and own property in its own name in Italy and enjoy different tax advantages (http://www.stranieriinitalia.it/attualita-l_italia_riconosce_ufficialmente_la_chiesa_ortodossa_romena_13743.html); Department of Information and Media. Romanian Orthodox Church Officially Recognized in Italy. Available at: http://episcopia-italiei.it/index.php?option=com_content&view=article&id=694:biserica-ortodox-roman-recunoscut-oficial-in-italia&catid=45:comunicate&Itemid=65&lang=it [accessed 25 October 2012].

meetings with the Diocesan Bishop, and annual assemblies gathering the Romanian Orthodox priests in Paris (Pr. Valdman, personal communication, Milan, 18 July 2007). Local parishes also maintain contact through personal ties and friendship among priests who call each other to ask for advice and to exchange or inform one another of experiences regarding parish life (Pr. Verzea, personal communication, Padua, 4 April 2008).

New Missions of the Romanian Orthodox Churches in Italy

Besides organisational adaptation, migrant religious organisations go through structural adaptation processes, which refer to the adaptation of migrant communities and organisations to legal, social, cultural and organisational structures of the new setting (Martikainen 2005: 125). Different from the role they play in the traditional homeland, migrant religious organisations act both as religious and community centres to be more responsive to needs of communities (Ebaugh and Chafetz 1999: 599). The transformative processes that the BOR parishes in Italy go through are no exception to this formulation.

The Romanian Orthodox Churches as Community Centres

Migrants have certain needs, expressed in 'the search for refuge, respectability and resources' (Hirschman 2004: 1208), for which they search in the religious space, since religious institutions are 'the gatekeepers of necessary resources' (Solari 2006: 322). The BOR parishes are the main institutions Romanian migrants turn to within the Italian context, not only to worship but also to get help, to meet or reach out to other Romanians and to preserve their identity. The Orthodox Church is a social space and community centre where Romanian migrants can meet, speak in their native language, exchange information regarding employment or other basic needs, share feelings, make new friends, have a sense of community, and not lose touch with Romania and their Romanian identity. Krindatch (2006a) argues that for Orthodox Christians the church is the place of worship and the idea of the church as sort of a 'social club' is foreign to them. Nevertheless, even though the BOR parishes' main mission and activities are within the religious sphere, the migration experience and transnational context turns them into community centres, confronting them with the need to take on social and cultural responsibilities.

The BOR parishes in Italy are the main reference points for Romanian immigrants whether they are practising Orthodox or not. From the very early stages of the Romanian migration up until today the BOR parishes continue to be the main place of gathering and socialising, where people can exchange information and share problems encountered in Italy: 'They come here to

36 *Orthodox Identities in Western Europe*

meet the brothers and they meet God' (Pr. Valdman, personal communication, Milan, 18 July 2007). Besides the urge to get information, problems also make people turn to the Church: 'Because unfortunately bad things make us turn to God. And here bad things are plenty' (Pr. Lupăştean, personal communication, Trento, 14 August 2008). Romanian migrants in Italy have all types of problems, from normal life issues to housing, from work to family. Care drain,[15] which has a severe impact on family relations and relations with relatives and friends back home (Sandri 2008: 111), and divided families are a cause of concern for priests both in Romania and Italy (Pr. Roşu, personal communication, Turin, 19 March 2008; Pr. Lupăştean, personal communication, Trento, 14 August 2008). Negative publicity about Romanians in the Italian media creating extra difficulties for the Romanian communities also compels the BOR parishes to be more active in order to undo the negative image.

The experiences of BOR parishes in Italy as community centres requires them to be more socially active and even to formulate a social doctrine to provide the parish priests with some guidance, despite the resistance within the Church against more involvement in the social sphere with the argument that 'the social doctrine sounds too Western' (Pr. Codrea, personal communication, Verona, 20 July 2007). The BOR parishes in Italy have to cater to different types of needs (religious, spiritual, material, social and psychological) and actively get involved to resolve problems (bureaucratic, economic, social) of the Romanian immigrants, a necessity which tests the BOR parishes ability to adapt to the receiving context. This structural adaptation process also has implications for the mother church and its social standing and doctrine.

Two-way Process: Integration and the Reproduction of Ethno-religious Identity

Resort to religion is an adaptive process that allows for the smooth integration of the migrant community to the new setting, while preserving the distinct ethno-religious identity of the migrant community and keeping migrants attached to the sending context. Transnational migration does not weaken the links with the home country but, by creating a particular attachment to the home country, strengthens it. The BOR parishes play a very important role in this. One priest argues: 'Being away makes them more attached' (Pr. Rîmboi,

---

[15] Feminisation of migration and the rise of female migrant-based care models for elderly, disabled and child care in the receiving countries of female migration lead to a care drain in the countries of origin. In Italy, the transition from family care to a 'migrant in the family model of care' leads to outsourcing of domestic and care services to migrants, particularly to migrant women (Bettio et al. 2006: 272). Female care workers contribute to the unity of the Italian family at the expense of their own families. While they migrate with family strategies to cater for the needs of their families, their absence creates problems for child and elderly care back home.

personal communication, Bologna, 24 May 2007). Therefore, adaptation is a two-way process, which leads to integration and maintenance of ethno-religious identity and transnational ties with the sending setting.

The BOR parishes emphasise the importance of integration of the Romanian community into Italian society. As compared to the other migrant communities, the Romanians have some commonalities with the Italians, which might facilitate and precipitate integration. The linguistic proximity and historical ties with Italy, such as the common Latin origin of the people and the language and commonalities in faith, create ambivalence in terms of being very similar but different at the same time. Pr. Valdman is of the view that the linguistic and cultural proximity can serve to facilitate integration; however, it can also favour assimilation (personal communication, Milan, 18 July 2007). Since it is easy for the Romanians to learn Italian in a relatively short period of time, younger generations drop out of school to go to Italy (Pr. Uţa, Ecclesiastical Relations Department of the Romanian Orthodox Patriarchate, personal communication, Bucharest, 28 March 2007). Similarities require the BOR parishes to be more prudent and proactive in maintaining the traits that make them distinct. Therefore, the BOR parishes have the difficult task of balancing two opposing tendencies: encouraging and supporting Romanian emigrants to be well integrated into the fabric of Italian society, while ensuring that the Romanian Orthodox faith, tradition, language, culture and identity are maintained through the local, translocal and transnational agency of the BOR parishes. However, keeping Romanians attached to the Orthodox tradition in the Italian setting is a big challenge, since both the BOR parishes and the Romanians coming from a setting where Orthodox Christianity is the majority faith, come into contact with a different kind of reality in Italy. Being in a minority position in Italy leads many of Romanian immigrants to devote more time and energy to their faith as it is questioned, challenged or contested in a new setting.

The priests are trying to teach the Orthodox faith and tradition first to their own people and then to introduce it to the Italians (Pr. Lupăştean, talk delivered at the Focolare Movement Meeting, Trento, 21 January 2008). Restrictions on practising religion under the communist rule in Romania, communist propaganda and restrictions on religious belief and practice had a negative impact on religious training of the people. Therefore, in some cases the priests have to engage in missionary activity within their own community. This makes pastoral work more challenging, complicated and demanding, particularly when some faithful lack basic knowledge. While teaching the Orthodox faith to Romanians serves a missionary goal, the urge to introduce it to the Italians does not aim at bringing new adherents into the flock. The BOR is interested in keeping its own community intact and tries to lessen the loss of members due to mixed marriages and conversion. The BOR, by introducing Romanian Orthodox faith and culture into Italian society, aims to underline the commonalities between two faiths and cultures and to facilitate the smooth integration of Romanians. It also seeks to prevent prejudices and discrimination against Romanians owing to their ethno-religious identity and language, which make them distinct. Therefore, the goal is to maintain religious and ethnic identity and to consolidate it, while integrating into Italian society and making a positive contribution to it.

Migrant religious organisations play a key role in the reproduction of traditions and ethnic culture in the receiving context. Gurvitch argues that the ethnic churches maintain the mythic-symbolic memory of the group in a different context than the original through the reproduction of 'social frames of cognition', which gives a sense to the individual migrant's existence. The liturgy and religious ceremonies become an expression of national, regional culture, identity and language mingled up with religious tradition and values. The sacred is a referent in mobilising people and resources for the formulation of transnational ties and space (cited in Berzano 2008: 3). Ethnic, cultural and linguistic identity is part of the religious identity and tradition, particularly for the Orthodox Churches. The BOR presents itself 'as the privileged *keeper* and *guardian* of national values' in Romania (Conovici 2006: 1). Within the transnational migration context and in a predominantly Catholic country like Italy, the role of the BOR as the guardian of national identity and language is accentuated. Keeping the Orthodox faith in Italy becomes an expression of the national identity and a way of articulating transnational spiritual ties.

National identity is an important element of the Romanian Orthodox liturgy. During the liturgy, besides the hierarchs and priests of the BOR, the priests and parishioners pray for the Romanian state, soldiers, people and land. Since the liturgy is in Romanian, the Church reproduces Romanian religious as well as national identity. Romanian national dishes are distributed after the liturgy. Many come to the Church to hear the liturgy in Romanian as well as to communicate and socialise in Romanian. Sometimes families bring their children to the BOR parishes dressed up in Romanian national costumes.

The Romanian language is one of the main factors that create a sense of community and familiarity within the Church space. The language issue is one of the main concerns of the first generation, while socialisation of the second generation into the religious traditions as well as the language and culture of the parents becomes one of the main tasks of immigrant churches (Martikainen 2005: 127). There is an important dilemma, particularly for the first-generation parents, who want their children to be well integrated into the new society. They want their children to have good educational skills and to speak the language of the receiving society well. However, they also want to transfer their ethnic and cultural heritage to their children and coming generations through their own language. First-generation parents turn to their religious institutions for the teaching of their mother tongue (Ebaugh and Chafetz 2000: 102). Therefore, religious organisations take on the task of teaching and transmitting religious, ethnic and cultural identity through language to the second generation. Most of the BOR parishes are trying to organise Sunday schools for the second generation to teach catechism blended with the Romanian language, history and geography, as in Verona, Turin, Bologna, Milan, Ivrea, Padua and Mestre. Upon the request of the families they also teach Italian and English at the BOR in Mestre. In some BOR parishes, the priests' wives take an active role in the teaching and organisation of courses, as in Padua or Verona. Since many Romanians have to work even on Sundays, there are very few volunteers. In the parochial school of Turin, teaching is mostly performed in a systematic way, with courses on catechism, Romanian language, history and geography, handicrafts and traditional dances.

Food is another important national element that is reproduced within the religious setting. Goldsmith talks about the 'centrality of food as a religious expression' (cited in Ebaugh and Chafetz 1999: 590). In congregations composed of one nationality, consumption of national food helps in reproducing and strengthening the ties between religion and national traditions (ibid.: 591), which is also the case in the BOR parishes in Italy. Bread is an indispensable element of parish life and it is customary to bring bread for the service. *Sarmale* – vine leaf rolls stuffed with minced meat, rice, onion and some spices – are a traditional dish served after the liturgy. *Colivă*[16] is a sweet introduced by a saint and distributed after the memorial service. Besides its religious function, sharing and serving food in the BOR parishes helps ethno-religious community building.

Romanian Orthodox Priests as Community Leaders

The main witnesses and protagonists of the structural adaptation process that the BOR parishes go through in Italy are the Romanian Orthodox priests. Thus, it is not only the religious organisation that is transformed by the process of migration but also the duties and area of activity of the priests. The priesthood consists of different type of duties and activities. The main vocation of the priest is his religious mission. Besides his religious and integrative roles (defining groups and organisations with which he will collaborate), the priest has practitioner roles such as 'preacher, pastor, teacher, priest, administrator and organiser' (Hoge 2000: 373). The priest is also a group leader and counsellor (Moberg 1962: 488–90). Within the migration setting certain roles of the priests are accentuated.

In most cases the priests ordained to serve in Italy, previously by the Metropolitan Church in Paris and now by the Diocesan Bishop of the BOR in Italy, are already in Italy for study purposes or work as deacons in a Romanian

---

[16] Traditionally its main ingredient is wheat, even though local recipes vary widely and it is also made with barley. It is a dish that symbolises death and resurrection.

40   *Orthodox Identities in Western Europe*

Orthodox parish church, since they are familiar with the setting, society and the language as well as the requirements of the Romanian Orthodox communities in Italy. However, transnational ties between Italy and Romania could also lead to the construction of a Romanian Orthodox parish and ordainment of a priest from a particular locality, as was the case for the BOR parish in Ivrea, established through the contacts of the Romanians in Ivrea and Suceava with the ordination of a Romanian priest from Suceava.

Romanian priests face many challenges in Italy. Initially they can be overwhelming. Even having work experience and a knowledge of the setting may not suffice. The BOR, which is the church revered by the majority of the population, becomes a minority or immigrant church in Italian territory and within the Catholic context. According to one priest, this creates a big challenge for the Romanian Orthodox Patriarchate; the Patriarchate should send the most capable as well as 'cultured and open minded' priests who can cope with this new context (Pr. Valdman, personal communication, Milan, 18 July 2007). While one clergyman argues that priests ordained in Italy should be ready to reach out to believers in a more 'modern' context compared to the 'traditional' one in Romania (ibid.), others argue that working in diaspora requires Romanian Orthodox priests to adopt a different pastoral strategy (Pr. Milăşan, personal communication, Bolzano, 18 January 2008), since the dispersed settlement, dimensions and composition of the parish community makes the pastoral work more challenging.

Pastoral work becomes more challenging especially on account of the limited resources of the Church. Financially the Orthodox churches are weaker compared to the Catholic and Protestant parishes.[17] Since the BOR parishes in Italy have limited resources and depend mostly on the contributions of the community, a 'greater sense of financial responsibility to the church' (Levitt 2001: 172) is required. The rent or the maintenance bills of the churches and the salaries of the priests of some BOR parishes are paid with the contributions of the Romanian Orthodox parish communities. Since the contribution priests get from the Patriarchate is meagre and symbolic, amounting to a mere 200 euros per month, most of the priests have to work during the week in order to get by and to maintain their families.[18] The need to work puts an extra burden on the priests in trying to cater for different needs and problems.

---

[17] Similarly, some of the Orthodox parish communities in the US fail to organise Sunday schools or other educational services due to limited resources and lack of volunteers (Krindatch 2008: 18).

[18] Among the challenges that the Orthodox priests in the US face are maintaining their families with limited income, heavy work load, limited support from the parishioners, difficulty in balancing power and authority within the church and lack of or limited administrative support (Krindatch 2006b: 25).

The priests visit prisons and hospitals, and provide information about jobs and accommodation. They give assistance regarding residence or work permit issues. They get to know the families in their parish better when they visit the parishioners to bless their houses. As they themselves go through similar problems with the members of their parish community and develop closer relations with migrants, they manage to come up with appropriate answers to the immigrants' problems (Pr. Lupăştean, personal communication, Trento, 14 August 2008). The involvement of the priests in the lives of the parish communities enables them to be active community workers, and the main reference point for the people to ask for advice or help. They actively engage in community building. This requires a lot of effort, patience and a conciliatory role, not only because the churches have limited resources, but also due to the fact that the members of the parish communities (the Romanians and Moldovans) come from different regions and have different religious practices and traditions. Therefore, the diaspora situation requires the priests to be innovative, 'read the territory well, to be always in contact with the spiritual but also daily needs of the people' (Pr. Roşu, personal communication, Turin, 19 March 2008).

The priests tend to approach the church services in innovative ways, particularly as they use the sermons to communicate with the parish communities. The sermon consists of two parts. The first part focuses on the chapter of the Gospel recited during the liturgy. The second part is devoted to parish life and certain issues or problems that concern the Romanian communities in Italy, communication of the messages of the metropolitan of the church or the diocesan bishop, and certain announcements (sometimes as a response to questions from the faithful via emails or phone calls) on religious practices, job announcements or the collection of money for those in need of help, migrant festivals and activities of the Romanian or Moldovan associations. The sermons also urge the faithful to learn more about their faith in order to strengthen it and to not to be so easily 'deceived'. Therefore, the sermon gains new and important functions within the Italian setting.

Migrant Religiosity

Religious institutions, besides social and material resources, provide emotional and spiritual resources, which have a very important function in the lives of immigrants in the receiving context (Cancellieri 2008). The habitual order and abilities fitting the context one is born into and is used to dissolves as one migrates. The challenge of adjusting to a new setting strains the migrants' mental and psychological abilities as they long for traditional order that they are used to (Zaretsky 1996: 96). Testimonies of the Romanian churchgoers confirm the need for psychological support, due to being away from their home and loved

42 *Orthodox Identities in Western Europe*

ones. This factor is also aggravated by the hardship of adapting to a new setting. Believing in God and going to church provides shelter and acts as a source of healing for those who suffer loneliness, anxiety or loss. The Church provides a space for prayers and relations that help immigrants gain self-respect and compensates for the loss of status. There are many Romanians willing to take part in the parish council, since they tend to equate the councillor duty with 'recognition' (Pr. Verzea, personal communication, Padua, 4 April 2008).

Overcoming difficulties within the migration context by turning to God is neither something specific to Romanians nor something new. Based on his two-year study of nineteenth-century immigrant letters, Dolan argues that talking about God was a common theme in immigrant letters (1988: 69). Migrants believed that God was watching over them in their lives in a new continent, helping, protecting and guiding them, and always close to them (ibid.: 69–70). Many Romanian churchgoers see their very presence in Italy, as well as their sufferings and hardships, as 'God's will', or a test of their belief. Moreover, in a migration setting the rites of passage 'help to cushion shock, carry people over crises and symbolise passage from one stage of life to the next' (Moberg 1962: 350) and strengthen the religiosity of the migrant. For many Romanian families the very presence of a Romanian Orthodox parish church can be the reason for settling in a town, as they want to get their children baptised in accordance with the Orthodox rite and raise them under the guidance of a priest. Among the parishioners, besides those that were practicing Christians, even under the communist rule, there are also some Romanian churchgoers, who have discovered the 'true meaning' of their faith in Italy. One such example is a young Romanian man who has found 'the only real and true friend', Jesus Christ, in Italy (parochial council member of the BOR parish in Trento, personal communication, Trento, 1 April 2008). For many, prayers or confession also gain a new meaning and become a means of providing psychological support and guidance for spiritual issues as well as economic hardships or practical problems.

Religiosity of the Romanians is not restricted to within the walls of the parish church. The icon cards they put in their cars or carry in their purses or pockets, icons they put in their bedrooms and kitchens or display on the wallpaper of their mobile phones, prayer booklets they carry with them in order to recite when they get a chance at home or in the work place, documentaries and sermons recorded from Romanian television or downloaded from the BOR websites, religious movies, documentaries and books exchanged with friends, icon bracelets on arms or the Orthodox crosses on necks, and even angel toys that recite prayers for the children are all different ways, means and places beside religious services.

Agency of the Romanian Orthodox Churches in the Construction of the Romanian–Italian Transnational Orthodox Space

The BOR, Romanian Orthodox priests and parish communities in Italy construct a Romanian–Italian Orthodox space coloured with elements from the Italian Catholic tradition. Migrant communities try to replicate the religious institutions they have back home, which externally and internally resemble native religious buildings in order to strengthen the feeling of being at home (Ebaugh and Chafetz 2000: 81). Certain other elements create a familiar feeling, such as announcements written in the native language or religious books sold inside the church (ibid.). Even though the architecture and internal structure of the churches are designed in accordance with the Latin Catholic tradition – for example, the pews, which one may not find in the Orthodox Church – the liturgy and the parish life as well as the iconostases, icons, incense, prayers and hymns in Romanian, prayer books, and Romanian embroidered covers around or under the icons, all convert and transform the building into a Romanian Orthodox church. Likewise, women covering their hair with scarves, people speaking in Romanian to each other in the church garden or whispering prayers in Romanian within the church and sharing Romanian food and jokes or problems during and after the liturgy render that space a Romanian Orthodox one, even if it is only for those three hours. Beyond the walls of the BOR parishes, the houses or cars decorated with small icons, crosses, candles, prayer books and icon cards, the Orthodox hymns, movies, documentaries and sermons of Romanian Orthodox priests on CDs or video cassettes, the prayers on the lips, in the hearts and minds of the believers when alone, working, walking or traveling are important elements of the Romanian–Italian transnational religious space.

In the case of churches shared with the Catholic parishioners, the religious space is under constant construction and redefinition. Rather than a full conversion of the Church space into an Orthodox one, the space becomes the scene of the construction of the Romanian–Italian religious transnational space. As stated by one priest: 'We have reached a certain point here that we cannot say this church is an Orthodox church or a Catholic church. It is our church' (Pr. Babula, personal communication, Ivrea, 21 March 2008). Through the BOR parishes, Romanian saints and spirituality are transferred to the new setting to become part of the parish life in Italy, as in the case of Sfântul Leontie in the BOR community in Ivrea (ibid.). Emphasising certain feasts or certain saints can also work to create a common ground for the Catholics and Orthodox Christians to come closer and walk together, while bringing new elements into the lives of the Romanian Orthodox Christians in Italy. A church shared by both Catholic and Orthodox communities could act as a space for discovering commonalities. On Easter, celebrated on the same day in April 2007 by both Catholic and Orthodox Christians worldwide, the Catholic and Romanian

Orthodox parishioners in Ivrea prayed together (ibid.). Venerating the saints of the 'undivided church', such as St Vigilius (San Vigilio), who now is in the Romanian Orthodox calendar of saints and feasts and is commemorated by the Romanian Orthodox parishioners in Trento, serves to bridge the gap that arose and widened between the two traditions throughout history (Pr. Lupăştean, talk delivered at the Focolare Movement's Meeting, Trento, 21 January 2008). While Romanians get acquainted with Catholicism, the presence of the BOR parishes in Italy in turn allows the Italian Catholics the chance to learn more about Orthodox Christianity.

Another feature of being a religious space under construction is the changing composition of the Romanian parish communities in Italy. Freedom of movement, while removing the selectivity criteria for the Romanian migration, allowed people from different parts and regions of Romania to migrate to Italy. Enhanced mobility of the Romanians within and out of Italy as EU citizens subjects the parish communities to constant change and makes it difficult for the priests to estimate the exact number of parishioners. Romanians are also very mobile within Italy, since many of them work with short-term contracts or without contracts. When a churchgoer finds a new job in a different city, he or she becomes a member of a different parish in Italy. When a new parish is established in a town, the Romanian faithful that used to go to a nearby town on Sundays to attend the liturgy, and therefore were members of a nearby parish church, become members of the new one. However, as some parishioners maintain their ties with the previous church, they take active part in the articulation of trans-local ties among different BOR communities in Italy.

Ties with the local priests in Romania are maintained even if the Romanian immigrants have been living in Italy for a long time, or plan to settle in Italy. The testimonies of the churchgoers in Italy are indicative of the fact that they keep their social and spiritual ties with priests in Romania. The faithful also help the BOR parishes in Italy to get in touch with local churches in Romania, as in the case of the churchgoer who became the link between the priests of the two parish churches in Trento and Botoşani (member of the women's committee of the BOR parish in Trento, personal communication, Trento, 13 May 2008). Sometimes relatives of immigrants come from Romania, other parts of Italy, or Europe to participate in a marriage or baptism ceremony. This allows for contacts, visits and exchanges among the members of the Romanian diaspora through churchgoing.

Monetary support – in the form of money for the construction or reparation of a church – sent to local parishes in Romania from the BOR parishes in Italy is another way of articulating transnational ties. Even though it may be limited and symbolic in some cases, these contributions and prayers reach a local parish in Romania and through the same process, letters and messages of gratitude are also sent to the BOR parishes in Italy. People also support the BOR parishes by bringing or sending priestly vestments or icons to the priest from Romania. Local ties and networks can also serve to link the BOR parishes in Italy and Romania. In some cases, upon invitation from the Romanian priests in Italy, the priests in Romania visit the BOR parishes, attend the liturgies and strengthen ties. Priests in Romania also get in touch with the BOR parishes in Italy through their family members in Italy (Pr. Matei, personal communication, Mestre, 29 May 2008).

The BOR parishes in Italy play important roles in community building and structuring migrant transnationalism in the Romanian–Italian transnational space. As one priest states, this 'continuous interaction' that starts through transnational migration can lead to transformations within the church: the BOR parishes in diaspora, as the 'branches that went beyond the frontiers', strengthen the trunk, the mother church, by utilising 'Western methodology' to maintain Eastern values. This paves the way for a 'broader vision' for mutual understanding, ecumenical dialogue, enrichment and peaceful co-existence, rather than conflict (Pr. Valdman, personal communication, Milan, 18 July 2007).

In Italy, BOR parishes become community centres – a space for the resolution of problems, the reproduction of Romanian Orthodox identity, and the generation of resources indispensable for the integration of the Romanian migrants – while religious reorganisation leads to the redefinition of the priest's role as well as the way the migrants relate to the Church and conceive their faith. Even though these transformations are developed as a response to local requirements and problems, transnational connections – already established or newly articulated – with localities in Romania sustain, affect and transmit the BOR parishes' experiences to different settings within the Romanian–Italian religious transnational space.

Concluding Remarks

Since it is migration that brought the BOR to Italian territory, the future of its parishes in Italy is tied with the future of the Romanian migration and migrant community in Italy. Factors such as the characteristics of the Romanian migration; socio-economic developments in Italy and Romania; local and national determinants constraining or extending migrant transnationalism; the extent of the Romanians' attachments to Italy developed through experiences, marriages, and children; the extent of their ties and relations with Romania; the agency of transnational secular and religious institutional actors; second-generation self-perception; and preferences regarding living transnational lives – all these would determine the durability of the Romanian–Italian transnational space and ties.

46 *Orthodox Identities in Western Europe*

The issue of language, which is one of the main markers and transmitters of culture and identity, poses a serious challenge to the BOR parishes in Italy. In some churches, liturgies or other church services are already conducted partially in Italian. Moreover, the BOR parishes need to balance their emphasis on preserving and transmitting the Romanian Orthodox identity to the second generation through the Romanian language with the need to make room for the second generation's self-perceptions and attachments. Therefore, the challenge is not only to teach the second generation Romanian language, culture and tradition within the migration setting, but also to do so in a globalising world by finding the right way of constructing dialogue with new generations.

Italian territory proved to be a fertile ground for Romanian Orthodoxy and churches to flourish. Through transnational migration the BOR parishes emerged as small Romanian islands in Italy (Berzano and Cassinasco 1999: 140), and as Romanian migration gains a permanent status, the Romanian Orthodox Patriarchate devotes more attention to Romanians in Italy and Europe based on the belief that the 'Orthodoxy in Italy has a future' (Piovano 2001: 92). In the near future the BOR and their parish communities are planning to construct or transform buildings into Romanian-style Orthodox churches. The construction of the church of the Romanian Orthodox Diocese in Rome has a symbolic meaning and constitutes the next phase in the construction of the transnational Orthodox space. The BOR, besides being a migrant church within the Italian and European landscape, is also a EU member state church, which affects its reconfiguration and agency within the Italian and European context and shows its propensity to upgrade its transnational agency within the EU transnational space.

Bibliography

Anghel, R.G. 2008a. Come hanno fatto i Romeni ad arrivare in Italia?, in *Stranieri in Italia: Trent'anni Dopo*, edited by A. Colombo and G. Sciortino. Bologna: Il Mulino, 19–49.

Anghel, R.G. 2008b. Changing Statuses: Freedom of Movement, Locality and Transnationality of Irregular Romanian Migrants in Milan. *Journal of Ethnic and Migration Studies*, 34(5): 787–802.

Baldwin-Edwards, M. 2008. Migration Policies for a Romania within the European Union: Navigating between Scylla and Charybdis, in *Migration, Mobility and Human Rights at the Eastern Border of the European Union: Space of Freedom and Security*, edited by G. Silaşi and O.L. Simina. Timişoara: Editura Universităţii de Vest, 257–88.

Berzano, L. and Cassinasco, A. 1999. *Cristiani d'Oriente in Piemonte*. Turin: L'Harmattan Italia.

Berzano, L. 2008. 'Etnicità' e Stratificazione Sociale nelle Chiese Etniche. Paper presented at the conference *Ethnic Churches in Italy: Theoretical Aspects and Fieldwork*, Faculty of Political Science, University of Turin, 14 March 2008.

Bettio, F., Simonazzi, A. and Villa, P. 2006. Change in Care Regimes and Female Migration: The 'Care Drain' in the Mediterranean. *Journal of European Social Policy*, 16(3): 271–85.

Bobrinskoy, B. 2003. La diaspora ortodossa in Europa Occidentale: Un ponte tra le due tradizioni europee?, in *L'Ortodossia nella Nuova Europa: Dinamich Storiche e Prospettive*, edited by A. Pacini. Turin: Giovanni Agnelli, 303–319.

Cancellieri, A. 2008. Immigrazione e Religione: Il Caso di Padova. Paper presented at the conference *Ethnic Churches in Italy: Theoretical Aspects and Fieldwork*, Faculty of Political Science, University of Turin, 14 March 2008.

Chiaramonte, E. 2008. *Le Chiese Etniche Pentecostali a Torino*. Unpublished Undergraduate Thesis, Faculty of Political Science, University of Turin.

Cingolani, P. 2007. Dentro e fuori dai confini del paese: La costruzione degli spazi sociali transnazionali e delle differenze tra i migranti Romeni a Torino, in *Un Arcipelago Produttivo: Migranti e Imprenditori tra Italia e Romania*, edited by F. Gambino and D. Sacchetto. Roma: Carocci, 37–64.

Cingolani, P. 2009. *Romeni d'Italia: Migrazioni, Vita Quotidiana e Legami Transnazionali*. Bologna: Il Mulino.

Ciobanu, R.O. 2008. Family Stories of the Romanian Transnational Migration to Spain. Paper presented at IMISCOE PhD Summer Workshop, Lisbon, 30 June–4 July 2008, 1–31.

Cionchin, A.C. 2006. Rapporti fra communità romena e società Italiana: Forme dell'integrazione, in *Cultura Romena in Italia: 80 Anni dalla Creazione della Prima Cattedra di Lingua Romena a Roma*. Proceedings of the Italo-Romanian Conference, 27–28 March 2006. Bucharest: Institutul Cultural Român, 143–211.

Colombo, A. and Sciortino, G. 2003. La Legge Bossi-Fini: Estremismi gridati, moderazioni implicite e frutti avvelenati, in *Politica in Italia: I Fatti dell'Anno e le Interpretazioni*, edited by J. Blondel and P. Segatti. Bologna: Il Mulino, 195–215.

Conovici, I. 2006. The ROC after 1989: Social Identity, National Memory, and the Theory of Secularization. Paper presented at the ISORECEA Conference *Religion and Society in Central and Eastern Europe*, Budapest, 14–17 December 2006.

Constitution of the Italian Republic. Available at: http://www.senato.it/documenti/repository/istituzione/costituzione_inglese.pdf [accessed 5 March 2013].

Department of Information and Media. Romanian Orthodox Church Officially Recognized in Italy. Available at: http://episcopia-italiei.it/index.php?option=com_content&view=article&id=694:biserica-ortodox-

roman-recunoscut-oficial-in-italia&catid=45:comunicate&Itemid=65&lan g=it [accessed 25 October 2012].

Dolan, J.P. 1988. The Immigrants and their Gods: A New Perspective in American Religious History. *Church History*, 57(1): 61–72.

Ebaugh, H.R. and Chafetz, J.S. 1999. Agents for Cultural Reproduction and Structural Change: The Ironic Role of Women in Immigrant Religious Institutions. *Social Forces*, 78(2): 585–612.

Ebaugh, H.R. and Chafetz, J.S. 2000. *Religion and the New Immigrants: Continuities and Adaptations in Immigrant Congregations.* Walnut Creek: AltaMira Press.

Hirschman, C. 2004. The Role of Religion in the Origins and Adaptation of Immigrant Groups in the United States. *International Migration Review*, 38(3): 1206–1233.

Hoge, D.R. 2000. Religious Leadership/Clergy, in *Handbook of Religion and Social Institutions*, edited by H.R. Ebaugh. Houston: Springer, 373–87.

Introvigne, M. 2012. Italy Enters into Concordates with Buddhists and Hinduists, who follow Mormons, Apostolic Pentecostals, and an Orthodox Church. Available at: http://www.cesnur.org/2012/mi1807.htm [accessed 5 March 2013].

Italian National Institute of Statistics (Istat). 2010. Popolazione Straniera Residente in Italia. Available at http://demo.istat.it/str2010/index.html [accessed 25 October 2012].

Krindatch, A.D. 2006a. What Makes the Orthodox Churches Strangers to American Mainstream Christianity. Available at: http://hirr.hartsem.edu/research/orthodoxarticle1.html [accessed 30 November 2010].

Krindatch, A.D. 2006b. Evolving Visions of the Orthodox Priesthood in America: A Study Report. Berkeley: Patriarch Athenagoras Orthodox Institute. Available at: http://www.orthodoxinstitute.org/files/evolvvisstudrepwebpost.pdf [accessed 30 November 2010].

Krindatch, A.D. 2008. The Orthodox Church Today: A National Study of Parishioners and the Realities of Orthodox Parish Life in the USA. Berkeley: Patriarch Athenagoras Orthodox Institute. Available at: http://www.orthodoxinstitute.org/files/OrthChurchFullReport.pdf [accessed 30 November 2010].

Levitt, P. 2001. *The Transnational Villagers.* Berkeley: University of California Press.

L'Italia Riconosce Ufficialmente la Chiesa Ortodossa Romena [Italy Officially Recognizes the Romanian Orthodox Diocese of Italy] (14 September 2011). Available at: http://www.stranieriinitalia.it/attualita-l_italia_riconosce_ufficialmente_la_chiesa_ortodossa_romena_13743.html [accessed 11 March 2014].

Martikainen, T. 2005. New Orthodox Immigration in Finland. *Yearbook of Population Research in Finland*, 41: 117–38.

Ministry of Religious Affairs. 1949. Statut Pentru Organizarea si Functionarea Bisericii Ortodoxe Române. Available at: http://www.legex.ro/Statut-Nr.4593-din-17.02.1949-198.aspx [accessed 1 February 2012].

Moberg, D.O. 1962. *The Church as a Social Institution: The Sociology of American Religion*. Englewood Cliffs: Prentice-Hall.

Morini, E. 2002. *Gli Ortodossi: L'Oriente dell'Occidente*. Bologna: Il Mulino.

Perrotta, M. 2007. Immigrati Romeni tra lavoro regolare e irregolare: Ricerca etnografica in un cantiere edile a Bologna, in *Un Arcipelago Produttivo: Migranti e Imprenditori tra Italia e Romania*, edited by F. Gambino and D. Sacchetto. Roma: Carocci, 95–132.

Phinnemore, D. and Light, D. 2001. Introduction, in *Post-Communist Romania: Coming to Terms with Transition*, edited by D. Light and D. Phinnemore. Basingstoke: Palgrave, 1–14.

Piovano, A. 2001. L'Ortodossia in Italia: Intervista a un protagonista, Traian Valdman, in *Religioni in Italia: Il Nuovo Pluralismo Religioso*, edited by F. Ballabio and B. Salvarani. Bologna: Editrice Missionaria Italiana, 89–94.

Richardson, A. and Bowden, J. 1983. *The Westminster Dictionary of Church Theology*. Philadelphia: Westminster Press.

Sandri, V. 2008. I Rumeni in Trentino Famiglie e Migrazioni Attraverso L'Europa. Unpublished MA Thesis, MA in Society, Territory, Environment, University of Trento.

Sandu, D. 2000. Circulatory Migration as Life Strategy. *Sociologie Românească*, 2: 65–92.

Schmidt di Friedberg, O. 2002. Musulmani nello spazio pubblico: Le associazioni Islamiche a Torino e a Trieste. In *Stranieri in Italia: Assimilati ed Esclusi*, edited by A. Colombo and G. Sciortino. Bologna: Il Mulino, 143–69.

Sciortino, G. and Colombo, A. 2003. Introduction, in *Stranieri in Italia: Un'immigrazione normale*, edited by G. Sciortino and A. Colombo. Bologna: Il Mulino, 7–21.

Silaşi, G. and Simina, O.L. 2008. Labour Market Distortions as New Challenges beyond the EU Enlargement: The Romanian case, in *Migration, Mobility and Human Rights at the Eastern Border of the European Union: Space of Freedom and Security*, edited by G. Silaşi and O.L. Simina. Timişoara: Editura Universităţii de Vest, 317–50.

Solari, C. 2006. Professionals and Saints: How Immigrant Careworkers Negotiate Gendered Identities at Work, *Gender & Society*, 20(3): 301–331.

Spini, V. 2003. Introduzione, in *Pluralismo Religioso e Convivenza Multiculturale: Un Dialogo Necessario*, edited by R. De Vita and F. Berti. Milano: Franco Angeli, 419–27.

Statutul Pentru Organizarea şi Funcţionarea Bisericii Ortodoxe Române 1989. 1990. *Biserica Ortodoxa Romana* [*Official Bulletin of the Romanian Orthodox Church*], 108(11–12): 222–7.

Zaretsky, E. 1996. *The Polish Peasant in Europe and America: A Classic Work in Immigration History*. Urbana: University of Illinois Press.

Chapter 2
The Myth of an Ideal Leader: The Case of the Syriac Orthodox Community in Europe

Naures Atto

The Syriac Orthodox Church of Antioch claims to have roots in the see of the ancient Patriarchate of Antioch, first occupied by the apostle St Peter. The patriarchal see of the Syriac Orthodox Church has moved several times since its establishment, and emigration has also been a characteristic of its members: first within the Syro-Mesopotamian area (later the Middle East) and, especially in the twentieth century, beyond their traditional boundaries to Western countries. As a consequence of socio-political changes and emigration, the Syriac Orthodox faithful have experienced a number of different political rulers, among them Romans/Byzantines, Persians, Arabs, Mongols and the Turks. They have never ruled themselves as a socio-political group. When writing about their own history, Syriac authors often refer to it as being a catalogue of oppression because they have always been subject to other people's rule, a situation which has never varied.

After their establishment in different Western countries, the members of the Syriac Orthodox Church have also been confronted with new challenges thrown up by contemporary modern secular societies. In fact, the already dispersed religious community in the Middle East has become even more dispersed after its emigration to Western countries. In the present day, the Syriac Orthodox Church has far more members living outside the historical homeland (different areas in the Middle East) and can therefore be considered a diaspora community, characterised by strong transnational relationships that have been developed at both family and institutional levels (religious and civic). The challenges with which the Syriac Orthodox Church has been confronted in the Western diaspora are a consequence of the emigration of this community from the predominantly agricultural societies in the Middle East, where religion played a central role in the organisation of life, to the modern, democratic societies in the West, where religion has become a private matter. In a nutshell, emigration has dislocated the collective identity of the people (Atto 2011). Awareness of this lurking danger means that in the process of settlement and thereafter, group identity has been a central point of discussion, both at religious and civic level. Elite members especially have done all that they can to heal the dislocated identity of their people (ibid.).

In this chapter I shall discuss how changes in the discourses about the collective identity of the members of the Syriac Orthodox Church have also altered the expectations of their religious leadership and commenced discourses arguing the need for secular leadership. In my work, I shall refer to the members of the Syriac Orthodox Church by the emic name *Suryoye*,[1] which they use when speaking both in their mother tongue Surayt Aramaic and in Syriac Aramaic.[2]

The fieldwork was conducted among *Suryoye* in Sweden. In it I have placed an emphasis on interviews with elite members, mainly during the period 2004–2005. I have defined the elite as the more highly educated, the clergy, the people on church boards and on the boards of *Suryoye* secular institutions, rich individuals whose ambition is to exert influence and the elderly who are in a position to exercise traditional influence. The choice of Sweden is for two reasons. It is acknowledge that Sweden is home to the largest concentration of *Suryoye* in Europe and elite members in Sweden have played a pioneering role in the debate about the collective identity of their people.

Religious Leadership in the Homeland

In the Ottoman Empire (after the occupation of Constantinople in 1453), minorities were defined within the framework of what has been referred to as the *millet* system, under which non-Muslims were considered subjects of the Empire and accorded *dhimmi* status, but were not subject to the Sharia law. This categorisation was based on the Islamic concept of the *Ummah*, the Muslim community or nation (implying a definition transcending modern national boundaries). *Millet* is therefore an inherently religious concept.[3] Accordingly, all Muslims in the Ottoman Empire were defined as the *Millet-i Hakime* (the dominant *millet*) and all non-Muslims were defined as *Millet-i Mahkûme* (the dominated *millets*) (Oran 2007; Soykan 2000).[4]

---

[1]   In Tur 'Abdin they used to refer to themselves as *Suroye*, instead of *Suryoye*. The latter name, which was formerly used in Tur 'Abdin but only in Syriac, has also come to be used by the diaspora when speaking in Surayt.

[2]   Surayt Aramaic is the spoken mother tongue of the *Suryoye*. Traditionally it has not been written, in contrast to Syriac Aramaic, which is considered the classical mother tongue of the *Suryoye* and which has been used in the liturgy of the Syriac Churches until today. Except for some works that have been published in Surayt during the last few decades, the literature produced has been in Syriac.

[3]   'Nation' in Turkish – group of co-religionists, from the Arabic *milla(t)*.

[4]   In modern Turkish, *Mahkûm* means the 'imprisoned', 'prisoner', 'inmate', 'convict'.

The latter group, organised into non-Muslim religious communities (*millets*), was considered to be made up of second-class subjects. Until 1882 the Syriac Orthodox Church was represented at the Sublime Porte of the Ottoman Empire by the Armenian patriarch. In 1882 it became an independent *millet* – the *Süryani Kadim Millet* (Ancient Syriac *Millet*). In the Turkish Republic, the religiously based definition of 'minority' and 'majority' identities has continued to be used as the main classification; members of minority groups are defined as 'non-Muslim citizens of Turkey'.

Each era and region has posed specific challenges to the Syriac Orthodox Church as an institution and to its members. In the Middle East, the clergy of the Syriac Orthodox Church had a religious role within the church alongside their task as spokesmen of a non-Muslim community in its communications with the state. The continuing existence of the Syriac Orthodox Church as an institution was highly dependent on the policy of the state towards the church. This history reveals how Syriac Orthodox clergymen have tried to negotiate the position of the church and the community with political leaders in the Middle East; often characterised by loyalty discourses.

The following example from Ottoman Turkey in the period after the First World War illustrates the working of the leadership of the Syriac Orthodox Church in relation to the Turkish rulers. The Syriac Orthodox patriarch deputised a delegation led by Archbishop Ephrem Barsaum[5] to attend the Paris Peace Conference (1919) where it was to submit the requests of the Syriac Orthodox community to the representatives of the Great Powers involved in the war. In his petition, the archbishop presented six requests on behalf of his people. Among his petitions, he put a case for their autonomy in Turkey, asked recognition for the losses suffered by his community in the broadest sense and requested compensation.

Similarly, in September 1919, Patriarch Elias had an audience with the Ottoman Sultan, Muhammad Rashid, in Istanbul on the occasion of the presentation of an official *firman* (decree) confirming his appointment as Patriarch. It is striking that during this audience the Patriarch submitted a long list of requests to the Sultan, which were discussed by the Cabinet (*Meclis-i Vükelâ*) on 22 November 1919 (Oral 2007; Hür 2007).[6] Among these requests were that those people who had been deported during the genocide should be allowed back to their homes and have their property restored, and that kidnapped women and children and all those who had been forcibly converted to Islam should be allowed to return to their own religion.

---

[5] The successor of Patriarch Elias III.

[6] For the official decision about the Patriarch's requests, see: Başbakanlik Osmanlı Arşivi Meclis-i Vükelâ Mazbataları (217), No. 553, 22 November 1919.

These requests of the Syriac Orthodox church leadership were made only a few years after two thirds of their population in the Ottoman Empire had been massacred, but not one was granted. Although the Patriarch also made these and other requests at the Paris Peace Conference, throughout his career he pointedly demonstrated his loyalty to the Ottoman authorities and later to the Turkish authorities.[7] Several sources (Ikdam 1922: 3; Akyüz 2005: 445; Nuro 1972) indicate that after the war, the Patriarch told his community members to obey Turkish policy and rule, and to refrain from cooperation of any sort with the Armenians. Especially after he had realised that the Western countries were not going to display much interest in the *Suryoye*, he tended to lean more towards the Turkish side and subsequently expressed his loyalty more explicitly to the members of the Turkish elite whom he happened to meet.

The Patriarch's cautious political approach was firmly rooted in a survival strategy and should be understood in the context of his own time. An excerpt from the interview by Abrohom Nuro with the Patriarch's secretary, Zakaria Shakir, clearly reveals that the Patriarch's intention was that he would deal with issues within the accepted political boundaries of the Ottoman and Turkish rulers (Nuro 1972; Atto 2011: 90). At the same time, as their supreme leader, responsible for his people, he negotiated political matters with *Suryoye* lay elites. Inherent in the role of these leaders was their advice to their community members to observe the 'correct attitude' to the state in which they lived. Although there may have been lay elites who took leadership positions upon themselves at local level, those who negotiated with the state were the highest ranking clergymen of the Syriac Orthodox Church.

Even after the Syriac Orthodox patriarch was expelled from Turkey in 1925, the strategy of the Syriac Orthodox leaders necessarily continued to be to devise tactics to adapt to their new position in Turkish society. Their attitude was characterised by their obedience to a succession of Turkish governments. This demonstrable loyalty was accompanied by attempts to de-politicise their community. To mention a more recent example, the present patriarch of the Syriac Orthodox Church, Zakka I Iwas (who resides in Saidnaya, Syria), voiced exactly such a discourse of obedience when he addressed his community members in the Zafaran Monastery (Mardin) during his visit in 2004:[8]

---

[7]   Outsiders have criticised him for this strong loyalty to the Turkish state. For example, Israel Audo (2004) refers to his attitude in terms of 'voluntary slavery'. See also Kurt (2010). For this sort of criticism see also Holmes (1923), who was the principal of the American Orphanage for Armenian children in Urfa at the time of the Patriarch's visit to Urfa in 1919.

[8]   Patriarch Zakka I Iwas was officially invited by the governor of Mardin to attend the meeting 'Kültürler Arası Diyalog Platformu', which was held in Mardin on 13 May 2004.

In order to be a true believer in God, first and foremost that believer should be a good citizen. If a believer is not loyal to his country, it is impossible [for him] to be a true believer in God. (cited in Akyüz 2005: 457)

The Patriarch's correlation between a 'believer' and a 'loyal citizen' provides a cogent illustration of how the clergy in particular have made use of loyalty discourses founded on religious arguments to encourage the members of their community to be loyal and obedient citizens. This religious discourse shows no deviation from the tradition of *Suryoye* clergymen, which has been to convince the faithful to accept any hardship and persecution. This strong clerical discourse of 'loyalty' betrays the fear which would have been gripping them and should be seen in the light of a survival strategy. To give an example, many books written by Syriac Orthodox clergymen in Turkey have a frontispiece showing a picture of Mustafa Kemal.

Suryoye as a Social Category in the Homeland

It is essential to emphasise some of the elements which reveal how *Suryoye* have categorised themselves and how others have categorised them spatially, according to the country from which they migrated. In their mother tongue Surayt[9] (a modern Aramaic language) they referred to themselves as *Suroye*, and in Syriac Aramaic as *Suryoye*. In Arabic and Kurdish they were referred to as *Suryani*,[10] and in Turkish as *Süryaniler*. What did these names mean in terms of a category of people? Nowadays, these names refer to those whom we know to be members of the Syriac Orthodox Church.[11] It is the same category which was known as the *Süryani Kadim Millet* under the Ottoman Empire.[12] As mentioned earlier, under the Ottomans, the religious affiliation of the group was the basis on which it was categorised. In the context of the modern Middle East, the former *Süryani Kadim Millet* continued to be organised along denominational lines. Therefore, in practical terms the *Suryoye* people (*'amo Suryoyo*) were a group of

---

[9]   See further Tezel (2003: 24) for his ideas about the derivation of Surayt. For the use of the terms 'Surayt', 'Turoyo' and 'Suryoyo' when referring to the spoken mother tongue, see Atto 2011 (Appendix 2).

[10]   The Kurds in Tur 'Abdin also used *Fellahi* (in the sense of Christians) to refer to them, because they were the main group of Christians in the area. Consequently, *Fellahi* came to function as a synonym for *Suryani*.

[11]   Depending on the context and discourse, these names can also refer to the Syriac Catholic and the Syriac Protestant churches.

[12]   The Syriac Orthodox Church added *Kadim* (ancient, old) to its name in order to distinguish itself from those members who converted to the Catholic Church but who continued to use the name *Süryani* (Kiraz 2005: 2).

Christians among a majority of Muslims – from their own perspective and from the perspective of the Muslim majority.

At this juncture, it is important to clarify the concept of *'amo* as a collective category among the *Suryoye* in the Middle East: the term *'amo* in Surayt means 'a people'; *u 'amaydan* means 'our people'.[13] In everyday life, it was not a category which was theoretically of any importance to the ordinary *Suryoye*. They did not pay much heed to it. They had an implicit idea of what 'our people' meant. Furthermore, the neighbouring 'others' knew who the *Süryani* or *Süryaniler* were. What mattered more to all groups involved was that they were Christians, hence different from the majority population of Muslims. Their status and position in a Muslim majority society has depended heavily on that category. From the perspective of the *Suryoye*, the Christian element in the category of 'our people' was therefore a key element in creating 'us' and the 'others'. Nevertheless, at other, more specific levels, there was still a sense of being distinct from the other Christian groups.[14]

Consequences of Emigration

Since the mid-1960s, *Suryoye* have emigrated in large numbers from countries with more traditional societies to countries which can be considered the most modern societies of their age. In their attempts to define themselves they have been confronted with conflicting concepts. The traditional method of identification and categorisation along religious boundaries as in the Middle East no longer seemed appropriate in the context of their new settlements. In Western countries, for over a century people have usually been categorised according to their national citizenship. Consequently, since their settlement in Western countries, *Suryoye* have been categorised according to 'country of origin', with the upshot that they have been recognised not as a distinct ethno-national category, but as Christians within that same category (such as in 'Christian Turks' and 'Christian Arabs').

---

[13]   *'Amo* can also be used with the meaning of 'people' or 'crowd', but here it is used with the meaning 'a people'.

[14]   To be *Suryoye* (here: Syriac Orthodox) also meant to be different from other Christians and included an unquestioned sense of collective identity and consciousness. For example, in Tur 'Abdin, Syriac Orthodox individuals who had converted from the Syriac Orthodox Church to Protestantism or Roman Catholicism in Midyad were no longer referred to by the ordinary people as *Suryoye* but as *Prut* and *Katholik* or *Kaldoye* respectively. The ordinary people no longer considered them *Suryoye* because of their new denominational affiliation. Therefore, to be *Suryoye* meant more than being Christian; it proclaimed that they were adherents of a specific form of Christianity which had consequences for the social category in the daily life of Tur 'Abdin.

The Myth of an Ideal Leader 57

Most crucially, the way in which *Suryoye* have been categorised in Europe has not set them apart from other national groups from the Middle East. Therefore, *Suryoye* have regarded the names and categories applied to them by Westerners (the new 'others') as misnomers. Religion has also lost ground as a boundary-setting element between the *Suryoye* and the new 'others' in the Western countries. To a certain extent, the 'others' have also become the Europeans whom they initially identified (from a traditional perspective) as Christians. The resultant paradox is that, if they were to include themselves in the same category as these Christians in Western countries, such a step would mean their absorption into this group, with the consequent loss of their group distinctiveness (often expressed as a collective of ancient history, Eastern Christianity, language and culture). On the horns of this dilemma, if they were to keep a distinct group identity it was essential for them to find new ways of positioning or identifying themselves as *Suryoye* in their new host societies.

At this juncture, an important characteristic of the new context in the host societies should be pointed out: freedom in relation to different aspects of life. In their new homelands, the *Suryoye* visibly began to enjoy the freedom to express their ideas about such topics as their collective identity and to negotiate this over time. They were no longer restricted to defining themselves within the narrow confines of the national ideology of the country in which they lived, as they had to do in the Middle East. This meant that they were no longer obliged to define themselves solely as a religious community.

Emigration has also changed the internal subject positions among *Suryoye*. In this sense, the new context has allowed space for the empowerment of lay elites, who are increasingly well educated and who have gained access to a variety of new sources. In the homeland, it could be said that the clergy were still far more influential and better educated than the lay elites. The central power was vested in the clergy who represented their church members. By and large, it was the clergy who made the major decisions affecting the *Suryoye* at a collective level. In the Western context, a number of factors, including the opportunity to gain a higher education, have been of major help to lay elites in increasing their influence in relation to the clergy. This relationship has undergone a sea change and the lay elites have become the competitors of clergymen for influence within the church community about matters within the ecclesiastical as well as civic spheres. The new lay elites have put topics on the agenda of their people which would never have been thought of in the homeland. In the new context, they have been the ones who have made the first statements about a distinct identity of their people (in terms of modern concepts) and who have used their new position as European nationals to speak out about the rights of the *Suryoye* as a people both in the homeland and in Europe.

Lay elites were also the ones who began to problematise the categorisation of their people by the new 'others' in Europe. In the beginning, among the ordinary

58 *Orthodox Identities in Western Europe*

people this categorisation played a role only from a more traditional perspective. To give an example, as far as the *Suryoye* are concerned, the majority groups in the Middle East are Islamic, and the *Suryoye* are not. Expanding this problematisation, educated elite members added the claim that they are also ethnically distinct from other national groups in the Middle East. The term 'ethnicity' refers to relationships between groups whose members consider themselves distinctive (Eriksen 1993: 6). As a matter of course, there is discrepancy between their self-identification and the categorisation by others. This touches on the political element of positioning oneself among other people.[15]

The young elites who were involved in the secular organisations took the lead in informing the new societies in which they lived about their 'distinct identity'. This has subsequently engendered a new cause: to be recognised internationally as a people, and therefore to be entitled to cultural, linguistic and religious rights so that they can survive among other nations (*emwotho*).[16] Quite clearly, a distinct identity is a central element here and is linked to the survival as a people in a worldwide diaspora.

It transpires that the relatively small number of members of the elite have managed to set out the path for a renewed national consciousness among *Suryoye* in Europe. Endeavouring to influence the community with their ideas about the past, present and future of their people, lay elites have been most vociferous in criticising their leadership more explicitly than they would have done in the traditional context.

Leadership Vacuum in the Diaspora

'We have become as a flock without a shepherd' (*Hawina khed qat'o dlo ru'yo*) is a phrase which the *Suryoye* commonly use when they want to express their sense of being leaderless. Indirectly this is a reference to Israel without kings or prophets without God.[17] But here, they use it more directly as a reference to Jesus as the Good Shepherd. In the case of the *Suryoye*, the lack of such a shepherd is sorely felt and is implicitly assumed. The phrase presumes that in the past they did have a shepherd (*ru'yo*). In contemporary societies they have become as an 'orphaned flock' which has lost its way home and cannot retrieve its *unity*. The leadership vacuum which developed, and which is felt as a palpable loss by *Suryoye*, is inextricably linked to their past and present sorrows. Apparently

---

[15]   For further information on this topic see Atto 2011.

[16]   The Assyrian Universal Alliance (AUA) has been a member of the UNPO (Unrepresented Nations and People Organization) since 1991.

[17]   Jesus uses it in Matthew 9:36: 'When he saw the crowds, he had compassion for them, because they were harassed and helpless, like sheep without a shepherd'. Here Jesus is referring back to Isaiah 13:14.

they do not feel that their *ru'yo ruhonoyo* (religious leader),[18] the patriarch of the Syriac Orthodox Church, meets their current expectations of what a *ru'yo* should be. The middle-aged teacher of Syriac, Shabo, says his grandfather drew a metaphor between the situation of the *'amo Suryoyo* and that of a 'chicken without feathers on its wings' (*gdaito da gefayda mpartene*). To be deprived of a 'shepherd' leaves a huge yawning gap waiting to be filled.

Several elite members responded to my request to identify the leadership of the *Suryoye* for me with the answer: 'Perhaps you expect me to say that the patriarch is the leader of the *Suryoye*, but he is not!'. Political activists and intellectuals are particularly vehement in their criticism, accusing him of not taking an explicit stance on the human rights of the *Suryoye* in the Middle East. Even the symbolic power of the patriarchate is perceived to be very weak. Given his established position, it is remarkable that such an individual as Shem'un, a member of the older generation, a deacon and former teacher of the Syriac language in church schools (*madrashyotho*), also shares this opinion:

> What leaders? Do we have leaders? The archbishop is a religious person who does his best to run his monastery. He is neither a king nor the leader of a country. He is not a secular but a religious person who is responsible for the church. Since all our secular people [leaders] have died, we all focus on the archbishop. We see him, a living person, and say he is the one who is alive. But this should not be the case ... The Turkish authorities maintain the archbishop as a communications partner because they do not want to talk to anyone else. They know that, when and if the going gets rough, they can request him to talk about religious matters only.

Shem'un is referring to the situation in which an archbishop functioned as a mediator between the Turkish State and the *Suryoye* people and to the way in which the archbishop has been used as a channel to steer his community members in the direction the Turkish authorities want. Therefore, he implies that the archbishop would never be able to defend the collective interests of his community. His statement also implies the need for secular leadership alongside that of the ecclesiastical leaders (as will be discussed in the next section).

Let us look more deeply into the common idea among *Suryoye*: 'We have no leader'. This statement by my respondents was generally followed by a critical tirade against the present community leaders, who are dismissed as being incompetent to meet the needs of the community in its relationships to different aspects of life. The sense of a leadership vacuum can often be traced back to a retrospective perspective on *Suryoye* history, ascribing it to 'dislocatory' events. Na'im, an academic and activist, illustrates the implicit parallelism he draws between what

---

[18]   Literally, *ru'yo ruhonoyo* means 'spiritual shepherd'.

he perceives to be the past failure of the traditional community leaders and their present inability to lead their people in the worldwide diaspora effectively:

> I believe that our people were burdened with a severe trauma at a time at which they were not prepared for this [calamity]: the roots of our people were hacked away [*qshi'enne*]! The killing of our people between 1914 and 1918 generated a situation in which they were no longer able to derive pride from being the *'amo Suryoyo* [*Suryoye* people] ... The *Seyfo* was the reason for the abandonment of hope ... The *Suryoye* had not been able to defend themselves; the *'amo* were on the point of being severed from their *shirsho* [roots] ... As victims of the *Seyfo*, our people lost their faith, not least in our leaders.

Sometimes, the great trauma caused by the genocide is imputed to the historical failure of the *Suryoye* leaders to defend their people at that juncture. Na'im has also not overcome his lack of trust in the leadership of his people. Following Na'im's line of reasoning, we see that his personal reflections on the disappointing quality of the leaders in charge also encompass the leaders of the *Suryoye* from the time before and during the genocide in the First World War in Ottoman Turkey. Na'im's retrospective reading of *Suryoye* history helps him to extend the failure of the clergy (in their position as 'leaders in charge') to the present context. They are castigated for their choice of accommodation with the political regimes of the Middle East (as discussed in the second section of this chapter). Broadly speaking, the elite members tend to use this argument when they construct their argument for the separation between religious and secular leadership. They judge the religious leaders to have failed to take strategic precautions to save their people from persecution in their home territories and also for having been unprepared to face the challenges confronting them in the diaspora. Bereft of strong leadership at a time when collective empowerment was required in the diaspora, Na'im wants to see the emergence of new lay figures to lead his people.

An example which expresses the shortcomings of today's clergy at a secular level is that given by Father Aday, himself a priest with an activist background. Arguing for the political involvement of clergymen instead of fighting their people's involvement in politics, Father Aday portrays Jesus as a political activist:

> I am delighted when priests show political *nous* [Greek: 'mind']. The clergy should understand that Jesus *did* political work. Jesus changed the religion of the area through his attitude. People converted to Christianity; this is politics. If Jesus is God Who came to earth and Who managed to change the world, why is a priest not allowed to have a political ideology?

The Myth of an Ideal Leader 61

This portrayal of Jesus as an activist is quite regularly heard among clergy and activists who were educated within the church. By analogy, aware of the central position Jesus holds among *Suryoye* (whether religious or secular), they want to legitimate their own activism. Especially in talking about the stance of the clergy for the national needs of their people, they attribute to Jesus the central role which they would like to give to clergy. This seems to be paradoxical, as activists usually take the stance that the clergy should only be concerned with religious matters. This latter attitude can be explained by their discontent with the way in which the clergy fulfil their role at the moment when they do get involved in non-religious affairs.

The ideal typical character which elites require of the 'Good Shepherd' has messianic features. Through a merging of moral virtues and personal authority, the Good Shepherd is portrayed as a 'saviour' who can overcome the vitiating inner dissensions and who is endowed with the ability to empower the *Suryoye* as a people, as more than simply a religious group. The different qualities with which a leader in charge should be endowed have been enumerated by the elite as follows: (1) competence to win the broad acceptance of his leadership; (2) a charismatic personality, willing to shoulder the 'struggle of this people'; (3) the ability to defend and sustain the *Suryoye* traditions and language; (4) humble, learned, a skilled diplomat, fair, open to criticism, possessing integrity and able to unify the people.

The qualities of an 'ideal leader' for the *Suryoye* have a relational and contextual character and are therefore not static. They are formulated to meet the present-day situation. The desired qualities are those which are absent in the present context. For instance, the proven ineffectiveness of the current leaders has inspired a desire for 'effective leadership'. The qualities are contextual because these leadership discourses have been formed in a European context in which secular, democratic leadership is considered to be of overriding importance. Contextual changes after the emigration of the *Suryoye* have influenced their image of what the 'ideal leader' for their people should be; people have begun to compare their leaders with Western politicians. It stands to reason that leadership discourses can also change over time.

Following the premises of poststructuralist discourse, the need for identification with something ('hegemonic projects', 'leadership discourses') is the result of the 'permanent' lack within the structure, that is, the lack of a 'full identity' (Laclau 1996: 92). The ontological lack of structures and subjects requires the hegemonic articulation of new projects, including leadership discourses. Therefore it is the discursive terrain which requires leadership discourses within identity discourses. There is a dialectical relationship between the 'representative' and the 'represented'. Representation is a necessary moment in the identification process which gives meaning to objects and elements. As Laclau puts it, 'the discourse of the representative must fill the gap in the identity

62 *Orthodox Identities in Western Europe*

of the represented' (Laclau 1996: 99–100). This also explains the articulated need for leadership in the identity discourses of *Suryoye* after their emigration to Western countries.

The problems which occur at the representation level of a discourse can be studied by applying the concept of the 'split subject'. As mentioned above, emigration to the Western countries led to the condition of the split subject among *Suryoye*. The implications of the 'dislocation' experienced have resulted in a crisis of identification and representation. This crisis can also be studied as a leadership crisis and hence a crisis of hegemony. From the view of discourse theory, hegemony implies the presence of a 'political and moral-intellectual leadership' (Torfing 2005: 11). The aim of discourses is to realise hegemonic leadership for ideological totalisation. Through identification with either previously weak discourses and/or with newly emerged discursive projects and leaderships, the split subject tries to find a solution to its crisis. Competition for hegemony also means competition for leadership and representation. In leadership discourses, the critique of the current leaders is a moment necessary to the construction of the *myth* of an 'ideal' and 'desired' leader. Laclau (1990: 61) refers to this in terms of a 'mythical subject'. The leadership vacuum is constructed through and in critical discourses in order to formulate the need for new and alternative leadership. This is the moment at which previously weak or new discourses endeavour to fix the meaning of the 'desired' leadership.

The Need for Secular Leadership

Quite independently of the question of whether *Suryoye* will someday have their own state, all respondents find it necessary to be represented by secular leadership. The main reason given is based on the argument that they are an ethnie, distinct from other groups and with a secular connotation the same as that of other national groups; a situation which implicitly requires secular leadership. As Father Aday puts it, 'We are a *'amo* and we should have a leader'. This unequivocally suggests a division between the secular and religious spheres. Certainly, the sense of a need for the division of the religious and secular responsibilities of clergy and secular leaders is high. Gabriel says: 'Throughout the entire world, the church and the secular world are divided. The priest has a function to perform in the church and the political organisations should deal with the secular issues and represent our people'. The academic activist Barsaumo relates secular leadership to being an *umtho* (nation):

> We should have a secular leader. As I see it, the church and the nation (*umtho*) are two different things. I can be a Christian and keep this in my heart; I do not have to display it to the outside world. However, the *umtho* is something compulsory. I

The Myth of an Ideal Leader 63

must say that I am a *'amo*, a person with a history, that I have a homeland (*athro*) from which I come and many other matters. My whole identity is based on the nation ... We are not less (*noqes*, implying 'less developed') than other people, so why can we not have one [nation]?

Without implying territorial self-government in the European diaspora, apparently the wish is to develop some kind of cross-denominational or secularly based collective representation. This intimates the depth of the desire to continue to retain their distinctiveness as a people among majority populations. This secularisation argument has a rhetorical dimension and can be understood as part of the modern dimension of living in secularly based societies in European countries denouncing religious hegemony, in which they seek accommodation as a group of people. At this stage, it could be said that the reason for this argument does not rely heavily on their highly developed secular values. Instead, the call for a division between the spheres of religious and secular influence can be perceived as a disagreement between the secular elites about the handling of certain issues, such as the struggle for the human rights of their people in the Middle East (as discussed above), by the clergy. Importantly, the 'secularisation' argument gives the lay elite an instrument that will allow them to develop their spheres of influence in a European context. Although the elites are scathing in their judgement of the capabilities of their present leaders, they express themselves more positively when they focus on the future needs of the *Suryoye* and when they put their reflections about the possibility of *Suryoye* leadership into words, perhaps an indication of their hope that one day they will indeed be represented by such a secular leadership. The realisation of such a leadership could mean a sudden, radical, positive and historical shift for them, which can be seen in relation to an imagined better future.

Suryoye lay elites who have assumed Assyrian ancestry adduce a more elaborate argumentation in favour of secular leadership than do their counterparts, who assume an Aramean ancestry for their people.[19] For example, the former argue that secular leadership will assist the development of an ethno-national (and cross-denominational) collective identity among the *Suryoye*, and this is what will prevent them from assimilating into Europe and eventually lead to the disappearance of the *Suryoye* as a distinct group. This can also be interpreted as a quest for recognition as a distinct people. Therefore, the elite members will accord any secular leader a strong role, expecting him to fill the gap in the inferred leadership vacuum.

---

[19]   For a broader discussion on this matter, see Atto 2011. Adherents of both ideologies trace their roots back to an ethnic relationship with either Assyrians or Arameans in pre-Christians times.

The lay elite are highly critical of the fact that many *Suryoye* give the clergy unquestioned authority. A champion of secular leadership, the activist Melke explains his argument for a cross-denominational approach as follows: 'If we do not have secular leadership, we shall become extinct. If we have only religious leadership, we shall be organised into different churches and disappear as a people'.

Melke's argumentation is a good illustration of how the discourse of secular leadership is constructed in strong contrast to the discourse of religious leadership. The argument for secular leadership is legitimated by referring to the risk and danger of becoming 'assimilated' and hence becoming 'extinct' as a people if *Suryoye* continue to be organised along denominational lines under a religious leadership. By dramatising the danger of becoming extinct (*gmeqsho'ina*) in the Western diaspora, secular lay elites are doing their best to hegemonise their political projects.

My respondents suggested two main alternatives to the organisation of secular leadership: a board of representatives (*si'tho mdabronitho*) or a parliament-in-exile with its own president. The first option implies the second, for the obvious reason that the first option would not have any political legitimacy in the countries of the Middle East. The parliament-in-exile would be expected to assume the function of representing the *Suryoye* in external collective affairs. The primary focus would be to accept the role of protecting the rights of *Suryoye* in respect of the regimes in the Middle East under which these *Suryoye* live. Proponents of this secular model assume that, as a people, the *Suryoye* would encounter fewer problems and that they would manage themselves better than they do today. The parliament-in-exile would be expected to assume the task of representing the *Suryoye* in external civic and political affairs.

Conclusion

The leadership discourses among *Suryoye* in Europe should be understood against the backdrop of migration. This cataclysmic experience has led them away from being a society in the Middle East where they were characterised principally by church affiliation, religious organisation, and leadership. The strong shift in the discourse about their identity, from ethno-religious to ethno-national, has altered the tenor of the discourse about the leadership of the *Suryoye*.

One can speak of an 'intertextuality' between *Suryoyes'* understanding of secularism and discourses about secularism in Western countries. The *Suryoye* lay elite in the diaspora have adopted the Western concept of secularism eclectically, without stopping to question it. The impact of this adoption is beyond the scope of this chapter, but further research among different Orthodox communities in

Europe (both as a single case study and from a comparative perspective) will develop our understanding of secularism among these groups.

Speaking about the impacts of emigration on *Suryoye* leadership, this chapter would claim that, despite the fact that emigration to Western countries has dislocated the hegemony of religious leadership, the secular leadership has not usurped the hegemony among the people yet. The *myth* of an 'ideal leader' has been constructed in and through discourses which have evolved in the diaspora. The emergence of a 'mythical leader' can be related to the shortcomings and failure of their religious leadership and to the absence of a leader who can provide solutions to the problems experienced in the Western diaspora. That is why the construction of the ideal leadership is fraught with a high level of demands and expectations. The 'ideal leader' is defined as the one who will heal the split subject, by uniting the people at present in a state of worldwide dispersion.

The leadership vacuum reflects the actual difficulties that *Suryoye* encounter at institutional level in their present state of dispersion. The conceptions and ideas they nurture of their actual and their ideal leadership are strongly related to other discourses which forge their collective identity. The ideas about what might be an effective and legitimate leadership for *Suryoye* shed light on the way elite members understand their dispersion today, how they interpret their history and see how they connect their past, present and future as a people. Here, the symbolic role of leadership betrays a great deal about how *Suryoye* reflect on their collective identity and how they would like to be perceived by the outsiders. Identifying a leader for their people who can represent them enshrines the possibility that outsiders might recognise them as 'a people'. From the perspective in which they would like to be positioned among other peoples, the absence of leadership is what makes them absent as a people.

Bibliography

Akyüz, G. 2005. *Tüm Yönleriyle Süryaniler*. Mardin: Anadolu Ofset.

Atto, N. 2011. *Hostages in the Homeland, Orphans in the Diaspora: Discourses of Identity among the Assyrian/Syriac Elites in the European Diaspora*. Leiden: Leiden University Press.

Audo, I. 2004. *Maktbonutho cal Rdufye da Kristiyone d Marde, w d Amid, w d Sacërd, w da Gziro w da Nsibin d bi sato 1915*. Jönköping: Ashurbanipal Bokförlaget.

Başbakanlik Osmanlı Arşivi Meclis-i Vükelâ Mazbataları (217), No. 553 (22 November 1919).

Donef, R. 2001. The Assyrian Genocide and Article 312 of the Turkish Penal Code: The Case of an Assyrian Priest in Turkey. Available at: http://www.atour.com/government/docs/20010926a.html [accessed 5 December 2009].

Eriksen, T.H. 1993. *Ethnicity and Nationalism: Anthropological Perspectives.* London: Pluto Press.

Holmes, M.C. 1923. *Between the Lines in Asia Minor.* Edinburgh and New York: Fleming H. Revell Company.

Hür, A. 2007. Hoşgörü Tarihimizden Bir Yaprak: Süryaniler. *Agos,* 590 (20 July 2007).

Ikdam [Turkish daily newspaper]. 1922. Süryani Kadim Patriki'nin Bir Tebliği. *Ikdam,* 8921 (15 January 1922).

Kiraz, G. 2005. Suryoye and Suryoyutho: Syrian Orthodox Identity in the Late Nineteenth Century and Early Twentieth Century. Paper presented at the PIONIER Project Seminar, Leiden University, 2005.

Kurt, A. 2010. The Secret Payment of Patriarch Elias Shaker for Denying the Assyrian Genocide Seyfo. Available at: http://www.atour.com/forums/religion/48.html [accessed 20 June 2011].

Laclau, E. 1990. *New Reflections on the Revolution of Our Time.* London: Verso.

Laclau, E. 1996. Power and Representation, in *Emancipation(s).* London: Verso, 84–104.

Nuro, A. 1972. Interview with Zakaria Shakir. Unpublished source.

Oral, M. 2007. Mardin'in Son Süryani Kadim Patriği Mar İgnatios III: İlyas Şakir Efendi, in *Makalelerle Mardin IV,* edited by I. Özcoşar. Istanbul: Mardin Tarihi Ihtisas Kütüphanesi Yayınları, 269–97.

Oran, B. 2007. *The Minority Concept in Ottoman Empire and Turkey.* Conference paper presented at the University of Utrecht, 2 April 2007.

Soykan, T. 2000. *Osmanlı İmparatorluğu'nda Gayrimüslimler: Klasik Dönem Osmanlı Hukukunda Gayrimüslimlerin Hukuki Statütüsü.* Istanbul: Ütopya Kitabevi Yayınları.

Tezel, A. 2003. *Comparative Etymological Studies in the Western Neo-Syriac (Turoyo) Lexicon: With Special Reference to Homonyms, Related Words and Borrowings with Cultural Signification.* Uppsala: Acta Universitatis Upsaliensis.

Torfing, J. 2005. Discourse Theory: Achievements, Arguments and Challenges, in *Discourse Theory in European Politics,* edited by J. Torfing and D. Howarth. New York: Palgrave, 1–32.

Chapter 3

The Transformation of Social Capital among Assyrians in the Migration Context

Soner Onder Barthoma

In many respects, the case of Assyrians in the Western diaspora provides an important example which makes it possible to understand how the identity of a Christian minority group from the Middle East has been transformed and redefined in the process of migration and settlement in Western secular societies since the 1960s (Deniz 2001, Cetrez 2005 and 2011, Atto 2011). During the integration process, not only have their socio-cultural norms and values changed, but their identity perceptions and the role of the Church within the community have also undergone a transformation. In their homeland, their identity was principally ethno-religious, meaning that the Church lay at the core of their identity and their social organisation; in the diaspora, they have acquired a more secular understanding of identity in which the hegemonic position of the Church has been displaced and new forms of social organisations have emerged.

In this chapter I shall illustrate how Assyrians in Sweden have built social capital and how the role of religion has assumed a different and less central role in their lives. I use the term 'Assyrians' (also known as 'Syriacs', 'Arameans' or in their mother tongue 'Suryoye') as a cross-denominational name, one of the accepted names used when referring to members of different churches of the Syriac tradition.[1]

Social Capital in a Nutshell

The World Bank (WB) defines 'social capital' as 'the norms and networks that enable collective action'; as 'institutions, relationships, and customs that shape the quality and quantity of a society's social interactions'.[2] The central thesis of social

---

[1] These churches are the (non-Chalcedonian) Syriac Orthodox Church, the Assyrian Church of the East (formerly known by the misnomer 'Nestorian'), the Chaldean Catholic Church, the Syriac Catholic and the Syriac Protestant Churches.

[2] World Bank. Overview: Social Capital. Available at: http://go.worldbank.org/C0QTRW4QF0 [accessed 2 November 2012].

capital theory is that 'relationships matter'. Social capital is broadly defined as networks and opportunities to mobilise resources which can facilitate outcomes. The core idea is that 'social networks are a valuable asset' (Putnam 2000). These interactive networks enable people to build communities. Trust between individuals (bonding) can evolve into trust between 'strangers' (bridging) and trust between a large composition of social institutions (linking). Eventually this evolves into a shared set of values, virtues and expectations within society as a whole. Here, trust is defined as an outcome of the whole process, but it can sometimes be seen as a 'reason' for the outcome. Theoretically, three types of social capital are distinguished: *bonding, bridging* and *linking*.

Bonding social capital refers to horizontal relations between people in similar situations and is largely to be found in such homogenous groups as extended family members and close friends. The 'bonding' is a reference to the idea of strong ties between similar members of a group which give this group its exclusionist character (Portes 1998: 15–18). Bonding relationships are 'inward looking' and reinforce 'exclusive identities'. Bonding social capital is the realm of mobilising solidarity and social trust among community members. Putnam (2000: 19, 22–3) notes that bonding social capital is good for 'getting by' and that bridging is crucial to 'getting ahead'.

Bridging social capital, in contrast, is much more heterogeneous. It covers horizontal relations between people with more remote ties – workmates, distant friends or students. The importance of bridging social capital lies in the fact that it cuts across 'diverse social cleavages'. This is the realm of creating broader networks and of generalising broader identities. Therefore, unlike its bonding counterpart, bridging social capital has an inclusive character. Putnam (ibid.) suggests that this form of social capital is useful in 'connecting to external assets'. Although 'bridging ties' are weaker and more diverse than 'bonding ties', they are nevertheless more important to 'getting ahead'.

Linking social capital is defined by Woolcock (2001: 13) as the vertical dimension of social capital and refers to ties between people or institutional bodies in dissimilar situations or from different 'strata of wealth and status'. Linking social capital also elucidates the relationship between civil society and government (Grootaert 2001: 20), and has a crucial role in understanding generalised trust, the rule of law and democracy.

How should these forms of social capital be understood? What are the links between them? There is an inherent tension between bonding and bridging forms of social capital, which evokes Ferdinand Tönnies' ([1887] 1957) dichotomy between a *Gemeinschaft* and a *Gesellschaft*. A *Gemeinschaft* produces more bonding social capital, based on community values, strong personal relations (grounded on trust) and the strength of collective ties (strong families, kinship, unity of will, shared place, belief or ethnicity). However, bridging and linking forms of social capital can also be found in a *Gesellschaft*, which is based principally on the complex relationships of modern societies, in which secondary relations replace personal relations, and conventions and State institutions take the place of strong collective ties (see Figure 3.1).

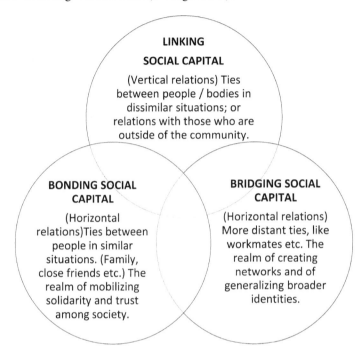

Figure 3.1   Relationships between different forms of social capital
Source: author's illustration.

Putnam (2000) has pointed out that bonding and bridging social capital should not be understood in terms of 'either/or categories', but as dimensions of 'more-or-less'. Uslaner (2001) notes that there is a shift from 'getting by' (bonding) to 'getting ahead' (bridging) in all societies, including diasporic communities.

Sociologists have found the concept of social capital useful when attempting to explain how ethnic-based forms of social organisation and collective action are embedded in interpersonal networks, and consequently how these forms of organisation and action generate and distribute resources (Sanders 2002: 330). In a case study of Chinatown in New York, Min Zhou (2005: 138–9) demonstrates the potential for 'upward mobility' in an ethnic enclave by making a distinction between an ethnic 'ghetto' and an ethnic 'enclave'. She stresses that an enclave, unlike a ghetto, is prone to be 'economically dynamic' and provides its inhabitants with cross-class relationships, job opportunities and models of academic and economic successes.

70   *Orthodox Identities in Western Europe*

In her study on the discourses of identity among the Assyrian elites in the European diaspora, Atto (2011) also notes that ethnic segregation and strong internal group ties among Assyrians in certain areas of Europe have been instrumental in encouraging the upward mobility and self-confidence of the group. She argues that this builds an important foundation for future relations and potential development in the European societies in which they have settled. Portes (1998: 13) also demonstrates the role of social networks in studies of ethnic business enclaves and ethnic niches. All these studies provide a foundation from which the conclusion can be drawn that immigrant groups, which have either ethnic or religious social formations in a *Gesellschaft* context, develop new forms of 'ethno-religious social capital' and that they apply these to the new situations they encounter.

The Migration and Settlement of Assyrians in Sweden

Assyrians are an ethnic minority group, originating in the Middle East. They were among the first people to convert to Christianity in the first century and derive great pride from their mother tongue, Aramaic. Throughout their history and into the current era, the church has been the main institution through which they have managed to protect their cultural identity. Therefore, their religious identity has been a fundamental part of their ethnic identity.

Today the Assyrian population is estimated to be approximately 3 million worldwide.[3] Most of the Assyrians have now settled outside their historical homeland and live dispersed in different countries.[4] Sweden has the most concentrated Assyrian population in the Western diaspora. The mass migration of Assyrians to Sweden took place during the 1970s and 1980s and led to an important transformational change in the socio-cultural structure of Assyrians. In the Middle East, they lived in a traditional society in which collectively shared values were central to their social relations. Subsequently, their confrontation with the societies in the Western countries has led to new acculturation processes (Deniz 2001, Cetrez 2005, Atto 2011).

---

[3]   Since there are no sound statistics it is hard to give very specific numbers of each church community in the worldwide diaspora. While there are several statistics, published mainly on the internet, it is hard to judge how accurate these are due to the question of self-identification, and because of the use of different categories for the registration of immigrants. For instance, in America one can choose one's ethnic origin in the census, while in European countries registration is based on 'former nationality'. Therefore, Assyrians and other immigrants who do not have a country of their own become invisible in the formal statistics.

[4]   In the European diaspora, the Syriac Orthodox Church has the largest congregation. In America and Australia, the Assyrian Church of the East and the Chaldean Church are the largest groups.

Of the approximately 100,000 Assyrians in Sweden, around 25,000 live in Södertälje, a small city west of Stockholm. Today, Assyrians have begun to refer to the city as 'New Midyad',[5] after the town from which most of the Assyrian inhabitants in Södertälje originated. Assyrian newcomers preferred to settle in this city because of the presence of already established community members (Björklund 1981: 103), resulting in the creation of their own society (*Gemeinschaft*).

Although Assyrians emigrated from an agrarian society, they have managed to develop new forms of social capital in their new society. By the first half of the 1970s, they had already established their first associations, churches and new forms of networks (Björklund 1981, Deniz 2001, Atto 2011). Assyrians have displayed an unusual flair for this networking activity. They have assiduously used their churches and civic associations to encourage activities which they value – for instance, setting up language classes in their mother tongue for children. Social gatherings have also functioned as a means by which to establish networks through which to develop and share in common collective goals. Today Assyrians are perceived to be among the most successfully 'integrated' groups in Swedish society. Besides their rapid economic establishment in a new country, they have managed to organise themselves around church organisations, federations, associations, women's and youth federations, student associations, aid and lobbying organisations and entrepreneurial networks. Södertälje is now home to two satellite community television channels, which can be viewed by Assyrians worldwide. Assyrians also have successful soccer teams (Assyriska FF and Syrianska FC), which have played in the Swedish premier league (*Allsvenskan*) in recent years.

Assyrians constitute an organised society, sustaining various associations. In Sweden, they have approximately 150 organisations with 50,000 to 60,000 official members.[6] They have become more engaged in Swedish politics, and in recent years especially, the number of Assyrian candidates in the national and local elections has increased visibly. Today, there are five Assyrian members of the Swedish Parliament (*Riksdag*).

---

[5]   Midyad is located in Tur 'Abdin (south-east Turkey) where Assyrians were the predominant population almost 40 years ago. Today, approximately 2,000 Assyrians still live in the geographical region of Tur 'Abdin.

[6]   The number of members and organisations was collected through internet research and informative interviews.

Results

The empirical data in this chapter were gathered by a web survey conducted in 2008, to which 349 respondents replied. The survey was distributed through the email list of ESNA (Eastern Star News Agency)[7] and published on *Hujådå* (an Assyrian online magazine) and on the website of the Assyrian Youth Federation. The majority of my respondents were members of the Syriac Orthodox Church who used the cross-denominational name 'Assyrian' to refer to their people. The results of the web survey were combined with interviews with elite members of the Assyrian community.[8] Some characteristics of my respondents are:

- Of those who completed the web survey, 62 per cent were men, 74 per cent were younger than 40, and 93 per cent were high school and university graduates. The respondents covered three age categories: those in the biggest group (42.8 per cent) were younger than 26 years, the second group between 26 and 40 years old (31.7 per cent), and the third group older than 40 (25.5 per cent). These categories are an important indicator of the up/down (fluctuating) tendencies in the building of social capital.

- A high percentage of the respondents (93 per cent) have completed secondary education. Although this says something about the general level of education among Assyrians, more importantly it is indicative of the specific group of respondents to this survey, and perhaps of their interest in this topic. Knowing that the largest group of respondents (40 per cent) was younger than 40, the educational level among them was not surprising when this fact is combined with the information obtained from my informative interviews and desk research. Over the last 15 years, there has been a visible tendency among Assyrians to participate in higher education (see, for example, Atto 2011).

To reach an understanding of the formation of different forms of social capital among the Assyrian community in Sweden, the empirical material was analysed in relation to three dimensions:

- Civic engagement (at micro or individual level): including density of membership of different organisations, characteristics of membership (active/passive) and participation in collective actions.

---

[7] ESNA had a comprehensive list of Assyrians living in Sweden.

[8] Interviews were conducted with members of the Assyrian Federation in Sweden (*Assyriska Riksförbundet i Sverige*), the Assyrian Youth Federation (*Assyriska Ungdomsförbundet*) and the Assyrian Women's Federation (*Assyriska Kvinnoförbundet*).

The Transformation of Social Capital among Assyrians in the Migration Context 73

- Norms (social trust, solidarity and reciprocity): these cognitive categories are discussed in terms of tendency.
- Social networks: with regard to the role of 'family', 'church', 'civic organisations' and 'different circles of friends'.

Civic Engagement

Putnam describes 'voting' as a crucial aspect of civic engagement. In some countries (such as the US, Canada and Great Britain), the voting tendency of different population categories is measured by making use of ethnic (and even religious) categories. However, most of the European countries eschew ethnic and race categories in their national statistics and registrations. Therefore, in my analysis of Assyrians' participation in elections (at local, national and European level) and their membership of Swedish political parties, I have depended heavily on my survey results. Furthermore, I have compared the survey results with the Swedish voter turnout statistics and with the turnout statistics of immigrants (as a general category).

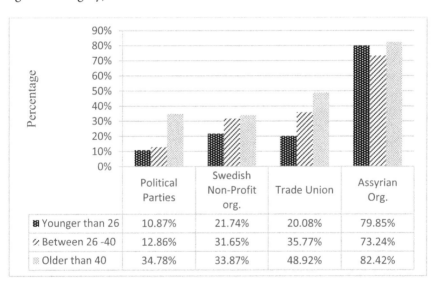

Figure 3.2   Membership

Membership   Membership of organisations and political parties is considered an important indicator of civic engagement. Putnam (1993: 88) emphasises 'active participation in public affairs' as an important source of democracy. The survey results (Figure 3.2) show that approximately 83 per cent of the respondents are 'official members' of an Assyrian organisation, including the

74   *Orthodox Identities in Western Europe*

Syriac Orthodox Church or the Church of the East; 44.48 per cent of them are members of a trade union; 34.52 per cent are members of a Swedish civil society organisation and 18.34 per cent of them belong to a political party.

The high percentage of membership of a community organisation – either religious or civic – is the result of the fact that the people on the list of contacts to whom I sent the survey were active participants in the Assyrian community. Furthermore, the associational life of Assyrians in Sweden has been noted as higher than anywhere else in Europe.

The rate of membership of Assyrian religious or civic organisations was considerably higher than their affiliations to other organisations in Swedish society. This might be an indication of the level of bonding social capital among Assyrians. The non-Assyrian organisations, as my interview respondents illustrate, were still considered 'external actors' with whom it was feasible to develop relationships in order to realise one's own organisation's goals. This reveals the perception of a degree of bridging social capital.

Membership of an organisation by itself is significant at the level of community participation. However, the character of membership, in terms of 'active' and 'inactive' also plays an essential role. Today, organisational membership has tended to deteriorate into merely 'formal membership', which often leads to a great number of passive members. At the same time, the fact that the importance of 'active membership' in many democracies has increased enormously can be observed. This is also related to the quality of social capital in a given example.

In my survey, I asked several questions related to this topic: 'How do you define your membership in terms of active or inactive?'; 'How often do you attend the meetings of your organisation?'; 'Do you vote in the elections of this organisation?'. To all of these questions, I obtained similar results: 55.83 per cent of the respondents defined themselves as 'active members'. Although the survey results exhibited a relatively high level of active membership in Assyrian organisations, my observations in the field have revealed a visible decline in the degree of 'active membership' compared to the 1970s and 1980s. This observation might indicate an important change: that the bonding relations of Assyrians today are less strong than they once were. It is remarkable that the first generation (69.05 per cent) was more active compared to the second generation (52.55 per cent). Consequently, the tendency towards less active membership of Assyrian organisations was more visible among the second generation.

Collective Action   Attending such collective forms of action as demonstrations and presenting petitions demonstrates the character of membership, in either active or passive terms. Collective action is one of the most important sources of the development of social capital. It is through collective action that a community strengthens internal ties, gains more social trust and mobilises its potential. To the question: 'How do you react when your organisation calls you up for a demonstration?', 40 per cent of the respondents answered, 'I prioritise this and go' (among those who defined themselves as 'active members', the number was almost twice as high, 74 per cent). In total, approximately 54 per cent gave a 'clear positive' response to this question.

These results demonstrate that in collective action, the self-definition of an individual plays a dominant role. Voluntary participation and sensitivity to public affairs on the basis of individual perceptions differ from collective action at the level of *Gemeinschaft*. When reflecting on the answer 'I prioritise and go', it is again remarkable that the first generation scores the highest (46.84 per cent) in contrast to the second generation (34.31 per cent). This might again be explained by the probable bias of the selective, very actively involved older age category who participated in this survey. The scope of this survey did not allow me to draw conclusions about the question of to what extent participation in collective action is based solely on individual choices. Nevertheless, from the contextual data gathered, I can add here that there is no forced collective action (such as collective group voting, patron–client relationship) in the traditional meaning among Assyrians in Sweden.

Participation in National Elections   The participation of the survey group in the national elections is 80.71 per cent. At the level of the municipality election, the response is less high, 76.42 per cent (Figure 3.3). Comparing these statistics with the general records of both Sweden and of Södertälje, it appears that the level of voting is lower than the general participation records (82 per cent) in Sweden show.[9] An interesting comparison is made in the statistics 'Participation in the Elections to the Riksdag in 2006 among those Born in Sweden and those Born Abroad by Sex'.[10] Among those whose parents were both born in Sweden, the participation percentage was 85.2 per cent, while those with two parents born abroad was 66.9 per cent, and those with one parent born abroad 81.8 per cent.

In Figure 3.3, I have displayed three sets of groups. I have used my survey group in order to say something about the voting attitude of Assyrians, although I am aware that it is not representative of the whole Assyrian population in Sweden. As Figure 3.3 reveals, the survey group differed in several aspects from the other categories. Firstly, in comparison with other immigrants, the survey group scored higher in all age categories, though there was a similarity in the

---

[9]   Statistics Sweden. Election to the Riksdag. Voting Rates among all those Entitled to Vote by Sex and Age (Survey). 18+ years, 4 age groups. Election year 2002–2010. Available at: www.scb.se [last updated 14 April 2011].

[10]   Statistics Sweden. Election to the Riksdag. Voting Rates among Swedish Citizens Registered in Sweden by Foreign/Swedish Background and Sex (survey). Election year 2002–2010' Available at: www.scb.se [last updated 14 April 2011].

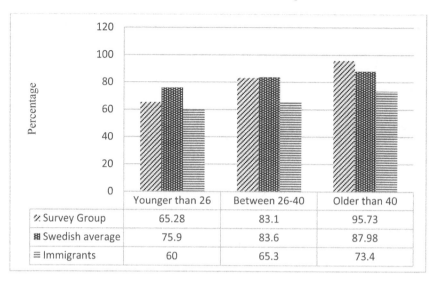

Figure 3.3   Participation in national elections

low percentage in the category of the age group below 26. Secondly, the score of the middle-age category was similar to that of the Swedish average. Thirdly, as previously mentioned, the first generation of Assyrians (older than 40) scored a very high (95 per cent) level of participation. The most important explanation of this is perhaps the following: Assyrians in this age group who responded to my survey are actively involved in both the Assyrian community and Swedish society. Their engagement explains their attitude to participating in voting. Among younger generations, the score of the survey group is close to the score of the general immigrant group, and is remarkably lower than the Swedish average.

Cross-tabulation between educational level and participation in elections (Figure 3.4) records a high percentage among the academically schooled group. These results do not differ from those in other societies: *the higher the educational level, the greater the civic engagement.* Hence, Putnam and other social capital theorists draw a direct positive relationship between education and the building of social capital.

Cross-tabulation between participation in elections and membership in an Assyrian organisation or Swedish non-profit organisations, trade unions or Swedish political parties shows very interesting results (Figure 3.5).

These results reveal that membership of a community organisation has a positive correlation with participation in elections (it affected the result by almost 10 per cent). Generally speaking, class-based trade unions scored the highest percentage. In the context of the social capital discussion, this difference exhibits the relationship between bonding and bridging social capital: the greater the bridging social capital, the greater the civic engagement. Although bonding (here: membership of a community

The Transformation of Social Capital among Assyrians in the Migration Context   77

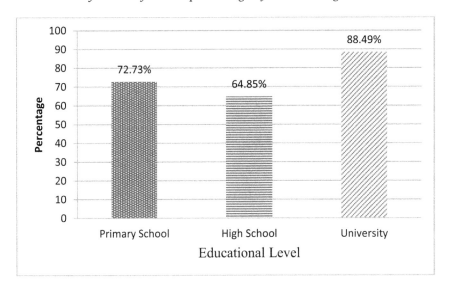

Figure 3.4   Participation in national elections and educational level

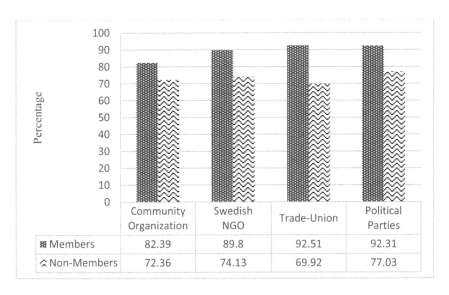

Figure 3.5   Voting attitudes and membership of an organisation

organisation) can have a positive effect on 'bridging social capital', it is the 'bridging capital' dimension in which 'getting ahead' has shown itself more clearly.

Norms of Social Capital

Social Trust   Putnam (2000) argues that 'social trust' is both a prerequisite for and a consequence of connecting with other people. Generally, measurement of social trust is based on one question: 'Do you feel you can trust most people or do you think that you have to be very careful in relations with other people?' (World Values Survey 2012). I have chosen a variable related to 'knowing someone's family'. The reason for this choice is based on my insight into the Assyrian community in the context of social relations between families. In my survey, I posed a hypothetical question: 'I can trust an Assyrian whom I don't know well, but whose family I know.' In the first instance, survey results could also shed some light on Assyrians' distrust of 'others'. Moreover, a strong positive correlation should logically be expected between the degree of internal trust and distrusted 'others'.

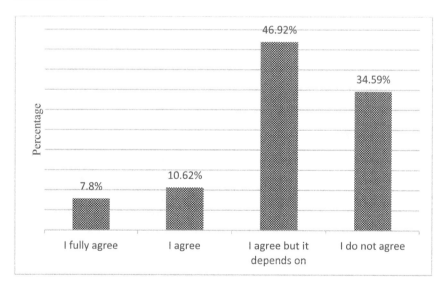

Figure 3.6   I can trust a community member

In this case, the respondents (Figure 3.6) who clearly opposed this hypothesis comprised 34.59 per cent of the total. The gender difference shows a distinctive result. Among the female respondents, 40.35 per cent answered negatively against 30.51 per cent of their male counterparts, again showing that Assyrian women have changed to a higher degree in the common traditional value of 'trusting one of us'.

The answers of those who can trust an Assyrian despite not knowing that person well can be divided into various degrees of positive answers. What elicits most discussions is none other than the high number (46.84 per cent) of the 'agree, but it depends' category. Since this category accepts the assumption only conditionally, the scope of this condition assumes greater importance. Although this can take many forms, I assume their answer is quite close to the confirmation of the hypothesis. Results from the cross-tabulations show that there is no big difference between the categories 'age' and 'education'.

The results demonstrate that:

a. Social trust values are *not* as high as might have been anticipated in the context of an inward-looking, closed Middle Eastern Christian immigrant group.
b. In comparison with social trust in Sweden (following from the statistics from World Values Survey), the survey results yield a lower proportion. However, the perception of 'trust' (knowing someone) among the Assyrian community differs from the understanding of 'trust' in Swedish society (*Gesellschaft*). The latter is based on an abstract 'generalised trust'. In contrast to this, in a *Gemeinschaft* trust as a value is founded on concrete personal interactions and relations on which the bonding of social capital is based.
c. The relatively high value of 'conditionality' can be seen as both an indicator of shift from a collectivist to an individualist approach and as a sign of 'bonding' ties.

Reciprocity Equating social capital with 'social connections' in his work *Bowling Alone*, Putnam (2000) emphasises the importance of 'reciprocity' for building 'social trust'. Generalised reciprocity which favours the public common good is the key to social capital. Putnam (2000) discusses the term 'reciprocity' using the idea of a 'service bank', to which everyone in a society contributes in some way and in turn receives something in return – a service. This process or structure is the main foundation of social trust building. We should also note that the perception of reciprocity is different in different societies. A remarkable differentiation can be seen between a *Gemeinschaft* and a *Gesellschaft*. In a *Gemeinschaft*, reciprocity is mostly between families (*not* individuals) and is mainly based on the idea of 'knowing someone'. This diverges widely from the understanding of reciprocity in a *Gesellschaft*, in which it is linked to contractual modern relations.

I formulated two questions in the survey in order to measure the tendencies towards reciprocity among Assyrians. The majority of the survey respondents

(69.5 per cent) answered the question: 'Do you go to another person's funeral without being directly acquainted to her/him?' negatively. This also indicates a shift from traditional norms and values towards a more modern approach in the Assyrian community. In answer to the second question: 'How important is reciprocity to you in your personal relations?', only 21.23 per cent of the survey respondents indicated that 'reciprocity is important' in their social relations; in their choice the remainder of the respondents perceived reciprocity negatively and associated it with a materialist interest. Therefore, those who considered reciprocity *not important* were those who approached this characteristic from a more 'moral' perspective or in terms of a 'duty' to the public good. An explanation for this is not hard to find when the characteristics of the survey group are taken into consideration. Despite the fact that my respondents did not value reciprocity highly, observing the intricacies of social life among them it is still possible to discern a fairly strong system of traditional reciprocal relationships. The results of this survey could show that reciprocity has become such a natural phenomenon that they might not always realise they are participating in it. This assumption is strengthened by the results of the comparison between the responses and relationship between reciprocity and self-definition in terms of 'individualism' and 'collectivism'. Those who considered themselves 'collectivist' (Figure 3.5) did not value reciprocity.

Self-definition   In this context, self-definition is related to aspects of 'individualism' and 'collectivism' (Figure 3.7). In sum, 8.6 per cent of the survey group identified themselves as 'individualist', 31.3 per cent 'mixed, but more individualist', 28.1 per cent as 'collectivist', 25.6 per cent as 'mixed, but more collectivist' and 6.4 per cent as 'none of these categories'. Concurring with my direct observations and desk readings, the collectivist approach is still quite strong among the Assyrian community.

For an understanding of the reliability of the responses to the question about 'self-definition', I also checked the results with a cross-tabulation between self-definition and the question: 'How important are traditional social relations for you?'. The results demonstrate that those who considered themselves 'individualist' still differed from the 'Western type of individualist'. To give an example, 67 per cent of the group which defined itself as individualist also chose 'I cannot imagine myself living without my family'. Only 11 per cent of the same group indicated that they could manage without any traditional social relations.

Tolerance and Solidarity   Two other key indicators of social capital research are 'tolerance' and 'solidarity'. In the questions related to tolerance, the survey group showed itself more tolerant of external issues and less of the internal questions. By 'external', we mean demonstrating an open and democratic approach to developments outside of the group. To the question: 'If a Turkish

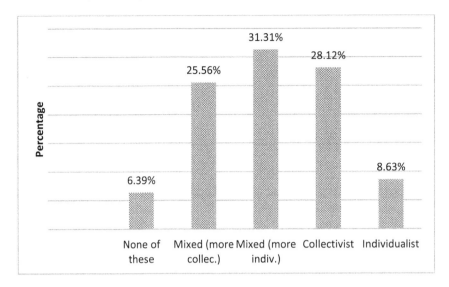

Figure 3.7   Individualist and collectivist attitudes

genocide-denier wants to give a speech and debate in your organisation, would you allow him?', 82 per cent of the respondents stated that they would be open to discussing the 'genocide' with a Turkish genocide-denier.[11] The highest record was among the second age category (26–40) with 88 per cent. Educational differences also affected the results. Academics were far more open to discussion with the genocide-denier (25 per cent) than those who had a primary school education only. In order to measure the internal dimension of tolerance, I formulated the question: 'If a gay organisation wants to give a speech about Assyrian homosexuals and human rights in one of your activities, how would you react?' 59.2 per cent of the group indicated that they were liberal and tolerant of such questions; the other categories could be interpreted as a range of negative attitudes: 7.9 per cent argued 'we do not have gays in our society' and 32.9 per cent stated 'this is not relevant to our agenda'. Women (65 per cent) again showed a tendency towards a more positive answer than men (48 per cent) and again their educational level played a role in the attitude of respondents. But, when it is all said and done, tolerance is a multifaceted term and can be best observed in practice.

To test 'solidarity', I formulated two questions taking the internal and external dimensions of solidarity into consideration: 'What kind of contact do you have with the new Assyrian refugees?' and 'If an Africa-related aid

---

[11]   I have deliberately formulated this question with an awareness that the genocide question is highly sensitive for the group.

82 Orthodox Identities in Western Europe

organisation wants you to participate in their solidarity activities, would you participate?'. In the results of the first question, 38.3 per cent of the respondents had only read something about the new refugees in the newspapers; 25.7 per cent of the group did not have any contact with them; 6.3 per cent had no interest in such problems and only 29.7 per cent of the group would try to show their solidarity with them. Statistically, this is a low rate of solidarity considering that almost 80 per cent of the respondents were members of a community organisation (perhaps formal members) whose major objectives are attaining collective goals. The new refugees are Assyrians, and hence considered members of the same group, but the majority are from countries different to those of the majority of my respondents (mainly Turkey and Syria). Therefore, in practice they are generally treated as 'outsiders'.

To the second question, 43 per cent of the survey group pointed out that they would attend an African-aid related activity; 17 per cent chose the option 'no'; and 40 per cent of the group gave no response.

Investigating 'group solidarity', it is particularly essential to study the role of the church and family in order to understand how such a group can mobilise itself in its efforts to realise projects for the good of the group. However, this group solidarity (bonding ties) has an 'exclusionary' character and affects the development of bridging social capital. The survey findings show that external solidarity is rather low. Therefore it is feasible to speak of less developed bridging social capital.

Social Networks and the Role of the Church

Social capital theory implies the importance of social networks and their vital role in democracy. 'Networking' mostly scores positive outcomes for both its 'members' and for 'bystanders' (Putnam 2000). The main questions in this context are: What kind of networks does the Assyrian community in the diaspora use to build social capital, and how does the choice of different networks affect the form of social capital? As mentioned in the background to this chapter, the church played a significant role in the social organisation of the Assyrian community in the homeland. Certainly the church was a place of worship, but it was also a haven where people would go when in need or when they were troubled. It would be true to say that the church was the main foundation of networking in the homeland. During the first years of settlement in Sweden Assyrians also used the church as an institution around which to gather and network. Therefore it can be plausibly argued that as an actor in Assyrian social capital the church did have a central role. Nevertheless, since settlement in Western societies this has changed and the church has had to forfeit its central role. Assyrians' settlement in Western secular societies has led to a secularisation process within the diaspora community, one consequence of which is that Assyrians have begun to use more ethno-national terms for their self-identification (See Deniz 2001, Cetrez 2005 and Atto 2011). The emergence of civil Assyrian organisations has reduced the central and omnipresent role of the church. Assyrians have become more literate, more individualistic and more critical of the role of their church and of their traditional norms and values. They have made use of some concepts of the Western secularisation discourse in order to redefine the role of the church (see Atto 2011). Notwithstanding this shift, it would be wrong to see this transformation as an abandoning of the past. Although the church has lost its central role within the community, it still has a very important role in the organisation of the Assyrian diaspora. In my survey, my aim was to observe the changing role of the church by looking at the frequency of church attendance and at the importance attached to the church in the survey group.

Only 17.3 per cent of the survey group attends church every Sunday.[12] Among the younger generation of the Assyrian community, the number of churchgoers (Figure 3.8) has decreased drastically in the diaspora. In interviews, as my respondents underlined, they do not find it 'meaningful' and 'necessary' to attend church every Sunday. A larger number of people among the second generation question the role of the church in the community and seek other ways to gather, socialise and network. Cetrez (2011) also underlines a similar point when he states that the religious values and practices among Assyrians in Sweden have declined from the first generation to the third generation. In his research, Cetrez (2011: 482) shows that the first generation scores more highly than the younger generations, and 'the role of religion for a system of meaning changes from playing a positive role in childhood to a more negative one in adolescence'.

Although the percentage of churchgoers has decreased markedly, particularly among the second generation, as an institution the Syriac Orthodox Church still continues to present an important network for social relations among the community. In contrast to the churchgoing attitudes in Western societies, every Sunday members of the Assyrian community fill their churches all over Europe and continue to build big, new churches – some of which can provide a worship space for more than 1,000 people at the same time – with their own financial sources. This is an important indication of the continued central role of the Church in the community.

Another important foundation for building social capital for the community is the role given to extended families. As the research clearly demonstrates, in the eyes of Assyrians 'family' is the most important aspect of social capital. Of the

---

[12] Onver Cetrez (2011: 483) achieved similar results in his quantitative research on religious participation. Accordingly, 19.3 per cent of the participants answered that they go to church 'very often', 29 per cent 'often', 45 per cent 'seldom', and 6.4 per cent 'never'.

survey group 95 per cent rated 'family' as a 'very important' or an 'important' part of their social existence. Moreover 'when they need something urgently', 69 per cent of the survey group sought help from the family. Only 44 per cent of the group indicated that the Church is important to them, which also reveals the changing tendencies, especially among the younger generation.

The choice of friends plays a certain role in this context. Trust, reciprocity and socialisation in general are connected to relationships between both families and friends. Here, I have consciously distinguished between Assyrian and non-Assyrian friends so as to be able to obtain clearer results about bonding and bridging social capital. Therefore I asked related questions to clarify the main concepts of some variables (such as family, church, civic organisations and friends). The survey group valued 'Assyrian friends' more than 'non-Assyrian friends'. A remarkable difference between gender categories is related to how a circle of friends is valued. The Assyrian female respondents showed a greater tendency towards 'bridging' relations and networking – a sign of horizontal relations with dissimilar people. Female respondents score 74 per cent on the importance of 'mixed friends', versus 57 per cent among the male respondents, who manifested a more 'inward-looking' approach.

The survey results of the networks used for finding jobs also demonstrate the importance of community sources and the changing attitudes among the group. 39 per cent of the survey group had found their jobs through community networks (church, civic organisations, families and friends); 25 per cent through non-Assyrian networks; and 36 per cent through the help of professional institutions. The community networks represent a key resource in

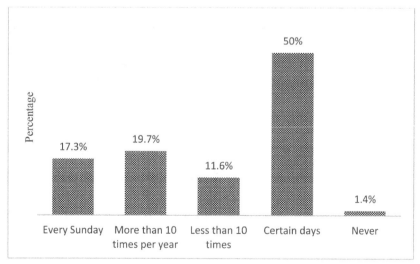

Figure 3.8   Frequency of going to church

job searches and indicate how bonding ties can be used. Nevertheless, the record for 'professional organisations' is also remarkable and indicates the development of linking social capital, namely the vertical relations among the group with the authorities.

Conclusions

As mentioned in the introduction to this chapter, the Assyrian case constitutes an important example for understanding the transformation of Middle Eastern Christian immigrant groups in the diaspora context. From a socio-historical perspective, Assyrians display the typical features of a *Gemeinschaft*: family-kinship based segmented relations, living in a collective, the presence of social control and the adherence to one main religious affiliation (in this case study predominantly Syriac Orthodox Christianity). Historically they used to materialise their everyday life with 'survival' strategies. Living in a Muslim society in different countries in the Middle East in which they had been used to being treated as a religious minority group, they developed strategies which enabled them to live as a self-organising, self-sufficient community. Certain boundaries with the 'others' were maintained in the homeland. However, all these features have undergone a transformation process after their emigration and settlement in Western secular societies. There are visible changes in their norms, values and attitudes, and hence in the formation of social capital among the group. Nevertheless, it would be wrong to argue that they have completely abandoned traditional values, norms and networks.

Speaking in terms of social capital, Assyrians in Sweden are more prone to build 'bonding social capital'. This form of social capital is heavily based on family-kinship relations. Bonding social capital had a positive impact on the rapid integration and establishment of Assyrians in Sweden and everywhere else in the Western diaspora. Bonding social capital has been a key source in Assyrian social networking and this can be seen in their everyday life, economic growth and 'competitiveness'. However, in later stages of their settlement it has become an obstacle to 'getting ahead', because of its 'exclusionary' character which tends to engender 'othering'. Together with the category of family, the church has been a crucial nodal point in the formation of their social capital in the diaspora, despite the fact that emigration and settlement have dislodged the previously hegemonic position of the church within the community.

Bridging social capital, in terms of relations with 'others', is less developed. Assyrians constitute a more self-oriented group. Inclusion of 'others', showing solidarity and tolerance towards the perceived 'others' and sharing 'new common values' can be designated 'problematic' issues at the collective level. Nevertheless, at individual level remarkable changes in the choices of individuals are observable– despite the fact that they are still not accepted openly at collective level, but are often 'tolerated' to avoid 'worse'. My survey results have shown that especially among the younger respondents and the more highly educated, a clear shift has taken place from 'getting by' to 'getting ahead'; a shift from a collectivist approach to a more individualist approach in a hybrid sense. Especially among the second generation and among women, it is feasible to speak of 'upward mobility' in terms of being more open and capable for building bridging social capital. The remarkable interest taken by Assyrians in politics over the last few years and in developing stronger relations with the authorities are significant indicators in understanding linking social capital in the Assyrian case. The tendencies towards more participation in elections and increasing membership in Swedish political parties can have positive outcomes in developing other forms of social capital beyond the resources of the group.

Bibliography

Atto, N. 2011. *Hostages in the Homeland, Orphans in the Diaspora: Discourses of Identity among the Assyrian/Syriac Elites in the European Diaspora*. Leiden: Leiden University Press.

Björklund, U. 1981. *North to another Country: The Formation of a Suryoyo Community in Sweden* (*Stockholm Studies in Social Anthropology*, Vol. 9). Stockholm: Department of Social Anthropology, University of Stockholm.

Blomkvist, H. 2001. Traditional Communities, Caste and Democracy: The Indian Mystery, in *Social Capital and Participation in Everyday Life*, edited by Paul Dekker and Eric M. Uslaner. New York: Routledge, 73–88.

Cetrez, O.A. 2005. *Meaning-making Variations in Acculturation and Ritualization: A Multi-generational Study of Suroyo Migrants in Sweden*. Doctoral dissertation. Uppsala: Uppsala University Press.

Cetrez, O.A. 2011. The Next Generation of Assyrians in Sweden: Religiosity as a Functioning System of Meaning within the Process of Acculturation. *Mental Health, Religion & Culture*, 14(5): 473–87.

Dekker, P. and Uslaner, E.M. 2001. Introduction, in *Social Capital and Participation in Everyday Life*, edited by Paul Dekker and Eric M. Uslaner. New York: Routledge, 1–8.

Deniz, F. 2001. *En minoritetsodyssé: Det Assyriska exemplet*. Gothenburg: DocuSys.

Grootaert, C. 2001. Social Capital: The Missing Link?, in *Social Capital and Participation in Everyday Life*, edited by Paul Dekker and Eric M. Uslaner. New York: Routledge, 9–29.

Grootaert, C. and van Bastelaer, T. 2002. *The Role of Social Capital in Development: An Empirical Assessment*. Cambridge: Cambridge University Press.

Hallberg, P. and Lund, J. 2005. The Business of Apocalypse: Robert Putnam and Diversity. *Race & Class*, 46(4): 53–67.

Johnston, R. and Soroka, S.N. 2001. Social Capital in a Multicultural Society: The Case of Canada, in *Social Capital and Participation in Everyday Life*, edited by Paul Dekker and Eric M. Uslaner. New York: Routledge, 30–44.

Portes, A. 1998. Social Capital: Its Origins and Applications in Modern Sociology. *Annual Review of Sociology*, 24: 1–24.

Putnam, R. 1993. *Making Democracy Work: Civic Traditions in Modern Italy*. Princeton, NJ: Princeton University Press.

Putnam, R. 2000. *Bowling Alone: The Collapse and Revival of American Community*. New York: Simon and Schuster.

Putnam, R. 2007. *E Pluribus Unum*: Diversity and Community in the Twenty-first Century. The 2006 Johan Skytte Prize Lecture. *Scandinavian Political Studies*, 30(2): 137–74.

Rothstein, B. and Stolle, D. 2003. Social Capital in Scandinavia. *Scandinavian Political Studies*, 2(1): 1–25.

Sanders, J.M. 2002. Ethnic Boundaries and Identity in Plural Societies. *Annual Review of Sociology*, 28: 327–57.

Statistics Sweden. Election to the Riksdag. Voting Rates among all those Entitled to Vote by Sex and Age (Survey). 18+ years, 4 age groups. Election year 2002–2010. Available at: www.scb.se [last updated 14 April 2011].

Statistics Sweden. Election to the Riksdag. Voting Rates among Swedish Citizens Registered in Sweden by Foreign/Swedish Background and Sex (survey). Election year 2002–2010' Available at: www.scb.se [last updated 14 April 2011].

Tönnies, F. [1887] 1957. *Gemeinschaft und Gesellschaft*. Translated by C.P. Loomis as *Community and Society*. East Lansing: Michigan State University Press.

Truzzi, M. 1971. *Sociology: The Classic Statements*. New York: Oxford University Press.

Uslaner, E.M. 2001. Volunteering and Social Capital: How Trust and Religion Shape Civic Participation in the United States, in *Social Capital and Participation in Everyday Life*, edited by Paul Dekker and Eric M. Uslaner. New York: Routledge, 104–117.

Woolcock, M. 2001. The Place of Social Capital in Understanding Social and Economic Outcome. *Canadian Journal of Policy Research*, 2(1): 1–17.

World Bank. Overview: Social Capital. Available at: http://go.worldbank.org/C0QTRW4QF0 [accessed 2 November 2012].

World Values Survey. 2012. 2010–2014 Questionnaire. Available at: http://www.worldvaluessurvey.org/wvs/articles/folder_published/article_base_136 [accessed 11 March 2014].

Zhou, M. 2005. Ethnicity as Social Capital: Community-based Institutions and Embedded Networks of Social Relations, in *Ethnicity, Social Mobility, and Public Policy: Comparing the US and UK*, edited by G.C. Loury, T. Modood and S.M. Teles. Cambridge: Cambridge University Press, 131–59.

Chapter 4

Orthodox Churches in Germany: From Migrant Groups to Permanent Homeland

Reinhard Thöle

Estimates put the number of Orthodox Christians living in Germany today at 1.5 million (KOKiD 2011: i). The number has thus tripled over the last three decades. Within a relatively short period, Orthodoxy has thus become the third largest Christian group in a country which until now was primarily characterised by the coexistence of Catholic and Protestant Churches. Further growth of Orthodox Churches in Germany can be expected. Orthodox expansion can also be observed in areas which were formerly part of East Germany, primarily in major urban areas, but less strongly than in West Germany.

Germany has clearly become a permanent homeland for Churches of Eastern tradition. We are about to witness a very interesting stage in that development: the transfer of Eastern Orthodox identities to countries of what used to be called Western Europe, which will involve drawing lines between their original identities and their new Western environment. For Orthodox Churches in Germany, it is indeed important both to uphold religious identities usually connected to national origins and to plant roots in the West. Taking future generations into consideration, they have to find ways of crossing national backgrounds and borders in order to keep alive their peculiar traditions of faith for their children. Looking at the historical background of Germany, the country had never been expected to someday become a permanent home for Orthodoxy. As recently as after the Second World War, the huge number of refugees staying in the country did not trust Germany to become a safe homeland; similarly, the first generation of foreign workers who had come at the time the Federal Republic was developing planned to return to their home countries after earning enough money.

Assessing Orthodox Presence in Germany: Statistical Issues

Statistical data on Orthodox faithful in Germany mostly rely on self-evaluation by representatives of Orthodox churches. Priests' estimates are based first on the number of families known to them as well as on experiences related to church attendance. Moreover, all those people who have immigrated to Germany from traditionally Orthodox countries during the last decades are usually added. Since there are no clear rules regarding church membership in those countries, and Orthodox Churches in those lands tend to include everybody not belonging to another religion in their flock, this model is then applied to the German context as well.

Data from population registry offices do not offer adequate information, since Orthodox Churches are not among those collecting church taxes (paid by members of their respective religious denominations, and collected by the State on their behalf in most cases) and many immigrants do not provide information on their religious affiliation. Moreover, a not insignificant number of immigrants belonging to Eastern or Oriental Orthodox Churches do not have a legal resident status in Germany.

It is difficult to assess how close the link between immigrants and their churches is, and whether it is defined by baptism or by cultural identity: thus the category 'church member' is difficult to circumscribe.

The largest group of Orthodox in Germany are Greeks (around 150 places of worship), followed by Romanians (around 50 places of worship), Serbs (79 places of worship) and Russians (63 places of worship affiliated with the Moscow Patriarchate and 45 with the Russian Orthodox Church Outside of Russia). Each of the other Orthodox churches (including Oriental Orthodox) are present with a lesser number of places of worship (around 10) (KOKiD 2011: 28–108).

There are seven small Orthodox monastic communities in Germany, one of them being for nuns (KOKiD 2011: 25–7).

This chapter is based on many years of observation and interaction with Orthodox churches, both in Germany and in other places. It is written from the perspective of a theologian (and Lutheran priest). We will take a look at the history of Orthodoxy in Germany, which will help us to understand the spectrum of various Orthodox identities influenced by different liturgical and ecclesiastical traditions, different languages, and different political and economic backgrounds (Thöle 1997). After a summary of some recent developments, we will also attempt to understand how Orthodox interact with other Christians in Germany.

Identity of National Churches and 'German' Orthodoxy

Immigrants usually organised Orthodox church communities on their own. Parishes were founded in populous areas. Immigrants asked priests from their homelands to come and serve them. Subsequently, dioceses were founded under foreign jurisdiction. Over the years, clergy in these dioceses looked for ways to cooperate at some level. Various initiatives can be listed in order to illustrate such cooperative efforts in Germany, as well as ecumenical initiatives which helped to further such purposes too.

The Ecumenical Committee for the Support of Orthodox Priests (Ökumenische Kommission für die Unterstützung orthodoxer Priester, KdöR) was launched in 1957, in order to provide financial support for the pastoral care of many refugees with Orthodox roots then living in Germany. In 1965 it received the status of a corporation under public law.

Regional conferences were initiated from 1966 onward by a circle of friends, called Philoxenia, under the guidance of Ilse Friedeberg (1914–1998), a former translator in Geneva. Orthodox priests were invited to speak about their homelands and the situation of their present parishes. Coming from different jurisdictions, the priests celebrated the Liturgy together in order to bring the congregations closer to each other despite their different backgrounds (Friedeberg 1973).

Around the late Archpriest Sergius Heitz (1908–1990), who used to live in Düsseldorf, the so-called Orthodox Fraternity (Orthodoxe Fraternität) came into existence; its aim was to promote cooperation across the different jurisdictions. It should also be mentioned that in 1974 the Ecumenical Centre (Ökumenische Centrale) of the Consortium of Christian Churches (Arbeitsgemeinschaft Christlicher Kirchen) hired an expert in charge of issues related to Orthodox Churches in Germany.

By May 1994, the Joint Committee of Orthodox Churches (later: 'of the Orthodox Church') in Germany (Kommission der Orthodoxen Kirchen in Deutschland, KOKiD) was founded. The KOKiD took responsibility for common tasks related to ecumenical issues, religious teaching at public schools and media work. Since 1997, its information service, *Orthodoxie Aktuell*, reports on developments in Orthodox Churches in Germany and around the world. The history of the Committee shows the difficulties for Orthodox groups to work together and follow a common path. However, while still looking for greater unity, Orthodox with different national backgrounds understand themselves as being together 'one Orthodox Church in Germany'. Obviously, this is possible thanks to the same traditions in matters of liturgy, faith and order (Basdekis 2001).

On 27 February 2010, a further step was taken with the founding of the Conference of Orthodox Bishops in Germany (Orthodoxe Bischofskonferenz

92 *Orthodox Identities in Western Europe*

in Deutschland) in Nuremberg. This allows Orthodox of the Byzantine tradition in Germany to progress significantly towards a joint appearance and presence. This fulfils the guidelines of the Fourth Pre-Synodical Pan Orthodox Assembly of 2009. Every decision of the Bishops' Conference has to be unanimous. Thirteen jurisdictions are represented in the Conference, with 17 bishops and vicar bishops (KOKiD 2011: 28, 124ff.). The President of the Bishops' Conference is the head of the Greek Orthodox Metropolis, Augoustinos (Lambadarkis, b. 1938), under the Ecumenical Patriarchate. The Conference is not allowed to interfere with the duties of the diocesan bishops in matters of administration or church order. The last instance of decision has to remain with the first hierarchs of each Church. How far and how soon the cooperation of Churches with different national backgrounds could lead to the goal of an autonomous, self-ruling Orthodox Church in Germany, cannot yet be foreseen.[1] At this stage, the Bishops' Conference has to find ways to balance between common local interests and views of each mother church.

It seems quite likely that the number of religious services celebrated in German as well as the amount of teaching materials in German will increase, in order to avoid losing the future generations. But the final goal of a 'German Orthodoxy' seems to be still more far off than before. This goal was more prominently advocated during the Cold War period. In Germany, members of small immigrant parishes, then in lesser number, were also thinking about ways to make Orthodoxy attractive for German people of non-Orthodox background. This would not have required them to belong in some way to another nation and to adopt another language (liturgical or otherwise) or to adopt foreign customs and traditions: the vision was one of German Orthodoxy, combining Orthodox and German identity.

This vision was most prominently advocated by the Russian Orthodox Archbishop Alexij van der Mensbrugghe (1899–1980) and Archpriest Sergius Heitz (1908–1990); the latter also made new editions of liturgical books in German available.[2] This approach also had its place in the Russian Orthodox Church Outside of Russia: prayer-books and other liturgical material in German were published.[3] In several places, German Orthodox congregations came into being. In some Russian parishes, liturgy was celebrated in German once a month. There is also the German Orthodox Monastery of the Holy Trinity (Deutsches Orthodoxes Dreifaltigkeitskloster) in Buchhagen-Bodenwerder; it

---

[1]   See the Statutes of the Conference of Orthodox Bishops in Germany, Essen, 13 November 2010. Available at: http://www.obkd.de/Texte/OBKD%20-%20Satzung.pdf.

[2]   See Heitz (1965) and publications that followed, for example *Der Orthodoxe Gottesdienst Band I* (Mainz, 1965), *Mysterium der Anbetung* (Cologne, 1986), *Mysterium der Anbetung III* (Cologne, 1988).

[3]   For instance the *Orthodoxes Gebetbuch*, published in Munich in 1989, including special prayers for the persecuted Russian Church.

belongs to the Bulgarian diocese. This monastery understands itself as a German Mount Athos and develops specific musical and iconographical traditions (Pfeiffer 1999).

The political change in former Communist countries of Eastern Europe was accompanied by a strong flow of new immigrants coming from there, and what used to be small parishes suddenly experienced a dramatic growth. Another consequence was that convert priests became a minority and their influence became modest. At the same time, a new generation of priests emerges, with young people who grew up or – for instance – belonged to families of Russians with German roots, who had the opportunity to settle in the country of their more or less distant ancestors.

Newcomers are looking for churches not merely because they are Orthodox, but sometimes even more with the expectation of finding a national home in a foreign environment. The idea of a German Orthodoxy is entirely foreign to them. This explains why Sunday services in German are often less well-attended and a number of priests nowadays lack understanding of the need for such services.

Overcoming the Past

The political situation created by Communist rule in Eastern Europe during several decades also had consequences for Orthodox Churches in Germany and elsewhere. Church structures created in exile had sometimes to live in separation from the patriarchates in the home countries. Much has changed since the end of the Communist regimes, but the legacy of those difficult years has not yet been entirely cleared.

On 17 May 2007, the two wings of the Russian Orthodox Church, the Patriarchate of Moscow and the Russian Orthodox Church in Exile, entered a new era of ecclesiastical unity by signing the 'Act of Canonical Union'; the event was marked by a joint celebration of the Holy Liturgy by the two First Hierarchs (Thöle 2007). In Germany, there is still a coexistence of ecclesiastical structures of both wings. Moreover, there is one parish belonging to the Russian Exarchate in Paris under Constantinople (a group that its members are keen to describe as 'independent', and gathering a number of congregations with Russian roots).

The Bulgarian Orthodox Church is present in Germany as a unified Church, thanks to the long-lasting work of Metropolit Simeon (Kostadinov), despite the difficulties in Bulgaria itself after the fall of Communism.

The situation of the various parishes of the Romanian Orthodox Church is different: to this day, they have not been able to reunite. The Bucharest patriarch's call in 2010 for the return of the separated Romanian parishes was rejected on the ground that Orthodox church organisation is based on the

94   *Orthodox Identities in Western Europe*

principle of territory much more than on the principle of nationality. While a number of Romanian parishes belong to the Metropolia of the Patriarchate of Bucharest, several older parishes, founded by Romanian exiles, are organised as a Romanian Vicariate under the Greek Orthodox Metropolia; moreover, two belong to other jurisdictions.

The situation of the Ukrainian Orthodox parishes is more complicated, as a consequence of the contested claim for independence from Moscow (autocephaly). There a few parishes in Germany under the Ecumenical Patriarchate, in addition to those belonging to 'non-canonical' bodies that will be mentioned later.

Coming to terms with the past remains an uncompleted task. It will require future generations in parishes issued from exile communities to overcome the fears and concerns that marked their parents due to their personal experiences during the Communist period. The emergence of new generations of hierarchs untainted by the past in the home countries will also help to heal past wounds (Thöle 1997).

The presence of smaller Orthodox groups belonging to so-called 'non-canonical' Churches should also be mentioned as an addition to the Orthodox landscape in Germany. Among them are three Ukrainian groups, each one with a few parishes in Germany: those belonging to the Patriarchate of Kiev, those under the Ukrainian Autocephalous Orthodox Church (led for some time by Archbishop Kyr Petro [1951–2011], a hierarch with ecumenical goodwill), and a bishopric of the Sobornopravna Synod (US). Regarding the Macedonian Orthodox Church, clergy ministering to its faithful in Germany mostly visit with tourist visas. There are also a few Old Calendarist groups. Moreover, the Orthodox Church of France (Église Catholique Orthodoxe de France, ECOF) has a parish in Germany that uses the Gallican rite.[4] Another Western-rite group belongs to the Communion of Western Orthodox Churches (Communion des Églises Orthodoxes Occidentales), an alliance of independent Churches following the Gallican, Celtic and Byzantine liturgical traditions.[5] The last groups gather few members, but may be attractive for potential converts looking for something other than the mainline Orthodox Churches in Germany, with their links to foreign national cultures.

Regarding the Oriental Orthodox Churches, they are in communion with each other and follow their respective different liturgical traditions. Estimates put the number of Armenian, Syriac, Indo-Syriac, Coptic, Ethiopian and

---

[4]   They have published a German translation: *Die Göttliche Liturgie unseres heiligen Vaters Germanus von Paris*, 2011.

[5]   They have also published their liturgy: *Göttliche Liturgie der Westlich-Orthodoxen Kirche vom Berg Karmel*, 2011.

Eritrean Christians at more than 100,000.[6] Those Churches have organised in Germany, but in recent times have suffered from intra-jurisdictional quarrels. The same holds true for the Assyrian (so-called 'Nestorian') Church of the East, which is present with only a handful of congregations in the Rhine-Main area (Schwarz 1995).

Ecumenical Outlook and Enrichment of Theological Views

From the very beginning, Orthodox Churches in Germany have attempted to be on good terms with the local Catholic and Protestant churches. This was not only due to a need for charitable support or for help with buildings where Orthodox religious services could take place. There were also far-sighted bishops, such as Metropolitan Irinaios (Galanakis), in Germany from 1971 to 1977, and Bishop Lavrentije (Trifunovic), in Germany from 1989 to 1991, who felt that the presence of Orthodox Churches in Germany should commit them to a mission of ecumenical encounter. Especially noteworthy is the fact that Germany has not been touched by the crisis that developed after 2000 between Orthodox and other member churches of the World Council of Churches (WCC). When Orthodox patriarchs visited Germany, they not only paid attention to their own churches but on every occasion attended also to other, non-Orthodox churches, seizing the opportunity for celebrations, talks and interdenominational prayers. Especially worth mentioning is the confession of guilt of Russian Patriarch Alexy II in the cathedral of Berlin, during his 1995 visit to Germany, regarding the suffering brought to Eastern Germany by the totalitarian Soviet regime (Thöle 2000).

The Orthodox Church belongs to the Consortium of Christian Churches (Arbeitsgemeinschaft Christlicher Kirchen); it is also present at the (Protestant) Church Congresses (Kirchentage) as well as at the Catholic Congresses (Katholikentage). At the Second Ecumenical Church Congress (Zweiter Ökumenischer Kirchentag) in Munich, 2010, a genuine Orthodox accent was set through the celebration of the *artoklasia* on the Odeonsplace: 10,000 guests at 1,000 tables were able to participate to this service. Orthodoxy in Germany can be seen as participating now 'in the very midst' among the circle of churches: it is 'no longer to be regarded as a sort of mere spectator, but as a true partner in life'.[7]

---

[6]   The Central Council of Oriental Christians in Germany (Zentralrat Orientalischer Christen in Deutschland), founded in 2013, quotes a number as high as 200,000, but it includes Byzantine and Uniate Christians from the Middle East.

[7]   See the statements by episcopal counsellor Nikolaj Thon and the person in charge of ecumenical relations, Archpriest Constantinos Miron, in *Orthodoxie Aktuell*, 14(6), 2010: 8, 9.

Furthermore, Orthodox presence in Germany has a theological impact for all Christians: next to Catholic or Protestant understandings of the meaning of 'church', there is now an Eastern ecclesiastical hermeneutic pattern, i.e. a church identifying itself through the Holy Eucharist. Such views could come into a fruitful dialogue with each other. It may conceal opportunities for new ways of expanding Catholic–Protestant togetherness towards the Eastern Orthodox. There are indications of initial steps in that direction. The Orthodox witness urges the Churches of the West, which often seem to remain lost in their own most beloved controversies, to look at themselves through different eyes. This could be tested on the questions of ministry and Eucharist, baptism and church, word and sacrament. It is a call to all Christian traditions to answer questions such as the following: 'What is the doctrine of Holy Scripture?'; 'What does the tradition of the Church mean really?'; and 'Of what importance is the celebration of the Holy Eucharist for the fellowship of the faithful?' (Thöle 2012). Only by doing so can they achieve a renewed and joint path towards unity and overcome hermeneutic difficulties and inherited reductions within their respective denominational legacies. By following such a path, old stereotypes and reductionism, which are cultivated as emotional blockades by conservative wings of all church families, can be put aside. Among such stereotypes, one could mention a few instances: worship versus revival, scripture versus tradition, patristic versus modern. Whether churches today do really want to enter into such deep dialogues, which might force them to change something, presents a significant question at a time when churches seem much more to be interested in keeping up their own traditional milieu – a time characterised by various crises, not merely the financial one.

Looking at history as a theologian, one sees not only the outcome of secular developments, but also ways in which God communes with his people: from such a perspective, the presence of Orthodoxy in Germany cannot be seen as a mere coincidence, but has to be received as God's guidance and gift. It would be a pity if the only result of this working of God would be a mere distant coexistence next to each other, at the very time when Europe is attempting to grow together in a globalizing world. The coming of various Orthodox ecclesiastical identities to Germany, despite all the difficulties and challenges this presents for the Orthodox themselves, should lead to promising steps forward, setting into motion changes in the identities of other Christian Churches in this ongoing process.

Bibliography

Basdekis, A. 2001. *Die Orthodoxe Kirche.* Frankfurt am Main: Otto Lembeck.
Friedeberg, I. 1973. *Philoxenia.* Marburg: Edel.

Heitz, S. 1965. *Der Orthodoxe Gottesdienst (Göttliche Liturgie und Sakramente,* Vol. 1). Mainz: Matthias-Grünewald-Verlag.

KOKid, 2011. *Orthodoxe Bistümer und Gemeinden in Deutschland,* 13th ed. Wuppertal: Orthodoxie Aktuell.

Pfeiffer, J. 1999. *Dass ihr anbetet in Geist und Wahrheit: Morphologie und Mystagogie des orthodoxen Tagzeitengebetes; nebst einer allgemeinen Einführung in die orthodoxe Liturgik und das Verhältnis von Liturgie und Mystik.* Buchhagen: Verlag des Klosters Buchhagen.

Schwarz, S. 1995. *Überleben in schwieriger Zeit: 4. Evangelisch/Orientalisch-Orthodoxe Konsultation.* Hanover: Kirchenamt der EKD.

Thöle, R. 1997. *Orthodoxe Kirchen in Deutschland.* Göttingen: Vandenhoeck & Ruprecht.

Thöle, R. 2000. Die Beziehungen der Evangelischen Kirche in Deutschland zu den orthodoxen Kirchen. *Reader zur EKD-Synode.* Available at: http://www.ekd.de/international/berichte/2000/oekumene_reader2000_09.html [accessed 20 July 2013].

Thöle, R. 2007. Kirchengemeinschaft zwischen Moskauer Patriarchat und Russischer Auslandskirche. *Materialdienst des Konfessionskundlichen Instituts (MdKI),* 58(4): 77–8.

Thöle, R. 2012. Warum es sich lohnt, sich mit der Orthodoxie auseinanderzusetzen. *Religion und Gesellschaft in Ost und West,* 40(7–8): 16–18.

Chapter 5

The Ambivalent Ecumenical Relations among Russian Orthodox Faithful in Germany

Sebastian Rimestad and Ernest Kadotschnikow

The Russian Orthodox presence in Germany has a long history, characterised by a vivid interaction with the existing Christian denominations – the Roman Catholics and Lutherans. Each individual Russian Orthodox parish in Germany has a unique history connected with the various settlement processes of Russian Orthodox faithful in Germany and the differing local circumstances. This chapter looks into these variations by analysing four parishes and their ecumenical engagement and relationship with the German environment. The four chosen parishes, all belonging to the jurisdiction of the Moscow Patriarchate, show various factors which can play a role in order to successfully integrate in the German social fabric and religious landscape. Before we turn to our case studies, however, we conduct a short historical overview of the Russian settlements in Germany as well as of the Orthodox participation in the local inter-denominational landscape.

Waves of Immigration

There were at least four waves of immigration from Russia or the Soviet Union throughout history. Already in the eighteenth century, there were settlements of Russian diplomats, merchants, nobles and their servants all over Germany, especially in the spa towns of the southwest and in the centres of power. The first Orthodox church buildings in Germany were thus embassy chapels, private chapels, memorial churches and places of worship for the spa guests. These places of worship did not all survive for a long time, but they initiated a tradition of Russian Orthodoxy in Germany that led to the foundation of parishes and building of churches also in other contexts.

The second immigration wave left Russia for different countries, including Germany, after the October revolution in 1917, fleeing Bolshevik persecution. Many of these emigrants hailed from the Russian intellectual elite and brought a new spiritual and intellectual impulse to the Russian Orthodox Church in the West, especially in Paris, but equally in various German cities. They founded new parishes or brought new life into existing ones. In the course of the Second World War, a third wave of Russian settlers arrived in Germany, mainly from the areas which came to the Soviet Union as a result of the war. These areas include the Baltic States, Western Ukraine and Belarus, the latter two being part of Poland in the interwar era. The Orthodox Church in these regions had developed rather liberally, especially in Estonia and Latvia (Rimestad 2012). Many inhabitants, not only Orthodox faithful, fled out of fear for Stalinist terror on the eve of the Soviet takeover. Germany was the first destination for most of the refugees. The bulk of them moved on to France, Great Britain, America or Australia, but some stayed.

The fourth and most recent immigration wave resulted from the break-up of the Iron Curtain, which led to an increased freedom of mobility between East and West. The emigration began even before the end of the Soviet Union, but intensified immensely once the Soviet Union ceased to exist. A large fraction of these new emigrants arrived in Germany, primarily due to the German legislation concerning the ethnic German 'late repatriates'[1] and the restoration of the Jewish contingent in Germany (Harris 2003). Both groups, the late repatriates and the Russian Jews, included a number of religiously assimilated individuals, i.e. Russian Orthodox faithful. Even where this was not the case, they often brought along Russian Orthodox family members. This resulted in an unprecedented sudden rise in the membership of the Russian Orthodox parishes; a significant number of new parishes are being founded to this day. The break-up of the Iron Curtain also resulted in an influx of students and migrant workers. Finally, a number of Germans found spouses in the former Soviet Republics, sometimes converting to Orthodox Christianity in the process.

The four waves are wholly unconnected, but the Orthodox Church provides an arena where the members of the various waves have to interact, and the integration process has not always been easy. The last immigration wave confronted the German parishes with a new challenge, since it consisted almost exclusively of people with a Soviet cultural background and a neophytic view of Orthodox Christianity.[2] Integrating these faithful in the existing parishes is a challenge, because of the difference of mentality to the long-established existing members. These tensions are much more apparent in the parishes belonging to the jurisdiction of the Russian Orthodox Church Outside of Russia (ROCOR)

---

[1] Those that could prove German descent had a right of entry to Germany and were granted German citizenship through a simplified procedure (Blahusch 1999: 109–133).

[2] The term 'neophyte' is used widely in the Russian Orthodox Church to denote often new faithful with a naive and incomplete understanding of the faith. They tend to exaggerate their commitment in various directions.

than in those of the Moscow Patriarchate, primarily since the ROCOR was the dominant jurisdiction in Western Germany until 1990 (Seide 2001: 171). The new parishes that have been founded since then are primarily parishes of the Moscow Patriarchate.[3]

Relations with Other Christian Communities

The Orthodox parishes in Germany entertain relations with other Christian communities against the background of the official ecumenical relations on the level of the church leadership. These relations are difficult to characterise briefly. In order to understand the case studies presented below more fully, we nonetheless attempt an overview. The Orthodox Churches have gathered in the German Conference of Orthodox Bishops since 2010. This organisation is the successor of the KOKiD, the Commission of the Orthodox Church in Germany, which was founded in 1994, so inter-Orthodox cooperation has a long history in Germany. There are numerous bilateral bodies consisting of representatives of different Orthodox, Catholic and/or Protestant churches, which mostly discuss theological issues. At a third level, there is a multilateral body, called the National Council of Christian Churches, which unites members of almost all Trinitarian Christian denominations operating in Germany. They discuss theological as well as organisational issues and represent the plural Christianity vis-à-vis the German state and society.

The ecumenical relations at the highest level do not work as smoothly, as the case of an agreement to mutually recognise baptisms from 2007 illustrates. The agreement was reached in the National Council of Christian Churches and solemnly celebrated in an ecumenical service in Magdeburg. It was originally supported by all denominations that accept infant baptism, including the Orthodox. The KOKiD mandated Bishop Longin of Klin to sign the agreement on behalf of 'the Orthodox Church in Germany'. Bishop Longin used to be a diocesan bishop in West Germany under the jurisdiction of the Patriarchate of Moscow, but with national reunification in 1991, the dioceses in Germany were also unified. The new role of Bishop Longin was defined as 'representative of the Moscow Patriarchate in Germany', a unique status in the Russian Orthodox Church that had never occurred before. However, once Bishop Longin had signed the agreement, the Patriarchate of Moscow promptly declared the signature void, for Longin had not conferred with the Patriarchate before

---

[3]   According to the official homepage of the German Eparchy of the Moscow Patriarchate, almost 40 new parishes have been founded since 1992, when the current bishop Feofan (Galinskiy) entered office. http://www.rokmp.de/eparhiya/ [accessed 27 March 2013].

signing (DECR 2007). Although there is no valid signature representing the Orthodox Church, this is hardly ever reflected in accounts of this 'hallmark of ecumenical cooperation'. Nevertheless, the incident puts a significant strain on the official ecumenical relations.

Similarly, the official position of Metropolitan Hilarion (Alfeyev) of Volokolamsk, head of the Department for External Church Relations of the Patriarchate of Moscow, maintaining that the Protestant communities cannot be called 'churches' in the full sense of the word, clouds the ecumenical atmosphere in Germany (EKD 2011). And it is not only Protestant Churches that have difficulties with Hilarion's explicit position. He is also responsible for retardation within the Joint International Commission for Theological Dialogue between the Catholic Church and the Orthodox Church. In 2007, the Russian delegation, headed by Metropolitan Hilarion, left a meeting of the Commission in Ravenna officially because of provocative conduct by the representatives of the Patriarchate of Constantinople. Inter-Orthodox conflicts thus spilled out onto the ecumenical scene. On the other hand, it can be said that there is some reluctance to fully embrace the ecumenical dialogue on the part of the Orthodox representatives. They arguably have a strategic interest in any pretext that leads to a stagnation of the ecumenical process. Thereby, they can reap the benefits of being involved in the ecumenical dialogue, such as cooperation in various fields and an increased network at the local level without having to fear the anti-ecumenical mood that prevails in much of the Orthodox community back home (Knox 2005: passim). The participants of the ecumenical dialogue, according to Hilarion and Patriarch Kirill, 'should not aim at doctrinal unity. Instead, they should search for ways to deliver a common witness in the world concerning the spiritual and ethical values of Christianity. The Saviour's commandment to full unity among his disciples is not abolished, but it is not given to us to know when it will be fulfilled' (Alfeyev 2010: 425).

Ecumenical relations, inter-Orthodox but also inter-denominational, are relevant not only at the level of the church leadership, but first and foremost at the level of the local parish. This is where ecclesiastical life is lived and not only discussed. Our four case studies are Dresden, Weimar, Frankfurt (Oder) and Hamburg. These four parishes are chosen primarily since they represent four different kinds of parish history and because they illustrate a variety of strategies and experiences when it comes to integration into the social fabric and religious landscape in Germany. The parish of Dresden is interesting, because it possesses a representative church building, the ownership of which has long been legally disputed between the Moscow Patriarchate and the ROCOR. In fact, the parish history may serve as an illustration of the history of the Russian Orthodox Church in Germany. The second parish, Weimar, also uses an Orthodox church building, without owning it. It is much smaller than the building in Dresden. There was an attempt to organise a room for celebrating monthly liturgies in neighbouring Erfurt, which will also be detailed during this case study. Frankfurt (Oder), the easternmost city in Germany, has an Orthodox parish that is led by a priest, himself converted from Roman Catholicism. The congregation used to celebrate liturgies in an unused kindergarten in the city centre, but was then granted a Roman Catholic church building some five kilometres outside of the city, where it now conducts worship. Hamburg, finally, is a case where a ROCOR parish co-exists with a recently founded parish of the Moscow Patriarchate. The latter has completely overshadowed the former parish, not least because of the successful acquisition of an unused Lutheran church building in the city centre and the priest's ability to initiate a vibrant parish life.

Dresden: A Bone of Contention between the Jurisdictions

The Russian Orthodox church building in Dresden was completed in 1874, financed mostly by Simeon von Wikulin, a Russian statesman living in Dresden, to be used by Russian diplomats and visitors to the Kingdom of Saxony (*Russische Orthodoxe Kirche* 2012: 39). The Russian Orthodox parish of Dresden, existing since 1860, moved into this new church and ensured a vivid parish life until 1915, when the German imperial government ordered it to be closed down due to the First World War. The official explanation was that 'there are concerns of national security, since the means are not available to monitor the Russian language services being held in this church, in order to avoid anti-German prayers and prayers for the Russian military forces' (quote from *Russische Orthodoxe Kirche* 2012: 17). When the church was reopened in 1921, the parish already encompassed a number of refugees, including noble officers, scientists and artists who had fled the Soviet regime. The active parish life that ensued involved interdenominational cooperation. The education of the refugee children in religion, Russian language and history took place in the parish hall of the neighbouring Lutheran church. This is an example of the optimistic attitude towards ecumenism within the Orthodox Church at the time, which also included the passionate participation at the founding of various organisations in the ecumenical movement (Zernov 2004).

In the course of the establishment of National Socialism in Germany, many of the Russian Orthodox parishioners moved on to France and America. This weakened all Orthodox parishes in Germany, but did not erase parish life completely. That was the situation in which the conflict between the ROCOR and the Moscow Patriarchate in Germany escalated.[4] Metropolitan Evlogii

---

[4] For the foundation of the ROCOR and its early history, see Seide 1983 and Pospielovsky 1984. The following narrative is taken from Seide 2001: 238–45.

(Georgievskii), who had been named Exarch of Western Europe[5] by Patriarch Tikhon of Moscow, also settled in Paris in 1922, entrusting the care of the parishes in Germany to Tikhon (Lyashchenko), whom he named Bishop of Potsdam two years later. A ROCOR Bishops' Council in 1926 decided to make Germany a diocese of its own. Metropolitan Evlogii disapproved of this decision and the development of the ROCOR and left this jurisdiction, eventually subordinating himself to the Patriarchate of Constantinople. Bishop Tikhon became diocesan bishop of the ROCOR diocese of Germany. The parishes in Germany were split between those supporting Bishop Tikhon and those following Metropolitan Evlogii, both of whom claimed ownership of all Orthodox property in Germany. The National Socialists, who came to power in the 1930s, decided to support the faction of Bishop Tikhon, because 'it is well known that the ROCOR gathers the most right-wing elements, the most nationally-minded faithful, those that are able to participate in the anti-Bolshevik struggle. The leadership of those following Metropolitan Evlogii are mostly left-wing, extremely liberal thinkers, who are not interested in fighting Bolshevism and the movements associated with it' (quoted in *Russische Orthodoxe Kirche* 2012: 22).

The parish of Dresden held to Evlogii and weathered all the official pressure to switch to the ROCOR jurisdiction, until a law from 1938–1939 officially gave all Orthodox property in Germany to the ROCOR under Bishop Tikhon (Seide 2001: 243–4). After the Second World War, Dresden was part of the Soviet zone of occupation, and the Orthodox parish priest asked Patriarch Sergii of Moscow to be let back into the mother church, the Patriarchate of Moscow, which was willingly granted (*Russische Orthodoxe Kirche* 2012: 23). During the communist regime in East Germany, parish life continued under difficult circumstances. There existed a kind of strategic alliance between the Christian denominations countering the official atheist ideology of the state. For example, a Catholic priest donated a church bell to the Orthodox parish in the 1970s, because the bells had been confiscated already during the First World War (*Russische Orthodoxe Kirche* 2012: 44). The renovation of the church building, which was began after the reunification of Germany in 1991, was financed by the Saxon authorities as well as both major churches in Germany. Ecumenical cooperation was thus always beneficial to the Orthodox Church, without concessions, apart from symbolic gestures. The parish of Dresden takes an active part in the Regional Council of Christian Churches of Saxony and entertains friendly relations with the other denominations in Dresden.

With regard to the inter-Orthodox dialogue, Dresden is an example of how the political circumstances of the Russian diaspora have been transposed to the ecclesiastical realm, leading to conflicts among the Russian emigrants, also

---

[5] An Exarch in the Russian Orthodox Church is a Bishop administering a peripheral region of the Church, which may consist of several dioceses (Klutschewsky 2010).

The Ambivalent Ecumenical Relations among Russian Orthodox in Germany   105

involving the German state agencies and courts. Since the unification of the two German states, a lawsuit has been fought, regarding the ownership of the church in Dresden. The ROCOR, under the leadership of Archbishop Mark (Arndt) of Berlin and Germany, claimed that the handover of the church of Dresden to the ROCOR from 1938 was still valid and thus that it was the legal owner. After several years of legal disputes, the court decided in its favour, but the acting parish priest (of the Moscow Patriarchate) refused to hand over the keys. Since in Germany there is a clear difference between the legal owner (*Eigentümer*) and actual owner (*Besitzer*), this refusal did not amount to a criminal case and further court sessions followed. The conflict lasted until 2007, when the two parts of the Russian Orthodox Church solemnly declared their unity. This unity rendered any legal disputes between the two jurisdictions theologically and morally unjustified, so the two parties agreed to recognise the status quo.[6] The pioneering role of Archbishop Mark in the negotiations leading up to the unification process made it even more important for him to get this lawsuit out of the way.[7]

The case of Dresden is thus a paramount example of an Orthodox parish in a nineteenth-century church building that has lived through the turbulent German history and the history of the Russian diaspora, with its many political splits and alliances. The parish retained continuity in spite of the difficult political inheritance. Archbishop Mark and Archbishop Feofan (Galinskyi), both of whom carry the denomination 'Berlin and Germany', pay joint visits to the parish of Dresden at special parochial events. This is the only case in Germany where such joint visits happen. It shows the ambiguity of its jurisdictional affiliation, where neither bishop wants to renounce his claim.

Weimar: A Long Tradition Develops in New Directions

The Russian Orthodox parish of Weimar uses, similarly to Dresden, an originally Orthodox church building in the middle of Weimar. Unlike Dresden, however, this building does not belong to the Orthodox Church, but is the property of the municipal museum of Weimar. It was built in 1862 as the burial church of Grand Duchess Maria Pavlovna of Russia, whose husband was the Grand Duke of Saxe-Weimar-Eisenach. The building was commissioned by her son,

---

6   Cf. a presentation of Archbishop Mark on 26 November 2009 at a round table in Paris: Orthodoxie.com. 2009. L'union canonique entre l'Eglise russe hors frontières et le Patriarcat de Moscou: Bilan et perspectives deux ans après. Available at: http://www.orthodoxie.com/actualites/france/lunion-canonique-entre-leglise-russe-hors-frontieres-et-le-patriarcat-de-moscou-bilan-et-perspectiv-2/ [accessed 9 April 2013].

7   For the unification process, see Stricker 2010: 109–121. For the preceding agreements between the two jurisdictions in Germany, see Seide 2001: 174–5.

Grand Duke Charles Alexander of Saxe-Weimar-Eisenach and, thus, was never church property, but belonged to the princely family.[8] Nevertheless, the Russian Orthodox Church was always allowed to celebrate the liturgy in it. After the Russian embassy in Weimar was closed in 1909, there was no functioning parish in Weimar until 1950. Since 1950, the Moscow Patriarchate has used this parish church to cater to all Orthodox Christians in Thuringia, not only those of Russian tradition.

Thus, the ROCOR never had anything to do with this parish and church. However, the current priest Mihail Rahr, who arrived in the year 2000, was originally born, raised and educated within the ROCOR in Germany and ordained a sub-deacon in its jurisdiction. For reasons of conscience, he left the ROCOR for the Patriarchate of Moscow, was ordained a deacon and priest, and eventually assigned the parish of Weimar.[9] For him, the Moscow Patriarchate, being in canonical communion with the other Orthodox churches, represented the canonically intact Russian Orthodox Church, and he felt that the isolation of the ROCOR was no longer justified. His father, Gleb A. Rahr, had already earlier had a difficult relationship with the ROCOR leadership in Germany, because of his pro-unification position.[10]

The parish in Weimar is also integrated into the local social and interdenominational discourse, primarily through the Regional Council of Christian Churches of Thuringia and even in the foundation 'Pro Oriente' in Vienna.[11] These fraternal relations with the other denominations enabled the Orthodox parish to establish dependencies in the neighbouring cities of Erfurt and Jena. The main difficulty in the establishment of these dependencies was the lack of suitable premises in which to celebrate the liturgy. In Erfurt, negotiations resulted in 2010 in a Roman Catholic church building being offered free of charge once a month for an Orthodox liturgy, including a storage room for the liturgical equipment and literature. In Jena, the Orthodox parish has rented a Lutheran church building for weekly liturgies since 2006. In general, the negotiations with the Roman Catholics in Thuringia could be characterised as unproblematic and their attitude as cooperative, whereas the Lutherans were more reserved, particularly concerning the financial aspects and liturgical

---

[8]   From the homepage of the parish of Weimar: [Anon.]. n.d. Die Russisch-Orthodoxe Kirche in Weimar. Available at: http://www.rok-weimar.de/html/geschichte.html [accessed 15 April 2013].

[9]   This section is based on numerous personal communications with priest Mihail Rahr over the last few years.

[10]   He is, for example, not even mentioned in Seide 1983, although he played an important role in the Russian diaspora.

[11]   'Pro Oriente' entertains a commission of young theologians for the dialogue between the Roman Catholic and the Orthodox Church, where a parish member participates.

forms.[12] As of April 2014, Father Mihail Rahr is unable to celebrate liturgies in Erfurt due to poor health. In Jena, the congregation is assuming an independent existence, due to an unaffiliated priest living in Jena. Archbishop Feofan granted him permission to celebrate, although he is not a member of the diocesan clergy. Thus, the situation is canonically ambiguous.

In the case of Weimar, the ecumenical cooperation is similar to the one in Dresden. Cooperation is largely a one-way affair, where the Orthodox parish benefits more than the other partner. In the canonical territory that the Russian Orthodox Church claims for itself, the latter has never and would never offer one of its houses of worship for use by Roman Catholic or Protestant congregations. This would be extremely difficult to justify from the point of view of canon law and lead to emotional dissonances among the Orthodox faithful. The only case that springs to mind where something similar has happened pertained to the Assyrian Church of the East, which was allowed to conduct services in an Orthodox church building in Moscow from 1992 until their own church building was completed in 1998.[13]

Frankfurt (Oder): An Industrious Convert

The parish in Frankfurt (Oder), the easternmost city of Germany, is an entirely different case. Contrary to the two previous examples, this parish does not have a long history or any originally Orthodox house of worship. The parish encompasses only the most recent wave of Russian immigrants to Germany, who arrived after 1990. Part of the history of this immigration wave in the region of Frankfurt (Oder) is the history of its Orthodox parish. The current priest, Georg Langosch, a convert from Roman Catholicism, used to be an active Orthodox parishioner in Potsdam, some 120 km away from Frankfurt (Oder).[14] Seeing the growing Russian community in his home town, he committed himself to the establishment of an Orthodox prayer group in Frankfurt (Oder). In order to do this, he contacted the other Christian denominations. These contacts bore fruit in that both the Lutheran Church and the Roman Catholic Church, at different stages, offered this group room in one of their houses of worship from 1995 onwards.

From 1998, the congregation rented a former kindergarten, where it arranged a small chapel for the exclusive use of the Orthodox parish. Several

---

[12] For example the use of incense, especially problematised in the Erfurt negotiations.

[13] From the official homepage of the Russian priory of the Assyrian Church of the East: Assyrian Church of the East. 2007. *Kratkii istoricheskii ocherk*. Available at: http://assyrianchurch.ru/publ/2-1-0-3 [accessed 15 April 2013].

[14] This section is based on numerous personal communications with priest Georg Langosch over the last few years.

108   *Orthodox Identities in Western Europe*

years later, the local Roman Catholic diocese offered the congregation a little used church building in a neighbouring village free of charge for permanent use. This offer was too tempting to refuse and the congregation moved into the church in Brieskow-Finkenheerd in 2004. The reason for this openness of the Roman Catholics may be sought in the existing connections between Georg Langosch and Catholic prelates and clergy, with whom he had studied at various theological institutions, including in Rome, before converting to Orthodox Christianity. The move to the village church proved to be a challenge for the parish life, since the place of worship was no longer as accessible from the city centre. Only the parish core remained in the Sunday liturgies and new arrivals no longer happened to pass by the church and involve themselves. The outreach to less religiously motivated potential parishioners especially suffered at the new location. Only immigrants with strong church affiliation were ready to travel to the village in order to acquaint themselves with the local parish. The missionary dimension thus disappeared.

Before Georg Langosch was ordained as an Orthodox priest in 1997, the parish was served primarily by a priest from the neighbouring Polish Orthodox Church in Gorzów. This example of inter-Orthodox cooperation is rather unusual, although the local Orthodox churches remain in Eucharistic communion and rhetorically emphasise their unity. After the ordination of Langosch, a section of the congregation decided to switch to the Gorzów parish, which led to conflict between parishioners and the priests.

Converted theologians and clergy tend to strain ecumenical relations, but in the case of Georg Langosch, the benefits of his personal connections within the Roman Catholic Church were much greater than the drawbacks of his conversion. Only the Roman Catholic priest of the parish including the dependency Brieskow-Finkenheerd has expressed his dissatisfaction.

Hamburg: A Story of Success

The Hamburg parish of the Moscow Patriarchate is also a young parish, which was founded in addition to the long-established ROCOR parish of Hamburg. The ROCOR parish has possessed its own typically Orthodox church building since the Second World War. The current house of worship was erected in 1964, financed by donations of the local population, to replace the existing expropriated church building. The previous church had been constructed on a plot of land donated by the high commissioner of the British Zone of Occupation in Germany.[15] Thus, the ROCOR parish in Hamburg has always

---

[15] P. Nikolai Wolper. Zur Geschichte der Russisch-orthodoxen Gemeinde in Hamburg. Available at: http://www.prokopij.de/Historie/geschichte_de.htm [accessed 10 April 2013].

The Ambivalent Ecumenical Relations among Russian Orthodox in Germany   109

benefitted from the generosity of Western non-Orthodox. This is also the case with the younger parish of the Moscow Patriarchate. It was founded in 2001, and originally celebrated liturgy in a Lutheran kindergarten, which had already served as house of worship for the Serbian Orthodox parish of Hamburg for 30 years.[16] However, in 2004, the parish acquired an unused Lutheran parish church in the centre of Hamburg, the 'Gnadenkirche' ('Grace Church'). The Lutheran Church in charge of this parish had already been looking for utilisation concepts for a number of years, because there were too few active parishioners to entertain such a large house of worship.[17] The current Orthodox priest, Sergei Baburin, has managed to attract a vibrant parish life to this church, including a pilgrimage centre, education facilities and a large parish hall. His organisational talent and extensive connections have furthermore enabled him to find sponsors for an elaborate renovation, making the church an Orthodox house of worship with an impressive fresco iconostasis and mosaics above the entrance.

The church was originally built in 1906–1907 to cater to the inhabitants of the new suburbs of Hamburg that resulted from industrialisation and urbanisation in the end of the nineteenth century (Konerding 2003: 129). Irony of fate has it that the church, in its neo-Romanesque style, fittingly recalls the time before Eastern and Western Christianity were divided. The Lutheran parish decided to give it up in 2001, primarily because of secularisation and dwindling church attendance. Its location on a traffic island in the middle of a busy road also made it less attractive to the parishioners. After three years of cooperation endeavours with various Christian groupings, art exhibitions and an unsuccessful search for a new utilisation concept, it was given to the Russian Orthodox parish for a symbolic sum. The owner, the North Elbian Lutheran Church, thereby avoided having to surrender the sacral building to secular purposes.[18] A couple of years after the handover, a new traffic concept for the area removed one half of the busy road isolating the church and turned it into a public open space, significantly enhancing its accessibility and appeal.

The official handover of the Gnadenkirche happened under the auspices of the bishop of Hamburg, Maria Jepsen, who, incidentally, was the very first female bishop in the Lutheran world. Moreover, she is known as a feminist theologian and supports equal rights for the gay community. In other words, she represents several characteristics which are extremely atypical for the Orthodox Church. Her own newspaper article on the occasion of the finished renovation

---

[16]   Church of St John of Kronstadt, Hamburg. *Kak poyavilsya nash prikhod* [How Our Parish Came About]. Available at: http://www.hamburg-hram.de/prihod [accessed 10 April 2013].

[17]   A conference on interior design and utilisation concepts for church buildings was held in the Gnadenkirche in 2001. Its proceedings were published in Brandi-Hinnrichs et al. (eds) 2003.

[18]   See, for example, the 'horror scenario' portrayed in Poser 2003: 141.

of the church emphasises that, although there are tensions on a theological level between the two churches, she is happy to establish such good ecumenical relations on a local level.[19] At the consecration festivities of the renovated church, the mayor of Hamburg, Ole von Beust, a professed homosexual, held a speech in which he expressed his gratitude to the sponsors and priest for having enriched the church landscape in Hamburg with such a lively parish, while letting his unhappiness with the general attitude of the Orthodox Church towards sexual minorities shine through.[20]

The parish in Hamburg is today among the most active Russian Orthodox parishes in Germany. It is a paramount example of the rather one-way ecumenical relations that the Orthodox Church enjoys in Germany. The Gnadenkirche is now the largest church building in the Russian Orthodox diocese of Berlin, and was acquired for the symbolic sum of €1. Not only the Russian Orthodox Church has benefitted from the plethora of Lutheran churches in Hamburg: other Eastern Churches, such as the Greek, the Bulgarian, the Ethiopian and the Coptic communities have reaped similar benefits. Each of them has taken over a previously Lutheran house of worship within the central precincts of Hamburg in the last decade, and now the Romanian Orthodox Church is also looking for a similar arrangement.[21]

Conclusion

All four case studies show that the Russian immigrants coming to Germany at all times encountered a benevolent attitude towards their religion, Orthodox Christianity. This benevolent attitude was expressed in the support they were given both from political authorities and from the two main religious bodies in Germany, the Roman Catholic and the Evangelical Lutheran Church. Instead of looking at the Orthodox Christians as strangers and outsiders, the Germans mostly considered them brothers in the faith in need of financial and political support. The Russian immigrants, on the other hand, have no problems accepting this help and participate actively in the cooperation projects they are offered. This includes on the one hand joint activities, which may lead to financial and material gifts, and on the other hand participation in the local ecumenical movement, such as the Council of Christian Churches, which exists in every federal unit in Germany.

---

[19] Maria Jepsen. 2007. Mehr als Kultur oder Politik. *Hamburger Abendblatt*, 122 (29 May 2007): 10.

[20] Natalie Bombeck and Matthias Schmoock. 2007. Gold, Gesänge und Geistlichkeit: Gnadenkirche Geweiht. *Hamburger Abendblatt*, 124 (31 May 2007): 10.

[21] Matthias Gretzschel. Warum in Hamburg die Kirchen die Konfession wechselten. *Hamburger Abendblatt* (19 February 2013): 6.

The Orthodox clergy and laity in Germany actively work towards establishing friendly relations with the other denominations and entertaining a network of connections across the denominational borders. This network is then activated in order to improve the situation of the individual parish. This is the case of all Orthodox communities. However, there is a difference in the openness towards ecumenical activities between the different national groups. The Russians and the Serbians are less apt to participate in ecumenical services than the Greeks or the Romanians, for example.

Our choice of case studies might not reflect the full range of scenarios available in the Russian diaspora in Germany, but they are representative enough to show the general benevolence of Germans to Orthodox Christianity. Obviously there are always negative experiences to be mentioned, especially those concerning the relations between the two dominant Russian church jurisdictions in Germany before their unification in 2007, but the positive aspects prevail.

In general, the Russian Orthodox willingness to engage in ecumenical cooperation seems to be much higher in Germany than in the area which the Moscow Patriarchate traditionally claims as its 'canonical territory', i.e. the former Soviet Union (Oeldemann 2008). A possible explanation for this more active ecumenical engagement might be that the Orthodox Church in the 'diaspora' context is more often on the receiving end than in an Orthodox context. In the former Soviet Union, being ecumenically engaged on the local level almost always means sharing Orthodox property or facilitating the spread of non-Orthodox denominations, which compete with the Orthodox Church for church members (Knox 2005: passim). In the diaspora, in contrast, the engagement is more likely to benefit the Orthodox Church at the expense of others. There is less material and ideological risk involved when the Orthodox Church is the minor partner.

Very important, moreover, is the fact that the Russian Orthodox community in Germany avoids ghettoisation. The Russian Orthodox faithful do not separate themselves from the rest of the German community, but actively attempt an outreach. Most of the Russian Orthodox parishes in Germany include German language readings and prayers in their Church Slavonic liturgies and some even celebrate German language liturgies regularly. This applies also to the non-Russian Orthodox community, whose members are welcome in all parishes of the Russian Orthodox Church in Germany. In some parishes, therefore, it is not unusual to have the occasional reading or psalm read (or sung) in Romanian, Serbian or Greek. There are also a handful of German-speaking parishes within the Russian Orthodox Church in Germany, which celebrate entirely in German.

Moreover, the other Christian denominations in Germany are open to innovations originating from Orthodox traditions. Since our focus is on individual Orthodox parishes, this openness cannot be fully appreciated within the scope of this chapter. However, several elements of Orthodox spirituality are increasingly becoming integral parts of ecclesiastical practice in the German Catholic, Lutheran and even Reformed Churches. This includes liturgical elements, such as the epiclesis during the Eucharist (Schnitzler 1969: 105, Bukowski et al. 1999: 361) or the use of various Orthodox hymns. Moreover, the use of icons and the Jesus Prayer in Western Christian contexts is becoming increasingly popular (Jungclaussen 1999). The use of Orthodox theological concepts in Western theology is another case of such transfer from Orthodox Christianity. This includes the fascination with *theosis* (Russell 2012), *oikonomia* in canon law (Belliger 2000: esp. 222–3) and increased willingness to concessions, like omitting the *filioque* in the Nicene Creed and others.

Our analysis covered four different trajectories describing how Russian Orthodox parishes interact with the local community and form part of the Christian voice facing the secular society through organs such as the Council of Christian Churches. They served to show that the situation of every parish is different, depending on the history of the parish, the accessibility to a church building and the personality of the priest. We could have analysed every single Russian Orthodox parish in Germany in this way, but the four chosen case studies show the typical issues facing the Russian Orthodox Church in Germany and some possible strategies their representatives pursue for coping with them.

Bibliography

[Anon.]. n.d. Die Russisch-Orthodoxe Kirche in Weimar. Available at: http://www.rok-weimar.de/html/geschichte.html [accessed 15 April 2013].

Alfeyev, H. 2010. *Patriarkh Kirill: Zhizn' i mirosozertsanie.* 2nd ed. Moscow: Izd. Mosk. Patr.

Assyrian Church of the East. 2007. *Kratkii istoricheskii ocherk.* Available at: http://assyrianchurch.ru/publ/2-1-0-3 [accessed 15 April 2013].

Belliger, A. 2000. *Die wiederverheirateten Geschiedenen.* Essen: Ludgerus.

Blahusch, F. 1999. *Zuwanderungspolitik im Spannungsfeld ordnungspolitischer und ethnisch-nationalistischer Legitimationsmuster.* Frankfurt am Main: Peter Lang.

Bombeck, N. and Schmoock, M. 2007. Gold, Gesänge und Geistlichkeit: Gnadenkirche Geweiht. *Hamburger Abendblatt,* 124 (31 May 2007): 10.

Brandi-Hinnrichs, F., Reitz-Dinse, A. and Grünberg W. (eds). 2003. *Räume Riskieren.* Hamburg: EBV.

Bukowski, P. 1999. *Reformierte Liturgie.* Wuppertal: Foeden.

Church of St John of Kronstadt, Hamburg. *Kak poyavilsya nash prikhod* [How Our Parish Came About]. Available at: http://www.hamburg-hram.de/prihod [accessed 10 April 2013].

DECR. 2007. Zayavlenie Sluzhby kommunikatsii OVTsS v svyazi s podpisaniem dokumenta o vzaimnom priznanii kreshchenia ryadom tserkvey v Germanii. Available at: https://mospat.ru/archive/36165.htm [accessed 30 August 2013].

EKD. 2011. Mann deutlicher Worte. Available at: http://www.ekd.de/international/friedenskonvokation/76703.html [accessed 15 May 2013].

Gretzschel, M. Warum in Hamburg die Kirchen die Konfession wechselten. *Hamburger Abendblatt* (19 February 2013): 6.

Harris, P.A. 2003. Russische Juden und Aussiedler: Integrationspolitik und lokale Verantwortung, in *Aussiedler: Deutsche Einwanderer aus Osteuropa*, edited by K.J. Bade and J. Oltmer. Göttingen: V&R Unipress, 247–63.

Jepsen, M. 2007. Mehr als Kultur oder Politik. *Hamburger Abendblatt*, 122 (29 May 2007): 10.

Jungclaussen, E. 1999. *Unterweisung im Herzensgebet*. St Ottilien: Eos.

Klutschewsky, A. 2010. Exarchate in der russischen Kirche, in *Kanon XXI*. Hennef: Roman Kovar, 136–53.

Knox, Z. 2005. *Russian Society and the Orthodox Church*. London and New York: RoutledgeCurzon.

Konerding, V. 2003. Das Schicksal der Gnadenkirche: Repräsentation und Isolation, in *Räume Riskieren*, edited by F. Brandi-Hinnrichs, A. Reitz-Dinse and W. Grünberg. Hamburg: EBV, 129–36.

Oeldemann, J. 2008. The Concept of Canonical Territory in the Russian Orthodox Church, in *Religion and the Conceptual Boundary in Central and Eastern Europe*, edited by T. Bremer. Basingstoke: Palgrave Macmillan, 229–36.

Orthodoxie.com. 2009. L'union canonique entre l'Eglise russe hors frontières et le Patriarcat de Moscou: Bilan et perspectives deux ans après. Available at: http://www.orthodoxie.com/actualites/france/lunion-canonique-entre-leglise-russe-hors-frontieres-et-le-patriarcat-de-moscou-bilan-et-perspectiv-2/ [accessed 9 April 2013].

Poser, W. 2003. Nutzung und Umnutzung von Kirchen, in *Räume Riskieren*, edited by F. Brandi-Hinnrichs, A. Reitz-Dinse and W. Grünberg. Hamburg: EBV, 141–5.

Pospielovsky, D. 1984. *The Russian Orthodox Church under the Soviet Regime 1917–1982*, Volume I. Crestwood, NY: St Vladimir's Seminary Press.

Rimestad, S. 2012. *The Challenges of Modernity to the Orthodox Church in Estonia and Latvia (1917–1940)*. Frankfurt am Main: Peter Lang.

Russell, N. 2012. Why does Theosis Fascinate Western Christians?. *Sobornost*, 34(1): 5–15.

Russische Orthodoxe Kirche zu Dresden: 1874–1999. Dresden, 2012.

Schnitzler, T. 1969. *Die drei neuen eucharistischen Hochgebete und die neuen Präfationen*. Leipzig: St Benno.

Seide, G. 1983. *Geschichte der Russischen Orthodoxen Kirche im Ausland von der Gründung bis in die Gegenwart*. Wiesbaden: Harrassowitz.

Seide, G. 2001. *Die Russische Orthodoxe Kirche im Ausland*. Munich: Kloster des Hl. Hiob von Počaev.

Stricker, G. 2010. *Geschichte der Russischen Orthodoxen Kirche in der Diaspora*. Berlin: OEZ.

VELKD 2007. Ökumenisch *den Glauben bekennen*. Hanover: VELKD.

Wolper, P. Nikolai. Zur Geschichte der Russisch-orthodoxen Gemeinde in Hamburg. Available at: http://www.prokopij.de/Historie/geschichte_de.htm [accessed 10 April 2013].

Zernov, N. 2004. The Eastern Churches and the Ecumenical Movement in the Twentieth Century, in *A History of the Ecumenical Movement, Vol. I: 1517–1948*, edited by R. Rouse and S.C. Neill. Geneva: World Council of Churches, 643–74.

Chapter 6
How do Orthodox Integrate in their Host Countries? Examples from Switzerland

Maria Hämmerli

The Orthodox population in Switzerland has more than doubled over the last 20 years, increasing from 71,501 in 1990 to 131,851 in 2000.[1] This is not the result of some sudden massive conversion of the Swiss population, but rather of successive waves of migration from Eastern Europe starting during the aftermath of the fall of communism. This rapid growth has involved not only an effort to create parishes in order to meet immigrants' religious needs, but also a whole process of adjusting ethnically diverse Orthodox churches to Swiss society, with its layers of social, linguistic, religious, legal and political complexity.

Literature on the adaptation of immigrant religious institutions to their host societies is generally focused on particular aspects of integration (cultural, structural, political, etc.) and on resources provided by religious institutions in the process of individuals' integration, such as social capital (Levitt 2007; Martikainen 2013; Ebaugh and Chafetz 2000; Foley and Hoge 2007). This chapter will explore some of the factors that impact adjustment, specific both to the Orthodox churches and to the Swiss context. I will ground my argument on findings from recent field research I conducted in Orthodox parishes located mainly in the French and German-speaking Switzerland (see Hämmerli 2011a).[2] Data was collected through semi-directed interviews and intense observation of parish life.

To begin, I will provide a brief overview of the Orthodox presence in Switzerland, its history, geographical spread, social composition and activity. Literature on this religious community is scanty; thus, I combine existing written sources (Ruffieux 2005; Grézine 1999; Baumer 2009) with data collected in

---

[1]   The source of this data is the 2000 National Census (see Bovay 2004). More recent data about Orthodox communities in Switzerland is not available, because of changes in the data collection system for the 2010 National Census.

[2]   The Swiss National Research Foundation (SNF) financed the research project *Multiple Dimensions of the Integration Process of Eastern Orthodox Communities in Switzerland*, in the framework of the National Research Programme 58: Religion, the State and Society, 2007–2011. The main applicant for this research project was Prof. François Hainard, from the Sociological Institute of the University of Neuchâtel.

A Brief Overview of the Orthodox Presence in Switzerland

Orthodox believers have lived, visited, or worked in Switzerland since the eighteenth century in the persons of Russian diplomats, aristocracy, and rich students, as well as Greek tradesmen. Yet the first parish was created only in 1816 in Bern, as a Russian embassy parish, with a more or less private status. This parish changed location several times before becoming established in Geneva, where in 1866 the Russian community, with financial help from home and local political support, built a traditional Russian-style cathedral, dedicated to the Exaltation of the Holy Cross. Another beautiful Russian church was built in 1878 with private funds by an aristocrat in Vevey, in memory of his young daughter Barbara, who died in labour. The church was named after Saint Barbara and served mainly the Russian aristocracy and royal family members spending holidays on Lake Geneva, as well as the Russian patients taking cures in the nearby Valais health centres.

As was the case more largely in the West, the Russian Orthodox population in Switzerland grew and diversified after the Bolshevik revolution in 1917, which chased away an important fraction of the country's aristocracy, military and intelligentsia. Two Russian parishes were established, in Zurich (1935) and in Bern (1944). After the Second World War, Swiss businessmen, craftsmen, and farmers who had migrated to Russia since the eighteenth century and converted to Orthodoxy, arrived back in the Lausanne area.[4] They created a community in Pully (Lausanne), which was not a parish in itself, but a dependency of Saint Barbara's in Vevey and which is served by the priest in Vevey to the present day.

At the end of the nineteenth century, the Lake Geneva Riviera attracted also wealthy Greek tradesmen and their families in search of a good education for their children.[5] This community was reinforced with new members at the beginning of the twentieth century, when many Greeks had to leave Asia Minor as a result of the conflict with Turkey. In the 1920s they built a Greek-style church in Lausanne.

Though the Orthodox presence was visible in public space through its three impressive worship edifices in the French-speaking area of Switzerland, numerically it was insignificant to the country's religious landscape. It was in

---

[3] Such parishes keep few archives, and even those are protected by restricted access.

[4] They were mainly from the Canton of Vaud: chocolate makers, farmers, nannies, hotel keepers, etc.

[5] The Pestalozzi method was world-famous at that time.

the 1960s and 1970s that new waves of labour migration, Greek and ex-Yugoslav ethnic groups, enhanced the Orthodox community and gave rise to the creation of new parishes, especially in the German-speaking regions: the Holy Trinity Serbian Orthodox parish in Zurich; the Cyril and Methodius Serbian Orthodox parish in Bern; the Holy Demetrios Greek Orthodox parish in Zurich and the Saint Paul Apostle of All Nations Greek Orthodox parish in Geneva.

During the same period, intellectuals, skilled professionals and political dissidents arrived from communist Romania and began to establish themselves in Switzerland (among them the royal family, forced to leave Romania in 1947). They created two parishes in the Geneva area: the Lord's Resurrection Romanian Orthodox parish in Chambésy (1975) and Saint John the Baptist Romanian Orthodox parish in Geneva (1979).

A more considerable Orthodox influx was caused by the fall of communism in Eastern Europe and the war in the former Republic of Yugoslavia. After the 1990s, numerous Romanian and Serbian parishes were established, especially in the German-speaking part of Switzerland, where former Yugoslavs settled, but also in the French and Italian parts, which were preferred by Romanians because of linguistic similarities.

Geographically speaking, most Orthodox believers in Switzerland live in the German-speaking part, around large industrial cities like Zurich, Winterthur, Sankt Gallen and Basel. In the French-speaking region of the country, the Eastern Orthodox presence is concentrated around the Lake Geneva region (Bovay, 2004).

In 2011, there were 42 Orthodox parishes in Switzerland, organised along ethnic lines as well as in relation to their respective mother churches: the Ecumenical Patriarchate of Constantinople, the Moscow Patriarchate, the Russian Orthodox Church Outside of Russia, the Romanian Orthodox Church and the Serbian Orthodox Church. There are also multi-ethnic parishes, some of which hold services in the local language. In the French-speaking part of Switzerland, seven parishes out of the 17 that I identified hold religious services in French, while the rest preserve the languages of their countries of origin. Paradoxically, in the German-speaking part, where the Orthodox population is more numerous, only one parish (the Russian Orthodox Church of the Resurrection, Moscow Patriarchate, Zurich) offers religious services in German, vespers and liturgy once per month (Hämmerli 2011a).

Seventy-eight per cent of the Orthodox population in Switzerland is of immigrant origin: ethnic Serbs from the former Yugoslavia, Russian-speaking people from the ex-Soviet Union, Greeks, and Romanians. The significant number of Swiss Orthodox (22 per cent) does not describe a group of native converts, although it includes them, but refers mainly to naturalised cradle Orthodox immigrants and their children (Bovay 2004; Hämmerli 2011a).

The population of the Greek Orthodox parishes that were part of my fieldwork can be described as middle class and upper middle class: members of the liberal professions, scientists, employees of multinational companies in the Lake Geneva region and students. Most have already acquired Swiss citizenship and some participate in the political activities of their host country. This does not imply disengagement from their relationship with the homeland, which often translates into high transnational mobility (many retain a residence in Greece) and strong social ties with family or monasteries.

First-generation Greek Orthodox immigrants are married to co-ethnics, maintain their Hellenic culture and language, and see the church as a place where their identity is preserved. Their offspring are less endogamous, engaging rather in intercultural and interdenominational marriages. This often reduces their religious practice, but does not disconnect them from their Orthodoxy as an important identity marker that they wish to pass on to their children by baptising them in the Greek Orthodox Church. Parish size is somewhat in decline because of the many return migrations of retired first-generation members, the lack of any significant renewal of migration waves and the secularisation process that affects culturally integrated members.

The members of Romanian Orthodox parishes originate from two major migratory waves, differentiated along historical lines in terms of before and after the fall of communism. While most of those who fled their home country during communism were highly skilled migrants, the migration patterns and profiles diversified after 1989: from lower middle class to students, artists and highly skilled professionals; temporary or permanent migrants. While the former group viewed their parishes as places to gather and express their resistance to communism and preserve their religious and linguistic identities, for the more recent migrations, their parishes are also places of socialisation in a familiar setting and venues for building social capital.

The social composition of Russian Orthodox parishes in the French-speaking part of Switzerland is very diverse, comprising descendants from the first Russian emigration waves after 1917, ethnic Serbs, Swiss converts and the so-called 'new Russians', i.e. post-Soviet immigrants. These actors carry different representations of the Orthodox Church, its relation to language and culture, and more generally its role in society.

Serbian Orthodox parishes comprise ethnic Serbs from all the countries of the former Yugoslavia. I identified four major generations of immigrants. First, in the aftermath of the Second World War, a political and social elite arrived who opposed the new political regime in Yugoslavia. Although few of them are still living, their parishes strive to keep in touch with them and organise activities directed to their specific needs. Second, from the 1960s to the 1970s, the Swiss economy needed a qualified labour force in the fields of healthcare and engineering, and ethnic Serb doctors and engineers found a place in these sectors of the Swiss labour market. Third, in the mid-1970s, low-skilled, seasonal workers started arriving. Their migration was not intended to be permanent and their families remained in the homeland. Fourth and finally, the migration pattern changed following the outbreak of war in the former Yugoslavia in the 1990s. Family reunification during the war and the deteriorating quality of life after the dissolution of Yugoslavia led to the final settlement of these immigrants in Switzerland. A new sociological profile emerged: young people who did not speak the local language and had no education and qualifications recognised in Switzerland. All these different categories of immigrants make use of the parish not only as a place of religious practice, but also as a venue for identity clarification and reconnection to their primary socialisation patterns.

Switzerland counts one Orthodox monastery, situated in Dompierre (canton of Vaud), under the jurisdiction of the Moscow Patriarchate. The small community is made up of two Swiss monastics and a German; it functions as a regular parish for people who live in the area, but other French, German and Russian-speaking believers maintain close contact with the monks. Yet the monastery has very limited means and small premises, which prevent it from playing one of the traditional roles that Eastern Orthodox monasteries commonly fulfil, i.e. receiving pilgrims or guests for retreats. In 2013, with the blessing of Metropolitan Joseph (Romanian Diocese of Western and Southern Europe), a nun came to Switzerland in order to establish a monastic community; the nascent monastery is currently looking for a stable place.

One noteworthy Orthodox institution in Switzerland is the Orthodox Centre in Chambésy, which was created by Ecumenical Patriarch Athenagoras of Constantinople in 1966 as a forum for rallying the Orthodox churches for ecumenical dialogue. The centre hosts a philanthropic foundation and a theological institute for postgraduate studies; most significantly, it is in charge of organising the coming Pan-Orthodox council. Although it was very dynamic when it began, its activities have decreased because of insufficient financial and human resources, severed by the recent Greek economic crisis which threatened at some point the very existence of the Centre.[6]

Orthodox communities in the German- and French-speaking parts of Switzerland differ in several aspects. First, their outreach to the Swiss society is very uneven, with Orthodox communities in the French-speaking area being more successful in recruiting members among the local population. This is due, on the one hand, to the longer history of Eastern Orthodox parishes in this part of the country and, on the other hand, to the use of French in their services and parish life. Also, the presence of the Orthodox Centre in Chambésy (close to the World Council of Churches in Geneva), the Ecumenical Institute in Bossey and other international organisations has given more visibility to the Eastern

---

[6]   The Centre used to receive considerable financial support from the Greek government.

Orthodox presence in the French-speaking part of the country. Second, in terms of cultural integration Orthodox parish members in French-speaking cantons feel more easily accepted into society than their fellow believers in the German-speaking part of Switzerland. This may be explained by linguistic reasons: a number of Romanians, Greeks and Russians were already familiar with French before they migrated, because their home countries have a long tradition of teaching French as a foreign language and are involved with the French-speaking world.[7] Being in command of the local language is a factor that improves the quality of the dialogue with the host culture. Moreover, eastern Switzerland challenges immigrants with its quasi-bilingualism: in private, people use the local Germanic dialects, which are becoming a strong identity marker; standard German is resorted to only in formal professional situations, the media, and in school for writing. Thus, immigrants have to acquire double linguistic skills. Another reason why Orthodox migrants experience easier cultural adjustment in French-speaking areas has to do with the implementation of the national integration policy, with a rather communitarian paradigm in the Swiss German cantons, whereas the Swiss French integration model leaves more space for cultural diversity.[8]

Despite their rapid numerical growth, Orthodox communities in Switzerland, like all Orthodox communities in the West, have been overlooked by academic research and are quite invisible also in their host societies. One can argue that this derives from a straightforward relation between this religious group and the host society and from their mutual acceptance of each other. What factors impact this successful adaptation?

External Factors that Impact Adaptation

The way Orthodox migrants relate to the host society and adjust to it differs with reference to the migration context that generated these communities: political hostility, religious persecution, economic hardships, etc. Migration waves provoked by political persecution in Russia or Romania brought to Switzerland a very different population than the exodus caused in the 1990s by a hard economic transition in Eastern Europe or war in the former Yugoslav

---

[7] Romania is a member state of the international French-speaking community, while Greece adopted French as the second foreign language to be taught in schools, and until 1961 French was the only foreign language taught in Greek public schools. Russia also has a long history of teaching and speaking French.

[8] This statement has to be balanced with some details: some French-speaking cantons (e.g. Valais) remain conservative with regard to migrant integration and citizenship granting, whereas other eastern cantons have made considerable progress in political migrant inclusion, e.g. Graubünden, Appenzell Ausserrhoden, Basel City (Matthey, 2006).

states. Political emigration usually presupposes that for a long period of time the homeland remains inaccessible and therefore people tend to consider integration in the receiving country more seriously, though parallel to a reflex of preservation of certain aspects of the ethnic identity (mostly language and religion). Labour migrants tend to establish contact with the host country through their interest in the labour market and consumer practices. Besides, new communication technologies and more rapid and accessible transportation means have diminished the geographical distance between the homeland and the receiving context, leading to a more intense relationship between the two.

For example, the Russian Orthodox Church Outside of Russia (ROCOR) was created by expatriates and refugees fleeing the Bolshevik regime after 1917. It separated from the mother church in Moscow, as a reaction to the growing control of the Soviet state. The forced migration and split in the church happened very soon after the Russian Orthodox Church had held an important council and revised the model of parish organisation. Two important consequences derive from this political and ecclesiastical context of migration: ROCOR developed a reluctance to become involved with political movements and state ideologies,[9] while focusing on keeping the purity of the Eastern Orthodox faith in its nineteenth-century Russian expression and tradition and to implement as accurately as possible the prescriptions of the 1917 Council (Nathaniel 1995).[10] Thus, parish life tended to reflect stricter, more conservative liturgical and ascetical norms. It is therefore through this lens that ROCOR approached the host society, searching for 'Orthodox elements' in its culture and history and being less involved in societal problems, ecumenical dialogue and political participation.

The picture is very different in Serbian Orthodox parishes. They are recently implanted in Switzerland and serve a large number of low-skilled economic migrants who have an unclear integration project and suffer from a negative image in Switzerland. This migration and reception context explains the need for Serbian Orthodox parishes to engage in social issues and approach integration in more pragmatic terms.

Yet it is not only the reason for migration that matters in the process of adaptation; the context of destination is also crucial. The political and economic

---

[9]   According to the two ROCOR bishops I interviewed, although ROCOR members may have a personal stand on political matters (and in its early history, ROCOR was not a-political, as it gathered czarists, White Army generals and extreme anti-communists), the Church as a religious institution is not supposed to get involved with the political life of the country.

[10]   Orthodox theologian Matthew Baker has drawn my attention (in a personal communication) to the fact that, in practice, ROCOR did not always implement the provisions of the 1917 council, such as those with respect to lay involvement in election of bishops.

situation in Switzerland at the time of the arrival of the Orthodox population offered an environment more or less conducive to integration. For instance, the Greeks who arrived in the 1920s after their forced exile from Turkey and the Russians fleeing Bolshevik persecution in the aftermath of the 1917 coup were both denied access to the labour market. They either left for the Americas or stayed and accepted unskilled jobs. This was very different from the situation after the Second World War, when the economic boom demanded a greater workforce than Swiss human resources could provide, creating the need for both low- and high-skilled foreign workers, especially in the fields of healthcare, construction and farming. During the 1950s and 1960s many Greek and ex-Yugoslav Orthodox settled in Switzerland, but the market was again saturated during the 1970s, when the migration policy became stricter and introduced seasonal employment. Many ex-Yugoslav Orthodox practised this kind of circular migration over 20 years, demanding family reunification, regularisation, and establishment only at the outbreak of the war at the end of the 1990s. At the present moment this category of people is experiencing a difficult integration process, as they have lived between two countries, with no particular feeling of belonging, and with a poor command of the local language, yet they are not able to return to the homeland. Their children arrived already as adolescents, with no recognised diplomas and not speaking any Swiss national language. Many go through an identity crisis, which they try to clarify by attending the local Serbian Orthodox parish where they get support.

Apart from the confusion resulting from the economic context in the receiving country, Serbian ethnics are subject to a rather negative image in Switzerland,[11] mainly caused by the war in ex-Yugoslavia, which led to a stigmatisation of Serbs as 'war criminals'. Serbian identity and image is further complicated by their being mistaken with Albanian Kosovars, who hold or used to hold Serbian citizenship. This is all the more detrimental for Serbs, as Albanian ethnics living in Switzerland are a population with relatively high criminal rates (especially among youngsters, pejoratively called 'Balkan Jugendliche').

Another specificity of the Swiss immigration policy is its strictness with respect to undeclared work and illegal, black market activities. Swiss law is highly restrictive both with employers and employees and stipulates cantonal and trade union control bodies. Thus the Orthodox immigrants I came in contact with had been subject to selection before they settled in Switzerland. In most cases, they had prospected an employment before migration. This explains why Orthodox parishes in Switzerland are not venues for economic integration, as is often the case in Italy and Spain.

---

[11] Especially in the German-speaking part of the country, where larger numbers of Serbian immigrants have settled.

Internal Factors that Impact Adaptation

Reflective Positioning

In his book *Elusive Togetherness*, Paul Lichterman (2005) analysed several religious groups and their capacity to reach out to the larger society and build bridges between different social segments. His findings point to the crucial role of reflexivity practised in a group, consisting in 'welcoming reflective talk about its concrete relationships in the wider world' (Lichterman 2005: 15).

Borrowing from Lichterman, I have noticed in my own field research that if parishes engage in discussing their relation to the host society, other religious groups, the state, or other social and political actors, this stimulates collective and individual thinking about the local society and elicits strategies of accommodating Orthodox identity to the local culture. Such reflective talk rarely involves the whole congregation. Depending on the topic, it concerns different categories: the clergy and the lay parish leaders, or the youth, women, the newly arrived, families, etc. Yet the outcome of reflective talk in a parish eventually touches the whole congregation, as it shapes a certain 'parish culture' with its ideological orientation, in which members are immersed.

Let me illustrate this with a few examples. In two different Serbian parishes, the bishop who was visiting and, in the second case, the parish priest, explained in their sermons how Serbs can be good Swiss citizens by remaining deeply Orthodox. Both clergymen emphasised elements of Orthodox spirituality to be mobilised in navigating the local culture: humility, love for one's enemies,[12] patience, non-judgement, etc. Serbian immigrants are encouraged to apply these values in their everyday interactions, so that they can guarantee peaceful relationships in their workplace or in their neighbourhood.

Another example is the Sunday school of a Romanian parish. Initially planned as a platform for teaching Romanian language and Orthodox religion, the Sunday school has grown into a place of debate about the children's Romanian ethnic-linguistic identity in relation to the civic education and social ethics they receive in Swiss schools or in multicultural families. In this way, children are shown similarities and differences between the two cultures and are encouraged to integrate them, rather than to contrast them as if black and white. The coordinator of this Sunday school said:

> children from mixed families should not be faced with the need to choose one cultural identity and exclude the other one, or picture it in negative terms. They

---

[12] This could give the false impression that the 'enemy' designates the Swiss population; actually, it refers to difficulties in social relationships with local people, often faced in early stages of migration because of cultural misunderstandings.

should not think that if they are Swiss, they have to exclude their Romanian roots, nor the opposite ... We need to show them the constructive side of living in two cultures.

Reflective talk about the larger society emphasises at times the distinctiveness of the respective community or stresses commonalities at other moments – points of encounter between the respective cultures and histories of the homeland and the host country. Sharing opinions and impressions about the local people's way of functioning and cultural codes helps Orthodox immigrants enhance their experience of the local society, though it rarely reaches beyond stereotypical representations. Parish members underline with humour and self-criticism the fact that they (Romanians, Russians, Greeks, etc.) are late, slow, or clumsy and Swiss are efficient, punctual, and hardworking, but also that they are more resourceful, spontaneous, and have a better sense of celebration. They find inspiration in Swiss cleanliness, tidiness, sense of organisation, reliability, and moderate consumerism.

When distinctiveness with regard to religion is underlined, on the one hand the Orthodox display a certain sense of superiority in relation to Western Christianity, which they perceive as 'dry', 'cold', 'soulless'. It might be assumed that this has further consequences on ecumenical relations, in which the Orthodox reportedly lack interest and enthusiasm. On the other hand, reflective talk reveals that the Orthodox strongly appreciate and admire the sense of organisation of the Western denominations, their way of building community and readiness to volunteer.

With regard to discussing commonalities, one of the Serbian parishes in Zurich stresses points of encounter between the Serbian and the Swiss culture by editing a bilingual (Serbian/German) magazine, *Buđenje/Das Erwachen*, which published, among others, articles about scientists, artists or other Serbian personalities that had been in contact with Switzerland throughout history. In the first issue of *Buđenje*, a substantive section was devoted to a parallel between the Swiss and the Serbian peoples as lovers of freedom and peace.

In their effort to find and cultivate commonalities with the host society, the Orthodox in Switzerland, just as their co-religionists in the West in general, have re-appropriated the local saints of the first Christian centuries, resulting in the construction of a common sacred memory. This provides a symbolic basis for recreating a spiritual home. For example, there are parishes that took the names of local saints like St Mauritius or St Maire and placed their parish activities under the protection of these patron saints. In the Russian Orthodox parish in Vevey, an icon of 'all the saints that flourished in the Helvetic lands' was painted. The late Bishop Ambroise, the former spiritual guide of this parish, composed a religious service dedicated to the Swiss saints, which is celebrated on a highly symbolic date: the day of the Federal Lent (*Jeûne fédéral*), in the second half of September. Another relevant example is the Zurich-based Eastern Orthodox initiative of reviving the memory of the city's patron saints: Felix, Regula and Exuperantius. Local Christian communities are invited to a procession from the site of the saints' martyrdom to one of Zurich's most famous churches, where an inter-Orthodox vespers is celebrated on this occasion every year on 11 September.

An important issue that is discussed in Orthodox parishes is their relation to the increasingly secular Swiss state: to what extent should the Church take advantage of local state funds aimed at migrant integration, in order to develop parish activities and projects that would stimulate parish life? Or should the parish ask for state financial support for the renovation of the precincts? What if financial help were to entail further state interference in the parish life and activity? Originating mainly from former communist countries that have suffered from forced secularisation, Orthodox Churches have developed some resistance to state interference in Church affairs. Yet simultaneously, in traditionally Orthodox countries, the Church seeks state support in the name of the historical principle of *symphonia*, which posits that the political and the religious authority should work together as complementary forces, in mutual respect. The tension between these two contradictory tendencies is felt also in parishes in Switzerland, though on a smaller scale. What further complicates the discussion about the relation to local public and political authorities is the Swiss system of regulating religion at the cantonal level: state–church relations differ from one canton to another, from total separation like in the French model of *laïcité* (Neuchâtel and Geneva), to the predominant model of state recognition of some communities (mainly Protestant and Catholic). Nonetheless, the Orthodox Church is a minority in Switzerland and does not hold recognition under public law.

There was an attempt of getting such recognition in the Canton of Vaud, which recently changed its constitution in order to allow religious groups other than Protestant and Catholic churches to obtain public law recognition. The Orthodox were believed to be eligible to claim it, but they failed to fulfil one key condition: namely, to have a common representation. At this point, reflective talk unfolded at the supra-parish, inter-Orthodox level, with clergy and some lay leaders trying to create an umbrella organisation that would represent the six parishes in the canton. Two obstacles prevented the creation of a common Orthodox body: first, an ecclesial one, deriving from the simple fact that there is no ecclesiastical correspondent of such an organisation reuniting parishes of different patriarchates. Moreover, as some bishops have residence in countries other than Switzerland, their coordination for supervising this special body was a very intricate issue. Second, there was a legal obstacle, as the respective Orthodox organisation would need to have legal statutes. These would need to match with each parish's legal and ecclesial statutes. Due to all these complexities,

126   *Orthodox Identities in Western Europe*

the project of getting public law recognition for the Orthodox Church in the
Canton of Vaud was suspended. Yet this was an opportunity for the Orthodox
leaders, clergy and laymen alike, to reflect on their legal situation in the long
term and on the future of their Church in Switzerland beyond their momentary
parish life.

Parish Organisational Culture

The orientation of parish life is very important not only for the religious practice,
but also with regard to the impact the parish culture can have on immigrants'
adjustment to the receiving society. For example, some parishes may emphasise
the importance of prayer and spiritual life, whereas others may be concerned
with the pastoral and secular needs of their members; or there are also parishes
prone to dialogue with other local Christian denominations and to engaging
with societal issues. The parish culture instils values that empower, or not,
migrant members in their effort of integration. I will mention here three parish
styles I have found in my field research:

First, the 'contemplative' style describes parishes centred on their members'
liturgical life. This is generally the case with ROCOR parishes. All Eastern
Orthodox parishes coalesce around the liturgy, since this is the primary reason
why they exist; but there are some other characteristics that are prominent in
'contemplative' parishes, in particular their reluctance to discuss and attempt
to solve social issues. This does not translate into a lack of empathy with the
dilemmas and problems that affect society. However, the solutions proposed to
these problems are approached at the spiritual level, which is perceived as being
the essence of the Church's message. The reflective positioning of 'contemplative'
parishes is thus situated in the area of theology and spirituality. One can argue
that this parish 'style' does not have much potential for engaging with the host
society. Yet, paradoxically, among the Eastern Orthodox ethnic parishes, it is the
ROCOR 'contemplative' ones that have had the most successful outreach to
local Swiss and have received many converts.

Second, the 'community building' style consists of special attention given by
parish leaders and priests to church members as a group, and to their common
problems and needs. It is the case with some Romanian parishes, some French-
speaking ones and most evidently with Serbian parishes. The latter develop not
only as providers of 'spiritual goods', but also as community centres that offer
various socially oriented services, e.g. counselling, libraries, entertainment
and cultural activities, thereby stimulating institutional and social integration.
The targeted groups are women, the youth and elderly people. Some of the
'community building' parishes orient their activities towards integration and
one of them has even formalised this aim by mentioning it in its legal statutes.
Their reflective positioning consists in identifying, discussing and solving

concrete problems that cause collective concern in relations between the migrant population and the receiving society.

Community building takes on a different meaning for French-speaking parishes, which are centred around their religious identity: the aim of the community is to nourish and perpetuate the Eastern Orthodox faith through the parish socialisation and theological education of both children and adults. The reflective positioning in this case refers to accommodating the Eastern Orthodox faith to the wider society and its increasingly plural religious landscape.

The 'community building' style is particularly propitious for engaging in a constructive dialogue with the host society by discussing the social, cultural and religious differences that mark the relations of the community with the wider society.

Third, the 'inter-ethnic networking' style describes parishes that focus on building co-ethnic transnational ties (particularly Greek and Romanian Orthodox parishes) or simply locally tied inter-Orthodox connections (French-speaking parishes). All ethnic Orthodox parishes are involved in transnational ties with their respective Western European dioceses or with ecclesiastical institutions in the homeland. Although these activities may appear as limiting the parishes to their ethnic church networks, they also give them the opportunity to compare different diasporic contexts and share solutions to certain difficulties. The circulation of ideas is paralleled by the circulation of various types of capital: poor parishes, monasteries or church-based organisations in the homeland benefit from the economic capital of their fellow parishes in Switzerland; conversely, parishes in Switzerland invite spiritual charismatic figures or bishops from the homeland in order to support the spiritual lives of their members who live in a non-Orthodox environment. Romanian Orthodox parishes organise youth camps and pilgrimages to monasteries back in their home country, thus offering children and adults the chance to stay in contact with monastic spirituality, which is a key element in Eastern Orthodox tradition.

Spirituality

Though the content of Orthodox spirituality was not initially part of my research interest, the data gradually pointed to the substantial role it can play in integration, by providing churchgoers with means of coping with challenges specific to the circumstances of immigration. I use the term 'spiritual capital' to describe Orthodox resources people mobilise in facing everyday difficulties related to adjusting to a new sociocultural reality. This includes prayer, fasting, the practice of virtues (repentance, forgiveness, love, humility, patience, hope, etc.), attendance of liturgical services, celebration of saints, etc.

The perpetuation of liturgical acts and practices gives their participants a sense of identity: dislocated from their cultural, social and geographical setting, immigrants find an element of stability in the immutability of religious practice.[13] Many Orthodox immigrant interviewees speak about the Church as the place where they are reconnected to their identity and their roots. Cattacin and Chimienti (2006) highlight the importance, in a migration context, of one's access to the identity forged during primary socialisation. Meanwhile, Bauman (2000) argues that our 'liquid modernity' engenders societies that favour change, pluralism and hybridisation and are thus unable to produce communities that fix identities. In such societies, the identity built during the primary socialisation allows individuals to 'surf on the waves of the society without limits' (Cattacin and Chimienti 2006: 36). Orthodox parishes are venues for reinforcing identity and a sense of community through collective worship, liturgical services, saints' feasts and family patrons' celebrations (*slava*). These practices, moreover, help individuals to situate themselves in a continuum with their ancestors, in a 'chain of memory' (Hervieu-Léger 2000). Religious practice thus reinforces a *Gemeinschaft* logic, which is necessary in order to better integrate the *Gesellschaft* (Proeschel 2010). Also, it is acknowledged that religion provides meaning to present individual situations by placing them in a larger cosmic and historical setting.

Moreover, spiritual values such as repentance, humility and love can also be interpreted as resources for integration, precisely as they invite the individual to a permanent self-questioning, self-renewal and self-discipline. The believer is urged to stop laying blame on the outside circumstances of hostility or injustice – often invoked by immigrants when they describe their condition as foreigners in a host country – and to overcome frustration and discomfort through personal change, adaptation and responsibility. Such values shape peaceful, respectful, optimistic conduct in society and they are a point of convergence with values cherished by the Swiss society.

Last, the Orthodox application of *oikonomia* – the practice of permitting formal adaptations while preserving the spirit encapsulated in Church canon law – allows Orthodox immigrants to adjust to very diverse social and cultural environments, without having to relativise their religious identity. Let us quote here a few examples. During the four fasting periods in the year, when Orthodox refrain from consuming animal products, Orthodox who eat in restaurants, canteens or are invited for meals in non-Orthodox contexts suspend their fasting rules. Or, take the case of monks: they have to wear a monastic black habit. In the canton of Geneva, however, such dress is traditionally prohibited in public

---

[13]   The use of the word 'immutability' points to the accurate perpetuation of rituals and their content and not to the fact that the religious services and practice remained completely untouched in the history of the Orthodox Church or in the process of migration. But the changes are not perceptible unless one is a connoisseur of the Orthodox liturgy. Most immigrants are not theologically literate.

spaces. Thus, in order to avoid shocking the passers-by or to be mistaken for Muslim traditionalists, some Orthodox monks who reside in the canton instead adopt a sober civil way of dressing and live an 'interiorised monasticism'.

Though the metaphor of 'spiritual capital' is very useful in describing religion as a resource 'people draw on to meet various challenges – sickness, political oppression, ethical choices, or social problems' (Woodberry 2003), relating spiritual capital to integration can raise two problems. First, it can suggest that church attendance and religious practice is a strategy immigrant believers appeal to in view of integration. It is an assumption of utilitarian usage of religion. Yet, people do not attend liturgy, confess, or celebrate saints' feasts in order to reach faster integration; the latter is rather a by-product of the former. In order to avoid such an erroneous utilitarian assumption, I consider spiritual capital only as a 'side-effect' of immigrant participation in a religious organisation and not as a purposeful, instrumental activity (Hämmerli 2011b).

Second, the 'benefits' of religion are not connected strictly to migration and integration issues, but constitute a part of what shapes the believers' *Weltanschauung*. It is therefore difficult to pry apart the application of religion in such a specific aspect and the more extensive significance of spirituality. This is further complicated by the fact that integration is a lengthy process, with different phases, corresponding to different mobilisations of the spiritual capital, all of which are difficult to grasp.

Conclusion

The integration of an immigrant religious community depends to a certain extent on external conditions (reasons for migration, context of destination – in terms of economic and migration policy, religious landscape, and state–church relations in the receiving country), but also on endogenous factors, such as organisational culture, the discussion of the relation of the respective religious community with the larger society and the content of the respective religion (its teachings and practices). The macro-level factors provide the framework for smaller scale and individual factors that impact the integration of Orthodox populations and their churches in Switzerland.

The Orthodox in this country have different national and cultural backgrounds, different migration patterns and trajectories. Their internal diversity overlaps with that of the receiving context, marked by multilingualism, religious pluralism, and multiculturalism. The integration process of this religious community unfolds unevenly, varying along ethnic lines (Greeks do not integrate in the same way and with the same pace with Serbs) and even within the same ethnic group, along waves of migration (Romanians before and after the fall of communism).

The Orthodox religious institutions struggle with self-organisation and coping with the pastoral needs of a recent immigrant population, which does not allow for much in the way of inter-Orthodox relations. The common representation of this community is impacted not only by its own complicated ecclesiastical architecture, but also by the diversity of the Swiss legal systems regulating relations between state and church. The Orthodox communities are in the process of redefining themselves in a non-Orthodox context, of finding a place in the Swiss religious landscape and reflecting on their future beyond the present first generation of immigrants.

Bibliography

Bauman, Z. 2000. *Liquid Modernity*. Cambridge: Polity.

Baumer, I. 2009. Unité et diversité des Églises chrétiennes d'Orient en Suisse, in *La nouvelle Suisse religieuse: Risques et chances de sa diversité*, edited by M. Baumann and J. Stolz. Geneva: Labor et Fides, 166–180.

Bovay, C. 2004. *Le paysage religieux en Suisse. Recensement fédéral de la population 2000*. Neuchâtel: OFS (Office fédéral de la statisque).

Cattacin, S. and Chimienti, M. 2006. Intégration: Un concept sociologique en politique migratoire. *Terra Cognita*, 6(9): 34–7.

Ebaugh, H. and Chafetz, J.S. 2000. *Religion and the New Immigrants: Continuities and Adaptations in Immigrant Congregations*. Walnut Creek: AltaMira.

Foley, M.W. and Hoge, D.R. 2007. *Religion and the New Immigrants: How Faith Communities Form our Newest Citizens*. Oxford: Oxford University Press.

Grézine, I. 1999. *Les Orthodoxes russes en Suisse romande*. Genève: Némo.

Hämmerli, M. 2011a. *Multiple Dimensions of the Integration Process of Eastern Orthodox Communities in Switzerland*. National Research Programme 58: Religion, the State and Society. Final Research Report. Available at: http://www.pnr58.ch/files/downloads/NFP58_Schlussbericht_Hainard.pdf [accessed July 2013].

Hämmerli, M. 2011b. Religion and Spirituality between Capital and Gift. *Religion and Theology*, 18: 195–210.

Hervieu-Léger, D. 2000. *Religion as a Chain of Memory*. New Brunswick, NJ: Rutgers University Press.

Levitt, P. 2007. *God Needs No Passport: Immigrants and the Changing American Religious Landscape*. New York: The New Press.

Lichterman, P. 2005. *Elusive Togetherness: Church Groups Trying to Bridge America's Divisions*. Princeton, NJ: Princeton University Press.

Martikainen, T. 2013. *Religion, Migration, Settlement: Reflections on Post-1990 Immigration to Finland*. Leiden and Boston: Brill.

Matthey, F. 2006. Le fédéralisme de l'intégration. *Terra Cognita*, 9: 72–4.

Nathaniel [Archbishop]. 1995. *Conversations on Holy Scripture and Faith*, Vol. V. New York: Russian Orthodox Youth Committee.

Proeschel, C. 2010. Identity Claims of a Religious Nature: An Obstacle or a Chance for Civic Integration? Draft paper for the XVII International Sociological Association World Congress of Sociology: Sociology on the Move. Gothenburg, 11–17 July 2010.

Ruffieux, N. 2005. L'Église orthodoxe en Suisse, in *Histoire de l'Église orthodoxe en Europe Occidentale au 20e siècle*, edited by C. Chaillot. Paris: Dialogue entre Orthodoxes, 75–85.

State Secretariat for Economic Affairs (SECO). Travail au noir. Available at: http://www.seco.admin.ch/themen/00385/01905/index.html?lang=fr [accessed October 2009].

Woodberry, R. 2003. Researching Spiritual Capital: Promises and Pitfalls. Spiritual Capital Planning Meeting, 9–10 October 2003. Available at: http://www.metanexus.net/archive/spiritualcapitalresearchprogram/pdf/woodberry.pdf [accessed October 2008].

Chapter 7

The Orthodox Churches in the United Kingdom

Hugh Wybrew

As a priest of the Church of England, I have had many contacts with the Orthodox Churches over the past 60 years: the Orthodox parishes in Oxford, the Romanian, Bulgarian and Serbian Orthodox Churches in their respective countries, where I served as a chaplain for Anglican expatriate congregations between 1971 and 1973. Later I spent three years in Jerusalem (1986–1989), where I had close contacts with the Greek Orthodox Patriarchate. In this chapter I will attempt to give an overview of the origins and present situation of Orthodoxy in the United Kingdom.

Little research has been done on the Orthodox churches in the British Isles. For their present state I have drawn on the scanty existing literature (Ware 2006; Ware 2010), on my own knowledge and direct field experience, on personal communications and comments of Orthodox friends, as well as on Orthodox sources (the websites of the various Orthodox churches in the United Kingdom, e.g. www.thyateira.org.uk and www.sourozh.org. uk; the 2013 Directory of Orthodox Parishes and Clergy in the British Isles and Ireland, published by the Orthodox Fellowship of St John the Baptist).

Reliable figures for membership of the various Orthodox jurisdictions are notoriously difficult to obtain. Church authorities tend to assume that all those of their respective ethnic communities are members of the church. A recent estimate of membership of the various Orthodox jurisdictions in the United Kingdom gives the following figures for 2010:[1]

---

[1]   Figures provided by Peter Brierley, independent researcher. Brierley, P. 2010. Introduction: Where is the Church Going?. Available at: http://www.brierleyconsultancy. com/church.html [accessed February 2012].

134   *Orthodox Identities in Western Europe*

Greek Orthodox: 233,120
Russian Orthodox (Moscow Patriarchate): 2,900
Russian Orthodox Outside of Russia (ROCOR): 17,000
Romanian Orthodox: 24,000
Serbian Orthodox: 4,050
Bulgarian Orthodox: 4,035
Antiochian Orthodox: 6,000
Georgian Orthodox: 2,000
Ukrainian Autocephalous Orthodox: 1,660
Byelorussian Orthodox: 2,400

The total of all Orthodox in the UK is given by the same source as 330,712. The numbers of those attending services regularly is considerably smaller. In his chapter 'The Orthodox Church in the British Isles', Metropolitan Kallistos Ware referred to an independent survey carried out in 1998, which concluded that on an average Sunday some 25,200 Orthodox of all jurisdictions attended church.

Numbers of places of worship, which roughly equate with parish communities, can be given with more accuracy. According to the 2013 Directory of Orthodox Parishes and Clergy, they are:

Patriarchate of Antioch: 18
Patriarchate of Bulgaria: 1
Ecumenical Patriarchate: 111
    (including Ukrainian Orthodox Diocese: 9
    and Belorussian Diocese: 2)
Exarchate of Orthodox Parishes of Russian Tradition within the Ecumenical
Patriarchate: 29
Patriarchate of Georgia: 1
Patriarchate of Moscow: 36
Patriarchate of Romania: 31
Russian Orthodox Church Outside of Russia: 11
Patriarchate of Serbia: 23

These parishes are served by 285 clergy.

Before the twentieth century Eastern Orthodox Christians were a rare presence in the United Kingdom, and confined to a very few places. By the end of that century, settled Orthodox communities had become a permanent part of the

Christian presence in all the four countries of the UK (England, Wales, Scotland and Northern Ireland), although most of them are in England. The vast majority are of immigrant origin, and all of them relate so far as jurisdiction is concerned to the ecclesiastical authorities of their mother church. There are British converts to Orthodoxy, most of whom have become members of the Russian Orthodox Church, which was the first to use English extensively in liturgical worship. A few have joined the Greek, Serbian or Romanian Orthodox Churches, while some are in the Patriarchate of Antioch. In addition, a few Orthodox are happy to attend their local Anglican church.

The Greek Orthodox Church

The Greeks were the first to establish an organised community in England in the seventeenth century. In 1677 Archbishop Joseph Georgirines of Samos, who was visiting London, was given permission to build a church to serve a small group of Greeks and their priest who had settled in London. The Bishop of London, Henry Compton, provided a site in Soho. However, relations between the bishop and the Greeks were not happy. The bishop forbade them to put up icons in the church, which in 1684 was taken from the Greeks and given to the Huguenots, before eventually becoming an Anglican chapel. From then until 1837 the Greek community was taken under the wing of the Imperial Russian Embassy. In that year a chapel was created in Finsbury Circus, in the City of London, in whose immediate vicinity many Greek commercial enterprises were situated.

In the course of the nineteenth century increasing numbers of Greeks came to live and work in Britain's rapidly growing commercial cities. In 1850 a new church was built in the City of London, and in 1877 the foundation stone of the present Cathedral Church of St Sophia was laid in Moscow Road in Bayswater. It was consecrated in 1882. The 1860s saw churches built in Liverpool and Manchester, and in 1906 the community in Cardiff built its own church. These four communities, though theoretically under the jurisdiction of the Ecumenical Patriarchate, had no direct contact with any autocephalous church. In 1908 the Patriarchate transferred these parishes to the Church of Greece, until in 1922 the Patriarchate created the Archdiocese of Thyateira and Great Britain.

Considerable numbers of Cypriot Greeks came to Britain during and after the Second World War, and again after the Turkish invasion of Cyprus in 1974. New parishes were created in many places in the United Kingdom, and by the beginning of the twenty-first century they numbered roughly 100. The archbishop is assisted by a number of suffragan bishops. The present archbishop, Gregorios, was elected by the Holy Synod of the Ecumenical Patriarchate in 1988. The parishes, served by over 120 clergy, enjoy a good deal of autonomy under the general supervision of the Archdiocese. They own the property they have acquired for religious and educational purposes. Some of the churches are purpose-built, others are buildings acquired from other communions, many from the Church of England.

The archdiocese is responsible for a number of institutions set up to promote educational and catechetical work, and to supply other church needs. In 2000 the first diocesan Greek Orthodox primary day school, St Cyprian's, was opened in Thornton Heath in the London Borough of Croydon, and the diocese supports other independent Greek schools. There are a number of officially accredited Greek Orthodox chaplains to British universities. A school of Byzantine music in Wood Green in London trains cantors for service in the archdiocese. Many parishes have informal language schools to teach Greek to children whose first language is now English. The archdiocese is engaged in charitable activity, its main organ being the Greek Orthodox Charity Organisation, and many parishes have their own charitable organisation. Youth work is an important feature of the archdiocese's mission, and there is an annual archdiocesan youth camp. As part of its educational work, the archdiocese sponsors a weekly religious programme on London Greek Radio.

While the majority of Greek Orthodox come originally from Greece or Cyprus, there are some English-speaking converts. Of the clergy serving in the archdiocese at the present, a little under a third are not native Greek speakers. While Greek is still the most common language used in liturgical worship, English is used to a greater or lesser extent in most parishes. Among English converts to Orthodoxy the best-known is Metropolitan Kallistos of Diokleia, one of the assistant bishops in the archdiocese. Metropolitan Kallistos is well known as one of the most distinguished theologians in the Ecumenical Patriarchate. For many years he taught in Oxford as Spalding Lecturer in Eastern Orthodox Studies. He has written a number of books, and receives many invitations to lecture in different parts of the world. At the time of writing he is the co-chair of the International Commission for Anglican–Orthodox Theological Dialogue and a member of the Orthodox–Roman Catholic Dialogue.

The archdiocese claims to be one of the few growing churches in the country. This is largely through immigration. That would be the case too with other Orthodox jurisdictions: considerable numbers of Russians and Romanians have settled in the United Kingdom in recent years. There have been relatively few converts to Orthodoxy in the Greek Archdiocese, in part because of its ethnic character and the prevalence of the Greek language in worship. This situation is gradually changing. An English translation of the Divine Liturgy has been published to meet the growing need of English-speaking Orthodox. Archbishop Gregorios of Thyateira and Great Britain has written: 'The Holy Liturgy is the cornerstone upon which our Church depends and continues its religious mission throughout the world ...We must bring this tradition of ours closer to

The Orthodox Churches in the United Kingdom

the new generation and to our people in general. The use of the English language in the diakonia is also becoming more necessary and obligatory'.[2]

Now under the jurisdiction of the Ecumenical Patriarchate is the Patriarchal Stavropegic Monastery of St John the Baptist at Tolleshunt Knights in Essex. It is both the oldest and the largest Orthodox monastery in the British Isles. Founded in 1958 by Father Sophrony Sakharov, a disciple of St Silouan of Mount Athos, it was at first under the Moscow Patriarchate before transferring to the jurisdiction of the Ecumenical Patriarchate in 1959. It is a community of nearly 40 men and women of varied ethnic origin. The variety of linguistic and musical traditions among members of the community made it difficult to follow the normal Athonite typikon. Fr Sophrony established a pattern of daily prayer, at the heart of which is the recitation of the Jesus Prayer morning and evening, for a total of some four hours each day, within the framework of Orthros and Vespers. This had the advantage of allowing more time than the typikon for personal prayer and other activities, such as the study of spiritual texts, as well as practising a form of prayer which Fr Sophrony believed possesses divine energy. The Divine Liturgy is celebrated three or four times a week. One of Fr Sophrony's aims was the publication of St Silouan's writings. His own books, some of which have been translated into more than 20 languages, have also been widely influential. The spiritual reputation that attaches to the monastery is mainly due to Fr Sophrony himself and to his books. Fr Sophrony himself died in 1993, and many regard him as a saint. Fr Kyrill, the present abbot, and Fr Zacharias, the community's spiritual guide, are also highly regarded, as were Fr Symeon, who died in 2009, and Fr Raphael, who now lives in Romania. The monastery's reputation has spread far beyond the United Kingdom.

Within the jurisdiction of the Ecumenical Patriarchate in the United Kingdom is a Ukrainian Orthodox diocese, whose bishop is based in Belgium, and a deanery of the Exarchate of Orthodox Parishes of Russian Tradition in Western Europe based in Paris.

The Russian Orthodox Church

From 1716 a Russian Embassy church existed in London and was the home of the parish of the Dormition. Following the Bolshevik revolution, the parish was under the jurisdiction of the Karlovtsy Synod, later known as the Russian Orthodox Church Outside of Russia. Membership of the Russian Orthodox Church grew as a small number of Russian émigrés eventually settled in England,

---

[2] Introduction to the 1995 English translation of The Divine Liturgy of our Father among the Saints John Chrysostom (Greek Orthodox Church 1995), issued at the initiative of His Eminence Archbishop Gregorios of Thyateira and Great Britain.

most in London, some in Oxford. In 1926 the Russian community split into two parishes. One remained within the jurisdiction of the Karlovtsy Synod, the other came within that of Metropolitan Evlogii in Paris. In 1931 the latter parish passed with Metropolitan Evlogii into the jurisdiction of the Ecumenical Patriarchate, but in 1945 moved to the Patriarchate of Moscow.

In 1950 the Russian Orthodox community in London received a new priest, Fr Anthony Bloom. Educated in Paris and trained as a medical doctor, Fr Anthony came to London in 1948 to be chaplain to the Fellowship of St Alban and St Sergius. The Fellowship had come into being in 1928 after the second of two theological conferences between Anglican and Russian Orthodox theologians held in St Albans. Among its founding members were Nicholas and Militsa Zernov, who settled in Oxford and were instrumental in setting up ecumenical houses there. The London parish acquired from the Diocese of London the church of All Saints in Ennismore Gardens in Knightsbridge and added the Dormition to its dedication. In 1962 the Patriarchate of Moscow created the Diocese of Sourozh to care for its members in the United Kingdom and Ireland, and Fr Anthony became its first bishop.

Subsequently Archbishop and then Metropolitan, Fr Anthony had a remarkable ministry. The diocese was free, as the Moscow Patriarchate in the Soviet Union was not, to put into practice the decisions of the Great Council of 1917–1918 with regard to church government. Anthony was eager to make Orthodoxy accessible to English people, and for many years was a familiar speaker on the radio and television. His books on prayer were widely read by Christians of other traditions, and he was highly respected as a speaker and as a spiritual counsellor. He attracted a number of converts to the Russian Orthodox Church. Parishes were formed, some of which were entirely English-speaking, and in the Cathedral of the Dormition and All Saints in London, English and Church Slavonic were equally used in services. By 2006 the diocese included some 30 communities in the United Kingdom and Ireland, most of whose clergy and members were English, and using English in worship. The two principal communities were in London and Oxford.

The situation began to change, however, with the collapse of communism and the Soviet Union, and the consequent freedom of Russians to leave the country. Increasing numbers of Russians came to the United Kingdom and Ireland, as elsewhere in Western Europe, and a considerable number has settled in Britain. For many, in their first years in the country, the church was a place where they could meet other new immigrants. Not all were at home with the way in which Metropolitan Anthony ran the diocese; they wished to see church life conform more closely to what they had known in Russia. Towards the end of his life Anthony asked for episcopal help in addition to that of Bishop Basil of Sergievo, and in 2002 Bishop Hilarion of Kerch came from Russia to London as an assistant bishop. However, Metropolitan Anthony found him difficult to

The Orthodox Churches in the United Kingdom 139

work with, and later that year asked him to leave. Bishop Basil, an American convert to Orthodoxy, who had long served the Russian parish in Oxford, was appointed administrator of the diocese of Sourozh after Metropolitan Anthony's death in 2003.

Anxious to conserve the ecclesial and spiritual heritage of Metropolitan Anthony, Bishop Basil came to the conclusion that the only way to do so was to transfer to the jurisdiction of the Ecumenical Patriarchate's Archdiocese of Orthodox Parishes of Russian Tradition in Western Europe. Not all the clergy and parishioners of the diocese wished to transfer, however, and the diocese split. In 2006 Bishop Basil and some of the parishes and clergy were received into the jurisdiction of Constantinople, while other parishes with their clergy remained with the Moscow Patriarchate. Bishop Basil became Bishop of Amphipolis in the Ecumenical Patriarchate. In 2007 a new bishop, Elisey, was appointed to the diocese of Sourozh, and after a court case, was confirmed in his possession of the cathedral in Ennismore Gardens. Not long after the split, in 2009 Bishop Basil retired, and the parishes which had transferred to the Ecumenical Patriarchate now belong to the Deanery of Great Britain and Ireland, within the Ecumenical Patriarchate's Exarchate of Orthodox Parishes of Russian Tradition in Western Europe.

In both London and Oxford the Russian parishes themselves split. Those who followed Bishop Basil in London now worship in an Anglican church, St Andrew's Holborn, while in Oxford a new Moscow parish of St Nicholas the Wonderworker was created. An appeal for funds enabled it to purchase a disused Anglican chapel and refurbish it as an Orthodox church. The Oxford parish of the Annunciation under Constantinople has continued to use the Church of the Annunciation and the Holy Trinity, consecrated in 1973, which it shares with the Greek parish in Oxford. Both English and Slavonic are used in worship.

Though relatively small, under Metropolitan Anthony's leadership the Russian Orthodox Church came to include by far the largest proportion of converts to Orthodoxy in the United Kingdom. Fr Anthony remained loyal to the Moscow Patriarchate, which he held needed and deserved the support of those outside the Soviet Union. He was, however, not uncritical of the positions forced upon it by the Soviet government, and made use of his freedom to speak out against some of its actions. Himself a Russian by birth and upbringing, he did not see the primary role of the Orthodox Church as a support for Russian ethnicity, but as the agent of the gospel and the authentic Christian tradition. His intention was to present Orthodoxy in a way that was accessible and attractive to British people, and it was that, as well as his own personality, which enabled him to attract several thousand converts to the Russian Orthodox Church. Now firmly under the control of the Moscow Patriarchate, the Diocese of Sourozh is principally concerned with the pastoral care of Russians living

The Serbian Orthodox Church

Serbs first settled in Great Britain in any numbers after the Second World War. The majority of them were former military men associated with British forces, who had no wish to return to Yugoslavia after the establishment of the communist regime there under Marshal Tito. Others soon joined them, refugees from the new government. It is estimated that some 40,000 Serbs settled in Britain after the war. But there had been earlier contacts in the course of the First World War. The distinguished monk and scholar Father (later Bishop) Nikolai Velimirovitch spent some time in Britain in 1915–1916. He travelled extensively, preaching in many Anglican cathedrals, including St Paul's in London. His mission was to make known the desperate wartime situation of the Serbian people and their efforts to preserve their nation's liberty, and he succeeded in winning much sympathy and material support for the Serbs. Towards the end of the war the Church of England welcomed some 60 Serbian theological students, who were able to pursue their studies at the theological college in Cuddesdon and at Oxford. At the same time Father Nikolai made many in Britain aware for the first time of Serbian Orthodoxy and its role in the history and life of the Serbian people.

During the Second World War the Yugoslav royal family and government in exile lived in London, where a Serbian Orthodox chapel had been arranged in a private house. A Serbian church community was formally set up in 1942. It was served by a priest, Fr Zhivoin Ristanovich, supported financially by the government in exile. In 1944 he was succeeded by Archpriest Miloye Nikolich, who remained the parish priest until 1975. In 1945 Patriarch Gavriil and Bishop Nikolai came to London for the baptism of King Peter's son Alexander. It took place in Westminster Abbey, and King George VI and his daughter Princess Elizabeth were godparents to the baby prince. During his stay in England the Patriarch was able to meet many of the leaders of the Church of England as well as leading politicians. Among the close friends of Bishop Nikolai was the Anglican Bishop of Gibraltar, Harold Buxton. With financial help the small Serbian community was able to buy a house and set up a chapel dedicated to St Sava. The Archbishop of Canterbury, Geoffrey Fisher, lent his support to the community, and was among those who spoke out against the persecution of the Orthodox Church in the new, communist Yugoslavia. Like other Orthodox communities, the Serbian parish was offered the use of Anglican churches for their services. In 1952 the former Anglican parish church of St Columba in Notting Hill in West London was consecrated as the Serbian Orthodox church of St Sava, and became the home of the Serbian parish in London. The parish's connection with the Yugoslav royal family in exile was symbolised by the presence in the nave of two thrones, one for the bishop, one for the royal family.

Next to the church a parish centre houses a number of cultural and spiritual activities. There is a flourishing Sunday school in which young people of all ages study the Serbian language as well as Serbian history and theology. It is served by ten volunteer teachers. A dance group, a church choir, a school of folklore, a youth group and spiritual group named after St Alypius the Stylite, contribute to the preservation and transmission of Serbian culture. The parish has good relations with the local community, and receives regular visits from local schools, designed to teach the children something of Orthodoxy and Serbian culture in general. The celebration of St Sava's Day features largely in the calendar of St Sava's, as of all Serbian parishes.

Parish communities were set up in other cities and towns in Britain to serve local Serbian communities. The only parish to have a purpose-built church is that of St Prince Lazar in Birmingham. Designed in a traditional fourteenth-century Serbian style and decorated with frescoes in the same style, it was consecrated in 1968. The parish was founded by Fr Milenko Zebic, who is now the episcopal vicar in the United Kingdom of the Diocese of Great Britain and Scandinavia. Since 1990 Serbian parishes have been part of the Serbian diocese of Great Britain and Scandinavia. Its bishop, Dositej, resides in Stockholm in Sweden.

The Romanian Orthodox Church

A chaplain had been attached to the Romanian Legation in London to serve the diplomatic community before the Second World War. But a Romanian community in London began to be formed only after the War and the formation of a communist government in Romania. In 1967 an agreement was concluded between the Romanian Patriarchate and the Church of England, which provided for an exchange of chaplains. With the consent of the Romanian government, a chaplain would be allowed to serve the Anglican Church of the Resurrection in Bucharest, and a Romanian priest would come to London to provide pastoral care for Romanians living in Britain.

A home for the new Romanian parish was found in the church of St Dunstan in the West in Fleet Street in London. Served at that time by the priest who was also the secretary of the Council on Foreign Relations at Lambeth Palace, St Dunstan's has several chapels, one of which became the Romanian Orthodox sanctuary. In 1966 it was provided with an iconostasis brought from the Antim Monastery in Bucharest. The Romanian community was at first not large, but has grown steadily. Since the collapse of communism in Romania, and the entry of Romania into the European Union, a considerable number of Romanians have come to the United Kingdom. The original parish has grown, and a second parish has been set up in London.

The Romanian parishes in the United Kingdom are under the jurisdiction of the diocese of Western Europe, whose bishop is currently Metropolitan Joseph, based in Paris. The Romanian Orthodox Church is closely linked with Romanian national identity, and the parishes are a focus for the growing number of Romanians in the country. Like the Romanian parish in London, other parishes often use Anglican churches or church halls for their worship. Traditionally there have been particularly warm relations between the Romanian Orthodox Church and the Church of England. Following a theological conference in Bucharest in 1935 the Holy Synod provisionally recognised the validity of Anglican ordinations; and while the Romanian Orthodox Church later acknowledged that such a recognition could properly be made only by the whole of Orthodoxy, some Romanian theologians and clergy still take the decision taken in 1935 as having authority.

The Patriarchate of Antioch

The Patriarchate has a Deanery of the United Kingdom and Ireland as part of the Antiochian Archdiocese of Europe. The deanery, which was set up in 1995, is under the care of Metropolitan John of Western and Central Europe. The cathedral church of St George is close to Regent's Park in London, and is the only Arabic-speaking congregation in the deanery, which otherwise consists mostly of a small group of former Anglicans who wished to become Orthodox. At first they were in contact with the Greek and Russian dioceses in Britain. But neither the Archdiocese of Thyateira and Great Britain nor the Diocese of Sourozh was willing to receive them *en bloc*, requiring instead individual conversions. Nor would either of these jurisdictions guarantee the ordination of Anglican clergy as Orthodox clerics. So they accepted the initiative of the Patriarch of Antioch to welcome them into his jurisdiction. The establishment of the Antiochian Deanery was opposed by the Greek and Russian diocesans, who saw no point in adding to the existing jurisdictions in Britain. Almost all the clergy as well as the members of the congregations are converts, using English in worship.

The Bulgarian Orthodox Church

Bulgarian Orthodox in the United Kingdom are under the jurisdiction of Metropolitan Symeon of Central and Western Europe. There are two parishes, one in London, the other in Dundee in Scotland, serving Bulgarian communities that have increased in numbers since Bulgaria's admission to the European Union in 2007.

The Georgian Orthodox Church

Since the collapse of the Soviet Empire and the independence of Georgia, an expatriate Georgian community has formed in the United Kingdom. In 2005 the Georgian Orthodox Church acquired a church in Clapton, London. In 2011 it was consecrated as the Georgian Orthodox Cathedral of the Nativity by the Catholicos-Patriarch of All Georgia, Ilya II, with the assistance of Archbishop Gregorios of Thyateira and Great Britain. At the same time the Catholicos also created the Diocese of Great Britain and Ireland, and appointed Bishop Zenon of Dmanisi as its first archbishop. In 2012 the newly formed Pan-Orthodox Assembly of Bishops in the United Kingdom and Ireland celebrated a pan-Orthodox Vespers on the Feast of the Sunday of Orthodoxy in the Georgian church.

Inter-Orthodox Relations

In Great Britain, as in other parts of the world, the Orthodox Churches are in an anomalous ecclesiological situation. Communities of different ethnic origin have remained within the jurisdiction of their mother churches. There are therefore parallel jurisdictions of all the Orthodox Churches represented in the United Kingdom. Acknowledging the unsatisfactory nature of this situation, and following the request of a pan-Orthodox consultation in 2008, an Assembly of Orthodox Bishops with Churches in the British Isles was set up in 2010. It is intended that it shall meet twice a year. It remains to be seen whether this development will lead to greater inter-Orthodox collaboration, at present symbolically expressed by the celebration of pan-Orthodox Vespers on the Sunday of Orthodoxy.

Meanwhile the Orthodox Fellowship of St John the Baptist, founded in 1979, brings together at its annual conference and study weekend members of all the Orthodox jurisdictions. In the academic sphere, a significant development took place in 1999 with the foundation of the Institute of Orthodox Christian Studies in Cambridge, the only Orthodox institution of higher education in the United Kingdom. It embraces members of the Orthodox Churches in Eastern Europe, the Middle East, Russia and Greece, and of Orthodox jurisdictions in the West. It aims to serve the needs of Orthodox parishes in Great Britain as well as providing worldwide opportunities for distance learning. Its principal is English, and so are some of the staff. Among those who teach as visiting lecturers at the Institute is Metropolitan Kallistos Ware. The Institute is a member of the Cambridge Theological Federation, which brings together 11 institutions, among them Anglican, Methodist, Orthodox, Reformed and Roman Catholic, providing theological and pastoral training for various forms of Christian ministry and service. The Federation is associated with the University of Cambridge. Formerly based in Wesley House, the Methodist theological college, the Institute has recently acquired its own building in Cambridge.

The Institute is the only Orthodox educational institution in Western Europe which teaches in English all aspects of Orthodoxy to students at various academic levels, pre-university, undergraduate and graduate. Its pan-Orthodox character anticipated the recent formation of the Pan-Orthodox Assembly of Bishops in the United Kingdom, and with the Assembly it is an instrument for enabling greater cooperation and unity among the country's different Orthodox jurisdictions. Its establishment in an ecumenical context means that it is well placed to train Orthodox clergy and laity to cooperate with other Churches and engage in dialogue with them.

Ecumenical Relations

Before the twentieth century contacts between Orthodox and British Christians were largely individual. In the largest of the British churches, the Church of England, interest in Orthodoxy developed in the nineteenth century as one consequence of the Oxford Movement, which from 1833 sought to emphasise the catholic character of the Church of England. Many of those whom it influenced came to look to the Roman Catholic Church as the model of catholic faith, worship and devotion. But some looked eastward, to the Orthodox Church. In 1864 the Eastern Church Association was founded to foster relations between the two traditions. It merged with the Anglican and Eastern Churches Union in 1914 to form the present Anglican and Eastern Churches Association, whose object is to pray and work for unity between Anglicans and Orthodox. The patrons of the Association are the Ecumenical Patriarch and the Archbishop of Canterbury, and its presidents are the Archbishop of Thyateira and Great Britain and the Bishop of London.

The Russian revolution interrupted the contacts that had been made with the Russian Orthodox Church in the course of previous decades. But it brought to Britain, as to other western European countries, Russian émigrés. In Paris they set up the Russian Orthodox Theological Institute of St Sergius. Among the émigrés who were enthusiastic about developing relations with churches of Western tradition was the dean of the new institute, Fr Sergei Bulgakov. In 1927 he took part, along with other Russian Orthodox, in a theological conference with Anglicans at St Albans in England. A second conference was

The Orthodox Churches in the United Kingdom 145

held in 1928, and from it was born the Fellowship of St Alban and St Sergius. Among the founders were Nicholas and Militsa Zernov, who were to make an important contribution to making Orthodoxy better known in Britain, and to building up friendly relations with Anglicans. The Fellowship is an informal society, enabling Orthodox and Anglicans to meet one another and learn about each other's understanding and practice of the Christian faith. In the years before and after the Second World War its annual conference was attended by distinguished theologians, and Orthodox and Anglican families took part in what included aspects of a summer holiday. In recent years the Fellowship has broadened its scope to include Eastern and Western Christians of all traditions. Together with the Fellowship's journal, *Sobornost*, the annual conference is still a central feature of its life, although with fewer participants. It is perhaps fair to say that the majority of the Fellowship's members in the United Kingdom are Anglicans or others interested in learning more about Orthodoxy. It was among Russian émigrés that enthusiasm for ecumenical contacts with Anglicans was most marked in the decades after the Russian revolution. With the passing of that first generation, ecumenical enthusiasm has perhaps somewhat waned; and subsequent developments in relations between the Anglican and Orthodox churches have contributed to a changed situation.

Both the Fellowship and the Anglican and Eastern Churches Association have pursued their mission within the broader context of relations between the two churches. A significant moment occurred in 1925, when the Church of England celebrated the 1600th anniversary of the Council of Nicaea. Representatives of the Orthodox Churches were invited to take part. Many senior Orthodox hierarchs gathered in London for the celebrations, which included a service in Westminster Abbey. A Joint Doctrinal Commission met in 1931, following earlier informal talks in 1920 and 1930 in the context of the Lambeth Conferences of those years; and in 1935 a conference was held in Bucharest between Romanian Orthodox and Anglican theologians. The Second World War interrupted such discussions between Anglicans and Orthodox, but contacts were resumed soon after 1945. In the 1962 the Archbishop of Canterbury paid an official visit to Patriarch Athenagoras of Constantinople. They agreed that a joint commission should be set up to examine agreements and differences in doctrine between the Orthodox and Anglican Churches. From 1966 to 1972 the two sides met separately to prepare the dialogue, and the Anglican–Orthodox Joint Doctrinal Discussions began in 1973 in Oxford. The earlier theological discussions had elucidated the principal points of divergence between the two Churches and prepared an agenda for the Anglican–Orthodox Joint Doctrinal Discussions; and it was widely thought that once these specific questions had been resolved, closer relations between them could be considered. The commission's first Agreed Statement was drawn up in Moscow in 1976, and summarised agreement on divine revelation and our knowledge of God,

146 *Orthodox Identities in Western Europe*

the inspiration and authority of scripture, scripture and tradition, the authority of the Councils, the *filioque* clause, the church as the Eucharistic community, and the invocation of the Holy Spirit in the Eucharist. Anglican members recommended to their churches the removal of the *filioque* clause from the Nicene Creed for historical and ecumenical reasons.

A crisis arose in 1977 over the ordination of women to the priesthood, which had already begun in the Episcopal Church in the United States. Some Orthodox representatives wished to end the dialogue at once, but the Orthodox Churches decided to pursue the dialogue, though now without unity as its goal. A special meeting of the commission took place in Athens in 1978, at which both sides set out their positions. Further discussions resulted in a second Agreed Statement, approved in Dublin in 1983. After a pause the dialogue resumed in 1989, renamed as the International Commission for Anglican–Orthodox Theological Dialogue. Metropolitan John Zizioulas of Pergamon was the Orthodox co-chair. Taking ecclesiology as its principal theme, the Commission was intended to discuss the thorny question of women's ordained ministry in the Church in the broadest theological context.

For the majority of Orthodox the ordination of women in the Anglican Communion is an insuperable obstacle to closer relations between the two Churches, and to it has been added more recently the liberal view of same-sex relationships among Anglicans. However, the dialogue continues, and its fourth phase has taken Christian anthropology as its topic. There is an acknowledgement among some Orthodox that the questions of women's ministry and human sexuality are important areas of contemporary concern, of which the Anglican Church has already had considerable experience and to which it has given a great deal of theological thought, from both of which the Orthodox might learn. The difficulties are of course not all on one side. Problems are posed for Anglicans as well as other Christian traditions by some Orthodox theological convictions, not least the Orthodox claim that theirs is the one, holy, catholic and apostolic church of the creed, from which all other Christian churches are separated, and the insistence on full doctrinal agreement as a prerequisite for unity. The growth of an anti-Western and anti-ecumenical tendency in some Orthodox churches in recent decades has added to such difficulties.

Theological disagreements have not, however, prevented the development of friendly relations between Anglicans and Orthodox at various levels. Successive archbishops of Canterbury have welcomed heads of Orthodox Churches on official visits to the Church of England, and have themselves paid visits to local Orthodox Churches. The Church of England has welcomed the presence of Orthodox communities, and has done its best to help them, not least by making available churches and other buildings for worship. An Orthodox observer is always invited to meetings of the General Synod of the Church of England, and is welcome to contribute to debates. Orthodox observers are invited to the

The Orthodox Churches in the United Kingdom

Lambeth Conference of all Anglican bishops, which takes place every ten years. Less well-known, but not insignificant, is the interest taken in Mount Athos by the Duke of Edinburgh, whose mother became an Orthodox nun, and by Prince Charles, who is Patron of the Friends of Mount Athos. They have both made a number of visits to the Holy Mountain.

It was perhaps to be expected that the Orthodox communities in Britain should give priority to relations with the Anglicans. The Orthodox, generally organised in national churches, felt a natural affinity with Anglicans as the established national church in England, though not in the other countries of the United Kingdom. Since the Second World War relations among the British churches, once cool and sometimes frosty, have gradually become warmer, and cooperation among them has slowly developed. In 1942 the British Council of Churches (BCC) was created, bringing together Anglican and Protestant Churches, and local councils of Churches were formed. In 1965 the Archdiocese of Thyateira and Great Britain became a member, and following the Decree on Ecumenism of the Second Vatican Council, Roman Catholic observers were invited to attend meetings. The Orthodox Churches have made a significant contribution to the theological reflection of the Council, not least to the work that was done in the 1980s on the doctrine of God as Trinity. Two booklets were published in 1989 with the title 'The Forgotten Trinity', one the Report of the BCC's Study Commission, the other a Study Guide on issues contained in the Report. Five Orthodox theologians were members of the Study Commission, among them Bishop Basil of Sergievo and Metropolitan John Zizoulas of Pergamon, who as a layman taught for some years in the University of Glasgow and later lectured at King's College, London.

In 1990 the British Council of Churches was replaced by Churches Together in the United Kingdom, in which the Roman Catholic Church was able to participate. There are Churches Together organisations in the four nations of Wales, Scotland, Ireland and England, and in almost every local community. Churches Together exists to enable the various Christian churches to deepen their fellowship with one another, to work towards greater visible unity, and to coordinate their witness and work in the wider community. Most of the churches in the United Kingdom participate in Churches Together, including all the Orthodox jurisdictions whose mother churches are members of the World Council of Churches and are involved in official bilateral ecumenical dialogues.

At the local level relations between the Orthodox and other churches are friendly. Practical cooperation, however, between Orthodox and other Christians is limited. Some Orthodox parishes still have a strongly ethnic character, and can be more concerned with strengthening their own community than with building up relations with communities of other Christian traditions. Differences of theology, language, and liturgical tradition hinder Orthodox Christians from joining in the acts of shared worship which take place among other Christian

148 *Orthodox Identities in Western Europe*

communities, particularly during the annual Week of Prayer for Christian Unity. Those Orthodox parishes, which are largely made up of converts from other churches, are understandably not always interested in developing relations with the churches they have left; there are, however, notable exceptions.

Conclusion

Over the years the Orthodox communities in the United Kingdom have put down deeper roots in this country. In longer-established communities, subsequent generations to the first immigrants have tended to assimilate to the culture in which they have been brought up, and within which they work and earn their living. The fact that they have attracted a certain number of indigenous converts has also helped to root them more firmly in British society. One sign of the indigenisation of the Orthodox churches is their appropriation of the saints of Britain who lived before the so-called Great Schism of 1054. In an address given in 2000, Archbishop Gregorios of Thyateira and Great Britain quoted St Arsenios of Cappadocia (1840–1924), who prophesied that 'The Church in the British Isles will only begin to truly grow again when it begins to venerate once more its own saints'. Saints of the first millennium have entered into Orthodox iconography, and their feast days have made their way into Orthodox liturgical calendars. In 2007 the Patriarchate of Moscow approved the commemoration on the third Sunday after Pentecost of the 'Synaxis of all the Saints who have shone forth in the lands of Britain and Ireland'. Such saints belonged to what is commonly called the undivided Church of the first millennium, and so are as much Catholic as Orthodox, and belong as much to the Church of England as to both. It is perhaps anachronistic to speak of them as Orthodox with a capital 'O'.

Among the symbols of the integration of Orthodoxy in British Christian presence and witness is a statue of the Grand Duchess St Elizabeth of Russia in a row of ten images of modern martyrs installed in 1998 in niches on the west front of Westminster Abbey. A granddaughter of Queen Victoria, she was married to the Grand Duke Sergei, the former Governor of Moscow who was assassinated in 1905. She became a nun, and founded the Monastery of St Martha and St Mary in Moscow. She was killed by the Bolsheviks in 1918, and subsequently canonised. The Dean and Chapter of Westminster decided for ecumenical reasons to include Roman Catholic and Orthodox as well as Anglican martyrs.

The integration of Orthodox communities into British life is also symbolised by the inclusion of their representatives at important national occasions such as the Service of Thanksgiving in St Paul's Cathedral on the occasion of the Diamond Jubilee of Her Majesty the Queen in 2012. Orthodox churches and their clergy are no longer rare and exotic phenomena; and the inclusion in the

European Union of eastern and south-eastern European countries of Orthodox tradition has increased significantly the numbers of Orthodox Christians who live and work in the United Kingdom. There are few large towns and cities where there are not one or more Orthodox parishes.

But the Orthodox jurisdictions in the United Kingdom are still much concerned with maintaining and passing on the cultural and religious traditions of their countries of origin. One sign of this is the felt need on the part of older generations to ensure that their children learn the language of their parents and grandparents, sometimes in informal schools attached to parishes. Particularly for new immigrants from Orthodox countries, the parishes of the different jurisdictions function as places where they can meet fellow countrymen already settled in Britain or other new immigrants. It is worth noting that while there is a significant proportion of convert clergy, many of the clergy who serve in Orthodox parishes come from the country of origin of their parishioners. Some have served in Britain for many years, others, like many of their parishioners, are more recent arrivals. The historically strong link between Orthodoxy and national identity is still a powerful factor in the life of the various Orthodox communities in the United Kingdom, reinforced by the wave of new immigrants since the collapse of communism and the entry of traditionally Orthodox countries into the European Union.

This is one reason for the general absence between Orthodox communities and other churches of the kind of cooperation which is increasingly common among the historic British churches. Anglicans and Free Church congregations sometimes share church buildings, as, less often, do Anglicans and Roman Catholics. Frequently Orthodox congregations worship in Anglican and other churches. But there can be no question of them sharing services, as Anglican and Free Church congregations sometimes do. Nor have Orthodox hierarchs been involved in the kind of collaboration that for some years has marked relations between the Roman Catholic and Anglican bishops in the Archdiocese of Westminster and the Diocese of London, whose bishops hold regular meetings to discuss pastoral matters. In 2011 and 2012, in a new development, the episcopates of the Church of England and the Roman Catholic Church in England and Wales held joint residential meetings. The Roman Catholic notion of a hierarchy of truths, enunciated by the Second Vatican Council, and the understanding of reunion as a gradual process, make such collaboration easier in the light of the degree of theological and liturgical convergence that has helped to overcome the oppositions of the past. Such forms of cooperation are less easy for the Orthodox, who regard themselves as the one, holy, catholic and apostolic church of the creed, and insist that there must be complete doctrinal agreement before closer relations are possible.

It remains the case that the majority of British people are unaware of the presence of Orthodox communities in British society. In 'The Orthodox

Church in the British Isles', Metropolitan Kallistos expressed the view that this marginalisation was mainly due to the jurisdictional fragmentation of Orthodoxy in Britain, unlikely to be overcome in the foreseeable future given the continuing strength of the ethnic character of the different jurisdictions. It is also the case that historically Orthodoxy is essentially Christianity as it developed in the political and cultural setting of the East Roman Empire and the Byzantine Commonwealth, a context very different from that in which Christianity developed in the West. That may make it seem an imported rather than indigenous presentation of Christianity. While continuing for a variety of reasons to attract a small number of British converts, the Orthodox churches in the United Kingdom are likely for the foreseeable future to minister for the most part to immigrant communities of traditionally Orthodox faith.

Bibliography

Brierley, P. 2010. Introduction: Where is the Church Going?. Available at: http://www.brierleyconsultancy.com/church.html [accessed February 2012].

Greek Orthodox Church. 1995. The Divine Liturgy of our Father among the Saints John Chrysostom, translated by Ephrem Lash. Oxford: Oxford University Press.

OFSJB. 2013. Directory of Orthodox Parishes and Clergy in the British Isles and Ireland. Orthodox Fellowship of St John the Baptist.

Ware, K. 2006. The Orthodox Church in the British Isles, in *A Short History of the Orthodox Church in Western Europe in the 20th Century*, edited by C. Chaillot. Paris: Inter-Orthodox Dialogue.

Ware, K. 2010 [1990]. Orthodoxy in Britain: Its Origins and Future. *Sourozh*, 106 (2010): 18–23.

Chapter 8

Population Movements and Orthodox Christianity in Finland: Dislocations, Resettlements, Migrations and Identities

Tuomas Martikainen and Teuvo Laitila

Orthodox Christianity has been present in the region known as Karelia since the eleventh century. At that time the name Karelia referred to the areas around the lakes Ladoga and Onega, and those now making up the south-eastern part of present-day Finland. Today Karelia is commonly understood to refer to the Russian Republic of Karelia as well as the north-eastern area of the Leningrad Oblast, and the south-eastern area of Finland.

The religious history of Karelia can be characterised as one of a borderland or 'contact zone' (Pratt 1992: 6–7), where the Orthodox and Roman Catholic, and, since 1527, the Lutheran Churches had their north-eastern European outposts, marking the great divide between the Catholic and Protestant north-western Europe and the Orthodox eastern Europe. Over the centuries, the region's Orthodox population have dwelt under Novgorodian, Swedish and Russian rule, and, since 1917, as citizens of the Republic of Finland and Soviet Russia, the Soviet Union or the Russian Federation.

This chapter will focus on the Orthodox population in and originating from Karelia, and on other relevant Orthodox population movements, from a historical and contemporary Finnish perspective. After a brief overview of previous research, we will focus firstly on the historical and contemporary dislocations, resettlements and migrations of Orthodox populations and the emergence of the Orthodox Church of Finland (OCF) as an outgrowth of the Russian Orthodox Church (ROC). In the closing section we will discuss changes in the social and organisational identities of Finland's Orthodox population and the OCF over the last century. Except for material concerning the last two decades, the chapter is mainly based on existing research.

Evaluation of Previous Research on Orthodox Population Movements

The history of Orthodoxy in Finland is rich in both voluntary and, in particular, forced migrations and resettlements. Whereas the general history of Orthodoxy

152   *Orthodox Identities in Western Europe*

in Karelia and Finland is already well documented (Purmonen 1981; Ambrosius and Haapio 1982; Kirkinen 1987; Kirkinen, Nevalainen and Sihvo 1994; Nevalainen and Sihvo 1998), considerations of the religious consequences of population movements and resettlements have not been as central as might be expected. The dislocations themselves have been noted and studied, but more often from economic, military and political perspectives, or as the life histories of refugees and political émigrés, rather than as triggers of religious transformation.

The earliest well-documented and studied population movements resulted in the seventeenth-century Swedish expansion into – as well as the Russo-Swedish War (1656–1661) in – Karelia. Pentti Laasonen, a specialist in Finnish Lutheran Church history, has traced the destinies of thousands of Karelian refugees, who fled either the Swedish forced conversion policy of the early 1600s or, after the Russo-Swedish War, Swedish reprisals due to the Karelian support for the Muscovite troops in their initially successful attack, as illustrated in the next section of this chapter (Laasonen 2005). However, Laasonen merely mentions the effect of the flight on the Orthodox in the Swedish-held Karelia, even though emigration significantly reduced their numbers and changed the religious balance of the region drastically in favour of the Lutherans.

Toivo Nygård, a Finnish history specialist, wrote a detailed study of refugees from the so-called Eastern Karelia (roughly the present Republic of Karelia in Russia) into Finland between 1917 and 1922 in connection with the Russian Civil War, but referred hardly at all to their Orthodoxy, and did not consider the refugees' impact on the Orthodox Church in Finland (Nygård 1980). Likewise, Pekka Nevalainen, also a specialist of Finnish history, authored an even more detailed study of the same refugees, though covering a longer period of time, up until the eve of World War II. He paid some attention to the ecclesiastical care of the refugees by the OCF but did not enter into a wider discussion of the Russian refugees' impact on the Church (Nevalainen 1999).

The latest study of the early twentieth-century Orthodox population movements in Finland thus far is Katja Hyry's doctoral dissertation (Hyry 2011) on East Karelian refugees from the region of Viena ('Belomorskaya Kareliya' in Russian, or 'Archangel Karelia'). Hyry collected refugees' stories of their experiences of and encounters with locals in Finland, focusing on refugee identity. She took into account their Orthodoxy, but did not discuss the refugees' role in relation to the OCF. The above four studies illustrate well how the specifically religious and ecclesial dimension of Orthodox dislocations and resettlements is under-represented, if not neglected, in research.

More recently, the study of Orthodox migrations has also focussed on Russian and other émigrés, immigrants and refugees, who moved to Finland during the Grand Duchy, after the October Revolution and since the 1990s. Of these studies we mention one on Russian life in Finland between the World Wars (Baschmakoff and Leinonen 2001), which includes a chapter on

Population Movements and Orthodox Christianity in Finland 153

ethnic Russians' religious life. However, it does not discuss the matter in the context of dislocation, but focuses on people who had already settled down in Finland. Another work, a history of the Helsinki Orthodox Parish, takes into account both the historical and newer Orthodox immigrants, portraying above all their economic importance for the parish, which was originally founded by local Russian merchants (Piiroinen 2002). Yet another study explains the impact of new immigrants in local parishes, but even there the broader impact of new immigrants on the OCF has not been in focus (Martikainen 2004; Martikainen 2005). Hence, a broader discussion on their impact on the OCF is still to emerge.

Orthodox Dislocations, Resettlements and Migrations Through History

Novgorodians, Swedes and Russians

Novgorodians adopted Orthodoxy from the Byzantines via Kiev around the end of the tenth century, and from the eleventh century onwards started to disseminate it in Karelia, where the pre-existing religion has been characterised as a form of shamanism (Siikala 2012). The key mechanisms for disseminating Christianity in Karelia were trade (transmission of Christian items and ideas in addition to commerce), forced conversions (the first of these to be documented in local chronicles took place in the Karelian Isthmus around 1227), and, evidently since the fourteenth century, mission work, carried out by locally based monks (the Valaam and Konevsky monasteries were both founded on islands on Lake Ladoga during this period) (Kirkinen 1987).

At first religion was used to link the Karelians to the Novgorodian trading and tax-collecting systems. This was effectuated by building churches and, later, monasteries, which functioned as centres for tax levying and fairs. Since the early thirteenth century with Swedish expansion into what is today southeastern Finland and the Karelian Isthmus, the Orthodoxy of Karelians grew in importance for Novgorod; they had to declare allegiance to the 'Novgorodian religion' to prove their political loyalty. But not until the late fifteenth century, after Muscovite Russia had taken control of Novgorod (in 1478) and rendered the Karelians its subjects, did religious activities such as attending church become more important (Kirkinen 1994).

With the Swedish expansion, Karelia became the site of a struggle for power between Novgorod and Sweden. The conflict ended with the Treaty of Nöteborg (in Finnish 'Pähkinäsaari'; in Russian 'Oreshek') in 1323, which divided Karelia into a Swedish area (roughly south-eastern Finland and the north-western part of the Karelian Isthmus) and a Novgorodian sphere of influence (the rest of Karelia). This border remained for the next two and a half centuries.

During the sixteenth century two rising powers – Moscow and Sweden, which was growing out of the Danish-dominated Kalmar Union – started to expand. A war between them broke out in 1579. After decades of intermittent war, Sweden gained the upper hand, and in the Treaty of Stolbova in 1617 secured the Karelian Isthmus and areas west and north of Lake Ladoga (Katajala 2005).

The overwhelming majority of the roughly 60,000 Karelians in the newly annexed areas were Orthodox (Kirkinen 1994: 134). For Sweden, which had adopted Lutheranism in 1527, the 'heretics' were a thorn in the side: to break away from its Catholic past Sweden had turned to a form of what is called Lutheran Orthodoxy (Tegborg 2002). Due to this, some zealous clergymen, including the bishop of the newly established Lutheran diocese of Vyborg (in Finnish 'Viipuri'), started to compel the Orthodox to embrace Lutheranism, at times using harsh methods of conversion. This provoked the Orthodox, and from the 1620s to 1640s some 25,000 of them fled to Russia (Laasonen 2005: 111). Orthodox Karelians also disapproved of the Swedish policy of transplanting Lutheran Finns from eastern Finland, mainly from the neighbouring region of Savonia, to western parts of Karelia. The policy led to conflicts between earlier inhabitants and the mainly Lutheran newcomers (Kirkinen 1982: 107–113; Laasonen 2005: 11–94).

Moscow was not willing to accept the loss of Ladogan Karelia. When in 1656 it embarked on a campaign for recapture, many local Orthodox supported the initially successful assault. However, the Swedes soon retook the area. At this point, perhaps as many as another 25,000 Karelians (Laasonen 2005: 111) followed the retreating Russian troops towards Moscow or, in lesser numbers, fled northwards to the Russian-held Olonets, east and north-east of Lake Ladoga. The escapees evidently, and most likely correctly, suspected that local Lutherans, as well as the Swedish government, would take revenge on them for their support for the Russians, particularly for their vandalising and plundering of non-Orthodox possessions (Kirkinen 1982: 107–113).

The war ended in the Treaty of Cardis in 1661, according to which the escapees were allowed to return, but few took that option. Large parts of Karelia remained deserted, and the ratio of Orthodox to Lutheran was reversed; in several places the majority of inhabitants were now Lutherans. To further increase the Lutheran population, as well as to repopulate the region, Sweden promoted immigration from Savonia. Consequently, only three parishes – Suistamo, Salmi and Suojärvi, all located on the northern or north-eastern shores of Lake Ladoga – were majority Orthodox by the end of the seventeenth century. Their religious belonging and activities were tolerated on the basis of so-called dissident paragraphs in the Treaties of Stolbova and Cardis, even though, officially, all people living permanently in the Kingdom of Sweden were required to be Lutherans according to the 1686 Swedish Church Law (Kirkinen 1982: 111–13). The outcome of these seventeenth-century population movements was thus a severe reduction in the number of Orthodox, the transformation of western parts of Karelia into all-Lutheran areas and the division of Swedish Karelia into an Orthodox East and an overwhelmingly Lutheran West.

The Great Northern War between Sweden and Russia broke out in 1700. After 20 years of intermittent skirmishes Sweden lost Karelia and most of south-eastern part of (contemporary) Finland in the Treaty of Nystad (in Finnish 'Uusikaupunki') in 1721. No major population transfers took place, but Sweden lost almost all of its Orthodox inhabitants, and a significant Lutheran population was left on the Russian side of the border. Only a small north-western section of Orthodox Karelia remained as a part of Sweden with a Karelian and Finnish-speaking Orthodox minority numbering 2,748 in 1795 (Osmonsalo 1945).

Subjects of the Russian Empire (1809–1917)

Russia first invaded and later annexed Finland in the Finnish War (1808–1809) as part of a broader political plan to counter Napoleon's advances and military threat. According to an 1809 imperial edict, basic Swedish laws remained in force in the conquered areas, now assigned as an autonomous Grand Duchy within the Russian Empire, headed by the Russian Tsar as the Grand Prince of Finland. Regarding religious affairs, no major changes took place. For example, permanent citizens and public office holders were still required to belong to the Lutheran Church. In practice this was changed so that by the late 1820s Orthodox Russians could also be appointed into public positions. However, their number remained insignificant. Karelian Orthodox, being mostly illiterate, were formally excluded from such offices.

Concerning the numbers of Orthodox, incorporation into Russia had two important consequences. First, the Russian military garrisoned major towns, particularly on the seashore. This increased the numbers of Orthodox. Immediately after the war the military numbered some 55,000, but quickly reduced to about 12,000. With the exception of the Crimean War (1853–1856), the number remained roughly the same until the eruption of World War I in 1914, when their numbers increased tenfold (Kurkinen 1985: 180).

In the garrison towns of Hanko, Hämeenlinna, Kuopio, Loviisa, Nikolainkaupunki (today Vaasa), Tampere, Tornio and Turku, Orthodox military churches were built (Raivo 1996).[1] The military presence and construction projects meant that Orthodoxy became visible for Lutherans in parts of Finland where it had previously been unknown or invisible. In addition to soldiers, the garrison towns hosted a Russian civil population – merchants, civil servants,

---

[1]   See also *Aamun Koitto*, 28 (1958); 13 (1962); 11–12 (1980); 4 (1986) for churches in Hanko, Loviisa, Nikolainkaupunki and Tornio, respectively.

manufacturers, and clergymen – numbering initially some hundreds and later a few thousand. However, the Russian military is seldom taken into account when speaking about the influence of Orthodoxy in the Grand Duchy of Finland.

The second and, retrospectively, more important Orthodox population change took place in January 1812, when the former Swedish Karelia or the so-called 'Old Finland' (the most south-easterly region of present-day Finland, the Karelian Isthmus and the western and northern shores of Lake Lagoda), was incorporated into the Grand Duchy. With it, roughly 25,000 Karelian Orthodox (Koukkunen 1968) became Finnish inhabitants and were put under the originally Swedish civil legislation of the Grand Duchy. However, ecclesiastically they remained under the Holy Synod of the Russian Orthodox Church, and, more precisely, as a part of the diocese of St Petersburg, until a separate diocese of Finland was founded in 1892 (Koukkunen 1977).

The transfer of Old Finland to the Grand Duchy also included the incorporation of three Russian-language civil parishes – Käkisalmi, Kyyrölä and Vyborg – to the Grand Duchy. All three were, broadly speaking, in the region of the Karelian Isthmus. Their members, numbering some two to three thousand, were mainly merchants, civil servants and, in Kyyrölä, peasants (Baschmakoff and Leinonen 2001: 20–30; Kemppi 1997).

In 1812, the Karelian Orthodox population of Finland amounted to some 30,000 people, around 3 per cent of the whole population of Finland (c. 900,000). Because they were almost totally concentrated in certain areas of Old Finland, whereas the Russian-speaking Orthodox predominated in several towns in Finland proper, the Grand Duchy was divided into groups of 'Russian' and 'Karelian' Orthodox, of which only the former were visible for most non-Orthodox Finns, and were also seen to represent Orthodoxy.

During the next 80 years their number increased, being about 50,600 in 1890. There are no statistics available with regard to their ethnic division, but if we presume that town-dwellers were as a rule Russians and country-dwellers Karelians, we could claim that roughly one fifth of the Orthodox in Finland were Russians. These figures do not include the Russian military (Loima 2001: 319; Baschmakoff and Leinonen 2001: 22). Rustic people were usually settled citizens, and their number was increasing, whereas townspeople were more or less provisional inhabitants, even though their number did not fluctuate that much.

The early decades of the twentieth century were a time of political turmoil. After the abolition in 1905 of the separate Finnish military, consisting merely of a few units, the number of Russian soldiers in Finland started quickly to increase. In 1910 it had almost doubled to some 20,000 men. During the First World War the military strength multiplied, peaking to some 125,000 on the eve of the October Revolution (Kurkinen 1985: 180). After the Finnish declaration of independence in December 1917 and the ensuing Finnish Civil War over the following few months, the Russian troops withdrew, leaving only some thousands of Russian civilians in the country.

To sum up, from the Orthodox viewpoint the most important population movements during the Grand Duchy consisted of Russian military and civilians moving to several Finnish towns, particularly to the southern and western coastal areas. In the popular Finnish imagination the result was that Orthodoxy, being already understood during the time of Swedish rule as the 'Russian' religion, was increasingly linked with foreign rule and military control (Laitila 2005). In addition, the fact that the Russians attempted to use the Orthodox Church as a tool for Russification towards the end of the Grand Duchy, as well as the general Finnish dislike of the Russification policies, did not improve the image of Orthodoxy or the Orthodox in the eyes of the rest of the population. Thus the Grand Duchy period bestowed upon the Karelian Orthodox the stigma of being Russians, and therefore enemies of the Finns (Nokelainen 1999: 103–104).

The Birth of the Republic of Finland and the Orthodox Church of Finland

Finnish independence from Russia and the official confirmation of the new country's borders were ratified by the Peace Treaty of Tartu in October 1920. Old Finland remained part of the new Finland, and the Petsamo area, along the Arctic Ocean, was also added to its territories, including the Petsamo Monastery (in Russian 'Petchenga'), as well as a few hundred Orthodox Sami (Ulkoasiainministeriö 1923).

As a part of the Finnish government's deliberate separation from Russia and Russian things, in November 1918 the Senate proclaimed the Finnish Orthodox diocese to be an autonomous Orthodox Church of Finland. To also validate the move canonically, the OCF leadership informed the newly re-established Moscow Patriarchate of the decision. Patriarch Tikhon confirmed the OCF's autonomy in February 1921. The Finnish government, not satisfied with this, instructed the OCF to completely sever ties with Moscow and to apply for autonomy from the Patriarchate of Constantinople, which also granted this in July 1923 (Nokelainen 2010).

However, neither the Finnish state nor the OCF could totally ignore Russia and its Orthodox population. The Russian Civil War (1917–1922) brought up to 44,000 Karelian and Russian refugees into Finland (Leitzinger 2008b: 171). Most of them were located on the Karelian Isthmus and in the cities of Vyborg and Helsinki; around 1,000 Karelians were also settled in the Orthodox parishes around Lake Ladoga. Although almost all the refugees were Orthodox, only a few joined the OCF, and then mostly in the area of the capital, Helsinki. The reason evidently was that most of them soon proceeded to continental Europe, especially to Germany and France, or returned to Russia. However, up until the

158   *Orthodox Identities in Western Europe*

outbreak of the Second World War Finland hosted 15,000 to 25,000 refugees. The OCF took pastoral care of the refugees in Karelia, but due to its small size and internal situation, could not do much (Hämynen 1993: 253; Nygård 1998: 128; Nevalainen 1999: 56–7, 181–8, 308).

Table 8.1 breaks down the number of refugees according to their ethnic backgrounds, as far as they are known or can be inferred from the official statistics. If we consider that the total number of Orthodox in Finland varied from 64,000 (in 1921) to 74,000 (in 1939) between the World Wars (Ambrosius and Haapio 1982: 517), numerically the refugees added some one fifth to one third to the whole Orthodox population. Had the majority of the refugees remained, it would also have altered the ethnic balance in the OCF, which at that time was waging a cultural war against the use of the Russian language in parish records, Church Slavonic in liturgy, and the Julian, or 'Old', calendar in the ecclesiastical reckoning of the year (Loima 2001).

Table 8.1   Russian and Karelian refugees in Finland 1918–1938 (Nevalainen 1999: 308; see also Nygård 1998: 129).

Year	Total	Russians	Karelians
1919	15,000	5,000	2,000
1922	33,500	15,000	11,000
1923	30,000	15,000	9,000
1925	21,500	13,000	6,000
1930	18,000	11,000	6,000
1934	18,000	9,000	6,000
1938	14,000	5,300	5,800

The OCF's cultural war was part of a deliberate policy of Finnicisation of the Church during the 1920s and 1930s. Finnish was used as an official and liturgical language. New churches were built according to an alleged 'Karelian', not Russian, model. Icon texts were gradually changed from Church Slavonic to Greek, later Finnish, and the clergy's liturgical vestments were reformed according to Greek, or Constantinopolitan, clues. Following their Lutheran counterparts, the Orthodox priests shaved their beards (Laitila 2004: 225–43). In the 1930s, even the Valaam Monastery claimed to represent the Byzantine tradition, and not its Slavic modification, in Karelia (Kilpeläinen 2000: 239–41).

The OCF supported Karelian-born refugees and neglected the Russians, as well as ignoring the Ingrians, who were Lutherans from the southern regions of

Karelia, numbering some 8,000 (in 1919) to 2,400 (in 1938) of the total refugee population (Nevalainen 1999: 308). The Church also attempted to turn the Russian minority within the OCF into Finns, or at least make them subservient to the Church's new 'Finnish' customs.

The fiercest battle was waged on the ecclesiastical calendar. The dispute concerning the use of the 'New' (Gregorian) and 'Old' (Julian) calendar had started in the Russian Church at the turn of the twentieth century. The issue divided Orthodox clergy and laypeople all over the Russian Empire, as well as in Finland, where the OCF decided to switch to the Gregorian calendar in 1921. In general, Russian-speakers stuck to the Julian calendar, but so did several Karelian communities, due to having close-at-hand connections with Russians, particularly in the most south-easterly parishes of Salmi and Suojärvi (Laitila 2004: 193–202).

For a few years, both calendars were used. The practice was approved by Constantinople. In the mid-1920s, the OCF leadership, heavily supported by the Finnish state, authorised the Gregorian calendar only, including for the Paschalion. Thus the Church detached itself from the 'mixed'[2] or 'Revised Julian' calendar, which was at that time adopted by several other Orthodox Churches on the initiative of the Patriarchate of Constantinople. In Finnish-language parishes the change went almost unnoticed, but Russian-speakers and many monks in the Valaam and Konevets monasteries protested. To begin with the latter, the joint operations of the OCF and the Finnish government forced the monks, who all seem to have been Russians, to give up (Frilander 1997). Rebellious monks with Finnish citizenship (they had had to apply for citizenship after Finnish independence), totalling 37, were removed from official monastic duties. Those who were not Finnish citizens, altogether 17, were expelled or volunteered into the Soviet Union or the Kingdom of Serbs, Croats, and Slovenes (Yugoslavia) (Panteleimon 1989: 287; Kilpeläinen 2000: 198). Those Russian-speaking members of the OCF not willing to conform to the Church's policy left and established two parishes of their own: Pokrova[3] (founded in 1926 in Vyborg, later moved to Helsinki) and St Nicholas (founded in 1927 in Helsinki). Both joined the ROC's Exarchate in Western Europe, headed by the Paris-based Metropolitan Evlogii. He joined the Patriarchate of Constantinople in the early 1930s. In 1945 the ROC asked the two parishes in Finland to return to her fold, which they did – as did Valaam, which remained under the

---

[2] The mixed calendar follows the Gregorian calendar, but counts the moving feasts around Easter according to the Julian or Meletian system.

[3] The parish's original name in Finnish was Yksityinen kreikkalais-katolinen kirkollinen yhdyskunta Viipurissa ('A Private Greek-Catholic Church Community in Vyborg'), which was changed to its current form on 18 August 2004.

Moscow Patriarchate until 1957 (Koukkunen 1982: 81–99; Baschmakoff and Leinonen 2001: 170–71).

Throughout the 1920s and 1930s, internal migration of the settled Orthodox population in Finland was low. Although refugees might occasionally remind the Lutheran Finns of the existence of the Orthodox in the country, the withdrawal of the Russian military had created an impression that there were no people of 'foreign' religion in independent Finland. Also some of the Orthodox buildings, above all some military churches, were transformed, either in order to be used for other purposes, for example as a public library (in Hämeenlinna), or completely destroyed (as in Mikkeli), thereby reducing the 'foreign' element in Finnish cityscapes (Raivo 1996: 114–17).

To sum up, the Russian refugees did not much affect the number of OCF members. But it seems evident that they intensified the cultural war that the OCF leadership was waging against Russian elements, or should we say, remnants, within Finnish Orthodox Church life. This, in turn, had concrete effects on the OCF. Russian-speaking members either voluntarily left or were forced to leave the Church, thus turning the internal divisions of the Church along ethnic and linguistic lines into an external fact: by the outbreak of World War II, the OCF had been effectively Finnicised and the Russian-speakers had been marginalised or forced out.

The Second World War and Loss of the Karelian Orthodox Heartland

The Second World War broke out in Finland in November 1939. The 105 days of the Winter War began with an undeclared offensive by the Soviets and came to an end in March 1940 with the Moscow Peace Treaty. During the war, some 420,000 Karelians, of which roughly 55,000 were Orthodox, had to leave their homes. The OCF lost two monasteries, one convent and the patrimony of 17 parishes, valued at up to 90 per cent of the total property of the Church. After some further transfers, in late 1940 the Orthodox evacuees were settled in areas of the middle region of Finland, reaching from the eastern province of Savonia to the western shores of the province of Ostrobothnia. Temporary parish centres were established to continue the work of those left on the Soviet side (Koukkunen 1982: 59–66).

This 'first resettlement' of Karelians particularly alarmed Finns in the coastal areas, where a substantial part of the population were Swedish-speaking. The matter has been studied only summarily, but it seems that in western parts of Finland, independently of their religion, Karelians were less welcomed than in eastern Finland. Furthermore, Orthodox people were also targeted due to their 'foreign' religion. However, the main reason for the hostility was not religion,

Population Movements and Orthodox Christianity in Finland 161

but a governmental order to accommodate the evacuees and, later, to yield them some farmland to secure their livelihoods (Prauda 2012).[4]

The resettlement of the Orthodox impacted not only population statistics but also religious geography. Let us provide a few examples. The Orthodox needed new places of worship to replace the lost ones. In many cases they could use Lutheran churches or local schools, but occasionally they had difficulties finding a place in which to officiate services. Moreover, the teaching of Orthodox religion in schools had to be organised – religion being one of the compulsory subjects. Here the problem was not where to teach, but how to find enough teachers. In Karelia, the Orthodox had been a compact group, but now they were scattered all over Finland, which increased the need for teachers of religion (Koukkunen 1982: 62–6).

Finland embarked on a war again in June 1941. The Continuation War was launched to recapture lost territories and to support the German large-scale offensive against the Soviets. Karelian evacuees started to return to the reconquered Karelia in the autumn of 1941, and by next spring about half of them, some 200,000, were already back in their former homelands (Koukkunen 1982: 66). The rest followed during the next 12 months. The returnees were able to stay in Karelia until early summer of 1944, when the Soviet general offensive forced the Finnish Army to retreat. Karelians were re-evacuated and, again, resettled into about the same areas as in 1940 (Laitinen 1995). The reconquered areas, as well as Salla and Petsamo in Lapland, were lost to the Soviet Union, which was officially confirmed in the Moscow Armistice of 1944 and the Paris Peace Treaty of 1947.

Local reactions to this 'second resettlement' were approximately the same as to the first one. Culturally the Orthodox were still considered more foreign than the Lutheran Karelian majority. In addition to those already mentioned, one further reason for this could be that, with the exception of the Karelians themselves, by 1944 Finns no longer cherished hopes of gaining Karelia back. Most people were convinced that the Karelian evacuees were there to stay, and not everyone was willing to accept them as their neighbours. This was particularly true with the Orthodox, who in some places were considered to be 'Russkies' (in Finnish, 'ryssä', a pejorative term for 'Russian'). Usually such name-calling was restricted to less official occasions; between grown-ups, it largely faded away over the course of the 1940s. But in schools and among children it continued throughout the 1950s, and sometimes even later (Hämynen 1996: 24–8).

Karelian resettlement was a huge task as the number of evacuees was about 10 per cent of total population of Finland. About half of them were agriculturalists, who were given small plots of land in different parts of the country. The rest found their way more independently into towns and other localities (Kirkinen,

---

[4]   On the first resettlement in general see Laitinen 1995: 52–62.

162 *Orthodox Identities in Western Europe*

Nevalainen and Sihvo 1994: 470–80). As stated above, roughly 12 per cent of the evacuees were Orthodox and their dislocation made Orthodoxy permanently a nationwide religion.

Post-war Reconstruction

The first quarter of a century following the war was a period of reconstruction for the OCF. The temporary relocation system of lost parishes was abolished at the end of 1949. The new parish system, effective from 1 January 1950, retained the two dioceses[5] of Karelia (relocated from the lost Karelian town of Sortavala to Kuopio in eastern Finland) and Vyborg (now relocated to Helsinki and bearing the name of the Finnish capital) and divided them into 25 parishes. The site of the archbishopric was settled on Kuopio. Some 40 new churches were built and the monastic life for monks and nuns was reassigned to two adjacent places (New Valamo – in Russian 'Valaam' – for men, and New Lintula for women) in Heinävesi, near Kuopio, as all the existing premises of Orthodox monasteries were now in Soviet Karelia or Petsamo (Raivo 1996: 166–8, 188–9).

In terms of social and cultural interaction, the loss of Karelia and the resettlement of the Orthodox population meant the dissolution of rather tightly knit Karelian Orthodox communities, except for in a few places in south-eastern Finland, as well as the loss of a sense of a particular Karelian identity. Karelians in general, and the Orthodox Karelians in particular, had to recreate an identity in their interactions with the culturally and, in the Orthodox case, religiously foreign Finnish majority (Kananen 2010).

For the OCF the resettlement had several consequences. It had to re-establish itself as a Finnish Church for the inhabitants of western and southern Finland. It had to fight for the preservation of the Orthodox faith among its members – mixed marriages in which the Orthodox spouse embraced Lutheranism were common – as well as for Religious Education (RE) in schools. As mentioned above, instruction in RE was compulsory, but its teaching depended on the number of pupils; only if there were a certain number of Orthodox pupils could they be taught in their own confession. Otherwise they had to participate in Lutheran classes. The required minimum quota per school was 20 – or, since 1958, 8 – pupils (Koukkunen 1982: 119–22).

The resettlement of the Orthodox population also led to an internal change. Until 1945, most Orthodox town parishes in western and southern Finland had had either a Russian-speaking majority or a substantial Russian minority. During the early post-war decades, and increasingly since the 1960s, Karelian Orthodox

---

[5] In 1980, the Helsinki diocese was divided into the (northern) Oulu and (southern) Helsinki dioceses.

evacuees headed for these towns. Thus Russians were pushed more and more to the background (if they ever were in the forefront in the independent Finland). However, the stain of foreignness did not fade away; it merely started to become somewhat exotic (see, for example, Piiroinen 2002).

For the OCF perhaps the greatest change – and also challenge – indirectly caused by resettlement was mixed marriages. In the three decades following the war, up to 90 per cent of Orthodox marriages involved a Lutheran partner. This endangered the future and vitality of Orthodoxy and greatly concerned the church leadership and the clergy. In addition, due to social pressure many parents baptised their children into the Lutheran Church and preferred a Lutheran to an Orthodox religious upbringing for them (Huotari 1975: 1–13, 159).

Consequently the OCF membership was in decline, as something approaching 1 per cent of its membership was lost annually from the early 1950s to the late 1980s, when the numbers leaving the Church decreased (see Figure 8.1). The number of those joining the Church started to exceed those leaving it by the late 1970s (Nguyen 2007).

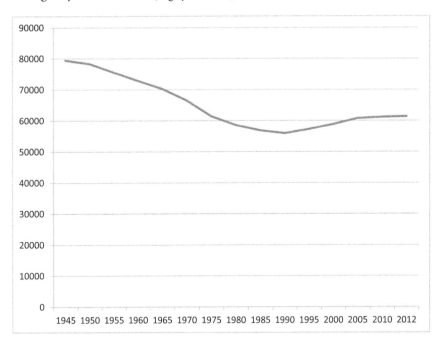

Figure 8.1 Membership in the Orthodox Church of Finland 1945–2012. The figure also includes members residing outside of Finland. Source: OCF Statistics.

In addition to mixed marriages and social pressure, the decrease of members may be explained by post-war social and economic changes that affected Finland as a whole. Until the early 1950s, Finland had been a mainly agrarian country, but over the following two decades a rapid process of urbanisation and industrialisation took place. These societal changes led to a 'third resettlement' for many Orthodox, as they followed others moving from the countryside to regional cities, and even abroad, as employment opportunities in rural areas were declining. Two thirds of those who were born in the former Finnish Karelia or who were their descendants were urban dwellers by the end of the 1980s, indicating a somewhat higher tendency for internal migration than among the rest of the population (Kirkinen, Nevalainen and Sihvo 1994: 478–80). Sweden had become a major destination for Finns, and these migrants also included Orthodox. It has been estimated that at the end of the 1950s there were 2,500 Finnish Orthodox in Sweden, a figure that grew to 6,000 by the end of the 1970s (Korkiasaari 2000: 425–7).

The third resettlement made Karelian Orthodoxy an urban and, thereby more broadly a Finnish, phenomenon. The late Archbishop Paavali (d. 1988), for example, emphasised that Orthodoxy is not only for the Karelians.[6] This happened at the same time that the popular view of Orthodoxy began to change; the 'Russian' image turned predominantly into a more 'oriental' one, be it Byzantine or otherwise. We see this shift as part of the global cultural and religious trends that began in the western world, beginning in the late 1960s, including the growth of new religious movements (NRMs), New Age and other new forms of spirituality.

In Finland, NRMs and New Age did not initially become very popular (Junnonaho 1996: 33–9). Instead, particularly younger intellectuals (artists, writers, etc.) found Orthodox mysticism and aesthetics through icons, which had become increasingly popular among Lutherans since the early 1970s, and via the New Valamo Monastery. The latter had since the 1950s been predicted to die out with the decease of the last Russian-born monks. Instead, a few Finns, many of them converts, took over its management, with the result that the dedication of the new main church in the summer of 1977 gathered hundreds of people and became a national feast. Since then the monastery, together with its Cultural Centre (opened in 1984 and organising exhibitions and national and international conferences, including inter-confessional ones) and Folk High School (starting in 1986 with short courses gathering annually some 2,500 students) became an increasingly popular spiritual (tourist) destination and resort, leading many to embrace Orthodoxy (Niinisalo 2005).

---

[6] Arkkipiispa Paavali Ilomantsissa: Ortodoksisuus ei ole tarkoitettu vain karjalaisille. *Aamun Koitto*, 17 (1985): 301.

Post-Cold War Immigration and Church Growth

Before the end of the Cold War at the turn of the 1990s and the collapse of the Soviet Union in 1991, immigration to Finland had been modest. In 1990, the republic had 26,200 foreign nationals and 63,000 people born in a foreign country. These figures grew to 168,000 foreign nationals and 248,100 foreign-born in 2010, as well as to some 130,000 Finland-born children with at least one immigrant parent. Hence, the share of the first and second-generation immigrants in the Finnish population was about 7 per cent by the 2010s and growing (Statistics Finland 1990–2011; Martikainen, Saari and Korkiasaari 2013: 48).

During the 1990s and 2000s, international migration has been a driving force in religious change in Finland in general. As East European migration, especially from the territories of the former Soviet Union and former eastern bloc countries, accounted for up to 40 per cent of all immigrants living in Finland in 2010, it is evident that among the migrants are many of an Orthodox background (Martikainen 2013: 4–5).

At least the following migration-related changes in the Finnish Orthodox scene can be identified so far. First, both the OCF and two ROC parishes, St Nicholas and Pokrova, received many new immigrant members from Russia, but also from other countries. Second, the presence of new Orthodox immigrants – of whom only a portion have joined existing parishes – is more significant in certain areas, particularly in the Helsinki region, in some larger cities in western and central Finland, and in south-eastern Finland. Third, the parishes have started liturgical, educational and other activities in Church Slavonic/Russian and, to some extent, other languages, to serve the immigrants and in order to gain new members. For example, several parish papers include Russian-language information on activities, and parishes with substantial Russian immigrant populations have services in Church Slavonic, too.[7] Fourth, the activities of the ROC, and other Orthodox Churches, have been on the rise in Finland. This had led to the formation of an unspecific number of ROC-related parish-type religious groups in some towns with immigrants of Russian origin.[8] Also, a small congregation, called Spaso-Preobrazhenskaya (the Transfiguration of Christ), was founded in the city of Tampere in 1994 by a Russian immigrant. The congregation has about 25 members and has been part of the Russian Orthodox

---

[7] See *Aamun Koitto*, 10 (1993): 18–19; 20 (1993): 6–7; 15 (1996): 11–13; 17 (1997): 18–20; 11 (2002): 10.

[8] In September 2008, the ROC consecrated a church (to St Alexander Nevsky) in Pori, on the south-western coast of Finland. In practice this meant the establishment of a new parish. See *Aamun Koitto*, 17 (2008): 8. There has been similar activity in some other parts of Finland as well, for example in the southern Finnish cities of Turku and Tampere, and in Kuopio in eastern-central Finland. See *Aamun Koitto*, 1 (2002): 28; 3 (2002): 20; *Analogi*, 5 (2004): 2, 5.

166 *Orthodox Identities in Western Europe*

Church Outside of Russia (Ketola 2008: 53–4). In 2004, the Ethiopian Orthodox Tewahedo Community ('Ortodoks Tewahdo yhdyskunta' in Finnish) was also founded, a member of the Ethiopian Orthodox Tewahedo Church (belonging to the non-Chalcedonian, or 'Oriental Orthodox' communion of churches) (Miettinen 2011; Finlex 2013).

Let us take a closer look at the effects of immigration on the OCF membership. As we stated above, migration has increased the number of registered members in both the OCF and the two ROC parishes. As Table 8.2 illustrates, the share of foreign-born members has grown in the OCF from 3 per cent in 1990 to 11 per cent in 2009. The proportional rise has been even larger in the Pokrova and St Nicholas parishes: from 800 (18 per cent foreign-born) in 1990 to 2,200 members (57 per cent foreign-born) in 2009. The table clearly indicates that the rise in membership is due to immigration, as the share of foreign-born has constantly been on the rise.

Table 8.2   Registered members and the share of foreign-born members in the Orthodox Church of Finland and the Russian Orthodox Church parishes from 1990 to 2009. Source: Statistics Finland.[9]

	The Orthodox Church of Finland		ROC Parishes	
	Members	Foreign-born (%)	Members	Foreign-born (%)
1990	52,627	3	800	18
1995	53,883	4	887	26
2000	55,692	6	1,115	40
2005	57,829	9	1,705	52
2009	58,539	11	2,226	57

A closer look at the linguistic diversity of members in the OCF and the ROC parishes shows that Russian is by far the most significant language for non-national language speakers.[10] Russian accounted for 80 per cent of all foreign-language speakers among the OCF and 94 per cent among the ROC parishes in 2008. However, within the OCF there are also several smaller language groups that most likely represent (former) members of several other national

---

[9]   The data in Tables 8.2–8.4 are unpublished and were provided to the authors by Statistics Finland upon request.

[10]   The official languages in Finland are Finnish, Swedish and Sami. The figures on language are based on information that is declared by parents at birth, and in the case of immigrants, when they register for permanent residency in Finland. It is allowed to declare only one language, and it most likely refers both to identification with and knowledge of the language. See Latomaa, Pöyhönen, Suni and Tarnanen 2013: 166–7.

Population Movements and Orthodox Christianity in Finland 167

Orthodox Churches, including the Romanian, Greek and Serbian. This is a new phenomenon, even though there certainly have been individual non-Finnish or non-Russian Orthodox in the past, too.[11]

Table 8.3   Members by registered language in the Orthodox Church of Finland and the Russian Orthodox Church parishes in Finland in 2008. Source: Statistics Finland.

Language	The Orthodox Church of Finland	ROC Parishes
National languages total	**51,615**	**603**
Finnish	50,824	548
Swedish	708	55
Sami	83	...
Foreign languages total	**6,830**	**1,488**
Russian	5,450	1,400
Romanian	279	...
Greek	206	...
Serbo-Croatian	113	...
Estonian	95	25
Ukrainian	93	40
Tigrinya	89	...
Bulgarian	80	...
Amharic	70	...
Arabic	55	...
English	43	...
Armenian	36	...
Macedonian	23	...
Georgian	22	...
German	15	...
Serbian	15	...
Belarusian	15	...
Languages total	**58,445**	**2,091**

Note: The symbol '...' was used in the original source to indicate fewer than 10 individuals in a particular language group.

---

[11]   Antero Leitzinger names several majority Orthodox nationalities in his overview of foreigners in Finland, but does not discuss closer their religious affiliations: Leitzinger 2008a.

The share of new immigrants varies greatly between different parishes, as shown in Table 8.3. The greatest shares are to be found in the OCF and two ROC Helsinki parishes, the region where most immigrants live, and in the OCF Lappeenranta and Hamina parishes located in south-eastern Finland close to the Russian border. The smallest shares are found in eastern, central-interior and northern Finland. Thereby the presence of new immigrant members largely represents the general distribution of Russian immigrants in Finland (Martikainen, Saari and Korkiasaari 2013: 40).

Table 8.4   Registered members in the Orthodox Church of Finland and the Russian Orthodox Church parishes by country of birth in Finland in 2009, as a percentage. Source: Statistics Finland.

Orthodox Parishes	Total	Country of birth (%)	
		Finland	Abroad / Unknown
The Orthodox Church of Finland	**58,539**	**89**	**11**
Hamina	1,212	75	25
Helsinki	18,794	85	15
Hämeenlinna	1,072	94	6
Iisalmi	1,172	98	2
Ilomantsi	1,049	97	3
Joensuu	5,550	95	5
Jyväskylä	2,278	90	10
Kajaani	1,781	92	8
Kiuruvesi	464	91	9
Kotka	861	83	17
Kuopio	3,891	97	3
Lahti	2,383	91	9
Lappeenranta	1,782	72	28
Lappi	1,060	96	4
Lieksa	695	99	1
Mikkeli	1,010	86	14

Nurmes	1,138	98	2
Oulu	2,208	91	9
Rautalammi	915	99	1
Taipale	1,774	98	2
Tampere	2,737	87	13
Turku	2,618	81	19
Vaasa	947	80	20
Varkaus	1,130	96	4
Lintula Monastery	11	100	0
Valamo Monastery	7	–	–
ROC Parishes	**2,199**	**43**	**57**
Pokrova	358	53	47
St Nicholas	1,841	41	59
Orthodox total	**60,738**	**87**	**13**

The figures in Tables 8.2–8.4 represent only those migrants of Orthodox background who have officially joined the OCF or ROC parishes. There are most likely many more Orthodox immigrants who have not become members of the churches. So far the only representative survey among immigrants from countries with significant Orthodox populations, including questions on religious participation and belonging, was conducted by Statistics Finland in 2002. In the survey, 30 per cent of the Russians and 9 per cent of the Estonians declared Orthodoxy as important for them (Pohjanpää, Paananen and Nieminen 2003: 222). In 2011, there were altogether 89,000 people born in Estonia (29,500), Russia (9,000) or the former Soviet Union (50,500), which, together with other immigrants from Orthodox majority societies, suggests that in Finland there might be between 20,000 and 30,000 immigrants with Orthodox backgrounds. In terms of actual membership, there were 7,680 registered foreign-born members in the OCF and ROC parishes in 2009 (Statistics Finland 2013).

The increasingly multi-ethnic and multi-language membership has already manifested itself since the 1990s in some OCF parishes. Besides the already-mentioned increasing usage of Russian and Church Slavonic, some other developments have taken place. In the Helsinki parish of the OCF, home to some one third of all OCF members, small-group activity takes place in the

170   *Orthodox Identities in Western Europe*

English, Greek and Serbian languages, as well as among Eritrean and Ethiopian immigrants (Helsingin Ortodoksinen Seurakunta 2002: 23–4). The Helsinki Parish also hosts the International Orthodox Community, St Isaac of Nineveh, which arranges, among other things, English-language events and twice a year publishes the *St Isaac's News*, an English-language newsletter, as well as forming networks around the country (Martikainen 2013: 128–9). Also, in the Orthodox Parish of Turku, services are held in Romanian language by the Romanian-born parish priest, and small-group activities directed at Ethiopian immigrants have been set up.[12]

In the Finnish public debate, however, the rising number of Orthodox immigrants has not received any great attention, even though it has occasionally been mentioned. Rather, in continuation of the above-mentioned changes starting in the 1970s, the OCF is seen in a positive light by the majority as a national, that is to say, Finnish, church. According to surveys on Finnish attitudes to different religions, Orthodoxy was seen in positive light by 50 per cent of Finns in 1989 and by 65 per cent in 2008, thereby being almost on par with the majority Lutheran Church. Furthermore, among those with a negative view of religions, Orthodoxy scored the least as it was negatively viewed by only by 7 per cent in 1989 and 3 per cent in 2008 (Ketola 2010: 45–6). So the changes in the ethnicity of the OCF membership have not changed its public image as a 'Finnish' Church. However, for other reasons, mainly related to internal disputes on economic issues and the allegedly authoritarian governance of the OCF, the public image of the Church has begun to tarnish over the past few years.[13]

Conclusion: Identities of the Orthodox Population and the OCF in the Republic of Finland

Over the soon-to-be 100-year history of the Republic of Finland, the Finnish Orthodox have never constituted a compact group, either territorially or in terms of identity. Territorially, until the Second World War, the Orthodox made up a majority in a few Karelian municipalities on the north-eastern shores of

---

[12] Personal information to Martikainen from the Orthodox Parish in Turku, autumn 2010. Other parishes having personnel with an immigrant background include Ilomantsi (south-eastern Finland; a Greek-origin priest), Tampere (central-southern Finland; a youth worker of Serbian origin, who speaks Russian too) and Varkaus (eastern Finland; a Romanian-origin priest). Personal communication to Laitila, March 2013.

[13] For example: Mitro Repo tarjoaa tuuletusta. *Demari*, 14 May (2009). Available at: http://www.demari.fi/arkisto?id=5731 [accessed 8 March 2013]; Valamon luostarin johtaja vaihtuu. *Helsingin Sanomat*, 9 November (2011). Available at: http://www.hs.fi/kotimaa/Valamon+luostarin+johtaja+vaihtuu++edess%C3%A4+tiukka+talouskuuri/a1305549006183 [accessed 9 March 2013].

Lake Ladoga, whilst in the Karelian Isthmus the Orthodox were overwhelmingly Russian. Elsewhere, the Karelian Orthodox were an important minority in some areas of the present-day south-eastern Finland. Elsewhere, if they existed at all, they constituted a tiny minority incorporating a substantial number of Russians (in Vyborg and some larger cities outside Karelia) or Skolt Sami (in Petsamo).

This territorial division has been coupled with a relative ignorance among the Lutheran Finnish of the Karelian Orthodox majority, a racially-coloured despising or hatred of the Russian Orthodox as 'Bolsheviks' (with no particular distinction being made between Russians in the USSR and in Finland), and a similarly racially-motivated contempt for the few hundred Skolt Sami (and the Sami in general) as a kind of 'Untermenschen' (Shenshin 2008; Lehtola 2012). Thus, when a large majority of Karelians and Skolt Sami had to migrate during and after World War II, they arrived in a foreign territory and faced various sorts of prejudice, including those which identified them as (culturally and ethnically) 'Russians'. Or, to put it another way, from the (Lutheran) Finnish viewpoint all Orthodox communities had one – foreign – identity, whereas in fact they were constituted of several different ethno-religious identities. This variety has thus far been almost completely neglected in studies of Orthodoxy in Finland.

What, then, were these Orthodox identities? Until the early years of Finnish independence a proportion of Karelians identified themselves as Russians on the basis that they had a common religion. In other words, separation from Lutherans, whom the Orthodox called 'ruotši' (Swedes, i.e. foreigners), was for them more important than a common Finnic background. On the other hand, a substantial proportion of the Karelian Orthodox, among them some leading figures, considered political differentiation from Russians to be the most important thing and allied themselves with the Finns – for example, by emphasising Finnish in place of Church Slavonic as the language of services. The latter identification gained momentum between the world wars, partly due to strong pressure from the Finnish government. Russian identity, which linked religion and ethno-cultural features, was downplayed among the Karelians, whereas the Skolt Sami identity, similarly making no particular distinction between faith and nationality, was not even discussed until the 1980s (Saarinen 1994).

The OCF emphasis on exclusively Finnish, and for a while after World War II also Karelian, identity had two important consequences. The first was that official Orthodox self-identification as Finns or Karelians increasingly separated them from the Russian Orthodox and Slavic heritage as a consequence of the claim that being Karelian was identical with being Orthodox, and that Karelian Orthodoxy had direct Byzantine roots, uncontaminated by Slavic influences (Kirkinen 1987: 28–66, 165–205; Laitila 2004: 225–43, 333–41). However, until around the 1970s, Lutheran Finns passed this by almost without noticing; if they bothered to ponder the matter at all, they dismissed the Orthodox as

Russians, or claimed that by living in Finland they should become 'Finns' (that is, Lutherans). Their disregard of the distinct Karelian identity of 'Orthodox Finns' was evidently a shock to the evacuees, and one reason why, after World War II, they left the OCF *en masse* and adopted a sort of lukewarm Lutheran identity (Prauda 2012).

The second consequence had to do with the Russian Orthodox identity. As we mentioned above, those who could not accept the Finnicisation of the OCF and the demolition of its Russian heritage severed ties with the OCF, established their own parishes (Pokrova and St Nicholas) and created an identity of their own. Those who accepted the OCF policy, among them the monk, and later archbishop, Paavali (née Georgii Gusev) either fully adjusted to the OCF and the Karelian, or Finnish, identity, or adopted additional new identities (such as Swedish, which had high status in Finnish society).

In the manner of many diasporas, after World War II the Karelian Orthodox re-created their lost territorial identity on the basis of images, customs and memories: since 1945 they have published countless recollections of (an idealised) life in forfeit Karelia. Thus the lost heartland was substituted with a sort of imagined homeland. This development was supported by a cultural fashion for Karelian, or Orthodox, things and customs, such as Karelian dresses and foods, and the use of icons, which has also spread among many Lutherans. Consequently, instead of a concrete territory and everyday mutual interaction, the 'Finnish' (or often, re-Karelianised) Orthodox now based their identity on an allegedly shared, but fictitious, Karelian tradition made up of memories, habits and rituals, including Orthodox services and ceremonies. This Karelian nostalgia effectively excluded the Russian and Skolt Sami Orthodoxies, as well as their languages and cultures, from the OCF.

The Karelian nostalgia flourished until roughly the early 1970s, when the acceptance, and even admiration, of Orthodoxy by a substantial number of Lutheran Finns reduced its importance as a basis of identity for the evacuees. At the same time, descendants of the often Lutheran-converted evacuees, who had left the countryside over the past two decades and resettled in urban centres, began to find the OCF and the religion of their grandparents. Interest in Orthodoxy was further fuelled with the reopening of Karelia to tourism from the late 1980s onwards, which in turn resulted in a resurrection of the imagined Karelia. Stories of the lost homeland were revived by evacuees during these visits and became a living history for their grandchildren. These tourist trips to Russian Karelia, although not amounting to an immigration, led to some of the Lutheran-baptised grandchildren joining the OCF. With the additional wave of the above-mentioned Lutheran converts and an increasing number of Orthodox immigrants from the former Soviet Union joining the OCF, the result was that the OCF's membership decline finally converted into an increase during the early 1990s. As we stated above, the same also happened in the two Russian parishes.

The increase of new Orthodox immigrants also rekindled the calendar question, which had been settled once in the late 1920s. As a rule, the new Orthodox immigrants have been accustomed to the 'Old', Julian calendar, whereas the OCF uses the 'New', unmixed, Gregorian one. Despite this difference, immigrants joining the OCF have either not regarded the 'New' calendar as a problem, or they have joined one of the two ROC parishes. However, over the past two decades a few Orthodox, both Finnish and others, who for some reason or another consider the ROC to be the 'true' representative of Orthodoxy, have claimed that the use of the Gregorian calendar is heretical. The accusation has been repeated in some Finnish–Russian interactions, especially in some monasteries, where Finnish Orthodox visitors have been blocked from taking part in services. The dispute was officially settled in OCF–ROC negotiations which took place in the early 2000s,[14] but disagreement on the calendar is still a potential bone of contention, particularly if the ROC authorities decide to get more involved with Orthodox immigrants in Finland.

In spite of positive signs in the encounters between the immigrants and the OCF, it seems obvious that the Church still faces major challenges. First, in response to the increase of Russian immigrants, a revived interest in 'Karelian nostalgia' has also taken place among many church members, which has strengthened Finnish and Karelian identifications. Second, the Church has been slow to develop any large-scale or coherent work or mission among immigrants, as most of the initiatives have been taken by individual parishes. Therefore, although several thousand immigrants have found their way to the Church, many more might have either discovered it abroad or, perhaps, even do not know of its existence. The 'concessions' that the OCF has launched (increase in the use of Russian in communication and of Church Slavonic in services, support of priests fluent in Russian in parishes with substantially immigrant populations) may slowly reach them, too. However, these measures might not be enough. In order to become a Church for the numerous Russian immigrants, the OCF needs to rethink its 'official' historical identities (Finnish, Karelian and Byzantine), to accept its Slavic past also and, for the first time since the early 1920s, to figure out how to coexist with a foreign, particularly Russian, immigrant population and the gradually growing ROC.

---

[14] *Aamun Koitto*, 17 (2005): 12–13.

174   *Orthodox Identities in Western Europe*

Acknowledgements

Tuomas Martikainen has written this text in association with the Åbo Akademi University Centre of Excellence in Research PCCR – Post-Secular Culture and a Changing Religious Landscape. We would like to thank Matti Saari from Statistics Finland for his help in obtaining statistics on contemporary Orthodox immigrants, Harri Tajakka from the Synodal Office of the OCF for statistics on the OCF membership, Kimmo Ketola from the Church Research Institute on data of Finnish attitudes towards different religions and Antero Leitzinger for checking some of the historical data.

Bibliography

Aamun Koitto ['The Dawn', semi-official magazine of the OCF]. 1958, 1962, 1980, 1986, 1993, 1996, 1997, 2002, 2005, 2008.

Aamun Koitto. 1985. Arkkipiispa Paavali Ilomantsissa: Ortodoksisuus ei ole tarkoitettu vain karjalaisille. *Aamun Koitto*, 17 (1985): 301.

Ambrosius (Fr) and Haapio, M. (eds). 1982. *Ortodoksinen kirkko Suomessa*. 3rd edition. Heinävesi: Valamon Luostari.

Analogi [Joint magazine for the Orthodox parishes in Hamina, Hämeenlinna, Kotka, Lahti, Lappeenranta, Tampere and Turku]. 2004.

Baschmakoff, N. and Leinonen, M. 2001. *Russian Life in Finland 1917–1939: A Local and Oral History*. Studia Slavica Finlandensia 18. Helsinki: Institute for Russian and East European Studies.

Demari. 2009. Mitro Repo tarjoaa tuuletusta. *Demari*, 14 May (2009). Available at: http://www.demari.fi/arkisto?id=5731 [accessed 8 March 2013].

Finlex 2013. Opetusministeriön päätös Etiopian Ortodoks Tewahdo yhdyskunta -nimisen uskonnollisen yhdyskunnan merkitsemisestä uskonnollisten yhdyskuntien rekisteriin. Available at: http://www.finlex.fi/fi/laki/alkup/2004/20040674 [accessed 14 March 2013].

Frilander, T. 1997. Ajanlaskukysymys ja Suomen kansallistuva ortodoksinen kirkko 1923–1927. *Ortodoksia*, 46: 80–103.

Hämynen, T. 1993. *Liikkeellä leivän tähden: Raja-Karjalan väestö ja sen toimeentulo 1880–1940*. Historiallisia Tutkimuksia 70. Helsinki: Suomen Historiallinen Seura.

Hämynen, T. 1996. 'Ortodoksi, se oli ryssä ilman muuta': Suomen ortodoksien identiteetti 1200-luvulta nykypäiviin. *Aamun Koitto*, 20 (1996): 24–8.

Helsingin Ortodoksinen Seurakunta. 2012. *Vuosikertomus 2011*. Helsinki: Helsingin Ortodoksinen Seurakunta.

Helsingin Sanomat. 2011. Valamon luostarin johtaja vaihtuu. *Helsingin Sanomat*, 9 November (2011). Available at: http://www.hs.fi/kotimaa/

Valamon+luostarin+johtaja+vaihtuu++edess%C3%A4+tiukka+talouskuuri/a1305549006183 [accessed 9 March 2013].

Huotari, V. 1975. *Ortodoksisen ja luterilaisen avioliitto.* Helsinki: Suomalaisen Teologisen Kirjallisuuden Seura.

Hyry, K. 2011. *Meistä jäi taas jälki: Miten Vienan pakolaiset etsivät paikkaansa, kertoivat kokemastaan ja tulivat kuulluiksi 1900-luvun Suomessa.* Acta Universitatis Lapponiensis 199. Rovaniemi: Lapin Yliopisto.

Junnonaho, M. 1996. *Uudet uskonnot – vastakulttuuria ja vaihtoehtoja: Tutkimus TM-, DLM- ja Hare Krishna-liikkeistä suomalaisessa uskonmaisemassa.* Helsinki: Suomalaisen Kirjallisuuden Seura.

Kananen, H. 2010. *Kontrolloitu sopeutuminen: Ortodoksinen siirtoväki sotien jälkeisessä Ylä-Savossa (1946–1959).* Jyväskylä Studies in Humanities 144. Jyväskylä: Jyväskylän Yliopisto.

Katajala, K. 2005. *Suurvallan rajalla: Ihmisiä Ruotsin ajan Karjalassa.* Historiallinen Arkisto 118. Helsinki: Suomalaisen Kirjallisuuden Seura.

Kemppi, H. 1997. Karnalan ja Petsamon ortodoksisten seurakuntien arkkitehtuuri, in *Karjalan ja Petsamon ortodoksiset kirkot ja kirkkotaide,* edited by K. Thomenius and M. Laukkanen. Etelä-Karjalan taidemuseon julkaisuja 18:1b. Lappeenranta: Etelä-Karjalan Museo, 39–165

Ketola, K. 2008. *Uskonnot Suomessa 2008: Käsikirja uskontoihin ja uskonnollistaustaisiin liikkeisiin.* Tampere: Kirkon Tutkimuskeskus.

Ketola, K. 2010. Uskontotilanteen muutos ja suomalaisten suhtautuminen eri uskontoihin. *Uskonnon ylösnousemus: Kirkon, uskonnon ja kulttuurin murros,* edited by T. Martikainen and V. Jalovaara. Helsinki: Magma, 40–51.

Kilpeläinen, H. 2000. *Valamo – karjalaisten luostari?: Luostarin ja yhteiskunnan interaktio maailmansotien välisenä aikana.* Helsinki: Suomalaisen Kirjallisuuden Seura.

Kirkinen, H. 1982. Ortodoksisen kirkon varhaisvaiheita Suomessa, in *Ortodoksinen kirkko Suomessa,* 3rd edition, edited by (Fr) Ambrosius and M. Haapio. Heinävesi: Valamon Luostari, 88–116.

Kirkinen, H. 1987. *Bysantin perinne ja Suomi: Kirjoituksia idän kirkon historiasta.* Joensuu: Ortodoksisen Kirjallisuuden Julkaisuneuvosto.

Kirkinen, H. 1994. Karjalan historia juurista Uudenkaupungin rauhaan, in *Karjalan kansan historia,* edited by H. Kirkinen, P. Nevalainen and H. Sihvo. Porvoo: WSOY, 13–171.

Kirkinen, H., Nevalainen, P. and Sihvo, H. 1994. *Karjalan kansan historia.* Porvoo: WSOY.

Korkiasaari, J. 2000. 1940-luvulta 2000-luvulle, in *Suomalaiset Ruotsissa: Suomalaisen siirtolaisuuden historia 3,* edited by J. Korkiasaari and K. Tarkiainen. Turku: Siirtolaisuusinstituutti, 135–496.

Koukkunen, H. 1968. Kreikkalaiskatolisen kansanopetuksen alkuvaiheet. *Ortodoksia,* 18: 49–88.

176   *Orthodox Identities in Western Europe*

Koukkunen, H.1977. *Suomen valtiovalta ja kreikkalaiskatoliset, 1881–1897*. Joensuu: Joensuun Korkeakoulu.

Koukkunen, H. 1982. *Tuiskua ja tyventä: Suomen ortodoksinen kirkko 1918–1978*. Heinävesi: Valamon Luostari.

Kurkinen, P. 1985. *Venäläiset Suomessa 1809–1917*. Helsinki: Suomen Historiallinen Seura.

Laasonen, P. 2005. *Novgorodin imu: Miksi ortodoksit muuttivat Käkisalmen läänistä Venäjälle 1600-luvulla?*. Historiallisia Tutkimuksia 222. Helsinki: Suomalaisen Kirjallisuuden Seura.

Laitila, T. 2004. *Uskon luotsi: Sergei Okulov Suomen ortodoksien vaiheissa*. Kuopio: Aamun Koitto.

Laitila, T. 2005. Ortodoksikarjalaiset idän ja lännen rajalla: Suomalaisuus, karjalaisuus, venäläisyys ja kansallisen identiteetin rakentaminen, in *Epäluuloista ekumeniaan: Ortodoksisen ja luterilaisen kirkon vuoropuhelu*. Etelä-Karjala-instituutti, Raportti 2, edited by Suvi Niinisalo. Lappeenranta: Etelä-Karjala-instituutti, 107–130.

Laitinen, E. 1995. Vuoden 1945 maanhankintalain synty, sisältö ja toteutus, in *Rintamalta raivioille: Sodanjälkeinen asutustoiminta 50 vuotta*, edited by E. Laitinen. Jyväskylä: Atena, 52–138.

Latomaa, S., Pöyhönen, S., Suni, M. and Tarnanen, M. 2013. Kielikysymykset muuttoliikkeessä, in *Muuttajat: Kansainvälinen muuttoliike ja suomalainen yhteiskunta*, edited by T. Martikainen, P. Saukkonen and M. Säävälä. Helsinki: Gaudeamus, 163–83.

Lehtola, V.-P. 2012. *Saamelaiset suomalaiset: Kohtaamisia 1896–1953*. Helsinki: Suomalaisen Kirjallisuuden Seura.

Leitzinger, A. 2008a. *Ulkomaalaiset Suomessa 1812–1972*. Helsinki: East-West Books Helsinki.

Leitzinger, A. 2008b. *Ulkomaalaispolitiikka Suomessa 1812–1972*. Helsinki: East-West Books Helsinki.

Loima, J. 2001. *Muukalaisina Suomessa: Kaakkoisen Kannaksen kreikkalaiskatoliset venäläisseurakunnat kansallisena ongelmana 1889–1939*. Helsinki: Yliopistopaino.

Martikainen, T. 2004. *Immigrant Religions in Local Society: Historical and Contemporary Perspectives in the City of Turku*. Turku: Åbo Akademi University Press.

Martikainen, T. 2005. New Orthodox Immigration in Finland. *Yearbook of Population Research in Finland*, 41: 117–38.

Martikainen, T. 2013. *Religion, Migration, Settlement: Reflections on Post-1990 Immigration to Finland*. Leiden: Brill.

Martikainen, T., Saari, M. and Korkiasaari, J. 2013. Kansainväliset muuttoliikkeet ja Suomi, in *Muuttajat: Kansainvälinen muuttoliike ja suomalainen yhteiskunta*, edited by T. Martikainen, P. Saukkonen and M. Säävälä. Helsinki: Gaudeamus, 23–54.

Miettinen, D. 2011. Orientaaliortodoksinen seurakunta perustettu Suomeen. *Kotimaa24.fi*. Available at: http://www.kotimaa24.fi/uutiset/kotimaa/5729-orientaaliortodoksinen-seurakunta-perustettu-suomeen [accessed 14 March 2013].

Nevalainen, P. 1999. *Viskoi kuin Luoja kerjäläistä: Venäjän pakolaiset Suomessa 1917–1939*. Helsinki: Suomalaisen Kirjallisuuden Seura.

Nevalainen, P. and Sihvo, H. 1998. *Karjala: Historia, kansa, kulttuuri*. Helsinki: Suomalaisen Kirjallisuuden Seura.

Nguyen, R. 2007. Converts – A Challenge and a Resource for the Church, in *Orthodox Tradition and the 21st Century*, edited by G.S. White and T. Laitila. Joensuu: University of Joensuu, 123–7.

Niinisalo, S. (ed.). 2005. *Ambrosius*. Helsinki: Ortodoksisen Kulttuurikeskuksen Säätiö.

Nokelainen, M. 1999. Suomen ortodoksit ja kansakunnan jäsenyys. *Teologinen Aikakauskirja*, 104(1): 102–107.

Nokelainen, M. 2010. *Vähemmistökirkon synty: Ortodoksisen kirkkokunnan ja valtion suhteiden muotoutuminen Suomessa 1917–1922*. Helsinki: Suomen Kirkkohistoriallinen Seura.

Nygård, T. 1980. *Itä-Karjalan pakolaiset 1917–1922*. Studia Historica Jyväskyläensia 19. Jyväskylä: Jyväskylän Yliopisto.

Nygård, T. 1998. *Erilaisten historia: Marginaaliryhmät Suomessa 1800-luvulla ja 1900-luvun alussa*. Jyväskylä: Atena.

Osmonsalo, E. 1945. Kreikkalaiskatolinen kirkko Suomessa 1800-luvulla: Eräitä piirteitä. *Suomen kirkkohistoriallisen seuran vuosikirja*, 31–32: 267–89.

Panteleimon (Hegumen). 1989. *Valamon paterikon: Luostarin isien elämäkertoja*. Heinävesi: Valamon Luostari.

Piiroinen, P. 2002. (ed.). *Ortodoksisuutta eilen ja tänään: Helsingin ortodoksinen seurakunta 1827–2002*. Helsinki: Helsingin Ortodoksinen Seurakunta.

Pohjanpää, K., Paananen, S. and Nieminen, M. 2003. *Maahanmuuttajien elinolot: Venäläisten, virolaisten, somalialaisten ja vietnamilaisten elämää Suomessa*. Helsinki: Tilastokeskus.

Pratt, M.L. 1992. *Imperial Eyes: Travel Writing and Transculturation*. London: Routledge.

Prauda, P. 2012. *'Isänmaallista yhteydentuntoa syventämään': Siirtolaisiin kohdistuneet asenteet sanomalehti* Ilkassa *sekä* Savon Sanomissa *vuosina 1939–1944*. Unpublished Master's Thesis in Orthodox Church History. Joensuu: Teologian Osasto, Itä-Suomen Yliopisto.

Purmonen, V. (Fr). 1981. *Orthodoxy in Finland: Past and Present*. Kuopio: Orthodox Clergy Association.

178   *Orthodox Identities in Western Europe*

Raivo, P. 1996. *Maiseman kulttuurinen transformaatio: Ortodoksinen kirkko suomalaisessa kulttuurimaisemassa.* Nordia Geographical Publications 25(1). Oulu: Department of Geography, University of Oulu.

Saarinen, T. 1994. Koltat, arktiset ortodoksit: Pieni kansa muutosten keskellä. *Aamun Koitto*, 17 (1994): 8–12.

Shenshin, V. 2008. *Venäläiset ja venäläinen kulttuuri Suomessa: Kulttuurihistoriallinen katsaus Suomen venäläisväestön vaiheista autonomian ajoilta nykypäiviin.* Helsingin Yliopisto: Aleksanteri-Instituutti.

Siikala, A.-L. 2012. *Itämerensuomalaisten mytologia.* Helsinki: Suomalaisen Kirjallisuuden Seura.

Statistics Finland. 1990–2011. Country of Birth According to Age and Sex by Region. Available at: http://pxweb2.stat.fi/database/StatFin/vrm/vaerak/vaerak_en.asp [accessed 12 February 2013].

Statistics Finland. 2013. Population by Religion and Country of Birth 2009. Unpublished Statistics (provided to the authors upon request).

Tegborg, L. (ed.). 2002. *Sveriges kyrkohistoria, 4: Enhetskyrkans tid.* Stockholm: Verbum.

Ulkoasiainministeriö [Ministry for Foreign Affairs]. 1923. *Suomen ja Venäjän välisten Tartossa pidettyjen rauhanneuvottelujen pöytäkirjat kesäk. 12 p:stälokak. 14 p:n 1920.* Helsinki: Ulkoasiainministeriö.

Chapter 9

Orthodox Parishes in Strasbourg: Between Migration and Integration

Guillaume Keller

The history of Orthodox communities in Alsace mirrors the establishment of Orthodox places of worship elsewhere in the West, following the influx of immigrants, and with new parishes organised after the end of Communist regimes in Central and Eastern Europe. This case study on the Orthodox presence in a French city, which also is one of the centres for European institutions, provides a local example of developments and issues for Orthodox Churches in Western Europe as they appear in other chapters of this book.

While Orthodox Christians have been present in Alsace since the beginning of the twentieth century, the first parish was only established after the Second World War. While being part of the French Republic, Alsace keeps local specificities at the legal level: the 1905 law of separation between Church and State has never been enforced and the 1801 Concordat still applies. While Orthodox parishes need to adjust to a specific local legal framework, which seems at first sight not to favour non-recognised religious bodies, in practice both civil authorities and established Churches have expressed a benevolent attitude toward Orthodox groups.

There are today eight such groups with regular celebrations in the Strasbourg area: two parishes under the Patriarchate of Moscow (a Russian-speaking one, with stavropegial status – i.e. directly under the Patriarch – and a French-speaking one), a parish of the Archdiocese of Russian Orthodox Churches under the Ecumenical Patriarchate in Western Europe, as well as Greek, Romanian, Serbian, Bulgarian and Georgian parishes.

This research has been conducted on three lines: interviews with clergy and laypeople active in local Orthodox parishes; a questionnaire circulated in those parishes where it was permitted; and research on the local media in order to identify articles on Orthodox presence in Alsace as well as Orthodox Churches in general. Our research has focused on five of the eight existing parishes. Three have opened their doors: they are those parishes that could be described as best integrated, as well as the best acclimated to the use of the French language (although most parishes include at least a few prayers in French in their celebrations). Two parishes have turned down our request, for various reasons,

180 *Orthodox Identities in Western Europe*

ranging from doubts about the results of a research of that kind to fears that it might create tensions within the respective communities. The two parishes that have been reluctant to agree to the presence of a scholar may also have thus exhibited the persistent legacy of fears going back to the period during which Communist regimes ruled their respective home countries.

Overview of Orthodox Parishes in Strasbourg

The first Orthodox parish was founded in Strasbourg in 1946; it belonged to the Russian Orthodox Church Outside of Russia (ROCOR). The parish lived without any legal status until 1981: it had not registered with the local registry of associations. However, from 1946 to 1981, the local authorities made a hall available to the parish, based merely on verbal agreement and without any formal lease.

Bearing the name of the Church of Christ the Saviour, a major challenge for the parish was the lack of clergy, since there were not many priests available in the Western European Diocese of ROCOR. Until 1974, a priest residing in Belfort travelled to Strasbourg from time to time. Subsequently, priests of various backgrounds served over the years. The parish used to gather around 100 faithful, with 10 to 15 regular churchgoers.

The parish lived through several crises linked to divisions between branches of the Russian Church. In 1995, on his own, a parishioner invited Bishop Guri, then representative of the Moscow Patriarchate in France, to visit the parish: the purpose was to transfer it under the Patriarchate. In 1998, according to minutes of a general assembly, those supporting continuing affiliation with ROCOR used to celebrate liturgies in Church Slavonic on Saturdays, while those in favour of the Russian Exarchate of the Ecumenical Patriarchate did it in French on Sundays. The parish as it was disappeared in 2006. Nevertheless, following the disputes within ROCOR regarding reconciliation with the Moscow Patriarchate, the place continued to be used for some time by a group of people who had rejected the reunion. This group still keeps a few adherents in Strasbourg, but apparently without a stable place for church services.

The French-speaking parish of St John Cassian has its roots in the ROCOR parish. This parish was born out of disputes regarding liturgical language (Church Slavonic or French) as well as jurisdictional affiliation in 1998. While some among the faithful wanted to stay with ROCOR, others inclined toward the Moscow Patriarchate, while a third group finally joined in 2004 the Russian Exarchate of the Ecumenical Patriarchate, with its Parisian headquarters at the famous St Alexander Nevsky Cathedral (Rue Daru). This third group started the French-speaking parish. It gathers twice a month for liturgical celebrations in a Protestant chapel. Among parishioners are found Romanians, descendants of Russian émigrés and several faithful of French origin; a number of people currently attending are students. A feature of the parish is that it includes several mixed couples (Catholic/Orthodox as well as Protestant/Orthodox), who are pleased to be able to attend liturgical celebrations in a language they understand. While the priest himself, like a number of his parishioners, has a Romanian background, he celebrates in French if there are French-speaking persons present, and otherwise in Romanian. On average, there are some 30 people, but that number can go up to 100 when a major feast is celebrated. This is a more general rule: in all parishes, attendance at least doubles on a feast day.

The birth of the Greek parish of the Three Holy Hierarchs was linked especially to the presence of Greek students at Strasbourg University. One of them wished to become a priest: in 1964, he turned to the Greek Metropolitan and was ordained. In 1965, the city authorities made a place available for holding services. At the city's expense, a room was refitted as a chapel and another one as a classroom for the Greek school for children (teaching of Greek language and catechism).

Keeping Greek as a liturgical language does not only reflect attachment of the parishioners to their national tradition, but it also serves a practical purpose. While Greek Orthodox parishioners in Strasbourg tend to be professionals or medical doctors, with a command of French, some of the faithful, who have a similar profile, come from nearby Kehl, in Germany, and have little knowledge of French. Regular attendance tends to be between 40 and 50 faithful.

The presence of a large university has also played a key role in the birth of the Romanian parish of St John the Baptist. During the second half of the 1970s, Romania reconnected with the practice of student exchanges with the University of Strasbourg, which had been suspended since 1939 due to political circumstances. From 1978 to 1990, several young Romanian theologians received grants from the French Government in order to allow them to come to Strasbourg and prepare for a doctoral degree there; one of them was the current Romanian Patriarch Daniel. Quite naturally, several Romanians settled in the area turned to them for liturgical activities. An association was founded for that purpose in 1984. But caution then marked the life of the community, both between believers and toward the outside world, due to fears inspired by the Communist regime then ruling Romania.

The irony was that the fall of Communism actually threatened the fragile balance existing in the Romanian Orthodox group in Strasbourg. Suddenly, a great number of new immigrants arrived from Romania. The chapel then in use soon became too exiguous. Thanks to the Roman Catholic archbishopric and the Sisters of Mary Reparatrix, the Romanian parish since 2007 has been given the use of a chapel for which – out of Christian solidarity – no rent is required (except for electricity and water costs). Except during holiday periods, the 120 seats in the chapel are all occupied every Sunday. It should also be mentioned that the priest of the Romanian parish serves as a chaplain for Orthodox inmates at the Elsau jail (30 out of 500).

The Serbian parish of St George was born in the 1990s, as the Serbian Orthodox Church was recovering its full freedom thanks to political developments. Serbian parishioners used to be guests first in a Protestant, then in a Catholic chapel. At the beginning, there were some 20 faithful, with a liturgy once a month; but the number soon reached 50. In 2003, thanks to the generosity of a female parishioner, the parish became the owner of a former farmhouse that was refitted into a chapel.

The Bulgarian Orthodox parish of St Cyril, St Methodios and St Benedict of Nursia was formed in December 1997, following a Vespers service at the Greek Church. The Bulgarian group continues to hold its celebrations in the Greek chapel.

The Georgian parish of St Ketevan came into existence around a priest who arrived in Strasbourg in 1998. It holds liturgical services in Georgian every week, but leads a discrete life. Services first took place in the hall of a Protestant church, and today in the chapel of a Catholic church.

Founded in 2003, the Russian parish of All Saints is the most recent. Since 2004, it has enjoyed stavropegial status, directly under the Moscow Patriarchate, due to its role as representation of the Patriarchate to the Council of Europe. Thus its founding was not merely an answer to the presence of Russian-speaking people in Strasbourg, but also reflected the desire of the Russian Church, especially Metropolitan Kirill of Smolensk (who became the Patriarch of Moscow in 2009), to play a role on the international scene, and more specifically in political developments at the European level. Such aspirations require the existence of a 'representative' place of worship in a city such as Strasbourg. The Patriarchate asked the city authorities to make a place available to build a church, in order to replace the converted garage currently used by the parish. On 17 January 2011, the city council unanimously agreed to give to the Russian Orthodox Church a piece of land in a central area of Strasbourg, close to the location of European institutions. The plan of the building has been designed by an architect from St Petersburg. A parish centre will be built next to the church. The building permit was obtained in December 2012. Currently, there are between 40 and 50 faithful attending liturgy on Sunday.

The French-speaking parish of St Gregory Palamas and St Attalia gathers mainly people without an Orthodox background who have embraced the Orthodox faith. The roots of this parish go back to a group of Alsatians who used to visit the Bethany Centre, a retreat centre located in Gorze (Lorraine). This group is led by Fr Alphonse Goettmann, a priest who then belonged to the clergy of the (Western rite) Orthodox Church of France (Église Catholique Orthodoxe de France, abbreviated ECOF), and later joined the Orthodox Church of the Gauls, a group that is not in communion with any canonical

Orthodox Church. The parish was founded in 1985. At that time, it was using the Liturgy of St Germain of Paris. There were around 40 parishioners (more than today).

In 2000, a group of parishes, including the one in Strasbourg, broke with ECOF and formed the Union of Western Rite Religious Associations (Union des Associations Cultuelles de Rite Occidental, UACORO), without having access to a bishop at that time. Deploring the existence of a 'canonical problem at the episcopal level' in the ECOF and 'facing the absence of a higher canonical authority', this group wished to regain communion with all Orthodox Churches and asked the Assembly of Orthodox Bishops of France to make such a move possible. The Assembly laid down various requirements, one of them being to accept and implement the whole liturgical, dogmatic and canonical tradition of the Orthodox Church, such as the celebration of the Liturgy of St John Chrysostom. Each parish was invited to approach one of the Orthodox dioceses existing in France.

Due to some encounters as well as the original Russian legacy of the ECOF, the parish in Strasbourg approached the Russian Church. From 2005, the parish gave hospitality in its chapel to the new, already mentioned Russian parish of All Saints, then freshly founded and without a place of worship. In 2006, the Diocese of Chersonese of the Moscow Patriarchate received the former ECOF parish in its jurisdiction. The deacon was ordained a priest in September 2007 and is the current rector. Some 20 people attend every Sunday. Since 2005, the parish has given up the Western rite and adopted the Byzantine.

While a number of Orthodox monasteries have appeared in France in recent decades, there are none in the local area. The closest is located in Godoncourt (Vosges), where a community of nuns under the Serbian Patriarchate resides.

One of the founders of the Greek parish and the chair of the parish council until 2004, Dr Asterios Argyriou (formerly professor of Modern Greek at Strasbourg University), had supported the idea of a single parish, without national, cultural or linguistic barriers: however, in Strasbourg as everywhere else, this dream faced the desire of each Church to have its own, distinct presence.

Orthodox Parishes and Local Legal Context: The Concordat and Religious Life in Alsace

The Concordat is more than two centuries old (Messner 1997). Regarding the relations between the State and the Roman Catholic Church, it was concluded between Napoleon and Pope Pius VII in 1801. In order to regulate similarly the Protestant religious activity in France, Napoleon had the Organic Articles passed for the Reformed Church and the Church of the Augsburg Confession in 1802. In 1808, following a congress of some hundred Jewish delegates, a

184 *Orthodox Identities in Western Europe*

similar arrangement was entered for them, following the model of the Protestant Consistory (i.e. the equivalent of a bishopric). The Concordat was abolished in France in 1905. At that time, however, the dioceses of Metz and Strasbourg (Alsace-Moselle) were under German control. Following the reintegration of those territories into the French Republic in 1919, after the Second World War, the area has kept and defended its specific legal framework for religious bodies, despite a temporary suspension of the Concordat during Nazi occupation from 1940 to 1945.

The Concordat remains widely supported by local public opinion. In 1998, a survey showed that nearly nine out of ten people saw benefits in keeping it (*Les Dernières Nouvelles d'Alsace* 1998). In 2001, another survey revealed that 66 per cent did not favour the extension of a similar regime to other religious bodies beside the existing beneficiaries. Among the 26 per cent supportive of such an extension, a small majority thought it should be extended to all religions. 18 per cent would like to see such a status granted to Islam (Orthodox Christians were not mentioned as such in the survey).

According to local law, the Concordat system thus applies to Catholic, Lutheran, Reformed and Jewish organised religious life. The clergy of each of those religious bodies has the same status as civil servants (Dagorne and Grisey Martinez 2007). Since Orthodox parishes are not considered as belonging to a statutory religious organisation, they do not belong to that category and have to organise themselves following the pattern of local associative law.[1] Since they do not benefit from a concordat, Orthodox priests are not paid by the State: they often need to have a second job beside their ministry – a situation quite often encountered by Orthodox clergy in Western Europe.

The legal capacity of associations under local law is not restricted: they are entitled to own investment property, receive donations and legacies, and engage legal actions. In Alsace-Moselle, buildings used for the purpose of worship by associations having as their sole purpose the practice of religious rites not belonging to the statutory category are exempted from property taxes.[2] In the same way, buildings used only for worship are exempted from housing taxes.[3]

---

[1] The French law regulating associations (1 July 1901) does not apply to Alsace. Regarding Orthodox parishes, the Greek Orthodox parish of Strasbourg presents a peculiarity, however. It is a subsidiary of the Greek Orthodox Metropolis of France, with headquarters in Paris. The Metropolis has the specific status of a religious association ('association cultuelle', law of 9 December 1905): this means that several French parishes directly attached to the Metropolis do not have a status of association of their own. This explains why the Greek parish in Strasbourg is not registered under the local law. Regarding taxes, both local non-statutory religious associations and religious associations under the law of 1905 ('associations cultuelles') are tax-exempt, insofar as their activity is exclusively that of worship.

[2] Code Général des Impôts (CGI), article 1382-4 (modified 1994).

[3] CGI, article 1407-I-2.

Non-statutory religious associations under the local law may be subsidised by local authorities, to the extent that there is a local public interest to do so (e.g. setting up a place of worship if there are a sufficient number of believers who express such a need).

In principle, local authorities do not have real duties toward Orthodox communities in Alsace-Moselle. Parishes do not receive financial support from local authorities. In practice, however, as we have seen, the authorities have helped Orthodox groups in practising their religion. The most obvious example has been the gift of a piece of land for building a Russian-style church in the city where the European institutions are located (*Les Dernières Nouvelles d'Alsace* 2010). When they visited Strasbourg in 2007, Patriarch Alexy II (since deceased) and the Chairman of the Department of External Relations of the Moscow Patriarchate, Metropolitan Kirill (who is the current Patriarch), asked the city authorities to provide piece of land for building a church. This was agreed by the city council in January 2011, and half a hectare of land was made available.

Under the concordat system, denominational religious teaching is provided in public schools for the 'established' groups, although a majority of pupils at the secondary level now opt out. With no concordat, Orthodox children and teenagers follow catechism in private settings. In both Romanian and Greek parishes, children are taught their national language at a Sunday school. In the Greek parish, this is provided by a teacher who is a Greek civil servant sent by the Ministry: children receive both language training and catechism. In the Romanian parish, the priest's wife – who happens to be a teacher herself – teaches Romanian language as well as a basic knowledge of religions in general and Orthodox catechism. Due to a limited number of children as well as lack of teachers and facilities, most other parishes do not provide such teaching on a regular basis. For instance, at the parish of St John Cassian, some eight children receive catechesis (on the Passion and Resurrection) only twice a year. In this case, it is true that age gaps between the children do not make such collective teaching easy. Moreover, the professional commitments of the priest (who needs to have a secular job) as well as of the faithful make it difficult to find convenient times for meetings. In Strasbourg as in much of the Orthodox diaspora in Western Europe, catechism becomes in fact delegated to parents.

Orthodox Immigrants in Alsatian Environment

The presence of a famous university has attracted Orthodox people to Strasbourg from the 1920s, although this does not seem to have led then to the founding of parishes. Both Catholic and Protestant theology departments offer reputable courses in Patristics, which continue to draw students. From 1927 to 1939, the

Catholic Theology Department of the University (Perrin 2004) maintained a home for Orthodox students and clergy: it was called St Basil College. The Dean of the Department between 1923 and 1945, Msgr Victor Martin, envisioned this college as an appendix to the international seminary (with an opening to Catholics from the Middle East from 1922). Msgr Pierre Dib (1881–1965) was its head. Of Lebanese background, he was convinced of the need to develop good relations with Orthodox Christians. He became the Maronite Bishop of Cairo in 1946 (Ziadé 1967). Unfortunately, no archives of this college are left; a total of some 70 students stayed there.

A significant number of students are found among practising Orthodox at local parishes. A minority of them have come for theological studies. Most of them study at the Catholic Department of Theology, although a few have attended its Protestant counterpart, as Patriarch Daniel did. In the Romanian parish, a majority of parishioners are students. After liturgical services, 10 to 15 of them meet with the priest for discussing various topics. Students of various disciplines can be found in all the other parishes too.

Small groups for ecumenical dialogue gather Orthodox with other Christians in Strasbourg. The existence of the university and the presence of some Orthodox priests willing to engage into ecumenical dialogue offer a favourable ground, although it should be added that the number of participants in such efforts remains a modest one.

One instance is the Group of the Seven Churches (Groupe des Sept Églises), which allows Christians of various denominations in Strasbourg to meet and compare their views on theological subjects, thanks to speakers that include Orthodox Bishops on a pastoral visitation or visiting Orthodox professors of theology. Moreover, a Council of Christian Churches in Strasbourg was launched in March 2002: it gathers representatives from the Catholic, Protestant, Anglican, and Orthodox Churches.

As we could see earlier, local authorities have proved several times to be quite cooperative in assisting parishes looking for a place of worship, such as renovating a place for making it available to the Greek parish or, more recently, giving a piece of land for the building of a Russian church. The peculiar legal situation helps to explain such an open approach. But help in this regard has also come from the mainline (Catholic and Protestant) churches in Alsace, as our short descriptions of several parishes have shown. This makes obvious the fact that the newly arrived Orthodox have been welcomed. It is true that Orthodox communities are not perceived as threatening in any way, be it religiously or socially. They rarely make the headlines of the media, and never in a sensational way.

Looking at the local media, there has been an increase in the (modest) number of articles on Orthodox Churches since the 1990s. According to a local journalist, this may be attributed both to a desire of some Orthodox living in

Alsace to be more visible and to greater curiosity of readers towards Central and Eastern Europe (including Orthodox Churches) after the political changes in those countries. In addition, journalists have started paying more attention to religious groups of immigrants.

The Place of Converts

Among Orthodox faithful in Strasbourg, one does not only come across descendants of people coming from foreign countries or new immigrants: there are also people drawn to the Orthodox Church in the context of spiritual quests, either temporarily or with a lasting anchoring. Some also become Orthodox after marrying an Orthodox spouse. There is no structured Orthodox catechesis for adults in France: Orthodox parishes in Strasbourg tend to use reference works such as *Dieu est vivant* (Catéchèse Orthodoxe 1979), a book that is also used by parents as an help for teaching their children,[4] and the books of the theologian Paul Evdokimov (1901–1970).

According to the priest of the parish of St John Cassian, 'a person who would like to convert to Orthodox Christianity should first participate in liturgical life for three years'. In that parish, all recent converts seem to have been people with Orthodox spouses.

A 70-year-old female parishioner of the French-speaking parish of St Gregory Palamas and St Attalia, who came from a pious Protestant family and joined the Orthodox Church in the mid-1980s, explained that she had been made aware of the Orthodox faith by fellow nurses, themselves converts, who belonged to the newly founded ECOF parish (1985). ECOF has been an easy-access door to Orthodoxy for French-speaking converts, and not only in Strasbourg.

This lady finally became Orthodox, quoting among her reasons 'a disappointment with the lack of asceticism and prayer of the heart, an absence of veneration for the saints and for the Holy Virgin' in her previous religious group. However, she acknowledges that her Protestant past has left a mark: for instance, she says that she tends to be more tolerant than official Orthodox positions on societal issues such as homosexuality or abortion. The parents of this lady witnessed her conversion and were not upset, since she remained a Christian. Her husband followed her. But her children were shocked: they see it as 'much too exotic'.

The interviewee explains that, considering language barriers, she would not have converted had there been no French-speaking parish. On the other hand, in the same parish, the rector's son and four parishioners (aged between 40 and 70)

---

[4]   Several subsequent editions of this book have been published, the most recent one in 2011.

188 *Orthodox Identities in Western Europe*

have in 2010 started attending courses for learning Russian and Church Slavonic, for the purpose of visiting Russia and also being able to take part more often in the services at the Russian parish, which belongs – like their own parish – to the Moscow Patriarchate.

According to people whom we interviewed, there was in Strasbourg between 1995 and 2005 a period with a more clearly marked interest for conversions to the Orthodox Church. There have been fewer conversions in the following years. It is, however, difficult to assess if this is related to local circumstances of the parishes themselves, or to wider social developments. It is also possible that the relatively long waiting time imposed upon potential converts by some priests deters a part of them.

Conclusion

The birth of several new parishes during the past 20 years gives evidence of an expansion of Orthodox presence in Alsace. The presence of a major university as well as European institutions has played an important role in the genesis of several such communities. Otherwise, the lives of these parishes reflect those of a large part of Orthodox communities in Western Europe: priests who often need to have a secular job beside their ministry in order to support themselves; the number of faithful rarely peaking above a few dozen on ordinary Sundays, with a much higher participation at the time of major liturgical feasts. One priest in Strasbourg observed that 'some Orthodox only come to church for the baptism of their child, and then we do no longer see them during several years' – definitely not an Alsatian peculiarity! The role of parishes for newly arrived immigrants is important: fellow believers provide them with help in finding their ways in a new environment.

Also similar to other places in Western Europe, jurisdictional problems have had an impact on the history of some Orthodox parishes in Strasbourg. There have been two changes in diocesan affiliation. The first was in the case of ROCOR parish: after an attempt by a few parishioners to go under Moscow, the parish finally joined the Archdiocese of Russian Orthodox Churches in Western Europe in 2004, while a small group of faithful refused the reconciliation between ROCOR and the Moscow Patriarchate. The other jurisdictional change has been the coming of a former ECOF parish under the Moscow Patriarchate (with an accompanying passage from the Western to the Byzantine rite).

Visibility of Orthodox parishes in Strasbourg is growing. Either with the help of city authorities or on their own, those communities refit or build chapels and churches, which will have over time an impact on the local religious landscape, such as the painted Serbian church in the Koenigshoffen area or – soon – the built-for-purpose Russian church. Relations with other Christian confessions are generally good, as made clear by the way Orthodox groups without a place of worship have been welcomed in Catholic and Protestant churches.

Only two Orthodox parishes in Strasbourg primarily use French in their liturgical services, although most priests are eager to insert at least a few words in French if they notice French-speaking people in attendance. A majority of parishes thus keep their particular liturgical language. As elsewhere in Western Europe, the life of Orthodox communities in Strasbourg remains under the sign of migration: nothing surprising, when considering that half of the parishes were founded after 1990 for serving the needs of new immigrant groups.

Bibliography

Catéchèse Orthodoxe. 1979. *Dieu est vivant: Catéchisme pour les familles*. Paris: Editions du Cerf.

Code Général des Impôts (CGI), article 1382-4 (modified 1994). Available at: http://www.legifrance.gouv.fr/affichCodeArticle.do;jsessionid=6C7C1 0C9A68E074DE9C23097856E26E2.tpdjo05v_1?idArticle=LEGIARTI0 00025092184&cidTexte=LEGITEXT000006069577&categorieLien=id &dateTexte=20140305 [accessed 12 March 2014].

Code Général des Impôts (CGI), article 1407-I-2. Available at: http://www. legifrance.gouv.fr/affichCode.do;jsessionid=6C7C10C9A68E074DE9C2 3097856E26E2.tpdjo05v_1?idSectionTA=LEGISCTA000006179806&c idTexte=LEGITEXT000006069577&dateTexte=20140305 [accessed 12 March 2014].

Dagorne, D. and Grisey Martinez, L. 2007. *Cultes non statutaires et régime associatif des religions*. Séminaire des droits des cultes, Palais Universitaire de Strasbourg, 24 January 2007.

Les Dernières Nouvelles d'Alsace. 1998. Les héritiers du Concordat. *Les Dernières Nouvelles d'Alsace* (9 October 1998).

Les Dernières Nouvelles d'Alsace. 2010. Strasbourg: Le projet d'église orthodoxe prend tournure. *Les Dernières Nouvelles d'Alsace* (1 December 2010).

Messner, F. 1997. Le statut des cultes 'non reconnus' en Alsace-Moselle. *Journal du droit local*, 20 (January): 11–16.

Perrin, L. 2004. Esquisse d'une histoire de la faculté de théologie catholique de Strasbourg. *Revue des sciences religieuses*, 78(1): 125–36.

Ziadé, I. 1967. Monseigneur Pierre Dib: Recteur du collège Saint-Basile à Strasbourg. *Paroles de l'Orient*, 3(1): 25–30.

Chapter 10
Orthodox Priests in Norway: Serving or Ruling?

Berit Thorbjørnsrud

According to Valerie Karras, there is a clericalisation process going on in the Orthodox Church in Europe and the Americas (Karras 2005: 2–3). Inspired by the clericalism that is influential in Western Christianity, Orthodox priests are presumably gaining prominence at the expense of lay people. As this challenges the Orthodox teachings on the roles of clerics and lay people as different but equally important to the functioning of the church, a clearly concerned Karras describes this development as an 'error' and a 'heresy' (Karras 2005: 2–3).

Based on my studies of the Orthodox Church in Norway, I agree with Karras that the priests have become very prominent, in the sense that much of congregational life tends to revolve around them. Whether this amounts to what can be described as clericalism at odds with Orthodox teachings is, however, another question. Karras herself does not provide any clear definition of the clericalisation she fears, but within Western Christianity it is generally understood to involve 'an excessive emphasis on the role of the clergy in the Church's internal affairs', 'clerical elitism' and 'the superiority of the priesthood over the laity' (*The Tablet* 2011).[1] Simply put, clericalisation involves clerics gaining power over lay people (Utgaard 2012: 170).

The Orthodox Church represents a very pluralistic institution, functioning within very different environments, and generalisations should only be made with great care. While Karras' critique may represent a correct analysis of what is happening in the USA, where she works, it does not necessarily follow that it fits the Norwegian terrain. Although the basic understanding of the relationship between priests and lay people is, in principle, shared by all Orthodox, such an understanding still has to be realised within quite different contexts, and consequently this relationship may develop differently. The question of whether there is in fact a clericalisation process going on must be studied empirically. Taking Norway as my case, I will discuss in this chapter the extent to which traces of such clericalisation may be observed.

---

[1] In the Catholic Church too, there are people worrying about a present clericalist backlash, reversing reforms from the Second Vatican Council.

As already mentioned, much of congregational life revolves around clergy. I will argue, however, this seems rather to involve an extension of their duties than an increase in their power. There are two particular factors that have to be taken into account:

- specific Norwegian laws regulating religious groups;
- the existence of parallel Orthodox jurisdictions, i.e. the so-called 'problem of the Orthodox diaspora'.[2]

On one level, these factors appear to increase the laity's power over the priests, in the sense that the priests are becoming dependent on the laity in new ways. The priests must, for example, prove themselves worthy of the laity's trust and respect in order to be both *accepted* as their priest *and* allowed to *remain* their priest.

There are approximately 12,000 Orthodox in Norway representing 15–16 different countries of origin, and there are 11 priests from 8 different countries (personal communication from the heads of the congregations, 2013). It is clearly impossible to compare the role of the priests in Norway with their roles in such a multitude of countries. What I will do is take the Orthodox teachings on priests, lay people and the relationship between them, demonstrate how these are being realised in the Norwegian context, and then discuss to what extent there are clericalisation processes going on that are comparable to those identified by Valerie Karras.[3]

---

[2] This is an expression used by church leaders and theologians. When they use the concept 'diaspora' they are referring to minorities living outside Orthodox boundaries, i.e. on territories traditionally belonging to the jurisdictions of other Churches or other religious groups. In this article, I will take my lead from their understanding of the concept and use it in this sense as a purely descriptive concept. Whether it is useful to apply 'diaspora' in the academic sense in this context is of course another question. Maria Hämmerli (2010) has, for example, argued against using 'diaspora' with regard to Orthodox minorities.

[3] I carried out fieldwork among the Orthodox in Norway during 2006 and 2007, particularly in Oslo where the majority live. I visited various congregations, attended different functions, joined pilgrimages and interviewed both clergy and lay people. Additionally, I have visited several major Orthodox centres (for example Moscow, Belgrade, Istanbul and Jerusalem) where I interviewed high-level church leaders. Altogether I have interviewed approximately 80 people. During the following years I have kept in touch with some of the congregations, and I have occasionally conducted additional interviews. This article represents a revised version of a much longer text in Norwegian (Thorbjørnsrud 2012).

Priests and Laity: They Cannot Do Without Each Other

In the Orthodox Church everyone who is baptised and chrismated is considered part of the 'royal priesthood'. In this sense all Orthodox are priests (Ware 2000: 80). Nevertheless, only those who have received the sacrament of holy orders gain access to the apostolic succession, the unbroken line of ordination from the apostles, and thus the right to administer the sacraments on behalf of Christ. Ordained priests have special rights and duties, but the interdependence between them and the general royal priesthood is strongly emphasised. In the words of Metropolitan Hilarion Alfeyev: 'as a congregation cannot function as a part of the Church without a priest, neither can a priest function as a priest without a congregation' (Alfeyev 2002: 105).

A priest must belong to a specific clerical hierarchy. He must be attached to a bishop, who is yet again attached to a patriarch serving as the head of one of the various autonomous Churches, which all together constitute the Orthodox Church. While priests may belong to parallel hierarchies, they all belong to the same kind of hierarchies and they are all considered canonical, i.e. as having the same right to administer the sacraments.

The Orthodox Church distinguishes between local, cultural traditions and the sacred Tradition that, it claims, represents a direct continuation of the revelation of Christ. While local traditions may be changed, attempts to change elements in the Tradition are easily considered heretical. To us believers, says the theologian John Meyendorff, 'it is not the 20th century, but the apostolic period which represents an absolute norm' (cited in Ware 2000: 67). Still, the Tradition is not to be copied blindly: on the contrary, the Church is supposed to engage in continuous efforts to better understand its true meaning (Ware 2000: 66). Such work is generally performed by high-level clerics, and local priests have no right to implement changes in any parts of the Tradition. If anyone tries to make such changes, they can easily lose their right to administer sacraments. Local priests are allowed to make changes regarding traditions, but as there is often some confusion among many lay people whether something belongs to a tradition or to *the* Tradition, the priests have to be careful. As I will demonstrate, although it is permitted to change, for example, the liturgical language, priests still have to be careful in doing so. Otherwise they will easily run into trouble with those among the laity who consider the choice of liturgical language as an issue belonging to the Tradition.

In order to be accepted into the priesthood a candidate has to prove that he has the suitable personal and educational qualifications, but he is not required to be without flaws. His human failings are not believed to interfere with the sanctity of the sacraments (Alfeyev 2002: 106). The authority of the priest is based not on who he is as a person, but on his office, in which he acts on behalf of Christ.

By gaining access to the apostolic succession, a priest is awarded what Max Weber called 'charismatic authority', i.e. authority based on what their supporters perceive as extraordinary qualities. In the Orthodox case, through ordination the priest acquires the capacity to enact, for example, the miraculous transformations believed to occur during liturgy. But the authority of the Orthodox priests is not, in principle, based on any form of personal charisma. Their extraordinary capacities are considered inherent in their priestly *office*, and the priests' authority represents, thus, a kind of 'institutionalised charismatic authority' (Thorbjørnsrud 2012).

Orthodox priests may, however, be ascribed additional 'personal charisma', based on how they, as individuals, are perceived by other clerics and the laity. If they manage to convince other Orthodox that they have become spiritually and morally advanced, they will be treated with more respect and they will more easily be listened to and obeyed. Obviously, in such cases they are categorised as increasingly different from ordinary people.

In the slightly chaotic diaspora in Norway, there are indications that not all lay people are entirely satisfied with the charismatic authority inherent in the office of the priests. As I will demonstrate, the priests who best succeed in gaining the trust and respect of laity appear to be those to whom a sufficient number of lay people ascribe personal charisma. Such priests are described as 'angels' or as 'saints for the next generation' and this of course augments their positions. However, as there is little general agreement on who deserves to be described as, for example, 'angels', it is very difficult to realise the potential authority inherent in the additional personal charisma.

Priests are supposed to teach and guide lay people, but with great care. Their mission is to empower people, and they are explicitly warned against dominating lay people or allowing lay people to obey them blindly. As stated by St John Chrysostom already in the fourth century, a good priest has to exorcise his potential desire to command people (Chrysostomos 1993: 76). Priests are also required to apply *oikonomia* in their pastoral care, i.e. to take into account people's general life circumstances and their actual spiritual level. Being too strict is considered destructive. The principle of *oikonomia* also serves as an important reminder of the emphasis on man's free will. Only those who freely choose God can reach salvation. Priests are supposed to inspire and support lay people, but they must absolutely not make peoples' choices for them or demand their submission.

Summing up, priests are considered to have a special kind of authority, but there are several restrictions on how it is to be exercised. The priests have acquired particular rights and capacities, but in order to perform these they depend on the work of the laity. In other words, the interdependence between clerics and lay people is heavily emphasised. According to Karras, this interdependence is

Orthodox Priests in Norway: Serving or Ruling? 195

presently being undermined and the priests are becoming too prominent. But is this the case in Norway?

Being an Orthodox Priest in Norway

When a young Orthodox priest arrived in Norway in 1997, he was confronted with a congregation which he later described as 'essentially a fiction'. It had nothing but a small group of enthusiasts. They had previously belonged to a congregation within the Russian Orthodox Archdiocese for Western Europe, a special jurisdiction attached to the Ecumenical Patriarch in Constantinople. These enthusiasts wanted, however, to switch to the jurisdiction of the Russian Orthodox Church of the Moscow Patriarchate (ROC-MP), and when they managed to convince ROC-MP of their needs, they left their old congregation, very much to the chagrin of its priest. The ROC-MP sent them a new priest, providing him with a room in which to live and a small monthly support. Otherwise, the new priest was on his own with no one to ask for advice. His clerical colleague, who had been abandoned by parts of his congregation, was deeply hurt and was thus in no mood to give the new priest in town advice.

Some of the enthusiasts were however deeply disappointed with the new priest, who did not satisfy their desire for 'a real Russian priest'. He was considered to be too young, and while he had been educated in Moscow, he was still 'only a Scandinavian convert'. These people opposed the priest openly, and apparently tried to gain control over the congregation and the priest. Although Norwegian laws require congregations to be governed by democratically elected parish councils cooperating with the clergy, this was clearly insufficient power sharing for some of those disappointed. They lobbied to get rid of the priest and the priest had to fight back. Eventually he won, and the agitators left the congregation.

Members active at the time explain that they had gradually realised that 'the lobbyists' only wanted to gain personal power over the congregation and the priest. The priest, on the other hand, they describe as having had to fight to protect his office, which was his priestly duty. When the majority of the initial enthusiasts reached this conclusion, calm was gradually restored and the priest was able to continue the laborious efforts to transform 'the fiction' into a dynamic congregation. By engaging some resourceful members he succeeded. The Russian jurisdiction has, at present, approximately 3,500 members and three priests serving in various parts of the country (personal communication from one of the priests in the Russian jurisdiction, 2013). In Oslo, the congregation has its own church in a chapel rented from the Norwegian Lutheran Church, a choir, people assisting the priest during liturgy, and an association for ethnic

Norwegian converts. It organises cultural activities and it participates in organisations together with representatives of other denominations.

When the first Orthodox congregation was founded in 1931 by refugees from the Russian revolution, they and their priests struggled in the same way (Johansen 2006). Later Greeks, Serbs, Bulgarians and Romanians also struggled to make their dreams of having congregations connected to their mother Churches come true. For all of them, it remains a difficult task to maintain and develop their congregations, and it is often the priests who have to carry much of the responsibility.[4]

The Orthodox are spread all over Norway and the priests have to lead a somewhat nomadic existence.[5] They move around in order to celebrate liturgy, baptisms, and weddings, to bury the dead, to give pastoral counselling or socialise with lay people who feel lonely in their new and unfamiliar country. Frequently the priests have to bring the necessary liturgical equipment in their travelling bags. It is clearly a demanding life, but the priests insist that it is absolutely necessary.

Whether the mother churches support their priests financially varies, and likewise it varies whether the local congregations are able to do so. Some priests have additional wage work, and if they are married it is sometimes their wives who support them financially.

The Bulgarian priest, for example, receives no financial support, neither from Bulgaria nor from his congregations in Scandinavia, and he works full time as a cleaner.[6] The congregation in Oslo, which he visits every fourth weekend, only pays his travelling expenses. When he arrives in Oslo he spends all his time serving the spiritual and social needs of the members, until he returns to yet another week of work, and as he says, to a phone which rings during most lunch

---

[4] The Russian congregation from 1931 belongs to the Russian Orthodox Archdiocese for Western Europe, a special jurisdiction attached to the Ecumenical Patriarch in Constantinople. It has approximately 1,000 members. The Greek congregation was established in 1965 and belongs to the jurisdiction of Constantinople: approximately 600 members. The Serb was established in 1992, and belongs to the jurisdiction of the Serbian Orthodox Church: approximately 4,500 members. The Bulgarian was established in 1995, and belongs to the jurisdiction of the Bulgarian Church: approximately 200 members. The Romanian was established in 1997, and it belongs to the jurisdiction of the Romanian Church: approximately 150 members (all figures based on personal communication from the heads of the congregations). There are approximately 3,500 members in the new Russian congregation(s) belonging to the Russian Orthodox jurisdiction (2013).

[5] Some of the jurisdictions have only one congregation, with members from all over Norway. The most numerous have several congregations covering different parts of Norway, but not all of these have their own priest.

[6] He lives in Stockholm, but serves Bulgarian congregations in the Scandinavian countries.

breaks. As he explains: 'there is always someone with a problem who needs to speak to the priest'.

In Europe, the Orthodox Church is the second largest denomination after the Catholic Church, but in Norway it is marginal (approximately 12,000 members). Most Norwegians are not aware of its existence, and if they are they tend to associate it with incense and bearded men in black robes, easily described as strange and exotic. In hospitals, for example, they have to fight to have Orthodox 'peculiarities' accepted. And while the Orthodox congregations are met with favour from the Norwegian Lutheran Church, which generously lends them premises for the celebration of services, they often feel as the 'exotic little sister' in such contexts too. Considering that the Orthodox perceive themselves as belonging to the *true* Church, which is presently both large and rapidly growing, it is of course challenging to be confronted with such marginality. As the priests in Norway, who belong to six different jurisdictions, rarely cooperate, and as they serve far from their mother churches, their sense of being marginal may of course be experienced as difficult. Several of the priests admit this, but in one respect they may experience their local marginality as an advantage. Religious leaders are not highly regarded by the majority in Norway, and their work is frequently treated with suspicion and criticised, particularly in the media (see for example Døving and Thorbjørnsrud 2012, Døving 2012). Orthodox priests may deplore the way religious leaders are 'demonised' in the media, and they may at such occasions question whether 'perhaps it is an advantage that so little attention is paid to the Orthodox'.

In their congregations the priests tend to participate in most activities. They administer sacraments and they participate in developing construction plans; they conduct pastoral care and participate in festivities; they are of course responsible for maintaining contacts with the mother churches; and they may also end up having to do such dreary tasks as tidying the premises after the members have gone home. Sometimes they may feel too much is left for them to do – once, one of the priests asked his congregation whether they regarded him as their caretaker. Clearly he felt that too many had forgotten the Orthodox concept of cooperation.

It is obvious that the Orthodox priests in Norway tend to become very important to their congregations. Their range of duties is, as noted, extensive, and much of congregational life revolves around the priests. The question is however, whether this allows them to use their authority in ways contrary to Orthodox ideals.

'In our congregations it is the priest who decides on everything', a man very active in his congregation replied when I asked him about the power of their priest. As we approached the issue in more detail, his views on what the priest actually decided on was however gradually reduced – not least when this man started taking into account the effects of Norwegian laws.

Priest and Parish Council: Who Decides over Whom?

In Norway all religious groups have the right to financial support from the state if they satisfy specific legal requirements.[7] Such groups must have statutes; regular democratic elections to the parish council and the council must be headed by a person fluent in Norwegian and with an acceptable knowledge of Norwegian society. Annual reports, election records and accounts must be submitted to the public office ('Fylkesmannen') which manages the financial support system. This system is meant to encourage democracy and transparency, but for many of the Orthodox immigrants it is clearly difficult to understand how it functions. And for new priests it may come as an unpleasant surprise that the system turns them into employees of the parish councils, and denies them the right to head 'their' congregation until they can prove their competence according to the prescribed requirements.[8]

New priests arrive because a congregation has worked, often for a long period, to get its own residing priest. Initially, therefore, the priests are received as honoured guests and treated with great respect. The priests bring the desired cultural and social capital, in the sense that they have expertise in Orthodox theology, ritual practice and a network of contacts in the mother churches. Once they settle in Norway they will, however, be far from some of the sources of their capital, and they will quickly be found lacking in terms of the cultural and social capital needed in order to function well in Norway. Consequently the priests become dependent on the capital the council members have acquired, and it is through them the priests have to learn how a congregation has to be run in order to receive the much needed public funding. The new priests have to learn what it means belonging to an almost invisible community in a secular/ Lutheran society not always friendly to immigrants. Furthermore, they have to learn how peoples' experiences in Norway have affected expectations towards themselves as priests. In other words, there is a lot the priests are required to learn and to learn quickly, in order to avoid problems. Particularly the first phase may turn out to be difficult.

In one congregation the honeymoon period lasted only briefly. A serious conflict erupted between the new priest and the parish council and its leader, and as a result the priest was dismissed. The priest applied however for legal assistance in order to retain his job. Apparently he had acquired knowledge of the Norwegian law regulating workers' rights, and he accused the parish council

---

[7] The Norwegian Lutheran Church, a state church until 2012 and now 'the people's church' ('Folkekirken'), is financed through tax money. In 1969 other religious groups acquired the right to compensation, i.e. they receive the same amount of money, for each member, as the Lutheran.

[8] If in doubt, the Fylkesmannen asks the religious leaders to come in for a personal check.

of breaking this law. The council, on the other hand, wanted the priest to leave, and as they knew his residency would be revoked if he lost his job, they were in fact applying the Norwegian immigration law against the priest. The mother church sent a bishop to mediate, but without results. Having no influence on any of the laws involved, the bishop eventually informed the congregation that although they could dismiss the priest, they would not receive another. This convinced the parish council that they had to make another attempt and gradually they ended up accepting the priest. He on the other hand invested considerable efforts in acquiring sufficient cultural and social capital in order to stabilise his position in Norway.

This particular priest managed to recapture his position, but he had to learn to cooperate with a council imposed on him by the Norwegian authorities. Not all priests manage to do so. One ended up asking his mother church for permission to return home to another post. Cooperating with the council and its leader had simply become too challenging. This priest was unable to consolidate his position and he did not gain the respect he as a priest apparently expected. He became lonely within his congregation and without its support he was unable to adapt to Norwegian society. Remaining in Norway became too painful and when his permission arrived he quickly returned to his home country.

If priests are to 'survive' the demanding initial phase, they have to grasp very quickly that being *appointed* as a congregation's priest only represents the first step; they have to *become* its priest too. In other words, they have to prove themselves worthy of the congregation's trust and respect. The priests have to establish good working relationships with the parish councils and they have to accept how their respective positions are defined in relation to the Norwegian system. Still, the priests must carefully identify how to balance between showing – in particular – members of the council the respect they feel they deserve, and being too respectful, i.e. ending up in a subordinate position as the young priest in the Russian congregation almost did.

The priests seem to be most vulnerable in the initial phase, but they continue to depend on the council's acceptance. After several years of service one priest was, for example, dismissed because the council considered certain aspects of his personal life unacceptable.

When a congregation wants to terminate their priest's service, they have to discuss this with their bishop. If they cannot reach an agreement and the congregation does not want to obey, the bishop has few sanctions available except denying them another priest. As the bishops are placed in other countries this of course complicates their mediation. And if the congregation refuses to obey even when threatened with the loss of a residing priest, it is risky for the bishops to actually implement such a sanction. The jurisdictional pluralism in the diaspora allows members of a congregation to transfer to another jurisdiction, and very few bishops want to risk losing members. Consequently bishops may choose to accept the will of a congregation even though this, as I will later demonstrate, may challenge the local priest. Some conflicts are even solved by moving a priest to another part of Norway assigned to a service which involves no one but his own family.

The Norwegian system can, unintentionally, reduce the potential for solving internal conflicts. Although the majority of members are relatively passive, those active are often competing to become members, or leaders, of the parish councils (Thorbjørnsrud, forthcoming). Such competitions may create serious conflicts, and they may eventually end at the public office responsible for funding religious groups, the Fylkesmannen. If, for example, the old and the new members of the council cannot agree whether the elections have been correctly carried out, this office stops transferring money to the congregation. What is very difficult for non-Norwegians to understand, however, is that while the Fylkesmannen has the power to stop their funding, its employees are not allowed to consider who is right and help to solve the conflict. Thus, all parties involved may write earnest letters pleading their case and ask for assistance, but the public employees relate only to the fact that some dispute whether the statutes have been correctly applied. In such cases the priests also struggle in vain to convince the authorities. In one case the only solution for the priest was to leave the non-functioning congregation and establish another; only then was he able to have the election of the obligatory parish council accepted by the authorities.

Whether a priest argues that one of the parties in the conflict is acting contrary to Orthodox doctrine (or is just acting irrationally) is irrelevant to the authorities. The priest is not regarded as having any authority in such cases, but is only identified as one of the parties. While there may be good intentions behind this non-interference policy, in some cases it clearly empowers people who simply refuse to step down, while it disempowers priests attempting to maintain order in the congregations.

Priests, who understand the importance of learning Norwegian and getting to know how the society works, usually end up as leaders of the parish councils and, thus, the congregations. If they achieve such a double set of capital the majority seems to consider them their natural leaders. Due to the turmoil in the diaspora, priests may, however, still be confronted with members leaving them in order to join other jurisdictions. In such cases the priests' authority as conveyer of the Tradition is challenged.

When Lay People Change Jurisdictions

In 1931 the Orthodox Church was (re)established in Norway by some Russian refugees, and for decades this congregation was the only one.[9] Then the Greeks, the Serbs, the Bulgarians, the Romanians and a new group of Russians established separate congregations.

Thus, there were six parallel jurisdictions on the same territory. The priests of the first congregation have repeatedly argued that such divisions are contrary to Orthodox ecclesiology, but members of the other congregations are clearly uninterested in listening and obeying.

The Orthodox Church consists, as mentioned, of several autonomous churches or jurisdictions. These are supposed to follow territorial boundaries and based on the concept 'one bishop in one city', it is unacceptable to establish two bishops, belonging to different jurisdictions, on the same territory (Meyendorff 1983: 117). The bishop represents Christ, and since Christ is one, only one person can fill his place. No bishop shall therefore move uninvited into the territory of another. Neither is ethnophyletism, i.e. organisation according to ethnicity, allowed. Admittedly some of the autonomous churches have become kinds of national churches, their territories following national borders. And instead of applying terms such as 'the Orthodox Church in Serbia', 'in Romania', etc., it is common to use designations such as the Serbian Orthodox Church, the Romanian Orthodox, etc. Although this may challenge Orthodox ecclesiology too, the problem is far greater in the diaspora.

The situation in the diaspora is often referred to as 'heresy' and it is argued that this represents the Church's 'most important challenge' (Binns 2002: 242). 'The problem of the diaspora' seems presently unsolvable, however, and frequently congregations belonging to specific jurisdictions are established in places where several others already exist (see Chaillot 2006). In Norway there are, as mentioned, six jurisdictions, and only a few years back a small group tried to establish a seventh attached to the patriarchy of Antioch. The priests in Norway could do nothing to stop the process. Neither could their superiors in the respective jurisdictions intervene. The diaspora is clearly considered a kind of no man's land and, thus, free for all. In this case however, Antioch refused to acknowledge the congregation and the project fell through.

The question of why church leaders maintain this system with parallel jurisdictions in the diaspora I will leave aside. What is of importance here is that although they

---

[9]   According to the Orthodox view, the whole Church was Orthodox until the schism in 1054, when the Roman Catholic Church broke away. As Norway was Christianised around year 1000, Norway too was originally Orthodox; thus the recent history involves a re-establishment.

may disagree about other church leaders' specific decisions, they themselves tend to continue to establish new congregations when lay people ask them to.

In Norway lay people have initiated or at least been very instrumental in the establishment of all of the six jurisdictions. They have of course no authority to make the final decisions, but they have clearly been very active in lobbying. This indicates that within the somewhat chaotic situation in the diaspora, lay people have found ways to satisfy what they perceive as the best answer to their needs, no matter whether the result is in accordance with Orthodox ecclesiology or not. All congregations are offshoots of the first congregation established in 1931, and as noted, its priests have, in vain, opposed the development. Generally active lay people appear very concerned about following the Tradition, and as I will demonstrate below, the priests have to be careful not to challenge their views on what constitutes a part of the Tradition. When some priests attempt to lecture lay people on the problematic ecclesiological situation in Norway, the majority relate to this message as 'noise' only. They insist that they are tired of having this message repeated time and again, and they argue that it only adds to the existing frictions. Even those who agree on the principles tend to argue that everyone has to accept the situation as it is and rather begin cooperating across jurisdictional boundaries.

The majority of lay people in Norway are first-generation immigrants or refugees who have arrived within the last two decades. Their priority is to establish Norway as their new home while simultaneously remaining in touch with their home countries. Their needs may thus be described as transnational. Clearly, for a congregation to represent a piece of the 'homeland' while in the midst of the demanding process of adapting to a new environment serves many important functions. As scholars like Ebaugh and Chafetz have demonstrated in their studies in Houston, Texas, ethnically based religious groups (or ethnically based networks within multi-ethnic groups) may actually help people adapt (Ebaugh and Chafetz 2000). My studies of Orthodox groups in Norway indicate the same (Thorbjørnsrud, forthcoming). There is a tendency to explain the presence of parallel jurisdictions in the diaspora as a result of nationalist loyalties (see, for example, Ware 2003: 179), but I argue that when lay people want a piece of their mother church in the new environment, this may better be understood as a pragmatic way of coping with a challenging situation.

What is important to emphasise in this context is that lay people find ways of disobeying a local priest. Rather than accepting that the priest has the authority to instruct them on their mistakes in relation to ecclesiology, many describe 'the lectures' as just another example of 'church politics' ('kirkepolitikk'). Church politics is a derogatory term applied to intra-Orthodox quarrels among local priests and/or among higher-level clerics. Its use implies that those involved are fighting to gain personal power. While theologians may describe the present situation in the diaspora as a sin, many lay people consider it more of a sin for clerics to waste their time fighting for personal power. And when clerics are perceived to be doing so, their authority as priests is undermined. Ironically, a priest who, in principle, has the authority to lecture on ecclesiology may end up undermining his own authority by doing so. It depends of course on *how* a priest is lecturing lay people, but it also depends on how lay people perceive the lectures. If such lectures contradict the needs lay people are attempting to satisfy, they may simply refuse to listen and rather accuse the priest in question of unacceptable behaviour.

When Priests Try to Overrule Lay People

In 2005, when the Serbian congregation was debating whether to buy their own building, it ended in a bitter conflict with 500 members leaving. After some deliberation, those 500 decided to remain within the Serbian jurisdiction, but only when their bishop allowed them to establish an independent congregation. When the conflict first began to escalate, many of the participants, even the priest, used a rather harsh rhetoric in order to convince their opponents. This made many members uncomfortable, but the priest's rhetoric in particular made many upset. Even some of his supporters later described this as 'unsuitable for a priest'.

The original Serbian congregation included all of Norway. It had only one priest residing in Oslo, but he travelled a lot. In Oslo, the Serbs celebrated liturgy in a church building belonging to the Greeks. But in order to develop the activities and the visibility of the Serbians, the priest and some of the members in Oslo wanted to buy a beautiful building for 18 million Norwegian kroner (approximately two million euros). Although all members seem to have been in favour of promoting the Serb presence in Norway, there was no agreement as to how. And many considered buying this building as too ambitious for a congregation consisting of immigrants and refugees. Additionally, Serbs in some other parts of Norway opposed spending all the resources in Oslo.

The priest was convinced that buying this house was the best solution, and he applied all of his priestly authority to convince everyone to take his advice. He argued, for example, that it was God who had led them to this particular house, and although it would be expensive, he described it as more or less a Christian duty to offer money. According to the priest, those who turned out to be 'stingy' didn't 'belong to the Church'. In his words: 'Do not allow your name not to be listed in the Book of Life, for how would you be able to live and survive such a thing?'.[10] In sermons and on the internet the priest advised on how much he

---

[10]   From the congregation's homepage: http://www.vasilijeostroski.no/. The text is dated December 2005, and was read in May 2006. The original is in Serbian. Apparently

considered good Christians should give, but the sums he mentioned, and the way in which he connected them to membership in the Church, made many people upset.

In interviews several Serbs described how they had observed members leaving the church crying. These members were struggling economically. Others better off wanted to contribute, but as the sums suggested were too high for them too, they stopped going to church. Some of them explained to me that the whole issue had become so tense, and framed as a question of Christian and Serb loyalty, that they felt unwelcome. Those who opposed the purchase challenged the priest and his supporters openly, but they lost the battle and then left the congregation. The priority of the priest was apparently getting a beautiful building, and not maintaining calm and order in the congregation. In this case, it ended with the congregation splitting into two.

The priest chose to use all devices available to him as a religious leader; he spoke of loyalty, of the necessity of being listed in the Book of Life, of spiritual survival, and he even enlisted God on his side, but still he did not convince everyone, and approximately 500 of the members left. His critics considered him to have gone too far. Even some of those supporting the purchase were critical. As one of those explained: 'no priest should speak like that; it is undignified!'. Apparently he was perceived as having exceeded the boundaries of how priests are expected to speak and behave. In other words, he was seen to have violated his priestly office. This turned him into just another human being, and thus the members too felt free to use a rhetoric they would otherwise have considered unsuitable when communicating with a priest. To them it was no longer a question of God's will; it became just another battle over power.

Among the Orthodox in Norway, it is unusual for a priest to behave like the Serb did in this case. When there are internal disagreements, the priests seem to have consensus as their main priority. Generally they tend to relate to all proposals for change with great care, and they seem unwilling to challenge the wishes of lay people.

Priests Treading Carefully

In 1924, the Orthodox Churches in Finland, Bulgaria, Greece, as well as in Constantinople, began to use the Gregorian calendar to determine the unmovable holy days, for example Christmas. This calendar, which is also used by the Catholic and Lutheran Churches, was introduced by Pope Gregory XIII in 1582 in order to correct the lack of precision in the Julian calendar,

---

the discussions became even more heated in less public contexts than the congregation's homepage.

which is 13 days behind the Gregorian calendar. While all Orthodox Churches celebrate Christmas on 25 December, there are actually 13 days between the celebration of Christmas in the Churches mentioned above and the celebration in all other Orthodox Churches still following the Julian calendar. However, all the Orthodox Churches, except the Finnish, use the Julian calendar to determine movable feasts like Easter.

The Orthodox Church distinguishes between the use of calendars in relation to the unmovable and the movable feasts. It is considered difficult, perhaps impossible, to change the way dates for Easter are determined, but determining, for example, the date for Christmas is considered differently by theologians. While Easter has to follow the Julian calendar, Christmas may follow the Gregorian. Many lay people oppose this distinction, however, and argue heatedly against any changes concerning when to celebrate Christmas.

In multinational congregations the members may have arrived with different Christmas traditions, and may have different views on the relationship between Orthodoxy and the use of a particular calendar. When this occurs, deciding when to celebrate Christmas may create frictions.

In Norway the majority celebrate Christmas on the evening of 24 December (according to the Gregorian calendar), but throughout all of December, people celebrate with various kinds of food rituals, Christmas feasts at work places, Santa parties for the children, and so on. Christmas Eve is celebrated as a family feast with special food and the exchange of gifts. As the Orthodox are, in principle, fasting for 40 days prior to their Christmas celebration (i.e. until 13 days after 24 December), the protracted local celebrations in which food represents such an important ingredient represent a challenge. Both ethnic Norwegian converts and those Orthodox who live in mixed families may experience Christmas as difficult: what to eat, what to teach the children, when to give them gifts, etc. Consequently, they may want to switch calendars in order to make the Orthodox and the Lutheran or secular Christmas overlap.

The oldest congregation is very multinational, and it has to quite some extent been 'Norwegianised'. Some wanted to 'Norwegianise' the calendar too, and a committee was organised to study the issue. Although the majority in the committee wanted a change and were perfectly able to argue for this change in terms of Orthodox theology, they abandoned the project. They realised that other members were not to be convinced. On the contrary these members continued to insist that the dating of all feasts must follow unchangeable principles, i.e. follow the Julian calendar.

When the discussion broke down, the congregation could have organised a vote and allowed the majority to decide, but this was apparently not an option. While it is the task of the priests to teach the congregations the differences between the changeable traditions and the unchangeable Tradition, the priest in this congregation made no attempt to lecture those opposed to a calendar

206 Orthodox Identities in Western Europe

switch. Aware of the potentially explosive force the calendar issue can have among the Orthodox, the priest and the other members refrained from making a decision they feared could make some leave the congregation.

The priest could have used his authority, but he did not. Neither do he or the other priests use their authority when it comes to the issue of liturgical language. The Orthodox Church has no sacred language, but some lay people consider, for example, Church Slavonic as sacred. Some have even explained to me that in order to profit fully from the liturgy, all Orthodox should learn this language. Orthodox with different views, and who may have children with no understanding of Church Slavonic, may argue in favour of a change. They do not however want to press the issue, and neither do the priests.

Such non-challenging strategies are typical of the priests serving in Norway. When they are forced to make a stand, it may happen that members, who dislike their decisions, transfer to another jurisdiction. The jurisdictions practise some of the ritual rules differently, and some members may decide to transfer because they like one way better than another.[11] And sometimes some decide to transfer simply because they are upset with the priest. In the diaspora, with all the tensions between the jurisdictions, such transfers are of course rarely easy.

The majority of the Orthodox remain within the same congregation, at least after having established a piece of their home church in Norway. Clearly the priests try very actively to make them do so by accommodating them.

Pastoral Care: Practising *Oikonomia*?

It is difficult to study pastoral care; what happens between a priest and a believer, whether in confession or in a private meeting, is intensely private. The only information available is thus what the priests and the faithful are willing to tell about their experiences.

When interviewed, some of the priests were quite outspoken about the dangers involved in pastoral care, particularly when meeting lay people who 'very nearly' ask them for 'orders about what to do'. The priests confirmed their belief in *oikonomia*, and they clearly considered it their duty to empower people, i.e. to help them reach their own decisions. As one said, 'I do not want to become a puppet master [dukketeaterdirektør]!'. No matter how strongly they may want, for example, a woman to leave an abusive husband, they insisted that their

---

[11] One man changed jurisdiction because he was uncomfortable having to confess every time he wanted to receive the Holy Communion. Although he liked doing so regularly, he complained he didn't always have anything to confess. As his original priest would not excuse him from such confession, this man transferred to another jurisdiction where he was allowed to decide himself when he needed to confess.

job was to empower such a woman so that she could decide for herself. Their duty was to teach people what the scriptures say and discuss with people, but to tell them what to do would, according to one priest, amount 'to a violation of their freedom, and this can, in the long run, destroy all mutual confidence'. Consequently, he said, 'even when some make choices I disagree with, I have to accept them!'. There is, however, a limit.

The Orthodox Church considers abortion unacceptable and a sin. One priest explained that if a woman confessed to having had an abortion previously, he would consider it less serious than if she had one after having discussed it with him. In the first case he would give the woman the benefit of the doubt; perhaps she wasn't aware of the Church's view, and he would give her only light spiritual work to do. In the case of the woman who consciously did the wrong thing, he would be much stricter and he would, for example, deny her the right to partake of the Holy Communion. Violations of Norwegian law are unacceptable too. And if somebody confessed to abusing children sexually, the same priest said that he would tell this person to stop immediately and then volunteer to follow him or her to the police. If the person refused, he would inform the police anyway.

Lay people whom I asked regarding their experiences with pastoral care confirmed what the priests said. No one admitted to having been pressured by the priests, and no one admitted to having transferred to another jurisdiction, i.e. another priest, because they disliked their priest's way of dealing with pastoral care. What some volunteered were rather stories of how their priests had helped them deal with difficult problems. A few even told me about priests helping them accept being gay.

When there is a conflict, or when somebody develops a dislike for a certain priest, the people involved naturally avoid asking him for pastoral care. Otherwise, people were clearly much more concerned about their priest's lack of time, than about his failing to apply *oikonomia*.[12]

Clericalisation – in Norway?

Service in the Norwegian diaspora is demanding. The priests are confronted both with problems created by the Orthodox themselves (parallel jurisdictions), and Norwegian rules challenging their position as leaders. These circumstances make it increasingly necessary for the priests to tread carefully. Clearly Karras is

---

[12]   It is of course possible that priests influence lay people's decisions much more than either party is willing to admit, or is able to admit. There is a fine line between convincing people to do the right thing and empowering them to do what is right for them, and neither the priest nor the believer is perhaps aware when the line is crossed. It is, however, important to emphasise that while the Orthodox in Norway do not seem to hesitate to criticise the priests for various reasons, no one has volunteered criticisms regarding pastoral care to me.

right when she claims that the priests have become very important. In the case of Norway they are often the centre of their congregations, and they are often those who move the congregations forward. It is doubtful, however, whether this actually increases their power. The combination of ideal and practical limitations seems to be too strong. Lay peoples' closeness to their own priest strengthens also their ability to evaluate him, and they seem perfectly willing to consider whether he is worthy of his office and, thus their trust, respect and love, or not.

To some extent it is rather lay people who have acquired more power. Whether this challenges Orthodox teachings represents another question. One may argue that lay people's contribution to 'the problem of the orthodox diaspora' challenges Orthodox ecclesiology. And the way they refuse to listen to priests, who attempt to teach them about ecclesiology, challenges of course the authority priests are meant to have. On the other hand, the contradictory messages given by high-level church leaders exempt – at least partially – lay people from such accusations. It is, after all, the leaders who extend permissions to ever more jurisdictions in the same place.

The presence of parallel jurisdictions contributes to a sense of competition. Priests naturally do not want to lose members, but presently such occurrences easily acquire an additional aspect of losing out to the competition. It also involves losing money, as public funding depends on the number of members. As the tensions surrounding the existence of parallel jurisdictions prevent the priests from cooperating, they end up with few or no colleagues in the vicinity, and thus they have to depend even more on the laity. Under such circumstances it is of course impossible for any kind of clerical elitism to develop.

The priests have the authority to administer the sacraments, and this involves deciding who is worthy of receiving them. As long as they apply the concept of *oikonomia* in their considerations, making such decisions represents an integral part of their priestly duties, and cannot be interpreted as a sign of clericalism.

A highly respected priest may perhaps convince the majority in his congregation that his proposals are always right. It is however difficult to find a congregation where all members share the same views on their priest. Consequently, it is only rarely that all members are equally willing to listen and obey. Priests have to be careful about antagonising members with different views, and they seem very concerned about maintaining order and harmony in their congregations. The Serb priest who decided that getting a new building was more important than searching for a compromise ended up losing the unsatisfied minority. The 500 members who left clearly did not consider their priest's point of view as superior to their own. Observing his loss confirmed, I assume, other priests' beliefs in the necessity of avoiding internal conflicts.

For the time being, the priests are too few and too divided for any clerical elitism to develop. Within each congregation there is only one priest, and it is thus very difficult to develop ideas of the priest as superior to the laity. Generally, the laity and their priest interact so closely that the priest will come across as a human being with ordinary flaws. The priests are, of course, not powerless in their interactions with the laity, but in the present situation they have to be careful when and how to use their power. There are consequently few traces of the kind of clericalism that Valerie Karras worries about in the USA. In Norway, for the time being, the priests are clearly not so much ruling as serving.

Bibliography

Alfeyev, H. 2002. *The Mystery of Faith: An Introduction to the Teaching and Spirituality of the Orthodox Church.* London: Darton, Longman & Todd Ltd.

Binns, J. 2002. *An Introduction to the Christian Ortodox Churches.* Cambridge: Cambridge University Press.

Chaillot, C. 2006. *A Short History of the Orthodox Church in Western Europe in the 20th Century.* Paris: Inter-Orthodox Dialogue.

Chrysostomos, J. 1993. *Om Prästämbetet.* Skellefteaa: Artos Bokförlag.

Døving, C.A. 2012. 'Pressens mørkemenn/troens tjenere' – posisjon og selvforståelse blant sunni-muslimske imamer, in *Religiøse ledere: Makt og avmakt i norske trossamfunn*, edited by C.A. Døving and B. Thorbjørnsrud. Oslo: Universitetsforlaget, 26–46.

Døving, C.A. and Thorbjørnsrud, B. (eds). 2012. *Religiøse ledere: Makt og avmakt i norske trossamfunn.* Oslo: Universitetsforlaget.

Ebaugh, H.R. and Chafetz, J.S. 2000. *Religion and the New Immigrants. Continuities and Adaptations in Immigrant Congregations.* New York: Altamira Press.

Hämmerli, M. 2010. Orthodox Diaspora?: A Sociological and Theological Problematisation of a Stock Phrase. *International Journal for the Study of the Christian Church*, 10(2): 97–115.

Johansen, J. 2006. *Den ortodokse kirke i Norge: Hellige Nikolai menighet 1931–1975 år.* Oslo: H. Nikolai Menighet.

Karras, V.A. 2005. Women in the Eastern Church: Past, Present, and Future. *The St Nina Quarterly*, 1(1). Available at: http://www.stnina.org/print-journal/volume-1/volume-1-no-1-winter-1997/women-eastern-church [accessed 26 March 2007].

Meyendorff, J. 1983. *Catholicity and the Church.* New York: St Vladimir's Seminary Press.

The Tablet. 2011. Dangers of Clericalism. *The Tablet* (21 May 2011). Available at: http://archive.thetablet.co.uk/article/21st-may-2011/2/dangers-of-clericalism [accessed 21 May 2011].

Thorbjørnsrud, B. 2012. Å løse-ikke binde: Ortotodokse prester i de troendes tjeneste, in *Religiøse ledere: Makt og avmakt I norske trossamfunn*, edited by C.A. Døving and B. Thorbjørnsrud. Oslo: Universitetsforlaget, 67–89.

Thorbjørnsrud, B. forthcoming. The Problem of the Orthodox Diaspora: The Orthodox Church between Nationalism, Transnationalism and Universality. *Numen: International Review for the History of Religions*.

Utgaard, A.H. 2012. Det permanente diakonat – bare for menn?, in *Hellig uro: 50 år etter Det annet vatikankonsil*, edited by P. Kværne and A.H. Utgaard. Oslo: Emila, 153–82.

Ware, K. 2000. Man, Woman and the Priesthood of Christ, in *The Ordination of Women in the Orthodox Church*, edited by E. Behr-Siegel and K. Ware. Geneva: Risk Book Series, WCC Publications, 49–90.

Ware, K. 2003. *Den ortodoxa kyrkan*. Skellefteaa: Artos & Norma Bokförlag.

PART II
Innovation

Chapter 11

Not Just Caviar and Balalaikas: Unity and Division in Russian Orthodox Congregations in Denmark

Annika Hvithamar

"Danes, converted to our faith, want to change everything". This is how JP-Copenhagen quotes [NN]. Note the usage: "Our faith". [NN] seeks to create the impression that Orthodox Christianity is a Russian speciality in line with balalaika music, vodka or caviar. [NN] creates, to the best of her ability, the idea that Orthodox Christian faith is best off if it is wrapped in folkloristic Russian robes. But this is not true. The truth is that the Orthodox Church is for everybody. The truth is that in the Church there is "neither Jew nor Greek, there is neither slave nor freeman". And the truth is that at no one, not even [NN], can claim to have a monopoly of Orthodox Christianity, let alone try to attach the Christian faith to a national romantic bandwagon.[1]

At the turn of the millennium the Orthodox congregations in Denmark underwent a division. Until the end of the twentieth century there had been a single congregation, based in the Alexander Nevsky Church at the centre of Copenhagen, which had been the only setting for Orthodox Christianity in Denmark. Today nine Eastern and Oriental Orthodox Church jurisdictions are recognised by the Danish state.[2] This chapter will address the schism that

---

[1]   [No author]. 2001. Fyrstelig fup og fidus [Royal bogus]. *Kirkebladet* 2, 87 (2001): 31–2. The names have been deleted for the sake of anonymity.

[2]   Including the Oriental Orthodox Churches, the churches represented are given here with the date of their recognition: The Russian Orthodox Congregation in Copenhagen (since 1982, ROCOR) – 1915; The Assyrian Church – 1992; The Macedonian Orthodox Church – 1995; The Coptic Church – 1996; The Romanian Orthodox Church – 1997 (as well as three subsequent Romanian congregations, individually recognised between 2010 and 2012); The Serbian Orthodox Church – 1998; The Russian Orthodox Church (Moscow Patriarchate) – 2001; The Armenian Orthodox Church in Denmark – 2005; The Orthodox Church in Denmark – 2011. Available online at: http://www.familiestyrelsen.dk/samliv/trossamfund/anerkendteoggodkendtetrossamfundogmenigheder/kristneogkristendomsinspireredetrossamfundogmenigheder/?tx_lffaith_pi1%5Breligion%5D=1&tx_lffaith_pi1%5Bdisplay%5D=community [accessed 22 June 2013].

214　　　*Orthodox Identities in Western Europe*

appeared in the Russian Orthodox congregations, and the ways in which the formation of an Orthodox congregation intent on integrating Orthodoxy into a Danish setting has influenced the outlook of Orthodox Christianity in Denmark. The chapter ends with a discussion of the role of converts in the dissemination of Orthodox Christianity in Western Europe, especially the influence exerted by the majority culture on the development of a 'Western Orthodox Church'.[3]

Princess Dagmar, Polish Immigrants and the 1917 Revolution

Counting Orthodox ecclesiastical buildings in Denmark is a manageable task. There is only one, the Alexander Nevsky Church.[4] This Orthodox Church, situated within a stone's throw of the royal castle of Amalienborg, has been the setting for Orthodox Christianity in Denmark since it was consecrated in 1883. Its distinguished history is, however, due more to the close connections between the royal houses of Russia and Denmark than to the impact of the Orthodox Church in this corner of the world. However, today this is changing. In the following, I will trace the history of Orthodox Christianity in Denmark and the role of ethnicity among its adherents.

Orthodox Christians have been sporadically present in Denmark since 1741, when the first Russian envoys brought along so-called transportable churches consisting of clergy and liturgical tools, when they were posted in Denmark.[5] Between 1780 and 1807, Denmark gave refuge to four brothers and sisters of the ousted tsar Ivan (1740–1741). For their use an Orthodox chapel was established in the mansion allotted to them in the city of Horsens, and Orthodox priests were brought to Denmark. However, the chapel was dismantled when the last of the royals died, and during this period proselytising among Danish citizens was prohibited (Friis 1895).

In the censuses of the Danish Bureau for Statistics, which recorded citizens from 1840–1901, the number of citizens claiming Orthodox Christianity as their religion is minute. The highest number of Orthodox is found in 1890 and amounts to 38 persons (Statens Statistiske Bureau 1903: 72f).

But three events changed this situation. The most visible one was the marriage of the Danish princess Dagmar to the future emperor of Russia in 1866. Until this point, the Orthodox believers that were in Copenhagen had held their services in a chapel set up in a rented apartment. But when Alexander III, on his first visit to Copenhagen, saw the deplorable state the rooms were in, he

---

[3]　An earlier draft of this chapter has been published in Russian (Hvithamar 2010).

[4]　The Church was constructed between 1881 and 1883, subsidised by the Russian government together with a private contribution from Alexander III (Koltscheff 1945: 1–4).

[5]　P. Hampton Frosell, unpublished manuscript (dated 1998).

Not Just Caviar and Balalaikas 215

ordered a proper church to be built. The marriage between the two royal houses also improved trade relations between Denmark and Russia and as a result more Russians moved to Denmark in the decades that followed. The censuses of 1901 and 1911 feature 106 and 256 Orthodox believers respectively (Statens Statistiske Bureau 1905: 73; Statens Statistiske Bureau 1913: 38). In the censuses of these years Orthodox are listed as 'Greek Catholics' – a term that even today is frequently used in Denmark to designate Orthodox Christians. This misnomer is somewhat unfortunate, as the term more properly describes the Eastern Catholic (pejoratively called 'Uniate') Churches of the Byzantine rite. There might have been affiliates of the Eastern Catholic Churches in Denmark as well, but since the Russian priest in the Alexander Nevsky church has listed himself as 'Greek Catholic' it must be assumed that this was the term used for all Orthodox Christians. This confusion between Orthodox Christianity and the Eastern Catholicism continued when a new group of supposedly 'Orthodox Christians' migrated to Denmark, as I will explain.

The second reason for the greater visibility of the Orthodox Church in Denmark was industrialisation. At the turn of the century Polish migrants from the Austro-Hungarian provinces of Galicia and Volhynia travelled to Lolland, in the southern part of Denmark, to work in the emerging sugar beet production. The substantial increase in his flock prompted an application for state recognition from the priest of the Alexander Nevsky church, Ivan Stchelkunoff, who had been born in Denmark. In his recommendation for state recognition, the Bishop of Zealand affirms:

> It has come to my knowledge that, apart from the approximately 200 members of this Church community who live in Copenhagen or nearby, there are, at least for several months of the year, around 2000 male and female farm workers spread all over the country. Their conditions, especially in regard to baptism and marriage ceremonies will be eased considerably. (Rigsarkivets Arkivalier 1915)

The Danish government granted the Orthodox Church the status of an 'acknowledged faith community' in 1915. But, in contrast to the definition of Orthodox in the censuses mentioned above, the Polish migrants were not Orthodox. They were affiliates of the Greek Catholic Church. As it turned out, one Danish Orthodox priest alone could not manage to serve the new prospective adherents. Instead, the Poles were served by Catholic priests, and when a larger group of the migrants eventually settled in the region over the years they became Catholics, not Orthodox. Hence this group of 'Orthodox Christians', who were the reason of the Danish state recognition of the denomination, has ceased to exist.

The third reason for the rise of the Orthodox Congregation in Denmark was the outbreak of the First World War and the Russian Revolution in 1917. In

216 *Orthodox Identities in Western Europe*

the aftermath of the turmoil, Denmark accepted several thousand refugees from Russia (Bertelsen 1995: 37). One vital reason for this relatively large number of Russian émigrés was the return to Denmark in 1918 of Maria Feodorovna, and her strenuous attempts to help fellow countrymen flee from Soviet Russia. In the next decade the former empress was the centre of the Russian diaspora, the social life of which was concentrated at the Alexander Nevsky Church. In this period the church and the setting around it offered the Russian immigrants the refuge, respectability and resources often associated with diaspora churches (Hirschman 2004: 1228). But with the death of Maria Feodorovna in 1928 the community disintegrated and most of the immigrants moved to France or the United States.

Thus, the early history of the Russian Orthodox Church in Denmark is a history of a tiny and scattered group of people. A few individuals stand out: the priest Ivan Stchelkunoff and the Empress Maria Feodorovna, both of whom played vital roles in the establishment of Orthodoxy in Denmark. However, as we will see in the following, the influential role of ethnic Danes has been symptomatic for the establishment of Orthodoxy in Denmark.

The Orthodox Church in Denmark in the Twentieth Century

During the first decades of the twentieth century most of the Russian émigrés who stayed in the country married Danish citizens and, gradually, like their Danish fellow citizens, limited their churchgoing primarily to baptisms, marriages and funerals – with the result that the next generation ceased to be practising Orthodox.[6] Today only a few descendants from the first generation of immigrants continue to attend the Orthodox Church. The high degree of assimilation of the Russian immigrants into Danish majority culture has resulted in a loss of language – and of religion. In time, divisions have developed within the congregation of the Alexander Nevsky church that have brought schism. Disagreements have centred, for example, around the right to the ownership of the church building, the right to define who could call themselves Orthodox, or the question of which ecclesiastical jurisdiction the congregation should be subject to. Thus, the Danish Orthodox congregation displays features seen in diaspora communities worldwide (Ebaugh and Chafetz 2000; Karpathakis 1994). In Denmark the environmental impact and the structural adaptions to the immigrant context is shown in the power struggles between the Russian clergy and the Danish churchwardens. In the history of the Alexander Nevsky Church, Orthodox priests, apart from the above-mentioned Ivan

---

[6] For an analysis of the development of the Orthodox diaspora in Denmark, see Hvithamar 2007b.

Stchelkunoff, have always been of Russian nationality or descent. They have come to Denmark for the purpose of working for the church and with no other network than Orthodox Russians. In contrast to the smooth integration of the rest of the congregation throughout the twentieth century, therefore, the priests seem to have been the least integrated members of the community. Records of the correspondence between Danish authorities and the congregation in the Alexander Nevsky church show that communication with the authorities are taken care of by the church warden or the parochial church council, while the priest is restricted to managing pastoral care, conducting the liturgy and other strictly religious duties (Rigsarkivets Arkivalier 1947). As such, his power has been limited to churchly matters; he did not serve as the bond between the church and the rest of the society. Rather, the priest was the guarantor for preservation of 'Russianness' – both the preservation of ecclesiastical tradition and the preservation of Russian language and culture.

The Public Office of the Danish State holds records of the communication between the state and some of the priests of the Orthodox Church. As it is one of the conditions for being an acknowledged faith community (see above) that the priest speaks and writes Danish, since it is he who is responsible for the parish register, the priest's lack of language skills is a matter of concern for the authorities. At one point, in 1947, the Ministry of Ecclesiastical Affairs recommended that recognition of the Alexander Nevsky Church should be withdrawn until they appointed a priest who 'masters the Danish language in writing and speech' (Rigsarkivets Arkivalier 1947). This never happened, but the case is illustrative of the seclusion of the Orthodox parish priest and of the role of language not only as a bond within the immigrant community but also as a vehicle for the acceptance of the community in the majority society.

Outside the church it was the churchwarden and the parochial church council who represented the church. For the greater part of the period since 1900 these have either been assimilated descendants of Russians or first-generation converts to Orthodox Christianity. This has made them more familiar than the priest with Danish culture and the public system – which has made it easier for them to influence the attitudes of the congregation.

One example of conflicts between the priest and the parochial church council is the transfer of the jurisdiction over the church from the Paris exarchate, which belongs to the Constantinople Patriarchate, to the Russian Orthodox Church Outside of Russia (ROCOR). Between 1961 and 1974 several lawsuits were brought before the civil court with the priest of Alexander Nevsky as plaintiff. The parish council wished to transfer jurisdiction and have the priest replaced, but, as the general assembly of the church could not be summoned in a way that was acceptable to both the priest and the parish council, the question of who the legal head of the church was sent to court. The Danish High Court only passed the judgment that a new general assembly had to be summoned,

218   *Orthodox Identities in Western Europe*

and consequently the case was only resolved in 1983, when the priest passed away. After this, the parish council effectuated the transfer to ROCOR. In the subsequent years there was a high turnover of priests, none of whom could find favour with the congregation, until 1997, when the present priest took over.

Due to such conflicts in the congregation, it may not really be possible to speak of a Russian Orthodox community in Denmark stemming back from the time of the revolution, although there has been a continuous congregation for all this time. The few sources describe the history of the Orthodox community in Denmark in the bulk of the twentieth century and talk about 'a tiny congregation, which, if there is not a fresh blood, will be extinct in a couple of years' (*Politiken* 1987).

But the history of the Russian Orthodox community in the twentieth century displays features known from other diaspora studies – debates concerning the definition of adherence to a religion, the assimilation of the second and third generation, and the new forms of authority that develop in the diaspora setting (Clifford, 1994). It also shows that the small size of the Danish congregation results in the traditional religious authority, the priest, being vulnerable because of his isolation and his role as the preserver of ethnicity, which contrast with the situation of the rest of the community.

The Millennium Divisions

With the ending of the Soviet Union in 1991 and the Balkan wars between 1991 and 1995, the Alexander Nevsky Church witnessed a new influx of Orthodox adherents from the former Soviet Union and what had been Yugoslavia. Some of these quickly formed national congregations (the Macedonian, Romanian and Serbian churches formed recognised religious communities during the 1990s), which now rent buildings or borrow churches from the Danish National Church, but the Alexander Nevsky church remains the centre for Orthodox Christians from a variety of nations who want to go to a 'proper' Orthodox church. Two main groups characterised the new immigrants – younger males, who in the turbulent 1990s sought a new life outside the former Soviet Union, and younger Russian women who had married Danish men (personal interview with the priest of the Alexander Nevsky Church, April 2013). In the 1990s a new group of ethnic Danish converts also started to influence the parish life of the Alexander Nevsky church, keen to accommodate the church to the Danish setting, to have more liturgies in Danish while at the same time questioning the relationship between 'Russianness' and Orthodoxy. These new factors led to inherent conflict, also typical for immigrant communities, breaking out between the immigrant community on the one hand, which saw the bond to Russia as an integral part of their belonging to the church, and the ethnic converts on the other, who aimed to ground their religious beliefs in the local setting (Gasi 2000).

This conflict soon proved to be too much for congregational unity, and at the turn of the millennium two splits occurred. In 2001 one congregation, led by the former churchwarden of the Alexander Nevsky church, formed 'The Alexander Nevsky Congregation, Moscow Patriarchate'. This name, although somewhat confusing, signals the focus of the conflict. The members of this new community felt that the Alexander Nevsky church (which, as mentioned above, was part of the ROCOR jurisdiction) had moved too far away from its Russian roots and had become too mainstream. In the opinion of its founders, the improved relationship between the Russian government and the Moscow Patriarchate meant that the precautions regarding the church–state relationship which characterise the ROCOR church were no longer necessary. Instead, in their opinion, the bonds between the Russian mother church and the Danish Russian Orthodox community ought to be tightened (personal interview with the churchwarden of the Alexander Nevsky Congregation, Moscow Patriarchate, December 2005).

Representatives of the opposite opinion felt that Orthodox Christianity should not be seen as 'a Russian speciality in line with balalaika music, vodka and caviar'. In 2002 this group, mostly ethnic Danish converts formed 'The Protection of the Mother of God Congregation'. The new community felt that it was time that Orthodox Christianity in Denmark ceased to be a community primarily defined as an exile church and instead took root as a Danish Orthodox Church – Russian in tradition but in a Danish location (personal interview with the priest of the Mother of God Congregation, September 2005). I will deal with this issue in the next section of this chapter.

Today Russian Orthodox Christians are disseminated across these three congregations. There remain a number of what could be termed 'potential Orthodox' (for example, immigrants from countries where Orthodox Christianity is in majority) who are members of any kind of Orthodox religious society (Hvithamar 2007b: 119). Most immigrants to Denmark with a background in countries with an Orthodox majority never attend church, or only do so at Easter and at important rituals (baptisms, weddings and funerals). In this regard these immigrants are very similar to the Danish population in general, of whom the great majority rarely attend religious services, although 78.4 per cent are members of the national church (Church Statistics 2014).[7]

---

[7] In Denmark only 10 per cent of the population attend church at least once a month, 31 per cent only at Christmas and 59 per cent less than once a year (see Andersen and Lüchau 2011).

220 *Orthodox Identities in Western Europe*

The Russian Orthodox Congregations

Today, three Russian Orthodox congregations function in Denmark. The oldest, and largest, is still the congregation of the Alexander Nevsky Church (ROCOR).[8] As it is still the only congregation that holds its services in an Orthodox Church built for the purpose, it is also this congregation that gathers Orthodox people of various nationalities who wish to participate in an Orthodox liturgy or to attend other kind of services. An average Sunday liturgy will attract between 150 and 500 regular churchgoers, and the Easter liturgy will attract 1,000 or even more. Despite its multinational composition, with representatives from Greece,[9] Serbia, Bulgaria and Macedonia, as well as Christian Palestinians, Libyans and Syrians, the church is predominantly a Russian Orthodox Church. The liturgical language is Slavonic, the clergy are of Russian nationality and most social gatherings are held in Russian. A small Danish group also attends – however they are predominantly first-generation converts. It has proved difficult for the Danish converts to continue the Orthodox adherence into the next generation (personal interview with the priest of the Alexander Nevsky Church, April 2013).

Today, the congregation of the Alexander Nevsky Church is dominated by a younger generation, with many regular churchgoers aged between 30 and 40 years and therefore many children. A regular Sunday school for children between 4 and 14 years, with education in tradition, scripture and Russian history (for example the role of the Romanov imperial family), is conducted after Sunday liturgy for the Russian-speaking part of the congregation. Children also participate as servers in the liturgy as a way to familiarise them with the Orthodox tradition. Finally, there have been a few examples of an Orthodox 'confirmation', where young men and women receive a special blessing and 'confirm' their Orthodox faith, mirroring the very widespread use of confirmation as an initiation ritual in Denmark.[10] However, the priest of the church expresses his concern about children, especially those of mixed marriages, who only have limited contact with the church or who do not have much chance to learn or practise Russian:

> We highly recommend that the children of mixed marriages learn Russian. But for
> some it is difficult, especially if the children do not have chance to speak Russian

---

[8] For the website of the Alexander Nevsky congregation, ROCOR, see http://ruskirke. dk (in Russian and Danish).

[9] Once a month an Orthodox liturgy in Greek is conducted, which is attended by a Greek-speaking congregation of around 30–50 people.

[10] In the Danish Lutheran Church, Confirmation, although not a sacrament, is an integral part of ritual practice and is sociologically speaking a major coming-of-age ritual. In 2012, 71 per cent of Danes in seventh or eighth grade were confirmed (Church Statistics 2012).

Not Just Caviar and Balalaikas 221

> with others than their parent. After the children turn 14 we lose them. Although some do return later. We believe that much is dependent on the parents. Whether or not they are practising Orthodox. And we believe that the foundation we create for the small children may be of use for them in the future. (Personal interview with the priest of the Alexander Nevsky Church, April 2013)

Despite the Alexander Nevsky church being the largest and oldest Orthodox parish in Denmark, its congregation is almost invisible in Danish public life. When it comes to the attention of the public, for example, in the mass media, it is solely when the occasional article on an Easter or Christmas celebration muses over its exotic setting under golden cupolas.

The other Russian Orthodox congregation is the Alexander Nevsky Congregation (Moscow Patriarchate).[11] This congregation is much smaller than the one at the Alexander Nevsky Church, partly because its services take place in a borrowed Lutheran Church (the Sailors' Church in the centre of Copenhagen), and it is much newer. Nevertheless it has formed contact with the secular Danish/Russian societies in Denmark fairly quickly and has been quick to form small parishes outside Copenhagen in order to serve Russians or those of the Orthodox faith living in other parts of the country. Since the rapprochement of ROCOR with the Moscow Patriarchate in 2007, cooperation between the two congregations has grown to some degree, but, in light of the troubled history of the two church jurisdictions, a union of the two congregations is still out of reach.

The Danish Orthodox Congregation

Whereas the two Russian Orthodox congregations are almost unknown outside the Orthodox community, this is not the case with the last congregation, the Protection of the Mother of God.[12] As the congregation was initiated with the explicit goal of rooting the Orthodox Church in a Danish environment, the language of the liturgy, its extra-liturgical activities and the outlook of the congregation have been Danish from the very beginning. The congregation belongs under the jurisdiction of the Paris Exarchate (Constantinople Patriarchate) and the majority of the congregation are first-generation converts.

Transposing Orthodoxy has meant that this congregation has had to adapt the Orthodox tradition to the Danish church tradition. This does not mean that the congregation are not strictly upholding the Orthodox tradition, but some

---

[11]   For a website on the Alexander Nevsky Congregation, Moscow Patriarchate, see http://www.ortodoxy.dk/ (mostly in Russian).

[12]   For a website on the Protection of the Mother of God Congregation, see http://ortodoks.dk (in Danish).

elements of the Lutheran tradition and of Danish majority culture have found their way into the life of the church.

In its liturgical life a visible change is the central role of the sermon. Whereas sermons in the Russian church have little importance and are sometimes even omitted, this is not the case in the Lutheran Church in Denmark, where the sermon, in a sociological perspective, is a very important part of Sunday worship. This is comparable with the Danish Orthodox congregation, where sermons are a vital part of the liturgy, and selected sermons are podcasted and published on the website of the congregation. Another trait is the communal singing which, particularly in Danish Lutheran Churches (but also in other Protestant and Catholic settings), contributes to the sense of community of the liturgical service. In Russian Orthodox churches it is, with a few exceptions, the choir that provides the singing, but in the Danish Orthodox church the whole liturgy is sung together. Also, partly because of practical reasons, the congregation has female readers (though they are not ordained). Finally the church room has an iconostasis, which is kept open throughout the liturgy. The priest of the congregation explains the changes with reference to cultural inheritance and to the sense of community among the congregation:

> In this congregation, and I do think the same is the case for other Scandinavian and Western European congregations, since many clergy and members of congregations are local people, we have a background that is inherently very different than the Russian or Greek one. ... In my view, it provides openness and it prevents that feeling you may sometimes get in some Orthodox Churches of a caricatured clericalism, that is a separation of clergy and congregation in two mutually independent groups.

All the changes have been brought before the archbishop in Paris, who has sanctioned the practice. And the possibilities for more changes of practices are discussed, not solely in the Danish congregation but more widely in the archdiocese. The most contentious is the possibility of reintroducing female deacons in the church and perhaps even female priests. However, whereas the diaconate is supposedly not unrealistic, the thought of female priests is not seen as feasible in a foreseeable future (personal interview with the priest of the Danish Orthodox congregation, December 2012).

Other changes are of a social character. The women of the congregation do not necessarily wear dresses and headscarves (which is the case in the two Russian Orthodox congregations). It is common to sit on a chair or on the floor during the sermon, and all Sunday liturgies are, like their Lutheran counterparts, concluded with a social gathering, where the congregation have coffee and a social talk. All such social adaptations are recognisable from a Danish majority culture as well as from the Danish majority church.[13]

Furthermore, the work of historical re-creation that takes place in the Danish congregation is illustrative of the merging with Danish majority culture. The Danish Lutheran Church is today as closely connected to the development of the Danish state and nation as the Orthodox Church in Russia is connected to the development of the Russian state and nation. Thus the origin of how Denmark was converted to Christianity in the tenth century plays a significant part of Danish national imagination. But where the standard version of the Danish conversion is that the Danes were converted through *Catholic* mission, in the Danish Orthodox congregation it is claimed that at the time when Denmark was converted it was by *Orthodox* Christianity, since the christening took place before the split between Rome and Constantinople in 1054. Another example is the use of symbols designating Danish nationality, such as the picture of the Jelling stone displayed such in the church room of the Protection of the Mother of God, or the Dagmar cross often worn by members of the congregation as their baptismal cross.[14] Thus, the Danish congregation is developing means to root its religious beliefs in the local environment by adapting Danish national symbols to their Orthodox faith. Adaptation to local culture is an inevitable trait of religion, not least for Christianity, and adaptations such as the above-mentioned are seen in other Orthodox congregations in Western Europe. In an Orthodox context, however, adaptations relating to gender roles, liturgical practices, and rules for clergy raise the theological question of what is part of the Orthodox Tradition and what is part of local culture, while also highlighting the fact that converts to Orthodox Christianity are not detaching their religion from their culture – only, in the case of the Danish Orthodox congregation, from the *Russian* culture.

---

[13]   For a further discussion of the accommodation of Russian Orthodoxy to Danish culture see Hvithamar 2007a.

[14]   The Jelling stone is a massive carved rune stone from the tenth century, with an inscription about the conversion of Denmark to Christianity. The stone is strongly identified with the creation of Denmark and is pictured on Danish passports. The Dagmar cross takes its name from the Danish medieval queen Dagmar (d. 1212), who was of Slavic descent. On one side it displays the crucified Christ, while on the other side it displays a Deesis formation of Christ with John the Forerunner and the Theotokos, and with John Chrysostom and Basil the Great. The cross gained wide popular usage after the Danish king Frederik VII (1808–1863) had a copy made for his daughter Alexandra's wedding with the heir to the British throne. Today the Dagmar cross is worn by Danish girls for their confirmation into the Lutheran Church, and is also given to children as a baptismal gift.

Lost in Translation? The Role of the Ethnic Converts

A small community such as that of the Danish Orthodox is very sensitive to the role of individuals. Personal conflicts, personal sympathies and charismatic personalities have a large influence on the course of events and on their history. The role of the individual is very visible in the development of Orthodox communities in Denmark. However, several traits of the Danish congregations mirror the developments seen among western European Orthodox congregations: the conflicts between various generations of immigrants, the debates between the jurisdictions, and the disputes about the degree to which congregations should stress their Russian heritage or should accommodate to their new homeland.[15]

Looking at the Orthodox congregations in Europe, it is striking to discover that the people who are the public face of these congregations are hardly ever Russian immigrants or the clergy who are appointed and come from Russia. From the largest congregation in Scandinavia, led by Fr Johannes Johannesen, to the Dutch pioneer of Orthodoxy, Fr Adriaan Korporaal, to the head of the Paris Archdiocese, Bishop Gabriel (de Vylder) and the author of the most widely known book on the subject, *The Orthodox Church*, Bishop Kallistos (Ware), all such figures have one thing in common: they are converts to the Orthodox Church. This gives them the advantage of knowing the culture, life and language of their respective homelands, which is only gradually learned by the emigrants and appointed clergy. Being converts, their desire to proselytise their new faith, to disseminate knowledge of Orthodox Christianity and to incorporate this branch of Christianity into their homelands seems to be even stronger.

The Danish Orthodox congregation exemplifies this. An interesting feature about the visibility of the Orthodox congregations is the way they are displayed in mass media. Infomedia, a Danish newspaper database that provides full texts of all newspaper articles in Danish newspapers from 2000 until today, figures only one article in which one of the priests from the Russian Orthodox congregation of the Moscow Patriarchate is mentioned and seven in which the priest from the Alexander Nevsky Church is mentioned. Apart from reports about the splits in the congregations, the topics they are interviewed about related to holidays like Christmas and Easter, and death notices. But whereas the two Russian congregations are virtually never heard of, the priest of the Protection of the Mother of God congregation is a prolific writer. Infomedia has registered 195 articles (Infomedia search, 26 November 2012). He participates actively in print, on radio and television, joining in the public debate on ethical questions, ecumenical issues and other subjects where 'the Orthodox point of view' is needed. As he 'masters the Danish language in writing and speech', it

---

[15] For an account of the European Orthodox communities, see Chaillot 2006.

is also he who is contacted by journalists wanting to hear views from minority Christians.[16] Although the Danish Orthodox parish is the smallest with regard to the number of adherents, it is by far the best known of the Orthodox communities in Denmark. This could also be interpreted as a translation of Orthodox Christianity to another culture. Whereas the Orthodox Church in Russia has traditionally tended to withdraw from public life, to regard involvement in public issues as problematic, and to consider ecumenical cooperation as being against the grain, the Lutheran Church in Denmark, like other churches in Western Europe, has pursued close contact both with media and social institutions. The result of these cultural differences is, however, that it is only this 'translated' form of Orthodoxy, which might have lost some of its Russian Orthodox features in the translation, which is known outside the small circle of adherents. The diaspora communities are invisible.

Secularised Danish society on the one hand, and on the other the Russian revolution, the anti-religious policy of the Soviet government, and the post-communist setting make up a specific background for the Orthodox community in Denmark. Taken as a specific case, the Russian Orthodox congregations in Denmark are so small that it is dangerous to conclude anything on a general level. But the communities in Denmark are also displaying features known from diaspora research: the transformation of the territorial homeland into a sacred place, the equation of nationality and religion and the conflicts between different waves of immigration, and the close connection between the local setting and historical development. And we have seen above another significant feature of Orthodox diaspora religion: namely, that it is converts who have represented the Orthodox Church to the general public and continue to do so. This is possible because of their familiarity with the language and public culture. In contrast, the ethnic representatives are almost invisible. This is a feature that is well known also from other parts of Europe. Orthodoxy now being disseminated is changing not simply through a geographical shift and by being in a minority church in a diaspora setting, but also, and most visibly, because the people representing the church in the public sphere are raised in the new country or are converts to the faith. Orthodox Christianity in Denmark is an example of how the people who represent a religion are the ones who shape it. And, while there is much more to ethnic communities than 'caviar and balalaika', their version of Orthodox Christianity may be hard to communicate to the majority society without the ability to 'master the language in writing and speech'.

---

[16] In articles printed in Danish newspapers between 1990 and 2008, 22 articles mentioned The Alexander Nevsky-congregation in Bredgade (from 1990–2008), while 37 mentioned the Protection of the Mother of God (2001–2008). The Russian priests are only cited a few times (the current priest has the most frequent appearance with five articles), the Danish priest is cited in or has published 151 articles (infomedia.dk, accessed 26 November 2012).

Bibliography

Andersen, P.B. and Lüchau, P. 2011. Individualisering og aftraditionalisering af danskernes religiøse værdier [Individualisation and De-traditionalisation of the Religious Values of the Danes], in *Små og store forandringer: Danskernes værdier siden 1981*, edited by P. Gundelach. Copenhagen: Hans Reitzels Forlag, 76–96.

Bertelsen, H. 1995. *Russiske flygtninge i Danmark, II: 1925–1995. En vellykket integration* [*Russian Refugees in Denmark, II: 1925–1995. A Successful Integration*]. Copenhagen: Attika.

Chaillot, C. 2006. *A Short History of the Orthodox Church in Western Europe in the 20th Century*. Paris: Inter-Orthodox Dialogue.

Clifford, J. 1994. Diasporas. *Cultural Anthropology*, 9(3): 302–338.

Ebaugh, H.R. and Chafetz, J.S. 2000. *Religion and the New Immigrants: Continuities and Adaptations in Immigrant Congregations*. Walnut Creek: AltaMira.

Friis, H.E. 1895. *Det Russiske fyrstehof i Horsens fra 1780 til 1807 samt deres Medlemmers og nærmeste families tidligere liv og fangenskab i Rusland* [*The Russian Court in Horsens from 1780 to 1807 and the Earlier Life and Confinement of its Members in Russia*]. Copenhagen: Andreas Høst & Søn.

Gasi, M.V. 2000. St Nicholas Greek Orthodox Church: Maturing Through the Generations, in *Religion and the New Immigrants: Continuities and Adaptations in Immigrant Congregations*, edited by H.R. Ebaugh and J.S. Chafetz. Walnut Creek: AltaMira, 258–71.

Hirschman, C. 2004. The Role of Religion in the Origins and Adaption of Immigrant Groups in the United States. *International Migration Review*, 38: 1228.

Hvithamar, A. 2007a. 'Nu skal vi tilbage til rødderne': Konversion til den ortodokse kirke i Danmark ['Let's Go Back to the Core': Conversion to the Orthodox Church in Denmark], in *Dansk konversionsforskning*, edited by J. Damsager and M. Mikkelsen. Århus: Forlaget University, 152–73.

Hvithamar, A. 2007b. De kristne ortodokse menigheder i Danmark: Tal fra diasporaen [The Christian Orthodox Congregations in Denmark: Numbers from the Diaspora], in *Tørre tal om Troen*, edited by M. Warburg and B. Jacobsen. Århus: Forlaget University, 110–26.

Hvithamar, A. 2010. Православие за рубежом. Русская Православная Церковь в Дании [Orthodoxy Abroad: The Russian Orthodox Church in Denmark], in *Будущее религии в Европе*, edited by O.K. Goreva and I.K. Maksutov. Moscow: Aleteya, 25–46.

Karpathakis, A. 1994. 'Whose Church is it Anyway?': Greek Immigrants of Astoria, New York, and Their Church. *Journal of the Hellenic Diaspora*, 20: 97–122.

Koltscheff, L. 1945. *Den Russiske Orthodokse Alexander-Newsky Kirke i København* [*The Russian Orthodox Alexander-Nevsky Church in Copenhagen*]. Copenhagen.

Manuscript Sources

Hampton Frosell, P. 1998. [No title]. Unpublished manuscript.

Rigsarkivets Arkivalier [Public Office of the Danish State]. 1915. Archive no. 16, 1st office, ref. 5 K, 934.

Rigsarkivets Arkivalier [Public Office of the Danish State]. 1947. *Kirkeministeriet*, Archive no. 16, 1st office, ref. 5 K, 934.

Rigsarkivets Arkivalier [Public Office of the Danish State]. 1962. *Kirkeministeriet*, Archive no. 16, 1st office, ref. 5 K, 934.

Printed Primary Sources

[No author]. 1987. En russer i Bredgade [A Russian in Bredgade]. *Politiken* (1 March 1987).

[No author]. 2001. Fyrstelig fup og fidus [Royal Bogus]. *Kirkebladet*, 2, 87 (2001): 31–2.

Statens Statistiske Bureau [Danish Bureau of Statistics]. 1903. *Folketællingen i Kongeriget Danmark, den 1ste Februar 1901* [The Census in the Kingdom of Denmark, 1 February 1901] *Statistisk Tabelværk V, A3*. Copenhagen: Statens Statistiske Bureau. Available at: http://www.dst.dk/pukora/epub/upload/19605/folket11901.pdf.

Statens Statistiske Bureau. 1905. *Befolkningsforholdene i Danmark i det 19. århundrede* [The Conditions of the Population in Denmark in the Nineteenth Century]. *Statistisk Tabelværk V, A5*. Copenhagen: Statens Statistiske Bureau. Available at: http://www.dst.dk/pukora/epub/upload/19256/Befolk1905.pdf.

Statens Statistiske Bureau. 1913. *Folketællingen i Kongeriget Danmark, den 1ste Februar 1911* [The Census in the Kingdom of Denmark, 1 February 1911] *Statistisk Tabelværk V, A9*. Copenhagen: Statens Statistiske Bureau. Available at: http://www.dst.dk/pukora/epub/upload/19603/folkt1.pdf.

Websites

Ankestyrelsens Familieretsafdeling [Division of Family Affairs, National Social Appeals Board]. Christians and Christianity-inspired Religious Communities and Congregations. Available at: http://www.familiestyrelsen.dk/samliv/trossamfund/anerkendteoggodkendtetrossamfundogmenigheder/kris tneogkristendomsinspireredetrossamfundogmenigheder/?tx_lffaith_pi1%5Breligion%5D=1&tx_lffaith_pi1%5Bdisplay%5D=community [accessed 22 June 2013].

Church Statistics. 2012. Konfirmerede 2012. Available at: http://www.km.dk/kirke/kirkestatistik/konfirmerede/ [accessed 11 March 2014].

Church Statistics. 2014. Medlemmer af folkekirken. Available at: http://www.km.dk/kirke/kirkestatistik/folkekirkens-medlemstal/ [accessed 11 March 2014].

Infomedia.dk [database with articles in full text from all Danish newspapers since 2000].

The Alexander Nevsky Congregation (Moscow Patriarchate). http://www.ortodoxy.dk/ [accessed 22 June 2013].

The Alexander Nevsky Church (ROCOR). http://ruskirke.dk [accessed 22 June 2013].

The Protection of the Mother of God Congregation (Constantinople Patriarchate). http://ortodoks.dk [accessed 22 June 2013].

Chapter 12

Mediating Orthodoxy: Convert Agency and Discursive Autochthonism in Ireland

James A. Kapaló

According to the 2011 census, Orthodox Christianity is the fastest growing religious grouping in Ireland, showing a growth rate of 117 per cent since 2006. It is also the fastest growing when viewed over the last 20 years, with an annualised growth rate of 27.4 per cent over the period (An Phríomh-Oifig Staidrimh 2012: 7). In 1991, there were just 358 Orthodox in Ireland according to the official record; by 2011, this had grown to 45,223. This considerable increase is largely the result of labour migration from Eastern Europe, but mixed marriages and a growing number of conversions to Orthodoxy also contribute to this trend. The presence of large numbers of Orthodox labour migrants is the result of the fall of the communist regimes in Eastern Europe and the subsequent accession of majority Orthodox countries to the EU. However, there are other strands to the Orthodox presence that stem from Ireland's close geographical and political connections with the UK, most notably the presence in the early twentieth century of a Russian émigré community, the arrival of Greeks and Greek Cypriots in 1950s, and the establishment of the Antiochian Orthodox Church in both Northern Ireland and the Republic of Ireland.

In this chapter I shall begin by briefly discussing the conceptual and theoretical problems related to researching the diverse migrant and convert Orthodox groups under a collective religious lens before going on to give a brief overview of the Orthodox presence in Ireland, summarising the historical waves of migration and the institutionalisation of the various Orthodox Churches. Following this I will explore the role and agency of local 'converts' to Orthodoxy, both as mediators of the local context and innovators within Irish Orthodoxy. Although the significant presence of Orthodox Christians in Ireland is the result of the recent mass labour migration, I argue here that the construction of Orthodox space in Ireland, both physical and conceptual, has been profoundly shaped by the agency of local 'converts'. I will explore here two aspects of this relationship, firstly looking at the role played by converts in the founding of congregations and the establishment of Orthodox institutions in Ireland, referring to the cases of the Romanian, Antiochian and Georgian Orthodox Churches. Secondly, I explore the phenomenon of 'discursive autochthonism' –

230 *Orthodox Identities in Western Europe*

and the practices that flow from this – amongst 'cradle' and convert Orthodox, a blend of historical revisionism and reimagining of the Celtic Christian past, and 'memory and meaning' making in the Irish Landscape. These two arenas of agency – institutionalisation and autochthonist discursive practices – amongst others, are contributing to the emergence of a 'fluid' intra-Orthodox space in Ireland.

This chapter is based on preliminary findings from ongoing research on Orthodox communities in the Republic of Ireland; in the future I plan to extend this to Northern Ireland. This research includes interviews with clergy in the priesthood and diaconate, lay leaders and parishioners from the Romanian, Antiochian, Greek, and Russian Orthodox Churches, observations at Romanian, Greek, and Russian Orthodox services and events in Cork and Dublin, and an analysis of the online presence of Orthodox communities in Ireland. Where necessary I have given the names of individual Orthodox clergy and community leaders in the text; however, in order to protect the anonymity of informants I have not attributed specific statements or testimonies to individuals. As this study constitutes the first systematic attempt to chart the immigration of Orthodox believers and to map the institutionalisation of Orthodox Churches in Ireland, inevitably there are some gaps in this preliminary summary.

'Orthodoxy' as a Category of Analysis in Ireland

Mapping Orthodoxy in Ireland is not a straightforward task as, much like elsewhere in Western Europe, Orthodox Christians are ethnically, linguistically, jurisdictionally and institutionally diverse. In the face of this diversity, it is reasonable to question the validity or usefulness of 'Orthodoxy' as a category of analysis for the disparate communities under discussion. The meaningfulness of the category should be tested on the basis of the contribution to our understanding of, on the one hand, Orthodoxy and, on the other, contemporary Irish society. I argue in what follows that in the Irish context research conducted through the religious lens of the category 'Orthodoxy' constitutes just such a meaningful category.

The reasons for investigating Ireland's disparate Muslim communities from a religious perspective have been explored by Oliver Scharbrodt in his research on Muslims in Ireland (Scharbrodt 2012). Some of these reasons which prove valid in the case of one religious community are however less relevant or persuasive when applied to others. Unlike in the case of Europe's Muslim migrants, 'religion' does not constitute a central marker of minority identity for the largely white Eastern European migrants, and neither does 'religion' operate as a platform for the pursuit of minority rights for the various Orthodox groups. There are some key reasons for this. Firstly, although Ireland's Orthodox Christians belong to migrant minority communities, many of them are also citizens of European member states. The European Union currently has four member states that are predominantly Orthodox in confession – Greece (accession 1981), Cyprus (2004), Romania (2007), and Bulgaria (2007) – with a further three with significant Orthodox minorities: Estonia, Latvia, and Lithuania (mainly ethnic Russians). This is important symbolically as these majority Orthodox states, for the first time in modern history, are playing a role in the construction of what it means to be European. The important symbolic division between the East and the West, which for many centuries reflected the state of schism between the Latin Catholic Church and their Greek and Slavic neighbours, has been recast, at least partially, in the new political reality of the European Union. EU citizens have voting rights and tap into all the social welfare benefits that Irish citizens enjoy once they are resident in the Republic of Ireland.

Secondly, the national, ethnic and linguistic distinctions that divide most Orthodox, and that are carried over into the migration context, preclude the emergence of 'solidarity issues' based on religious, social, political or cultural terms (Hämmerli 2010: 97). There is ample evidence that historical animosities and rivalries that characterise inter-state and inter-Church relations in Orthodox Eastern Europe have not been overcome in the migration context. Even under some of the most desperate and difficult circumstances, for example in prison and refugee camps during and immediately after the Second World War, when inter-Orthodox solidarity could have alleviated suffering and hardship, Orthodox peoples showed little solidarity with one another and where possible rejected the establishment of multi-ethnic congregation (Smith, 1969: 321). Ethnic exclusiveness remains characteristic of Orthodoxy in migration, ensuring that 'Orthodoxy does not operate as a coagulator of consciousness and agency'. In her problematisation of the concept of an 'Orthodox *diaspora*', Maria Hämmerli asserts that, despite displaying '*diaspora*-like tendencies', because of the ethnic divisions and the lack of solidarity the Orthodox presence in Western Europe should be characterised as 'a co-habitation of national diasporas' rather than a single religious *diaspora* (Hämmerli 2010: 101).

Both of these points hold true in the case of Ireland. There are, however, some clear arguments in favour of the application of an 'Orthodox' religious lens with regard to Orthodoxy in the Irish context and more generally. Firstly, although institutionally decentralised, in terms of religious practice and ritual Orthodoxy is remarkably uniform and consistent across national and ethnic communities. Through a shared ritual life and religious calendar, a common use of sacred space and experience of the material dimensions of practice as well as certain religiously reinforced patterns of social interaction, Orthodoxy presents a relatively unified religious system that has been said to 'structure[s] the community at all levels' (Hann and Goltz 2010: 5). Therefore, anthropologists have suggested that 'Orthodoxy' as a category of analysis has potential, especially when seeking to explore the interrelationship between Christian cosmology and ecclesiology on the one hand, and social and political identities on the other. Related to this is the question of the relationship between individual and collective identity in Orthodox theology and social practice. A number of scholars and theologians affirm the presence of a significantly different notion of the self and the self's relationship to the religious community and wider society in the Orthodox imaginary and in practice, one based on 'relationality' and loving communion within the Church.[1] Decentralised, dispersed and 'virtual' or 'online' Orthodox communities in the Western European migration context may force Orthodox theologians and scholars of religion alike to question these beliefs and assumptions in relation to the way that Orthodoxy can or should function in its new environments.

My second argument in favour of an inclusive category of analysis for all Irish Orthodox relates to the existence of what we may term a 'common Orthodox discursive space' or a 'shared universe of discourse'. Orthodox Churches and their members address one another in a 'common language of Orthodoxy' and in Ireland, as in most other European countries, the Orthodox Churches are affiliated to an Orthodox network. The Orthodox Churches also participate in ecumenical initiatives and forums together, and are quite visible in Ireland in this context. An important aspect of this discursive space, shared by both convert and cradle Orthodox alike, is the 'autochthonist discourse', the character of which is unique to the Orthodox minority experience in Western Europe.

Thirdly, although the various Orthodox communities in Ireland organise themselves separately there are significant inter-community contacts and groups of Orthodox believers that move between the various ethnic Church communities. One reason for this is the wide dispersal of both cradle and convert Orthodox throughout the country, meaning that members of one ethnic Church may regularly attend the liturgy of a different Church. Another example would be in the case of citizens of the Republic of Moldova, who constitute a significant proportion of members of the Romanian Orthodox Church in Ireland, many of whom, for historical reasons, are fluent in both Russian and Romanian and are familiar with both churches' liturgical traditions. As one young Moldovan in Cork explained to me: 'In Dublin I attended the Russian Church but here in Cork I attend the Romanian. Moldovans pick and choose, I like the Romanian community here and that is why I attend this one in Cork. A lot of Moldovans do the same, it just depends how they feel'. Also, converts to Orthodoxy can be found in each of the ethnic Churches and tend to have a more 'fluid' attitude. Finally, the Monastery of St John the Baptist in Essex in

---

[1]   For a summary of twentieth-century Orthodox thought on the problem of personhood and community, see Papanikolaou 2008.

Mediating Orthodoxy

England is visited by members of all Orthodox communities in Ireland and as such functions as another common meeting point and point of reference.[2]

My final point relates to the very public role that religion and religious discourses play in Ireland. Both the public role of the Roman Catholic Church in Ireland – still very strong despite the recent controversies over clerical abuse and a steady decline in Church attendance – and Ireland's history of conflict related to religious difference encourage society to view 'the other' in terms of religious affiliation – the assumption on the part of both the Catholic Church and the state is that religion is important to the country's new migrant population. Also, the majority Catholic Church's dominant presence in the primary and secondary education system and in other public services such as health care ensures that Orthodox migrants experience religious 'otherness' on an almost daily basis (Shanneik 2012: 90). Having briefly outlined the basis for my use of an inclusive category of 'Orthodoxy' for my research in the Irish context, I will now summarise the historical waves of migration and the institutionalisation of the various Orthodox Churches on Irish soil.

Mapping Orthodoxy in Ireland

Despite the arrival in the UK during the nineteenth century of significant numbers of Greek merchants from Asia Minor, there is little trace of Orthodoxy in Ireland prior to the twentieth century. Orthodox parishes were established by Greek merchants in London, Manchester, Liverpool and Cardiff that eventually, in 1922, came within the jurisdiction of the Ecumenical Patriarch. The census records from 1901 and 1911 for Ireland, however, show little evidence that these merchants crossed the Irish Sea and established themselves in the port cities of Ireland. The exception to this are the few Armenians:[3] one by the name of Serope Biman Seropian from Constantinople (Istanbul, Turkey), a merchant who married a Church of Ireland woman in 1892 and later settled in county Tipperary; the second, Harutan Batmazian, a confectioner from Urfa (Edessa, Turkey) who settled in Cork City and became famous for his Turkish Delight. Batmazian is, however, recorded as a Congregationalist rather than Orthodox.

---

[2]   The Patriarchal Stavropegic Monastery of St John the Baptist in Maldon, Essex, was founded in 1959 and is today under the jurisdiction of the Ecumenical Patriarch, after first being part of the Diocese of Sourozh of the Moscow Patriarchate. The monastic community is comprised of both monks and nuns from several different Orthodox countries and jurisdictions.

[3]   The Armenian Apostolic Church belongs to the non-Chalcedonian or so-called 'Oriental Orthodox' communion. The Oriental Orthodox churches did not accept the Christological definition formulated at the Council of Chalcedon in 451 CE and have since remained distinct from and not in communion with the Eastern Orthodox Churches discussed in this chapter.

234 *Orthodox Identities in Western Europe*

Besides these two businessmen there are just a handful of Greek- and Russian-born sailors and dockworkers recorded at Irish ports such as Dublin, Derry, and Cloomonad, County Mayo.

The mass economic emigration from Russian Orthodox lands in the late 1880s to 1910s numbered in the millions and included groups of religious dissenters such as the Molokans and Stundists, all bound for the United States but having little impact on Britain and Ireland. We can only really begin to speak of an Orthodox presence in Ireland following the 1917 Bolshevik Revolution when a handful of White Russian and Ukrainian émigrés settled in Ireland (O'Donnell 2008: 80). This period of Orthodoxy in Western Europe, which lasted from the 1920s to the 1940s, demanded 'rapid, extensive, and often contradictory adjustments in congregational structure, methods of financial support, religious education, ministerial recruitment and theological perspective' of the new exiles in their new homelands. This period also marked the beginning of today's familiar inter-Orthodox problems of 'jurisdictional rivalry, ethnic jealousy and inter-faith competition' (Smith 1969: 312). One figure from this period had a significant impact on Orthodox life in Ireland. Nicholas Couriss was a member of the minor nobility who fled Russia after the revolution and eventually found his way to Ireland via England, where he settled, had a family and eventually, following the death of his son and wife, and after studying at an Orthodox seminary in the United States, became parish priest of the first Orthodox parish in Ireland. By this time he was already at an advanced age. The Russian Orthodox Church Outside of Russia (ROCOR) established the parish of Our Lady's Holy Protection in 1969 and, following several moves, was finally located at 45a Pembroke Lane in the house where Fr Nicholas lived. The parish and its tiny house chapel closed with the death of Fr Nicholas Couriss in 1977 (O'Donnell 2008: 81). Fr Nicholas received some local Irish into the Russian Church; after the closure of the Russian parish they worshipped for some time with the Greek community.

During and after the Second World War other Orthodox communities began to settle in Ireland, most notably Greeks and Greek Cypriots, who by 1964 had founded the Hellenic Community of Ireland.[4] The first Greek parish, led by the Romanian priest Fr Ireneu Crăciun, was founded in 1981. As was the case with the Russian parish, the Greek community found it difficult to find a permanent home; only in 1994 was the current Greek Orthodox Church of the Annunciation at Arbour Hill consecrated (O'Donnell 2008: 82). The post-war exodus from Orthodox lands, of which the Greeks and Greek Cypriots were part, contributed to the creation of the 'canonical tangle of incredible complexity' that came to characterise Orthodoxy in Western Europe and the United States (Smith 1969: 319). In Ireland, however, numbers of Orthodox remained tiny

---

[4] See: http://www.helleniccommunity.ie/ [accessed 10 January 2013].

Mediating Orthodoxy 235

in comparison with the UK or France, and the various nationalities – Greeks, Romanians, Georgians, Serbians and local Irish – worshipped together in the Greek Church in the 1980s and early 1990s. The last of the Russian émigré community also found a home here when their own parish closed. The large number of Romanians that arrived in Ireland from the late 1990s during the so-called 'Celtic Tiger' economic boom years, which according to one informant 'swamped the Church', have since found 'their own home'; thus, the Greek parish today, numbering in the region of 500, is largely comprised of Greeks and Greek Cypriots once again, with only a small number of Palestinian, Georgian, and Serbian members.

Unlike the Greek community, which has a large number of professional people and students, the Romanian migrants who began arriving in the 1990s are largely from rural and working-class backgrounds with very few professionals. Today, Romanians make up the largest Orthodox community in Ireland. There were 11,447 Romanians by nationality who were Orthodox by religion in the 2011 census. This constitutes fully one quarter of all Orthodox in Ireland. However, precise figures are difficult to calculate as, in addition to this, a large proportion of those recorded under the category 'Other European Countries' and 'Orthodox' by religion may be from Republic of Moldova (Ukrainians and Russians are recorded separately) and therefore may also be ethnically Romanian. Their inclusion would add perhaps another 1,800–2,000 to this figure. Finally, an equivalent proportion of the nationally Irish Orthodox population, numbering 8,465, should be added to account for the children and spouses of Romanian citizens that are Irish and naturalised Romanian Orthodox in Ireland, adding approximately another 2,000 (An Phríomh-Oifig Staidrimh 2012: 105). This brings the approximate total of Romanian Orthodox in Ireland to 15,547, which equates to 34.4 per cent of all Orthodox, one full third of the Orthodox community. This, of course, by no means represents the number of active Church members. According to Romanian Church community leaders there are a great many nominal Orthodox who only make contact with the Church at times of need or crisis.

Since the arrival in 2000 of the first Romanian Priest to be sent by Metropolitan Iosif of the Romanian Metropolis of Western and Southern Europe, Fr Călin Popovici, the Church has expanded to establish a total of six parishes around the country: three in Dublin, one in Cork, one serving Galway and Limerick, and one serving Ballymena and Belfast (O'Donnell 2008: 83). Romanian priests and parishioners estimate there are in the region of 2,500 active Church members around the country, served by nine priests and two deacons. Attendance at weekly Divine Liturgy in the larger of the Dublin parishes can number in the hundreds. The parish in Cork regularly has between 40 and 70 attending liturgy.

The Russian Orthodox presence in Ireland has also been growing rapidly in recent years, with the census data showing 2,430 Russians of Orthodox faith. Russian Orthodox parishes, however, also serve Ukrainians, Belarusians, Moldovans and Latvians. If we add in the statistics for these national groups the figure is closer to 10,000.[5] As was the case with the Romanian community, the Russian community, following the death of Fr Nicholas Couriss and the closure of the first ROCOR parish, found a home in the Greek Church in Arbour Hill and began regular Russian services there in 1999 with Fr Michael Gogolov. 2001 saw the founding of the first Russian parish at Harold's Cross in Dublin, which was opened following the visit to Ireland of Metropolitan Kirill of Smolensk and Kaliningrad, later to become (in 2009) Patriarch of Moscow and All Rus'. Consecration of the church followed in February 2003 (Church of Holy Apostles Peter and Paul 2009). Jurisdictionally the Russian Church in Ireland belongs to the Russian Orthodox Diocese of Sourozh of Great Britain and Ireland and has since expanded from the Dublin parish of the Holy Apostles Peter and Paul to hold regular liturgies in Athlone, Belfast, Cork, Drogheda, Galway, Limerick, Sligo and Waterford as well as Stradbally, where a joint community with ROCOR has been formed (see below) (Diocese of Sourozh, n.d.). These parishes and communities are served by three Orthodox priests, headed by Fr Michael Nasonov as Dean, and one Deacon. The Dublin parish also supports both a Saturday school that teaches Russian language and culture for the Russian-speaking families and a Sunday school for Orthodox religious instruction. In comparison with the other Orthodox jurisdictions, the Moscow Patriarchate has provided most material support for the establishment of parishes in Ireland.

As mentioned above, the Russian Orthodox Church attracts Russian speakers from a number of countries, including Ukraine, Belorussia, Moldova and Latvia. Many of the younger people in these parishes are experiencing an institutional relationship with Orthodoxy for the first time in the migration context. As one young Russian explained: 'back home my family was not religious at all, only my grandmother went to church so a generation was missed out. I only started going to the Orthodox Church here in Ireland as a cultural thing really. Now I am very involved, it is somewhere I can feel comfortable surrounded by other Russians'. The migration context has encouraged some young immigrants to engage with Orthodoxy as part of their cultural heritage, which, as another young Russian student explained, blurs the boundaries between the so-called 'cradle' Orthodox and converts. This phenomenon is in contrast with the Romanian community, members of which tend to more to be more thoroughly 'churched', at least in terms of the local religious practices in their home region of Romania. Points of contention over the form of practice and worship arose quite frequently in the Romanian Orthodox Church precisely because members

---

[5] The census records report 5,486 Latvian Orthodox, 2,362 Ukrainian Orthodox, and 1,671 Lithuanian Orthodox. See An Phríomh-Oifig Staidrimh 2012: 105.

of the community, who come from disparate parts of the Romania and the Republic of Moldova, were the repositories of 'local knowledge' which they sought to actualise in the migration context, sometimes in contention with the parish priest. These differences in terms of congregational make-up between the Russian and Romanian Orthodox Churches offer an interesting point of comparative analysis for future research on community dynamics.

Independently of the parishes founded by the Russian Diocese of Sourozh, the Russian Orthodox Church Outside of Russia (ROCOR) has also had a presence since the 1990s. The first purpose-built Orthodox place of worship in Ireland, St Colman of Oughaval Chapel in Stradbally, was built by local landowner and Church of Ireland convert to Orthodoxy, Adrian Crosby of Stradbally Hall. The Church was consecrated by ROCOR in 1994. Today, the parish is jointly run by both branches of the newly reunified (2007) Russian Orthodox Church. However, with the absence of a significant local Orthodox population and as the only purpose-built Orthodox Church in Ireland, it is becoming popular with other Orthodox Churches as a site of pilgrimage and for youth camps for Orthodox children.

The most recent Orthodox Church to be established in Ireland is the Antiochian Orthodox Church. The Antiochian Church is quite different in character to the other Orthodox Churches in Ireland in that it is largely composed of non-cradle Orthodox. Part of the Antiochian Orthodox Deanery of the United Kingdom and Ireland, this Church has been the main Orthodox Church to attract both convert priests and laity in the UK and Ireland. Although there are several Syrian Orthodox Christians who attend liturgies in the various Orthodox parishes around Ireland, active members of the Antiochian Orthodox Church in Ireland are very largely non-cradle locals. Conversions in the West to Antiochian Orthodoxy began in the early twentieth century but then accelerated from the end of the 1970s, especially in the United States. In the UK and Ireland the Antiochian Church established a deanery especially to cater to converts from Anglicanism; this was partly precipitated by the controversy over the ordination of women and the question of homosexuality. There are currently two Antiochian parishes operating in Ireland, one in Belfast, established in 2004, and one described as Dublin/Cork, established in 2008. These congregations are served by a team of convert priests and deacons, most from a Catholic background. Despite their reputation for being more evangelical in spirit (Abu Mrad 2008: 257), the Antiochian community in Ireland does not actively proselytise in the strict evangelical sense, as one member of the church explained: 'we can't make it happen, it is nothing we are consciously doing' but 'something is happening to us nonetheless, we are growing'. The strongest community is in the counties of Cork and Kerry in the south-west of Ireland, a dispersed but active group of mainly non-cradle Orthodox who travel many miles to attend Orthodox liturgy in the cities of Cork, Limerick and

Galway. Part of the Antiochians' 'openness' means they attend Romanian and Russian Liturgy as well as Antiochian services. One Antiochian Orthodox man explained their influence in the following way: 'You see converts are a bit more fluid, we move around, the various ethnic Orthodox communities are becoming increasingly interconnected'. This far-flung community, which also boasts its own Orthodox Mission Chapel in the small village of Ballydehob, is sustained by strong contacts with Mount Athos and with the monastery of St John the Baptist in Essex.[6] Ancient Faith Radio, based in the United States, is also an important resource mentioned by members of the community.

There are many members of each of the Orthodox communities mentioned above that attend liturgy of other Orthodox parishes; for example, Russians, who only have one monthly liturgy in Cork, often attend the Antiochian liturgies. Nearly all the communities, as mentioned above, also have contacts with the Orthodox Monastery of St John the Baptist in Essex, which has Romanian, Greek, Russian, Bulgarian, and Syrian monastics, as well as English-speaking convert monks and nuns. These factors increase the points of contact between the various ethnic groups and converts in a way that may not happen in a more densely populated or more urban context.

Converts as Mediators

Conversion is a complex issue in the study of religions with a range of contradictory or conflicting approaches that privilege different aspects such as the person, the cultural and social environment or the theological dimensions. The topic of conversion is also controversial amongst 'non-cradle' Orthodox, many of whom are ambivalent toward the category and sensitive to pejorative connotations that may be attached to it. Non-cradle Orthodox often tend to question the relevance of the distinction between 'convert' and 'cradle' Orthodox, understanding their new faith identity as a return or 'reversion' (rather than conversion) to an original state of being in the universal Church. Accounts that would generally be referred to by scholars of religion as 'conversion narratives' are often described by Irish Orthodox as their 'personal journey' where the arrival at Orthodoxy is explained and understood in relation to an often protracted period of encounter and engagement with Orthodoxy. The publication of conversion narratives, both in print and on prominent online Orthodox websites, under the heading 'Journeys to Orthodoxy' supports this tradition of referring to and seeing this process as a 'journey' amongst the 'newly' Orthodox.[7]

---

[6]   See http://www.antiochireland.org/ballydehob/ [accessed 12 December 2012].

[7]   See in particular the 'Journeys' posted on the Antiochian Orthodox Deanery of the United Kingdom and Ireland website: http://www.antiochian-orthodox.co.uk/Journeys/

Mediating Orthodoxy

The theoretical approach to the problem of religious conversion that seems most in tune with 'non-cradle' Orthodox self-understanding and self-representation is the 'narrative' approach, which takes seriously the narrative construction by the individual of a new biography that gives meaning to their life story in the light of the beliefs, practices and community of the adopted religious tradition (Rambo 1999: 265). According to Margaret Somers it is 'through narrativity that we come to know, understand, and make sense of the social world, and it is through narratives and narrativity that we constitute our social identities' (Somers 1994: 606). Somers approach points to the ontological dimension of narrative and its significance for identity formation and understanding human agency. She describes our ability to construct meaning from a range of disparate events through 'emplotment'. Emplotment gives significance to 'episodes' that are not dependent on their chronological or categorical order for their place in the narrative. 'Causal emplotment' tries to account for *why* a narrative has the story line it does (Somers 1994: 616). This narrative approach advocated by Somers can help make sense of the way in which the key touch-points of the 'journeys to Orthodoxy' form the particular narrative constructions they do. Once again, there is no space in this short chapter to explore this fully, but an awareness of this particular understanding of the relationship between diverse biographical events, meetings and influences, and how, through the 'meaning-making' that goes on in narrative, these are translated into new religious orientations and agency on the part of the 'journeyed' can be instructive. That is to say, close analysis of these 'journeys to Orthodoxy' can help us understand the orientation and agency of Irish converts.

It is worth mentioning a few of the touch-points that recur in Irish 'journeys to Orthodoxy', some of which may be particular to the Irish experience. The impact of Vatican II features in narratives of the older generation who witnessed the removal of statues and elimination of many familiar elements of devotional life in what they consider to have been an 'overzealous' attack on the sensual and material aspects of religion. It is in this context that some Irish converts, when encountering Orthodoxy and Orthodox worship on holiday or working abroad in Greece, Cyprus or Russia, refer to the sensorial dimension of the Orthodox liturgical experience – icons, candles, incense and liturgical music as one of the key attractions of Orthodoxy. There is a sense that Orthodoxy, for some converts, contains an element of nostalgia and recaptures the drama and mystery of the Irish Catholic Church pre-Vatican II.

'Journeys to Orthodoxy' often include periods of 'spiritual seeking', sometimes involving Buddhist practice, encounters with Islam or Evangelical and Charismatic forms of Christianity. Ireland in the 1980s and 1990s, especially

---

journeys.htm [accessed 13 December 2012]; and on OrthodoxWiki: http://orthodoxwiki.org/Journeys_to_Orthodoxy [accessed 13 December 2012].

the West coast, saw an influx of British and other European people, many of them members of sub-cultural or 'hippy' groups, who brought a new 'spiritual' openness and the possibility of religious 'experimentation' to parts of rural Ireland. For the first time, with various spiritual or religious options available in the form of Buddhist retreats, yoga, and Christian charismatic missions, some people began to question their attachment to the Roman Catholic Church.

Another prominent component of 'journeys' in the Irish context, similarly to the UK, is the presence of a 'fall' narrative or reference to the 'surrender of Orthodoxy' in relation both to the Irish Catholic Church and the Church of Ireland (Ireland's main Protestant denomination, part of the Anglican communion). Essentially this relates to the perceived erosion of the authority of the traditional churches, especially the clerical abuse scandals that have rocked the Catholic Church in Ireland, and liberalisation in terms of social teaching and the role of women in the church in the case of the Church of Ireland.[8] Finally, the relationship between the ancient Celtic monastic heritage of Ireland before the Great Schism forms an important point of reference for many local Irish Orthodox. I shall return to this point in the following section.

Within these 'journey' narratives a set of broad attitudes that help define non-cradle Orthodox identity in Ireland also emerge. The most prominent of these is a rigorist approach to Orthodox doctrine and practice. Unlike rigorist groups in Greece, Russia and Romania, however, this is combined with an ecumenical spirit, both in terms of inter-Orthodox cooperation and relations with other Christian groups. Non-cradle Orthodox also tend to reject the 'feminisation' of Christianity pursued by some Protestant denominations whilst displaying an orientation towards the mystical and miraculous aspects of Orthodoxy. Converts to Orthodoxy also emphasise the need for clarity in terms of doctrine and spiritual progression. Orthodoxy is seen to provide answers and certainty where other more accommodating religious options simply supplement the confusion of modern life. General reflections on the state of anomie in contemporary society and anxiety about the excesses of late modernity are particularly frequent. As one informant described it: 'I am talking about the reality of Christianity, not the pick 'n' mix type – warts and all. I suppose the only way for humanity to get a hold of itself now is to get back to basics, and that's where Orthodoxy comes together'. Another non-cradle Orthodox man described his disillusionment with the 'rock 'n' roll mentality', the idea that 'man can improve the world without recourse to God', and described the need for a 'clear authoritative voice'.

---

[8] These ideas are especially common in the UK and Ireland, and feature in many of the personal 'journey to Orthodoxy' narratives I have collected and which feature on the website of the Antiochian Orthodox Deanery of the UK and Ireland: see in particular http://www.antiochian-orthodox.co.uk/Journeys/journey21.htm [accessed 13 December 2012].

Some of the early converts to Orthodoxy from the 1980s have gone on to take holy orders or lay leadership roles and have been instrumental in shaping and facilitating the institutionalisation of the Orthodox Church in Ireland. Their contributions included locating places of worship and negotiating with Catholic and Protestant church authorities over their use, facilitating the arrival of Orthodox priests from the various home communities, founding and heading intra-Orthodox councils and encouraging ecumenical contacts, and finally serving as priests and deacons for immigrant communities. I will restrict myself to a few examples to illustrate how these activities have shaped the Orthodox landscape in Ireland.

In the case of the Romanian Orthodox Church, contacts and discussions between the Romanian Orthodox bishop for Western and Southern Europe and a local non-cradle Orthodox, Godfrey O'Donnell, an ex-Jesuit priest, facilitated the arrival of the first Romanian priest in Ireland in 2000, organised his accommodation and postgraduate theological training at Milltown Institute and also secured, through his Jesuit, Irish Catholic and Methodist contacts, for the first and subsequent Romanian Orthodox parish churches. Later, in 2004, Godfrey O'Donnell was raised to the priesthood and has since played an instrumental role, not only in founding new parishes and expanding the Romanian Orthodox Church to other parts of Ireland, but also in creating ecumenical contacts and facilitating intra-Orthodox cooperation. Fr Godfrey O'Donnell was elected chairperson of the Dublin Council of Churches in 2008, helped found an Irish Network of Orthodox Churches, and has taken a lead in raising the 'visibility of Orthodoxy within the country' and, in his words, 'educating members of the Orthodox Church ecumenically' (O'Donnell 2008: 87). The leadership role taken by Fr Godfrey can be partly accounted for by the poor preparedness, lack of training and language skills of the Romanian Orthodox priests arriving in Ireland. According to one member of the community, the selection criteria for the priests 'do not seem to match the requirements of the job. Selection is by a panel of the bishop and monks who have no idea what it means to run a parish, let alone a parish in a foreign country!'. A similar situation in the Georgian Church also prevented the community from finding a suitable Georgian priest, with the candidates dispatched from Georgia proving ill prepared for the role.

In addition to Fr Godfrey in the Romanian Church, there are local Irish, non-cradle Orthodox priests and deacons serving in three other Orthodox Churches in Ireland. The two ordained clergy in the Antiochian Church in the Republic of Ireland, Fr David Lonergan and Fr Deacon John Hickey, as well as having founded the Antiochian parishes in Dublin and Cork, also serve, at the request of Fr Malkhaz Kumelashvili, the Georgian community in Dublin since his departure in 2009. As was the case with Fr Godfrey in the Romanian Church, they have played an instrumental role in securing a permanent place of worship for the Georgian community in Dublin. The Greek Church is also

242   *Orthodox Identities in Western Europe*

served by a local Irishman, Fr Tom Carroll, who was ordained to the priesthood in 2007. Fr Tom is a long-standing member of the Greek parish, and thus shares with Fr Godfrey (before his ordination in the Romanian Church) and John Johanson, a tonsured reader who was instrumental in establishing the Russian parish in Cork, a common experience of Orthodoxy in Ireland centred around the very multi-ethnic context of the Greek Orthodox community at Arbour Hill in the 1980s and 1990s. These men are all of the same generation and share a non-sectarian vision of Orthodoxy in Ireland, and in these various ways have acted as significant mediators between the migrant Orthodox churches and between Orthodoxy and Irish society. The points made above seek to demonstrate that the agency and local knowledge of non-cradle clergy and lay members Orthodox Churches are shaping the character of an emerging Irish Orthodoxy. In her article on Irish converts to Islam, Yafa Shanneik has argued convincingly for the continuation amongst these converts of an Irish Catholic *habitus* (Shanneik 2011: 505). Undoubtedly, the Catholic religious and social experience of Irish converts in the 1980s and 1990s has profoundly shaped the way that they understand and engage with Orthodoxy. Having been part of majority 'universalist' Catholic Church, for example, partly explains the strong desire for pan-Orthodox unity and ecumenical dialogue. For some convert Orthodox, Orthodoxy's future in Ireland is therefore is often linked not to the sustainability or the internal dynamics of communities of Orthodox, both cradle and non-cradle, but rather Orthodoxy's ability to 'make a difference' to Ireland's religious landscape.

The Discourse and Practices of Autochthonism

Having discussed the 'institutional space' as a site of mediation, I will now explore the Orthodox 'discursive space' shared by convert and migrant Orthodox actors and communities in Ireland and the phenomenon of 'autochthonism'.[9] What follows are some preliminary remarks delimiting a 'discursive autochthonist' space amongst cradle and convert Orthodox. This discursive space is characterised by a blend of 'revisiting' and 're-visioning' of the Celtic Christian past and is linked to 'memory and meaning' making in the Irish Landscape. The arrival of Orthodoxy and Orthodox migrants in the West has given rise to a process of reinterpretation of the West's religious past as prototypically Orthodox. This discourse, and the practices that flow from it, can serve to strengthen a sense of

---

[9]   Autochthonous means 'indigenous' or 'native to this place'. I use the term 'autochthonism' in this article, in preference to 'indigenism', in order to echo the preferred term used by some East European traditionalist political movements that similarly claimed continuity in a given territory.

Mediating Orthodoxy 243

belonging amongst migrant Orthodox, who have a means of conceptualising themselves as representatives of the ancient past of their new homeland, tapping into an local 'Orthodox memory' and 'imaginary', and at the same time can also operate to legitimise the religious choices and identities of local Western converts to Orthodoxy.

Celtic Christianity, including the early Churches of Ireland, Wales, and Scotland, has been mined by a whole range of religious writers and movements in search of and in the hope of reconstructing or recapturing a Celtic spirituality for the modern age. These actors have identified a whole range of distinctive features, such as God's mystical presence in everyday activities, the exaltation of the minutiae of creation, man's relation to the natural world, the spirit of community expressed through early monasticism and the figure of the *anamchara*, or the 'spiritual friend', said to have originated in Druidic tradition but to have been preserved in the early Celtic Church (Gierek 2011: 305–307). In addition, there are those that have identified in the early Celtic Church a more egalitarian form of Christianity that affirms the feminine and can act as a site of liberation for women from later patriarchal forms of religion (Condren 1989). The ancient texts, historical sites and local folk traditions of 'Celtic Christianity' offer a resource for a whole range of alternative spiritualities and liberationist theologies, especially those disillusioned with the traditional authority structures of the mainstream Catholic and Protestant traditions. These authors and activists have, according to Donald Meek, been 'prone to romanticising, sentimentality and misinterpreting history' which he attributes to a 'lack of academic knowledge of the sources' (Meek 2000: 19, cited in Gierek 2011: 304).

Orthodox theologians and writers have also engaged with these same sources in their search for points of contact and continuity between the contemporary Orthodox East and the distant past of the Celtic West. Orthodox commentators, however, are engaged in a hermeneutic different to these sources, one that expands the existing conceptual boundaries of *territorio orthodoxiae* into a lost Western realm. The historical spiritual traditions of the Irish, Welsh, Scottish and also early Anglo-Saxon churches become assimilated into a contemporary Orthodox *habitus* and landscape, a case of '*your* past is *our* perpetual present'.

Orthodox clerics and writers, both in the West and in the Orthodox East, give explicit expression to these ideas. One such example is Fr Gregory Telepneff, a traditionalist Orthodox priest in the USA, who is the author of *The Egyptian Desert in the Irish Bogs: The Byzantine Character of Early Celtic Monasticism*, in which he writes:

> For the Eastern Orthodox, in particular, Celtic Christianity holds a special appeal, but not because it is somehow 'exotic'; rather, the faith of the ancient Irish has an air of familiarity for an Orthodox, a certain quality which he intuitively identifies with his own faith (Telepneff 2001: 9).

In addition to expressing this perceived affinity, other Orthodox writers outline the necessity for and the means by which to bridge past and present. The following comes from 'A Brief History of the Irish Orthodox Church', published by a convert monk online:

> The task of the Orthodox Christian convert in the West today is to bridge the gap between our time and the neglected and forgotten saints of Western Europe, who were our spiritual forebears. As St Arsenios of Cappadocia (†1924) said: 'Britain will only become Orthodox when she once again begins to venerate her saints' (Nikodemus, n.d.).

The saints of the Celtic (and Anglo-Saxon) traditions are one of principal means, according to the Monk Nikodemus, by which to recapture Orthodoxy in Ireland and Britain. But he warns against engaging with this in as an 'intellectual or aesthetic exercise' in the way modern 'spiritualities' do, and instead viewing them as 'alive' as 'our friends and spiritual mentors'. Awareness of these views on the status of the ancient Irish Church and her saints is not restricted to the clerical elite. One of the first members of the Romanian Orthodox Church I met in Ireland informed me: 'the ancient Irish Church was Orthodox you know. This is an Orthodox land at heart'.

As these extracts illustrate, Irish (and British) Orthodox are able to draw on the historical links between Coptic Egypt and the Byzantine Empire to present a model of Celtic Christianity that is congruent with contemporary Eastern Orthodoxy, especially in relation to the 'otherworldly' and miraculous lives of Ireland's saints. The need to 'return' on the part of local Christians to the ancient tradition is often explained or justified in terms of a 'fall narrative' or a gradual erosion of an original, authentic Christian message, a 'surrender of Orthodoxy'. Narratives and re-readings of history produced by some Orthodox in the West are related to the historical Great Schism between the Eastern and Western Churches, but also significantly draw on aspects of history particular to Britain and Ireland. For example, Fr Andrew Phillips, an Englishman who converted to Russian Orthodoxy in the 1970s and a priest in ROCOR, presents in his book *Orthodox Christianity and the English Tradition* a 'fall' narrative constructed around the Norman conquest of England (and later of Ireland) which brings about the end of Celtic and Anglo-Saxon Orthodoxy. Historical accuracy aside, this discourse generates a discursive rupture in the continuity of the local Churches, the Church of England and the Roman Catholic Church, which requires bridging by 'reverting' to Orthodox belief and practice.

The act of bridging this rupture and reconnecting with the Orthodox past and its local landscape takes on material, visual and ritual forms in contemporary Ireland. That is to say, various practices flow from the discourse of Orthodox autochthony. Perhaps the most visible of these practices is the naming of Orthodox parishes after local Celtic saints. For example, a number of the parishes of the Romanian Orthodox Church are dedicated to Irish saints or include Irish saints in their dedication: the parish in Blanchardstown in Dublin is named after St Columba; a Romanian Orthodox parish in Galway in named after St Nicholas and St Brigit of Kildare (Ireland's most revered woman saint); and similarly, the Cork parish of the Romanian Orthodox Church is named after a pair of saints, this time including St Patrick, Ireland's patron saint (Parohia Sfântul Ierarh Calinic de la Cernica și Sfântul Patrick). The Russian Orthodox Church has dedications to St Colman of Oughaval in Stradbally. St Finnian of Clonnard in Belfast and the Antiochian parish in Dublin is dedicated to the Three Patrons of Ireland, St Patrick, St Columba and St Brigit.

Related to the dedications to Irish saints is the popularity icons of Irish saints painted according to Eastern Orthodox convention. Through the production of icons of local saints the Orthodox visual aesthetic has entered the Irish religious landscape, with icons of St Brigit or St Patrick appearing entirely natural to both Orthodox as well as local Catholics. Ireland has its own association of iconographers,[10] and the well-known Icon Chapel at the Benedictine Abbey at Glenstal plays an important role in promoting both the veneration of icons and, as the statement describing the role of the Chapel highlights: 'The monastic call to prayer for the unity of all Christians, especially in the east' (Glenstal Abbey, n.d.).

In addition to the naming of new places of Orthodox worship after local saints, local Irish Orthodox, migrants and converts alike, visit the ancient religious sites of the Celtic Church to venerate the saints attached to these places and to pray. The Antiochian community in southwest Ireland is particularly interesting in this regard, as this small group of Irish Orthodox takes advice from a monk on Mount Athos, Fr Chrysostomos Koutloumousianos,[11] with whom they are in regular contact, over which particular holy sites should be visited.

> Fr Chrysostomos gives us advice on which places to visit. For example he was keen that we go to where St Declan was baptised. [...] A group of us get in the car and visit some of the ancient sites, we pray the Jesus Prayer in places where it might never have been prayed before.

The same member of the Antiochian community also referred to the phenomenon of Orthodox monks travelling from Russia quite frequently to

---

[10] See http://www.iconofile.com/default.asp?dir=guide&page=showresource&SupplierID=44 [accessed 5 December 2012]. A fairly exhaustive gallery of icons of British and Irish saints can be found at http://www.oodegr.com/english/istorika/britain/British_saints.htm [accessed 5 December 2012].

[11] Fr Chrysostomos is the author of two comparative works on the Celtic Church and Eastern Orthodoxy (2008 and 2009).

visit Skellig Michael, one of the most well-known early monastic sites in Ireland situated on a remote craggy island of the coast of County Kerry. The website of the Antiochian Mission of St Phillip in Ballydehob in west Cork provides a link to a website on early Christian Ireland, to which members of the Orthodox community have contributed (http://www.antiochireland.org/ballydehob/ [accessed 4 December 2012]). These points illustrate that Ireland's Orthodox communities are, through the legacy of the Celtic Christian tradition in the landscape and through the lives of her saints, able to simultaneously 'colonise' Ireland's Christian past and tap into a pan-European Orthodox imaginary.

One local member of the clergy warned, however, 'there is a danger in all this of Orthodox romanticising. The practices within the Orthodox community should not take on the "egoic" characteristics that it has amongst some Catholic women's groups'. He went on to explain:

> I am in two minds about that, if I go to an early Christian site to venerate or adore God, you know, it doesn't really matter where I am, if I am in a field or some ancient monastic site, it makes no difference, but if I try to resurrect the past then it becomes an intellectual exercise which probably has no benefit at all, it would probably be an "egoic" thing.

The discourse of autochthony and the related practices briefly described above are part of the 'furniture' of the new Orthodox presence in Britain and Ireland. We have yet to see to what extent the symbolism, saints and ancient sites of the Celtic Church will 'indigenise' the practice of Orthodoxy in Ireland. However, the pan-European connections described above and the process of 'meaning-making' in the migration space form an important aspect of contemporary Orthodox narrative constructions of identity in Ireland.

Conclusion

Following an overview of the Orthodox presence in the Republic of Ireland, this chapter has focused on two aspects of the formation of Orthodox institutions and subjectivities in Ireland: the role of local Irish coverts as mediators of the migration space, and the discourse, shared amongst convert and migrant alike, on the autochthony of Irish Orthodoxy. There are surely many points of comparison with other European countries in terms of the recent migration of Orthodox populations and the establishment of Churches in the migration context. The prominent role, however, that local 'mediators' have played in establishing Orthodox parishes and later serving those parishes as priests, deacons and readers is, I believe, distinctive of the Irish context. Prior to the 1990s, the minimal presence of institutional Orthodoxy meant that many of the local converts that went on to be active within the various Orthodox Churches had some shared experience of Orthodoxy centred around the Greek Church in Dublin. The fact that a number of convert clergy and lay people have a keen interest in pan-Orthodox cooperation and unity is also helping to create a relatively fluid attitude towards Church affiliation. The demography of Ireland, with very few urban centres and hence very dispersed Orthodox communities, is also a not inconsiderable factor in encouraging inter-Orthodox contacts.

Many migrant families do not have the benefit of financial security, stable places of work or permanent homes and so *some* of the tasks of establishing Orthodoxy in Ireland have naturally fallen to those that are better placed, both financially and in terms of local knowledge to contribute. In this regard it is too early to speak in terms of a distinctive Irish inter-Orthodox space taking shape, but the subtle influence of non-cradle Orthodox identities is being felt. Also, there are now a large number of Orthodox children of school age – 7,839 according to the 2011 census (An Phríomh-Oifig Staidrimh 2012), some of whom are Irish-born but of mixed Irish-migrant Orthodox parentage and who constitute the first generation of Irish Orthodox. Many of these children, according to parents, are growing up as predominantly English speakers. A minority situation always entails the self-conscious production of an identity for the next generation. Irish Orthodox understanding of Orthodoxy and their identity as a religious minority in Ireland will inevitably find expression in unique ways. The discourse and practices of autochthonism may play, in future, a significant role in determining how local Irish Orthodox understand their place in Irish society and in the Irish landscape. The production of 'neo-natives' from members of migrant and convert communities through the incorporation of 'Irish sites' within a 'pan-Orthodox transnational space' may form a distinctive aspect of these identities.

Bibliography

Abu Mrad, N. 2008. The Witness of the Church in the Pluralistic World: Theological Renaissance in the Church of Antioch, in *The Cambridge Companion to Orthodox Christian Theology*, edited by M.B. Cunningham and E. Theokritoff. Cambridge: Cambridge University Press, 246–60.

An Phríomh-Oifig Staidrimh [Central Statistics Office]. 2012. Profile 7: Religion, Ethnicity and Irish Travellers. Dublin: CSO.

Antiochian Orthodox Deanery of the United Kingdom and Ireland. n.d. Journeys to Orthodoxy. Available at: http://www.antiochian-orthodox. co.uk/Journeys/journeys.htm [accessed 13 December 2012].

Church of Holy Apostles Peter and Paul. 2009. Iz Istorii Khrama [From the History of the Parish]. Available at: http://www.stpeterstpaul.net/index.

php?option=com_content&view=article&id=50&Itemid=59&lang=en [accessed 1 December 2012].

Condren, M. 1989. *The Serpent and the Goddess*. New York: Harper and Row.

Diocese of Sourozh. n.d. Directory of Parishes and Places of Worship. Available at: http://www.sourozh.org/parishes-eng/ [accessed 5 December 2012].

Gierek, B. 2011. 'Celtic Spirituality' in Contemporary Ireland, in *Ireland's New Religious Movements*, edited by O. Cosgrove, L. Cox, C. Kuhling and P. Mulholland. Newcastle upon Tyne: Cambridge Scholars, 300–316.

Glenstal Abbey. n.d. The Icon Chapel. Available at: http://www.glenstal. org/?page_id=146 [accessed 5 December 2012].

Hämmerli, M. 2010. Orthodox Diaspora?: A Sociological and Theological Problematisation of a Stock Phrase. *International Journal for the Study of the Christian Church*, 10(2–3): 97–115.

Hann, C. and Goltz H. 2010. Introduction: The Other Christianity, in *Eastern Christians in Anthropological Perspective*, edited by C. Hann and H. Goltz. Berkeley and Los Angeles: University of California Press, 1–29.

Koutloumousianos, Ieromonk Chrysostomos. 2008. *Ο Θεός των Μυστηρίων. Η θεολογία των Κελτών στο φως της ελληνικής Ανατολής* [*The God of the Mysteries: The Theology of the Celts in the Light of the Greek East*]. Mount Athos: Koutloumousiou Monastery.

Koutloumousianos, Ieromonk Chrysostomos. 2009. *Οι Εραστές Της Βασιλείας. Συνάντηση Κελτικού & Βυζαντινού μοναχισμού* [*The Lovers of the Kingdom: The Meeting of Celtic and Byzantine Monasticism*]. Mount Athos: Koutloumousiou Monastery.

Lucas, P.C. 2003. Enfant Terribles: The Challenge of Sectarian Converts to Ethnic Orthodox Churches in the United States. *Nova Religio: The Journal of Alternative and Emergent Religions*, 7(2): 5–23.

Macourt, M. 2011. Mapping the 'New Religious Landscape' and the 'New Irish': Uses and Limitations of the Census, in *Ireland's New Religious Movements*, edited by O. Cosgrove, L. Cox, C. Kuhling and P. Mulholland. Newcastle upon Tyne: Cambridge Scholars, 28–49.

Meek, D. 2000. *The Quest for Celtic Christianity*. Edinburgh: The Handsel Press.

Nikodemus. n.d. A Brief History of the Irish Orthodox Church. Available at: http://orthodoxinfo.com/general/irishorthodoxchurch.aspx [accessed 2 October 2012]).

O'Donnell, G. 2008. The Orthodox Church in Ireland 2008, in *Inter-Church Relations: Developments and Perspectives*, edited by B. Leahy. Dublin: Veritas, 80–90.

OrthodoxWiki. n.d. Journeys to Orthodoxy. Available at: http://orthodoxwiki. org/Journeys_to_Orthodoxy [accessed 13 December 2012].

Papanikolaou, A. 2008. Personhood and its Exponents in Twentieth-Century Orthodox Theology, in *The Cambridge Companion to Orthodox Christian*

Theology, edited by M.B. Cunningham and E. Theokritoff. Cambridge: Cambridge University Press, 232–45.

Pochin, M.D. 1966. Roman Road to Orthodoxy. *Focus*, July (1966): 153–5.

Rambo, L.R. 1999. Theories of Conversion: Understanding and Interpreting Religious Change. *Social Compass*, 46(3): 259–71.

Scharbrodt, O. 2012. Muslim Immigration to the Republic of Ireland: Trajectories and Dynamics since World War II. *Éire-Ireland*, 47 (Spring/Summer): 221–43.

Shanneik, Y. 2011. Conversion and Religious Habitus: The Experiences of Irish Women Converts to Islam in the Pre-Celtic Tiger Era. *Journal of Muslim Minority Affairs*, 34(4): 503–517.

Shanneik, Y. 2012. Religion and Diasporic Dwelling: Algerian Muslim Women in Ireland. *Gender and Religion*, 2(1): 80–100.

Smith, T.L. 1969. Refugee Orthodox Congregations in Western Europe, 1945–1948. *Church History*, 38(3): 312–26.

Somers, M. 1994. The Narrative Construction of Identity: A Relational and Network Approach. *Theory and Society*, 23(5): 605–649.

Telepneff, G. 2001. *The Egyptian Desert in the Irish Bogs: The Byzantine Character of Early Celtic Monasticism*. Etna, CA: Center for Traditionalist Orthodox Studies.

Toulson, S. 1990. *The Celtic Alternative: A Reminder of the Christianity We Lost*. London: Ryder.

Chapter 13

The Great Athonite Tradition in France: Circulation of Athonite Imaginaries and the Emergence of a French Style of Orthodoxy[1]

Laurent Denizeau

The Bolshevik Revolution and the advent of Soviet communism in Russia, as well as the Greek exodus from Asia Minor, caused significant immigration waves in Western Europe and in France: numerous Russians settled in places like Paris and Nice. In the course of inter-socialisation, many French people discovered Orthodoxy. The depreciation of the Second Vatican Council among some Roman Catholics also led to conversions to Orthodoxy. Orthodoxy in France thus tends increasingly to distance itself from cultural and ethnic identities, though these nevertheless continue to cause some canonical paradoxes.

This relatively recent development of Orthodoxy in France has benefited from the existence of monasteries, which act as privileged vehicles for Eastern Christian spirituality. This chapter focuses on the creation, in France, of several monastic dependancies of the monastery of Simonos Petra on Mount Athos (Greece), and more specifically on the *metochion*[2] of Saint-Antoine-le-Grand, situated in a small valley in Vercors. In this diaspora context, the notion of tradition – an unavoidable reference of the Orthodox faith – constitutes the identity pillar of a dispersed religious identity. The tradition discussed here is connected to locality, but, paradoxically, a de-territorialised locality, as it refers to the Athonite monastic tradition – in France. In such a context, tradition is not so much related to a place (Mount Athos), but rather to a network of agents capable of building locality beyond a geographical setting, in order to generate an enlarged community: one Church. The monks I met spoke of the establishment of this kind of monastery as a return to Western Christian roots,

---

[1]   I would like to thank Maria Hämmerli for the English translation of this text and Matthew Baker for his comments and proofreading.

[2]   Plural: *metochia* – a monastic dependancy (from the Greek *meta echo*: 'which partakes to').

252   *Orthodox Identities in Western Europe*

as the restoration of Orthodoxy in France via the Eastern Christian Athonite spiritual experience. The founder of these Athonite communities, a Frenchman himself, describes the emergence of Orthodoxy in France – initially related to immigration waves but no more so – as 'a pilgrimage to the roots'. He describes this in the phrase 'a Western expression of Orthodoxy' (*Orthodoxie d'expression occidentale*), which reveals a universal message in local colours. The means for conveying this message borrow from pre-schism Western spiritual works, as well as the Athonite tradition, via Russian theologians and writers. It is the transition from one style to another, rather than the focus on the positive character of a so-called original culture, that is considered in view of creating a local Church.

The Athos Outside of Athos: French Foundations of Simonos Petra

The existence of the 'Great Athonite Tradition' in France is tightly connected to the remarkable monastic life story of Fr Placide Deseille, which spans over the second half of the twentieth century. Fr Placide is preparing to celebrate 70 years of monastic life, spent between the Trappist tradition in the Roman Catholic Church and the Athonite tradition in the Orthodox Church. It all began in September 1942, when France was under German occupation and the future Fr Placide withdrew from the world and entered the monastery of Bellefontaine in Anjou. He was only 16 years old. The young monk who was in charge of his education introduced him to the teachings of the Desert Fathers. A Romanian monk visiting the monastery of Bellefontaine strengthened Fr Placide's interest in Orthodox monasticism and awakened the curiosity of another monk, Fr Dominique, who was to be very close to Fr Placide all the way through. He spent his first years in the monastery studying the main monastic writings. His deeper understanding of Thomistic theology led him gradually to turn away from scholastic thinking, considering it too narrow an approach to divine mystery. Thus he decided to extend his knowledge about Orthodoxy by attending courses at the Institut Saint-Serge in Paris.[3] Subsequently, the abbot general of the Cistercians assigned him the task of producing a bibliographical collection of the French translations of Western monastic writings from the fifth to the thirteenth century. Fr Placide joined the editors of the series *Sources chrétiennes* for this project. Increasing knowledge of the Desert Fathers' theology and his fascination with the Orthodox liturgy led Fr Placide to create a Byzantine-

---

[3]   Founded in 1925, this theological institute, affiliated with the Russian Paris Exarchate under the Ecumenical Patriarchate, is a private higher education institution which trains Orthodox priests. Since its creation, Saint-Serge has contributed to disseminating Orthodox theology in France, especially through the works of renowned theologians. The institute has become a point of encounter between the Orthodox and the non-Orthodox.

The Great Athonite Tradition in France   253

rite Catholic community in 1966 – the Monastery of the Transfiguration at Aubazine, in Corrèze. Fr Dominique followed him in this adventure, which sought to reconnect with the original monastic lifestyle. Several disciples joined them. The two monks were also in charge of liturgical services in a nearby Eastern-rite Catholic ('Uniate') women's monastery, which was later to convert to Orthodoxy and create the Monastery of the Burning Bush at Villardonnel. On their land the monks erected their own wooden monastic dwellings. Each member of the community occupied a small hermitage and joined the others for religious services and meals.

For its tenth anniversary, the community in Aubazine made a pilgrimage to traditionally Orthodox countries. In 1971, Fr Placide and other members of the community went for the first time to Mount Athos, which was going through an unexpected revival. It is then that they experienced a life-changing encounter with Fr Aemilianos from Simonos Petra. The idea of conversion emerged gradually, with the strengthening of the belief that the Roman Catholic Church had estranged itself from the tradition of the Desert Fathers. Fr Placide and some other members of the Aubazine community, including Fr Dominique, entered the Orthodox Church on 19 June 1977. To avoid insinuating a break with his past, Fr Placide preserved the name given to him when he took the habit in Bellefontaine. Fr Dominique became Fr Seraphim. They stayed for almost one year at Athos before returning to France, upon request of their *hegoumen*, in order to create *metochia* of Simonos Petra. This is how the Monastery of Saint-Antoine-le-Grand came to being, in a valley in Vercors. Another Aubazine companion, who had become a monk in Simonos Petra under the name of Fr Elias, created a female monastic dependancy in Dordogne.

Starting in 1981, new people with a monastic call presented themselves at Saint-Antoine-le-Grand. But they were women. Initially, the three fathers were to create a male *metochion* (Saint-Antoine-le-Grand) and a female one (the Monastery of the Transfiguration), according to the request of their *hegoumen*, Fr Aemilianos. The women candidates to monastic life were received as novices under Fr Placide's spiritual guidance, giving thus rise to a third *metochion*, the Monastery of the Protection of the Theotokos (known as the Monastery of Solan, from the name of the village where the monastery is implanted). New monks arrived later, beginning in 1987. At the time of writing this chapter, the community counts five professed monks, despite the eventful history of successive candidates presenting themselves to Saint-Antoine-le-Grand, the majority of whom were French converts to Orthodoxy, with a former Catholic or Protestant background. This indicates that the Monastery of Saint-Antoine-le-Grand, which is by default under the jurisdiction of the Ecumenical Patriarchate of Constantinople by virtue of belonging to the Simonos Petra monastic family, is not thereby the product of the Greek diaspora in France.

254 *Orthodox Identities in Western Europe*

Besides the monastic community, many other believers take part in the life of the monastery, which they attend as their regular parish. Former Roman Catholics, members of the Orthodox diaspora (Greek, Romanian, Russian, Serbian), converts introduced to Christianity through the witness of the Fathers – all these people benefit from the daily services in the French language,[4] the teachings of Fr Placide, the spiritual presence of the monks and children's catechism. Fr Placide's spiritual charisma attracts also many Orthodox clergy or various lay people, who may come from abroad to meet him or simply to be on retreat at the monastery. In a diaspora context, the monastery appears as a resourceful place for immigrants. As a *metochion* of Simonos Petra, the Monastery of Saint-Antoine-le-Grand is also a centre of attention of the Greek Orthodox diaspora.[5]

Orthodox monasteries being so scanty in France (about 20 of them, affiliated with different patriarchates), other immigrants from traditionally Orthodox countries also come to visit or stay at the Monastery of Saint-Antoine-le-Grand. Some Orthodox clergy attend the monastery because of its Athonite identity, which testifies of 'the Great Athonite Tradition'. Also, Fr Placide's life story attracts other Christians wishing to find a venue for dialogue with the Orthodox Church. Besides this spiritual interest in the monastery, the frescoes in the monastery church cater to a significant number of tourists. The iconography of the church provides an opportunity to speak about the Christian understanding of the world to an audience which has a rather imprecise knowledge of Christianity. This role of the monastery, which one might want to qualify as missionary, is reinforced by a rich publishing activity which presents Eastern Christian spirituality to the French public. The French monks like to point out that they live as if in a 'mission land', as they put it. It could be said that the different activities of this French Orthodox monastery reach far beyond its walls. It functions not so much according to a centripetal logic, which implies withdrawal from the world, but according to a centrifugal logic, in which the monastery contributes to invigorating the spiritual life of the Orthodox people living in the world, especially in a cultural context marked by secularisation.

The spiritual influence of this handful of monasteries can be explained by the exceptional personality and charisma of their founder, but also by their affiliation with Simonos Petra, one of the 20 sovereign monasteries on the 'Holy Mountain'. Thanks to their prestigious monastic ascendance, these *metochia* appear as the warrants of an authentic testimonial to the 'Great Tradition'.

---

[4] This presupposes considerable translation work, and the monks have tackled the job since the foundation of the monastery.

[5] This point is explicitly mentioned in the statutes of the monastery, approved by the Ministry of the Interior: 'The main activities of the order refer to [...] the reception of guests in need of moral help, particularly students of Greek origin residing in France'.

The Great Athonite Tradition in France   255

Since the separation with Rome, this has been a distinctive characteristic of Orthodoxy, as the 'Church of the Seven Councils', which claims to be the heir of the undivided Church.

On account of its history, Mount Athos is subject to social imaginaries that present the peninsula as the heart of the early monastic tradition. The monastic presence on Mount Athos is said to date back to the seventh century, when Islamic expansion supposedly caused monks to move from the Egyptian desert into safer Mediterranean areas (particularly in Cappadocia). As the number of monks was increasing subsequently, the Byzantine emperor Nicephorus II Phocas (921–969) assigned his father confessor to gather the hermits dispersed on the peninsula in monastic communities. Thus Athanasios founded the first Athonite monastery, the Great Lavra, in 963. This is considered to be the foundation date of the Monastic Republic of Mount Athos (Paléologue 1997), which boasts of more than a millennium of uninterrupted monastic life, rooted in the very tradition of the first Egyptian monasteries. Athonite monks like to note that at Athos, 'a thousand years are like yesterday',[6] underlining once more the continuum of a tradition based on early monasticism. Moreover, in 1046 the Byzantine emperor Constantine IX Monomachos (980–1055) issued a 'chrysobull' [edict] forbidding access to 'any woman, any female creature, any eunuch, any young smooth-face'. Safeguarded from the developments of the 'world' by a strict enclosure, Mount Athos is considered a special place, outside the world and out of time, and is often presented as a shrine of the 'Great Tradition' of the Orthodox Church. Through their prestigious Athonite filiation, the Simonos Petra dependancies in France guarantee 'authenticity', a recurrent word in many visitors' discourse, and are a resource for lay people and secular clergy and a representative of this 'Great Tradition' in France.

The phrase 'the Athos outside Athos', which the French monks use in order to describe their monastery, implies that here, in France, as well as there, at Mount Athos, the monastic experience relies on the same tradition. The same tradition in an isolated valley in Vercors, where the Athonite *metochion* started 30 years ago, and on a 60-kilometre-long Greek peninsula populated by monks since the seventh century. The Athonite tradition in France and Greece: do we speak of the same monastic experience? At least this is what the French monks believe; for them, this tradition is not so much precisely Athonite, but rather the 'Great Tradition' of the primitive Church preserved at Athos. The French monks explain their practice in terms of a specific tradition defined by its localisation: Mount Athos. But the circulation of religious landscapes in the context of globalisation results into the de-territorialisation of this localisation; consequently, the monks live the Athonite tradition outside of Mount Athos itself. Instead of trying to determine whether the monks are really faithful to the

---

[6]   This image is inspired from Psalm 89.

256 *Orthodox Identities in Western Europe*

Athonite heritage or whether the latter is really connected with the primitive Church, I prefer to focus on the circulation of tradition and on how the monks have built an Athonite monastic experience in France. The question that arises is the following: what elements of this 'Great Athonite Tradition' circulate?

How Tradition is Transported and Implanted

Monasticism is a privileged vehicle for tradition in the process of the recent implantation of Orthodoxy in France. Monasteries become warrants of traditionality, places where lay people can revitalise themselves and experience God's presence in a way that is identified and acknowledged as 'authentically' Orthodox. The implantation of these monasteries is less about transplanting the Athonite tradition than it is about translating the 'spirit of this tradition' in a specific cultural context. The French monasteries do not reproduce the Athonite tradition, but take their inspiration from it. Translation implies staying faithful to the original message, though never saying exactly the same thing. The French monks live the same monastic life as their Athonite seniors, but in the context of a secularised society, where Orthodoxy is not only a minority religion, but also one resulting from recent immigration. The monks' affiliation with the Orthodox Church is the result of conversion: they have been raised as Roman Catholics, Protestants, Jews, or even with no confessional background. Therefore living an Athonite life outside of Mount Athos implies a permanent dialogue between the Athonite tradition and the adjustments generated by its implementation in a specific cultural context. The challenge here is to be able to do things differently while keeping in line with the Athonite tradition, by differentiating between aspects of Greek culture and hesychast spirituality. Thus tradition consists in a process of translation, an accurate one, despite the need to innovate – or rather precisely because of this need. Far from being a mere literal repetition, the spirit of tradition allows for creativity. Its adaptability is incompatible with a literal transmission. The mediators of tradition, i.e. the elders – those who have already acquired this 'spirit' – are only repeating the same thing in a different way.

This de-territorialised tradition, the Athos outside of Athos, is being re-territorialised in the process of its implementation in France. The French monks claim the same tradition links them with their Athonite fathers, yet living this tradition in France differs significantly from living it on Mount Athos: though the monastery Saint-Antoine-le-Grand is committed to the 'Great Athonite Tradition', it does not follow all its practices and customs. Firstly, the *metochia's* missionary vocation of witnessing the Orthodox spirituality in France implies that their monastic enclosure is in no way commensurate with the Athonite one. Numerous families attend the monastery, and children can receive catechism. Women can come for spiritual retreats and liturgical services[7] to the male monastery of Saint-Antoine-le-Grand, and generally speaking everyone is welcome to attend the different religious services. This functioning as a regular parish led the monks to introduce the Gregorian calendar,[8] for the faithful to benefit from liturgical feasts, instead of the Julian calendar in use at Mount Athos. For the same reason, monks do not observe the Byzantine time as at Athos, where the liturgical day starts at the sunset and not at midnight like in the civil time division. The local dimension of the Athonite tradition is expressed also in the great efforts of translating the liturgical prayers into French, which involves the adaptation of the Byzantine music, in adjusting the ascetic practices (according to the visitors) and in the missionary activity of explaining Orthodox spirituality (in publications, conferences and welcoming tourists' visits to the church).

Monastic life in France is radically different from Athos, and sometimes opposed to the very foundations of the monastic engagement, in order to enable the experience of the same tradition in a specific context. That is because the implantation of Athonite monasticism in France means dealing with a legislative system that has nothing to do with that of the Monastic Republic of Mount Athos. Relations between the French state and religious institutions have been sometimes strained, resulting in the separation into two spheres of action: the state regulates public affairs whereas religious institutions operate in the area of private life. Central to these relations is the 1905 law which introduced *laïcité* as a constitutional principle, stating in Article 2 that 'the Republic does not recognise, nor pays for salaries, nor supports financially any religion'.[9] This French version of secularity is a recurrent theme in social debates related to the presence of religion in the public sphere. In this legislative context, monastic communities have to lead a true legal crusade involving some administrative subtleties in order to obtain legal recognition. The 1905 Law does not repeal Title III of the 1901 Law, under which fall religious orders (*congrégations*) that wish to get legal recognition. The 1901 Law states in Article 13 that:

> any religious order can be granted legal recognition upon decree issued in agreement with the Council of State; the provisions on the previously authorised

---

[7]   Female visitors reside not in the guesthouse situated on the monastic premises, which is for men only, but in another guesthouse, situated a few kilometres away from the monastery.

[8]   Or rather, the so-called 'Revised Julian Calendar', which still follows the older Julian calculation for the movable feasts, for example Easter, Pentecost, etc.

[9]   'La République ne reconnaît, ne salarie, ni ne subventionne aucun culte': Excerpt from the 9 December 1905 Law on Church–State separation, published in *Journal Officiel de la République Française* on 11 December 1905. The laws to which I refer are available online: www.legifrance.gouv.fr.

orders apply also in this case. Legal recognition can be granted to any new establishment by virtue of a Council of State decree ...[10]

The orders that had obtained legal recognition before 1901 uphold their authorisation, but recent orders can be granted legal recognition by the Council of State,[11] as long as they comply with Article 19 of the 16 August 1901 Decree regulating their statutes: 'The statutes must contain the same indications and engagements as the registered public associations [...]. The statutes must also contain: 1. The order and its members are subject to the jurisdiction of the local ordinary ...'.[12] The necessity of this obedience is restated in Article 20 of the same Decree, which stipulates that 'the application must include also a statement of the local diocesan bishop, who commits to taking the respective order and its members under his jurisdiction'.[13] Hereby, the State acknowledges the spiritual authority of the local diocesan bishop, but it must be noted that the above-mentioned orders can only be Roman Catholic. The authority of the ordinary became problematic the moment when recognition was requested by non-Catholic religious orders, as in the case of the Orthodox monasteries. As a consequence, submission to the authority of the ordinary extended with the recognition of a third party, such as the Orthodox inter-episcopal committee in the case of the Orthodox monasteries.[14]

Despite the resort to recognition by a spiritual authority, granting legal recognition to an order differs from religious recognition. The spiritual

---

[10] 'Toute congrégation religieuse peut obtenir la reconnaissance légale par décret rendu sur avis conforme du conseil d'Etat; les dispositions relatives aux congrégations antérieurement autorisées leur sont applicables. La reconnaissance légale pourra être accordée à tout nouvel établissement congréganiste en vertu d'un décret en Conseil d'Etat': Excerpt from Title III, Article 13 of the 1 July 1901 Law on the Contract of Association, published in *Journal Officiel de la République Française* on 2 July 1901.

[11] Though subject to the 1901 Law, orders must be recognised by the Council of State and not simply by the local Prefecture.

[12] 'Les projets de statuts contiennent les mêmes indications et engagements que ceux des associations reconnues d'utilité publique [...]. Les statuts contiennent, en outre: 1. La soumission de la congrégation et de ses membres à la juridiction de l'ordinaire [...]'. Article 19 of the 16 August 1901 Decree establishing public regulation for the implementation of the 1 July 1901 Law on the Contract of Association, published in *Journal Officiel de la République Française* on 17 July 1901.

[13] 'La demande doit être accompagnée d'une déclaration par laquelle l'évêque du diocèse s'engage à prendre la congrégation et ses membres sous sa juridiction': Excerpt from Article 20 of the 16 August 1901 Decree establishing public regulation of the implementation of the 1 July 1901 Decree on the Contract of Association, published in *Journal Officiel de la République Française* on 17 July 1901.

[14] The recognition of a Buddhist monastery raised the same problem; in that case, the spiritual reference was the Dalai Lama, through his representative in France.

The Great Athonite Tradition in France   259

authority only approves the statutes of the applicant order. Applications for legal recognition are addressed to the Ministry of the Interior. The application is signed by the founders and is accompanied by supportive documents (such as the statement of the spiritual authority, the opinion of the local authorities and the prefect's report) and a draft of the statutes. The statutes of the Order Saint-Simon-le-Myroblite (the juridical name of the Monastery of Saint-Antoine-le-Grand),[15] which are approved by the Ministry of the Interior, state that the aim of this association is 'the practice of religious life according to the monastic rule derived from the traditions of the Orthodox Church and the customs of the Monastery Simonos Petra on Mount Athos (Article 1)'.

But there is no mention of two key elements of the monastic profession, namely the taking of perpetual vows in a public ceremony and the vow of obedience to the monastery's superior. This is a deliberate omission, which fulfils the requirement of a decree dating back to 13 and 19 February 1790, which forbids perpetual vows and which has never been repealed since. Its Article 1 states that 'the royal constitutional Act does not recognise any monastic vows ... taken by persons of either sex; consequently, religious orders or regular orders where such vows are taken, are and will remain cancelled in France, with no possibility for anything similar to be established in the future'.[16] The goal of this article is to refuse any final engagement perceived as contrary to 'enjoying natural and imprescriptible human rights'.[17] The solemn profession of monastic vows is understood as contrary to human fundamental freedoms, despite the recurrent insistence on the candidate's free choice in the tonsure service. The strict application of this decree would entail the absolute ban of monastic orders; in practice, it is only stated in the report by the Council of State, which specifies that there can be no mention of perpetual or final vows in the civil statutes of those orders aspiring to legal recognition (Boyer 1993: 167).

Though missing from the statutes of the order, perpetual vows are mentioned in the monastery rule: 'Starting with their monastic tonsure, the brothers commit for life before God to observe their engagements. According to the teachings of the holy Fathers and the tradition of the Holy Mountain, no ecclesiastical authority can grant valid exemption from these'.[18] Let us note, with Alain Boyer, that 'the decision which founds the religious community differs in the civil law

---

[15] Referring to the founder of the Monastery Simonos Petra.

[16] 'La constitutionnelle du royaume ne reconnaîtra plus de vœux monastiques sciennels des personnes de l'un ni de l'autre sexe; en conséquence, les ordres et congrégations réguliers dans lesquels on fait de pareils vœux sont et demeurent supprimés en France, sans qu'il puisse en être établi de semblables à l'avenir'. Conseil d'Etat (France). 1824. *Tables générales des lois, arrêtés, décrets, ordonnances du roi, arrêts et avis du conseil d'état et réglemens d'administration publiés depuis 1789*, Volume 1. Paris: Ménard et Desenne fils, p. 13.

[17] Article 1 of the Declaration of Rights from the 24 June 1793 Constitution.

[18] Excerpt from the Rules of the Monastery, Article 16.

260   *Orthodox Identities in Western Europe*

and canon law' (Boyer 1993: 167). Perpetual vows are the foundation of the monastic tradition, but they are purposely ignored in the statutes of the order, so as to ensure the gain of legal personality. This leads Orthodox monasteries in France to develop a double, and at times contradictory, discourse: on the one hand there is a tradition with its own canon law and on the other hand there is the French legal system with its civil law – the result of a troubled history of church–state relations. Another relevant example is the treatment of deceased monks. The Athonite practice consists in exhuming the body three years after the burial, and placing the remains in an ossuary. French law forbids exhumation and therefore Orthodox monasteries cannot observe this traditional custom.

While the implementation of the Athonite tradition in France means maintaining a flexible general outline in order to allow for experimentation, there exists nevertheless the risk of a shift from adjustment to compromise. Adjustment implies that monastic practices adapt to a cultural background that differs from that on Mount Athos. Compromising could occasion the emergence of the worldly logic, which the monks strive to flee, in the organisation of monastic experience. In the former case, the monastery adapts its practices in order to avoid locking itself in strict observance and marginalising the community vis-à-vis lay people and more broadly the host society, and thereby fail its mission of witnessing Eastern Christian spirituality in the West. In the latter case, the logic of 'the world' would shape ascetic practice and would contribute to their redefinition, with the risk of dissolving the Athonite tradition. This is in fact the main criticism that convert monks or lay people with a formerly Roman Catholic background direct against Catholicism: the reproach of being too much in tune with the present social developments, as reflected in the *aggiornamento* introduced by the Second Vatican Council. And that is precisely one reason why the convert monks are so fond of tradition. But instead of considering merely what tradition 'says' in its texts, the monks find it more relevant to travel the 'backroads', which allow them to bypass a rigid itinerary and make adjustments which, while preserving the 'spirit of tradition', provide a more flexible framework for the monastic experience, making it possible here and now. The whole challenge of the circulation of tradition is to show that the same reality (the 'Great Athonite Tradition') can be lived differently.

Towards a French Style of Orthodoxy

The Orthodox presence is not totally new in the West; the first Greek church opened in London in 1677 and in North America there have been Orthodox ever since the eighteenth century (Ware 2002). Yet this presence has become significant only beginning with the twentieth century. The communist regime in Russia and the civil war in Greece generated significant immigration waves from Orthodox countries to France. In the 1960s, Olivier Clément documented some 150,000 Orthodox people in France (Clément 1965: 32). These figures have continued to increase, as attested by the Machelon Commission in charge of the relations between religion and public authorities, which listed 300,000 Orthodox in its report to the Ministry of Interior and Territorial Planning on 20 September 2006 (Machelon 2006). Besides, about 20 monasteries were established under the authority of different patriarchates.

With the immigrant Orthodox desirous to preserve an ecclesial connection to their homeland, the patriarchates provided their respective 'diasporas' with priests and bishops. This is how Orthodox churches with national titles (Greek Orthodox Church, Romanian Orthodox Church, etc.) multiplied on the same territory – in contradiction to the Orthodox canonical principle of unity expressed in the presence of one single bishop for a defined geographical territory. The Church very quickly became a venue for immigrants to keep a link with their homeland, a place where they can speak in their mother tongue and practise their customs. The close relation between culture and tradition originates from the integration of the Church in a geographical territory as a local Church.[19] In the context of globalisation, the local Church is no more confined to its national territory, yet religious identity remains strongly connected to national identity.

Nikos Kokosalakis notes that in Greece, Orthodoxy is inextricably bound to 'the Greek ethnic identity', as a consequence of the Ottoman domination and of the nationalist movement in the nineteenth century (Kokosalakis 1996: 137). Furthermore, the Greek Church plays an important role in the politics of the nation state and political institutions frequently draw on local religious representations in order to write a new chapter in the nation's history (Seraidari 2001). Affiliation with the Orthodox Church is therefore often associated with cultural identity. Thus tradition is torn between a strong local anchorage and the universal vocation of Christianity.

This raises a number of questions in the case of French (and, more generally speaking, Western) converts, whose Orthodox identity is the result of a spiritual journey: do they need to become Russians or Greeks in order to be Orthodox? Though it may sound provocative, it is not rare to sense surprise or even disapproval among cradle Orthodox at the idea that French people could identify themselves as Orthodox and at the same time be ignorant of the local customs. Here we encounter a confusion between faith and cultural customs. Kallistos Ware reports the statement of one bishop at the Council of Carthage in 257: 'The Lord said "I am the Truth"; He did not say "I am the custom"'

---

[19]   The integration of the Church in a defined geographic territory goes hand in hand with its integration in the history of that place. Thus the Orthodox tradition defined itself according to its geography (Eastern Christian spirituality), which in its turn was linked to the history of the respective place (the Schism with the Catholic Church and with Rome).

(Ware 2002: 254). The challenge for the planting of Orthodoxy in France is to move beyond national identities in order to create a 'French style of Orthodoxy', to quote the founder of the French *metochia* of Simonos Petra. This means to find a local expression of a message which is supposed to be universal, a Western way of living the teachings of the primitive Church.

Fr Placide's biography provides important information for the understanding of Athonite monasticism in France and of what is at stake in the relations with Mount Athos. The stages of Fr Placide's conversion led him to interpret this conversion as a return to the origins of a Christian tradition that the West and the East used to share. Consequently, he likes to draw parallels between the works of the first monks in the West and the tradition of the 'Holy Mountain'. In this respect, the rules of the monastery Saint-Antoine-le-Grand states the following:

> The present 'Rule of monastic life' (*typikon*) is based mainly on texts from all over the monastic tradition, chosen according to the spirit and necessities specific to our monastery; following Saint Nicodemus the Hagiorite, we borrowed from the spiritual tradition of the West, where we are called to live, while carefully ensuring that these texts are perfectly consistent with the Orthodox doctrine.[20]

The analogy between his conversion and the orientation of the French monasteries echoes the affinity between Western Christianity and the Orthodox tradition, lost since the eleventh-century schism. The two religious traditions are joined in Fr Placide's life story and relate to each other in a form of 'elective affinity', in Weber's understanding of the term (Weber 1994). Michael Löwy defines this as 'the process by which two cultural forms – religious, intellectual, political or economic – attract, influence and reinforce each other in active convergence, based on certain significant analogies, intimate similarities or closeness in meaning' (Löwy 2004: 100).[21] The closeness in meaning (*affinité de sens*) refers not so much to the territory (Mount Athos), but rather to a de-territorialised tradition, which exists now on Mount Athos just as it used to exist in France. Pierre Erny notes that the contact with immigrant populations in France gave rise to the idea that:

> it should be possible to renew the pre-Roman ecclesial tradition and the 'deep Orthodoxy' of our countries ... Theoretical proposals and concrete attempts have often failed. But it became obvious that it is possible to recover the ancient

---

[20] Excerpt from the prologue of the Rules of the Monastery Saint-Antoine-le-Grand, p. 2.

[21] 'Le processus par lequel deux formes culturelles – religieuses, intellectuelles, politiques ou économiques – entrent, à partir de certaines analogies significatives, parentés intimes ou affinités de sens, dans un rapport d'attraction et influence réciproques, choix mutuel, convergence active et renforcement mutuel'.

The advent of Orthodoxy in Western Europe is more often than not perceived as a potential spiritual regeneration, to the extent to which Orthodoxy in France is envisaged as a potential return to the pre-schism Orthodoxy in Western Europe. Thus the foundation of Athonite monastic dependancies in France is understood not as the implantation of an exotic tradition but as the creation of a French-speaking Orthodoxy (*Orthodoxie d'expression française*). In this respect, Fr Placide's speech at the inauguration and blessing of the monastery's premises illustrates this project:

> It is mainly from our regions that Christianity spread in the Gauls, during the apostolic times, when Christianity was Greek and Oriental. Our Orthodox Church stands in close continuity these first Christian generations. The presence of an Orthodox monastery in this Catholic region recalls our common origins, inviting us to focus on the roots of our traditions and the Christian origins of France. Yet this does not mean we should remain stuck in the past. When the oak tree deepens its roots, it is not in order to become an acorn again, but in order to raise higher its branches. This monastery is a sign of hope. The presence of the Orthodox Church, though it evokes the primitive Church, the Church of the Fathers and of the great councils, invites us to look to the future, to the Europe of tomorrow. If this Europe wants to stay faithful to its origins and preserve its identity, it should not limit itself to the Western nations, of Catholic and Protestant tradition. Orthodoxy is an essential component.[23]

---

[22]   'L'idée a germé qu'il devait être possible de renouer avec la tradition ecclésiale anté-romaine et "l'Orthodoxie profonde" de nos pays [...]. Propositions théoriques et essais concrets ont souvent tourné court. Mais l'idée en elle-même est devenue incontournable: celle qu'il est possible de retrouver l'ancien modèle de vie ecclésiale en s'inspirant certes de l'expérience des Églises d'Orient, mais sans s'inféoder à elles et en redonnant vie à la tradition orthodoxe autochtone'.

[23]   'C'est surtout à partir de nos régions que le christianisme s'est implanté dans les Gaules, dès l'époque des apôtres. Un christianisme qui, alors, était de tradition grecque et orientale. Notre Église orthodoxe se situe dans une continuité étroite avec ces premières générations chrétiennes. La présence d'un monastère orthodoxe dans cette région catholique rappelle nos origines communes, elle nous invite à regarder vers les racines de nos traditions, vers les origines chrétiennes de la France. Mais parler de ressourcement ou d'enracinement, ce n'est pas seulement inviter à se tourner vers le passé. Quand un chêne enfonce plus profondément ses racines dans le sol, ce n'est pas pour redevenir gland, c'est pour élever plus haut sa ramure. Ce monastère est un signe d'espérance. La présence de l'Église orthodoxe, si elle évoque l'Église des premiers siècles, l'Église des Pères et des grands conciles, nous

264 *Orthodox Identities in Western Europe*

This is not about a Western Orthodoxy, but about a Western version of Orthodoxy (*d'expression occidentale*), which means it is the local expression of a universal message, a Western way of living the teachings of the Church of the Apostles and the practice of the first Christian centuries. There is a shift from an Orthodox presence in the West to an Orthodoxy of Western expression, which is not confined exclusively to immigrant populations. The emergence of Orthodoxy in France is understood as a return to the Orthodox foundations of France, which are nothing else than the local expression of a universal Orthodoxy which France lost in the course of its history. The French saints in the iconography of Saint-Antoine-le-Grand indicate the will to unify the Christian Churches by linking up with the local, pre-schism Orthodoxy.[24]

The emergence of Orthodoxy in France, at first the result of immigration but no more confined to it, is in the image of Fr Placide's interpretation of his own conversion, namely a 'pilgrimage to the roots', the return to a common origin, identified as the primitive Church. This idea is not new however. In 1937 the Orthodox Catholic Church of France (Église Catholique Orthodoxe de France, ECOF) was intended as a restoration of the Orthodox Church of the West as it was before the schism, with its attempt to repristinate the ancient Gallican liturgy, dating from before the expansion of the Roman rite (see Mayer in this volume). This, however, runs the risk of tradition becoming a mere myth. At the present moment, ECOF is no more recognised by any Orthodox jurisdiction. It is precisely in order to avoid such pitfalls that the monks prefer to draw their inspiration from the living Athonite Tradition for accomplishing the return to the roots of Orthodox Christianity in the West.

Conclusion

What elements of tradition circulate? The term 'tradition' is commonly understood as territorial identification based on local customs reproduced in a certain context. As such, faithfulness to a particular tradition amounts to faithfulness to a body of norms and customs within a territory and on the background of historical permanence. But tradition implies the relation people

---

invite aussi à regarder vers l'avenir, vers l'Europe de demain qui se construit. Cette Europe, si elle veut être fidèle à ses origines et garder son identité, ne peut pas se limiter aux nations occidentales, traditionnellement catholiques ou protestantes. L'orthodoxie en est une composante essentielle'.

[24] I refer here to a representation of Saint Cassian the Roman (fourth–fifth century). He sailed from Egypt to Marseille, where he founded two monasteries with monastic rules inspired from the Egyptian tradition. The monks constantly parallel the evangelising mission this saint fulfilled for France through his witness of the Egyptian monasticism and their own present implantation in Vercors.

have with the past, and on which they base their engagement with the present, rather than the simple reproduction of some forms of the past. Thus the notion of tradition is not to be understood as the sheer persistence of the past and its influence on the present, but rather as the relation with what was before.

Tradition cannot be separated from the agents who create it. In this sense, tradition is not an immutable content in time and space, but a content that is passed on from one generation to another, through the mediation of elders, who play a highly important role in Orthodoxy. Tradition is not limited to a series of practices or customs, but a relational context in which spiritual filiation can unfold and develop. For it is within filiation that tradition is being built, on account of which it does not amount to just a heritage of the past, but provides a perspective on the past that helps us to understand the present. This is what makes tradition alive, for it is expressed in the framework of a filial relationship, in which present generations draw their heritage from the experience of their predecessors. Tradition reaches far beyond local identities, revealing a bond perceived as essential precisely as it unites present actors to past generations and thereby creates the Church.

Bibliography

Boyer, A. 1993. *Le droit des religions en France*. Paris: Presses Universitaires de France.

Clément, O. 1965. *L'Église orthodoxe*. Paris: Presses Universitaires de France.

Conseil Constitutionnel. Art. 1, Declaration of Rights, Constitution of 24 June 1793. Available at: http://www.conseil-constitutionnel.fr/conseil-constitutionnel/francais/la-constitution/les-constitutions-de-la-france/constitution-du-24-juin-1793.5084.html [accessed 18 March 2014].

Conseil d'Etat (France). 1824. *Tables générales des lois, arrêtés, décrets, ordonnances du roi, arrêts et avis du conseil d'état et réglemens d'administration publiés depuis 1789*, Volume 1. Paris: Ménard et Desenne fils.

Denizeau, L. 2010. *Petite ethnographie d'une tradition monastique, à propos de la foi et de la pratique religieuse*. Paris: Téraèdre.

Denizeau, L. 2011. Du silence de soi à la parole de l'ancien: Savoirs monastiques et acteurs de la 'Grande Tradition de l'Athos' en France. *Archives de sciences sociales des religions*, 154: 79–99.

Deseille, P. 2010. *Propos d'un moine orthodoxe: Entretiens avec Jean-Claude Noyé*. Paris: Lethielleux.

Erny, P. 1993. Premiers pas d'une orthodoxie d'Occident, in *Ethnologie des faits religieux en Europe*, edited by N. Belmont and F. Lautman. Paris: Editions du CTHS, 463–71.

266 *Orthodox Identities in Western Europe*

Kokosalakis, N. 1996. Orthodoxie grecque, modernité et politique, in *Identités religieuses en Europe*, edited by G. Davie and D. Hervieu-Léger. Paris: La Découverte, 131–51.

Legifrance. Art. 13, Law of 1 July 1901, published 2 July 1901. Available at: http://www.legifrance.gouv.fr/affichTexte.do;jsessionid=A48C4CA9D C8359AFD48132DC191BABBA.tpdjo12v_3?cidTexte=JORFTEXT00 0000497458&dateTexte=20090506 [accessed 18 March 2014].

Legifrance. Art. 19–20, Decree of 16 August 1901, published 17 July 1901. Available at: http://www.legifrance.gouv.fr/affichTexte.do?cidTexte=JORF TEXT000000668093&fastPos=2&fastReqId=767519860&categorieLien =id&oldAction=rechTexte [accessed 18 March 2014].

Legifrance. Art. 2, Law of 9 December 1905, published 11 December 1905. Available at: http://www.legifrance.gouv.fr/affichTexte.do?cidTexte=JORF TEXT000000508749&fastPos=1&fastReqId=84908798&categorieLien =id&oldAction=rechTexte [accessed 18 March 2014].

Löwy, M. 2004. Le concept d'affinité élective chez Max Weber. *Archives de sciences sociales des religions*, 127: 93–103. Available at: http://assr.revues. org/document1055.html [accessed 25 May 2007].

Machelon, J.-P. 2006. Les relations des cultes avec les pouvoirs publics. Available at: http://www.ladocumentationfrancaise.fr [accessed 10 December 2012].

Paléologue, A. 1997. *Le Mont Athos: Merveille du Christianisme Byzantin*. Paris: Gallimard.

Seraidari, K. 2001. La Vierge de Tinos: Le cœur sacré de l'État grec. *Archives de Sciences sociales des Religions*, 113: 45–59.

Ware, K. 2002. *L'orthodoxie: L'Église des sept conciles*. Paris: Cerf.

Weber, M. 1994. *L'Éthique protestante et l'esprit du capitalisme*. Paris: Plon.

Chapter 14

'We are Westerners and Must Remain Westerners': Orthodoxy and Western Rites in Western Europe

Jean-François Mayer

Since the nineteenth century, there have been attempts to create Orthodox Christian communities using Western liturgical forms. In some cases, the impetus came from believers who already were Orthodox faithful; in other cases, people or groups joining the Orthodox Church asked for permission to continue to use the liturgies they were accustomed to, with adjustments required to 'orthodoxise' them. Most of these undertakings would never have taken place had there not been already the presence of emigrant Orthodox Churches in the West; in addition, in one particularly significant case in France, the initiative was a direct outcome of an encounter with the reflections and aspirations of young Russian émigrés interested in the liturgical revival of the ancient Christian legacy of Western Europe. There are currently two Orthodox jurisdictions having Western rite parishes: the Antiochian Orthodox Church and the Russian Orthodox Church Outside of Russia (ROCOR); moreover, a few parishes under the Serbian and Romanian Orthodox Churches occasionally use Western rites, beside the Byzantine one.[1] Most recent developments in the field of Western rite in canonical Orthodox Churches have taken place in North America, but it has not disappeared from Western Europe.

Sometimes rejected by critical voices as 'uniatism in the reverse', the use of Western rite adds one more layer to issues of identity discussed across this volume. At an individual level, for a convert to the Orthodox Church, the need to affiliate with a denomination often associated with a national background can create hurdles: the wish of most converts is to embrace the Orthodox faith, and not another, new national identity. A convert with roots in Western Christianity needs also to deal with that legacy, even more so due to the fact that Orthodox claim the pre-schism, first millennium of Christianity in Western Europe as

---

[1] There are probably a few additional, isolated cases: one that has come to our knowledge after completing this article is a parish in Argentina, under the (canonical) Ukrainian Orthodox Church of South America.

268 *Orthodox Identities in Western Europe*

their own and venerate Western saints of that period. Very early after they had to go into exile, some Russian émigrés were keen to develop a knowledge and veneration of such saints. In parishes across Europe, there are Sundays marked for All Saints of England, All Saints of Germany, All Saints of Switzerland, and so forth, and offices have been composed in honour of these saints.

But should the Orthodox legacy of Western Christianity include specific liturgical expressions? And then, some dare to suggest, does 1054 mark a complete break, or could even some elements from post-schism Western Christianity also find their way into Orthodox piety and worship? Ultimately, this leads to a question not without consequences for dialogue with other Christians: should the Orthodox Church be perceived as 'the Eastern Church', or as the fullness of the Christian Church? If the second statement is true, why could it not also integrate non-Byzantine liturgical traditions? But immediately another question arises: can the Orthodox ethos as it has developed be properly conveyed through forms which have for centuries been associated with another tradition? Thus, the Western rite raises issues related to the identity of the Orthodox Church, as perceived by itself as well as by outsiders.

This chapter will provide an overview of efforts to find a place for Western rites within (canonical) Orthodox jurisdictions.[2] It is based primarily on the study of written material, but also on observations during visits to some Western rite Orthodox parishes in Europe and North America as well as written exchanges with people active in such parishes. While the focus will be on Europe, developments in North America will need to be briefly summarised, since there have been some reciprocal influences.[3]

Early Converts as Pioneers of the Western Rite

There are two ways to practise a Western rite in the Orthodox Church today: either 'orthodoxise' an existing rite or recreate an old, pre-schism rite. Although there were few practical consequences at the time, those two options became clear already in the nineteenth century.

---

[2] Part of this historical presentation is based on research published in an earlier article on Orthodox Western rite attempts (Mayer 1997). For an overview of existing literature in English, see Turner (2009). Jack Turner (University of South Carolina) has written a doctoral thesis on Western rite Orthodoxy and is preparing a book on the subject, to be published by Northern Illinois University Press.

[3] We will not take into consideration the case of communities that joined the Orthodox Church with the Western rite in Central Europe (Poland and Czechoslovakia) between the two world wars and their subsequent histories, since those episodes had no impact on developments in Western Europe that are discussed at the core of this chapter.

Orthodoxy and Western Rites in Western Europe 269

The first approach was promoted by Julian Joseph Overbeck (1821–1905). A German by birth, ordained a Catholic priest in 1845, he became Protestant in 1857, married, settled in England and worked there on the editing of Syriac manuscripts. In 1865, Overbeck decided to join the Orthodox Church,[4] although he was formally received in the Church only in 1869: he had originally planned to take that step only after his request for the restoration of a Western Orthodox Church would be accepted, but later realised he could not make it a precondition (Kahle 1968: 21–2). He would remain a faithful Orthodox until his death.

From the beginning, the project of Western Orthodoxy was at the heart of Overbeck's vision. He did not believe in a (re)union between the Orthodox Church and other Christian bodies, but foresaw individuals joining the Church. He stressed that the Orthodox Church was *the* Catholic Church, while all other forms of Christianity were heterodox.[5] Due to historical circumstances, 'Eastern Church' and 'Orthodox Church' were temporarily overlapping, but it was not meant to remain so. While attending Byzantine services in existing Orthodox parishes as long as there was no other option, Overbeck and those supporting him rejected as a matter of principle any 'Easternisation' of Western converts to Orthodoxy and did not favour the creation of Byzantine rite parishes using local languages for them:[6] 'We are Westerners and must remain Westerners' (Overbeck 1876: 112). Overbeck felt that the right way was to transform the heterodox, Western tradition into an Orthodox one by setting aside everything that was heterodox in its teachings and liturgical books: the result would be a return to the pre-schism Western Church. The first step would be the revision of the *Ordo Missae*, and then all the other parts of the Western liturgical books would be revised step by step in the same way; in the meantime, the Eastern rite could be used for dispensing sacraments. Around 1871, he published in Latin and English a *Liturgy of the Western Orthodox-Catholic Mass.*[7] It follows the ordinary of the Roman Mass, but with a few changes in order to 'orthodoxise'

---

[4]   Overbeck launched in 1867 the *Orthodox Catholic Review*, which continued to be published until 1891.

[5]   Nevertheless, Overbeck repeatedly attempted to get his Roman Catholic priestly orders recognised by the Russian Church and petitioned for being reinstated in his holy orders – but his wedding after he had left the ranks of Catholic clergy made such a request problematic from an Orthodox perspective (Kahle 1968: 81–3).

[6]   Overbeck bitterly opposed Stephen Hatherly (1827–1905), an Oxford graduate who was received in the Orthodox Church through baptism in 1856, was ordained a priest in Constantinople in 1871 and established an English parish using the Byzantine rite. Overbeck did not see both approaches as complementary, but as mutually exclusive (Kahle 1968: 69–73, 285–7).

[7]   Overbeck's Liturgy had been approved by the Holy Synod of the Russian Church. It is very hard to find this 24-page brochure, but it has been reproduced in the (also hard-to-find) privately published research volume on the Orthodox Western rite by Thomann (1995).

270   *Orthodox Identities in Western Europe*

it: it includes the Trisagion after the Gloria – 'in remembrance of our union with the Orthodox Church'; the *filioque* is removed from the Creed; there is no elevation of the host and chalice after the Words of the Institution;[8] and an epiclesis[9] is introduced.

Overbeck invited Roman Catholics of the West to return to the Orthodox Church and faith. He asked those interested to associate their names to a petition to the Russian Church which he had already sent to the Patriarch of Constantinople in 1868: the purpose was to ask Orthodox hierarchs to restore a Western Orthodox Church with priests celebrating a Western liturgy, since Divine Providence had originally formed a true Western Church congruent with the Western mind (Overbeck 1871b: 30). Moreover, the missionary argument was given, that would reappear later throughout the history of Orthodox attempts at a Western rite: few Westerners had joined the Orthodox Church, but many more would do so if allowed to keep their liturgical inheritance (Overbeck 1871b: 32).

The petition was sent to the Holy Synod of the Russian Church with 122 signatures in September 1869; signatories resided mostly in the United Kingdom, a majority of them with Anglican background plus a few Roman Catholics. 'Upon reception of the petition, the Metropolitan of St Petersburg, Isidore Nikol'skij (1799–1802), immediately formed a commission to study the question. The Synodal Commission was presided over by the Metropolitan himself. Overbeck was appointed a member by personal letter of the Metropolitan'. Overbeck was then invited to Russia: the Synod approved the principle of Western Orthodoxy (Abramtsov 1961b: 13).

Despite such promising beginnings, the project would never materialise. As Florovsky tells the story, 'a final decision was postponed in connection with the

---

[8]   'The Roman Catholics here elevate and adore the Host and the Chalice, but this is wrong, because the Consecration is only accomplished by the Invocation of the Holy Ghost' (Overbeck 1871a). Ironically, despite such an explicit rejection by a respected pioneer, a number of Western rite Orthodox parishes using variations of the Roman liturgy retain the elevation today (Turner 2012a).

[9]   The epiclesis ('invocation') is a prayer asking the Father to send the Holy Spirit upon the bread and wine and to make them into the Body and Blood of Christ. While the epiclesis is characteristic of Eastern liturgies, it is not explicitly present in the traditional Roman Canon of the Mass. The fourteenth-century Byzantine theologian Nicholas Cabasilas (canonised as a saint by the Ecumenical Patriarchate in 1983) was of the opinion that the prayer 'Supplices te rogamus' in the Roman canon (in which it is asked that the angel take the offering to God's heavenly altar, so that the faithful may receive Christ's body and blood) was in fact an 'ascending epiclesis'; modern Orthodox uses of Western rites, however, have not generally reflected this understanding, and have usually insisted on the addition of an Eastern-style epiclesis, following either personal convictions or requirements from Orthodox bishops before approval.

Orthodoxy and Western Rites in Western Europe 271

further development of the Old Catholic movement. The Synod was anxious to ascertain whether there were a sufficient number of people in the West to join the project in question' (Florovsky 1989: 134). Moreover, the Russians wanted other Orthodox Churches to approve of the plan. It seems to have been positively received in Constantinople, but led to a protest from the Church of Greece. 'Perhaps Overbeck's scheme was conceived on too grandiose a scale. He continually emphasised that he was not interested in acquiring a few converts for the Orthodox Church but in restoring a whole Church. If he had spoken of establishing Western Rite parishes within the jurisdiction of the Russian Church the Synod would perhaps not have been so hesitant and not have disturbed the Greeks with the question' (Abramtsov 1961b: 15). In 1884, the Synod decided not to pursue further. A few people used to gather with Overbeck in London for praying the hours together each week until the early 1880s, but they finally despaired of seeing the realisation of Overbeck's scheme and so instead were absorbed into existing, Eastern rite Orthodox parishes.

Needless to say, Overbeck's insistence on conversion to the Orthodox Church irritated those who envisioned other ways for the future of Christianity, such as Anglicans eager to pave the way for communion with the Orthodox Churches. From the start, dreams of a Western rite in the Orthodox Church thus provoked suspicions in circles eager to promote ecumenical relations.

Already in the nineteenth century, the option of resurrecting an older rite (and thus avoiding liturgies tainted by late medieval or post-Tridentine developments) was considered too. Wladimir Guettée (1816–1892) was an erudite Roman Catholic priest of Gallican and Jansenist leanings, who was received as a priest in the Russian Orthodox Church in 1861 (Besse 1992). Like Overbeck (1869: 50–51), with whom he had good relations, Guettée had become convinced that the Christian bodies of the West had become heretical and that the Orthodox Church was the true Church of Christ (Guettée 1889: 367–9, 405). But for the very reason that Rome had drifted away from the Orthodox faith, Guettée did not think that the existing Roman Catholic liturgy could just be appropriated by the Orthodox Church with a few minor adjustments. While the Canon of the Mass was pre-schism and should be seen as Orthodox (Guettée 1866: 450), and while the Roman Mass had kept the essential parts of Orthodox liturgy, it had retained 'neither the beautiful harmony nor the mystical meaning' of Orthodox liturgy, and had been vitiated by reformers lacking liturgical sense (Guettée 1866: 453–4). The fate of Anglican liturgy had been even worse (Guettée 1866: 431–2, 454, 457–8). Guettée contrasted this with the ancient Gallican liturgy, that had Eastern roots and was much closer to the Eastern rite, and was then Romanised from the ninth century; similarly, the Ambrosian liturgy in Milan or the Mozarabic liturgy in Spain had more affinities with the Eastern one (Guettée 1866: 430). Guettée worked on the restoration of the Gallican liturgy: he celebrated it in 1875 in

St Petersburg with the blessing of the Holy Synod of the Russian Orthodox Church. But there were no further efforts in this direction, and apparently Guettée usually celebrated in the Byzantine rite.

Thus there were in the nineteenth century some people who laid the ground for the vision of Western rite Orthodoxy. From that time, two liturgical options were considered, which would continue to accompany subsequent attempts to this day. But no Western rite Orthodox parish was born during that period. There was an interest in Orthodox circles for developments in the Christian West and for dialogue with Western Christians sympathetic to Orthodoxy. But rather than creating an Orthodox Western rite ecclesiastical structure, attention was paid to possibilities of restoring communion with sections of Western Christianity: first, there were philo-Orthodox High Church Anglicans and Episcopalians, who saw themselves as the perpetuation of an authentic local church of the West; then there were hopes raised by the Old Catholic movement.[10] Overbeck's venture had showed that there were not so many Westerners willing to convert to the Orthodox Church at that time.

Russian Emigration as Cradle of a Restored Gallican Rite

However, the issue of the Western rite would not die: in part because it raised significant questions regarding the identity of Orthodoxy along with its role outside of its traditional geographical areas, but also due to the existence of Western religious seekers with various longings. A few decades later, new impulses came from France, at the crossroads between thinking of Russian émigrés and quests on the fringes of the Roman Catholic Church.

In January 1925, eight young Russians living in exile in France founded in Paris the Confrérie de Saint Photius (Brotherhood of St Photios), originally with the goal of defending the Orthodox faith, but very soon – from 1926 – turning its attention to the restoration of Orthodoxy in the West and proclaiming accordingly that 'the Orthodox Church is not merely Eastern, but is the Church of all the peoples on earth' (Bange and Bange 2013: 20–21). The members of

---

[10] A few years after Old Catholicism was born, Overbeck (who had originally welcomed the movement) had come to the conclusion that hopes raised by that movement had been misplaced and could not be the way to a rebirth of the Orthodox Church in the West, but was rather inclined to assimilate with Anglicanism, the 'most dangerous form of Protestantism' (Overbeck 1876: 106–107, 116). Still, there were some Orthodox who continued to advocate rapprochement with the Old Catholics, such as General Alexander Kireev (1832–1910) (Novikoff 1914, Basil 1991). Eugène Michaud (1839–1917), a French priest and theologian who had been close to Guettée and had joined the Old Catholic movement, played an important role in promoting communion between the Orthodox and the Old Catholic Churches (Dederen 1963: 226–45).

the Brotherhood of St Photios were among those Russians who felt that there should be some providential purpose behind the events that forced some many people to leave their country, and that the Russian emigration was meant to bring something to the Western world (Pnevmatikakis 2012). Some members of the Brotherhood, such as the theologian Vladimir Lossky (1903–1958), who became a member in 1928, later became well-known figures in the Orthodox Church. Two of the founders, Evgraph Kovalevsky (1905–1970) and his brother Maxime Kovalevsky (1903–1988), would play a key role for the Western rite: the first was to become the charismatic leader and liturgist of the rebirth of Western Orthodoxy in France; the second, a gifted musician who adapted liturgical music for that purpose (and whose musical work had an impact in wider Christian circles).

The Brotherhood was involved in efforts for establishing in Paris an Orthodox parish using French as its liturgical language. However, from the start, it was also interested in the restoration of Western liturgical forms within the Orthodox Church. Thus, during a three-day meeting in April 1929, three liturgies were celebrated: Roman, Gallican (using Guettée's text) and Byzantine (in Latin!). A majority of the members apparently decided that the Gallican was the best option, but much work remained to be done for building upon what Guettée (who was not really a liturgiologist) had undertaken.[11] Evgraph Kovalevsky attempted to immerse himself in the liturgical tradition of the West – no easy task for one reared fully in the liturgical tradition of the East: 'I learnt the Roman Mass by heart, I attended ceremonies, I read the breviary, I let Latin penetrate into my soul. Often, the call of the East was so strong that I had to fight psychologically with myself – since in order to love something, one needs to give up something else' (quoted in Bourne 1975: 101).

In the 1930s, a relation developed with a small independent Catholic group gathered around Louis-Charles (later Irénée) Winnaert (1880–1937), a priest who had left the Roman Catholic Church following the turmoils of the modernist crisis (Bourne 1966). Winnaert had founded in 1922 a 'Free Catholic Church', received the episcopacy from James Ingall Wedgwood (1883–1951) of the (Theosophical) Liberal Catholic Church, and had then broken with that group and organised an 'Evangelical Catholic Church'. Suffering from the isolation of his group, he came in touch with Orthodox circles through Fr Lev Gillet (1893–1980), who was to become famous under the pen name 'A Monk of the Eastern Church' (Behr-Siegel 1993: 251–75). Winnaert applied to the Russian Church in 1936, was accepted, and the group was formally received in early February 1937, a month before its founder passed away. In March, Evgraph

---

[11] The Gallican rite was not seen as the only rite for Western Orthodox: Evgraph Kovalevsky hoped that the Roman Church would someday come back to Orthodoxy, and then it would obviously be with the 'orthodoxised' Roman rite (Bourne 1978: 43).

274   *Orthodox Identities in Western Europe*

Kovalevsky was ordained a priest of the Russian Church (Moscow Patriarchate) for the service of Western Orthodoxy.

The decree taken by Metropolitan Sergius (Stragorodsky) (1867–1944) of Moscow on 16 June 1936 had recognised Winnaert's priesthood, but not his episcopate. His parishes were to be considered as 'Western Orthodox Church' and were allowed to keep the Western rite, but texts would have to be expurgated from what would not be compatible with Orthodoxy. Priests to be ordained for those parishes would wear Western liturgical vestments, and would be allowed to wear either Western or Eastern vestments when attending an Eastern rite service (translation in Kovalevsky 1990: 395–400).

Not everybody understood the liturgical work ahead the same way. The rector of the Western rite parish in Paris, Fr Denis (Lucien) Chambault (1899–1965), wanted to keep the Roman rite as it was, with minimal adjustments; he had no interest in a Gallican rite. This disagreement would soon lead to a split. In 1939, Metropolitan Sergius agreed that there would be two groups: the former parish of Winnaert under Chambault, and another group with Kovalevsky as priest. The Metropolitan stressed that the reintroduction of the Western rite was still at an experimental stage in the Orthodox Church, that nothing was yet fixed, since there was room for improvements, and that the parallel use of two different types of liturgy was not to be seen as a problem; at the same time, he also encouraged the development of a French-speaking Orthodox parish in Paris, both for new generations of Russians settled in France and for converts who would prefer the Byzantine rite (Kovalevsky 1990: 79–80).

Chambault continued on the same way until his death, remaining faithful to the Moscow Patriarchate. He opened in Paris a small Benedictine priory, but it never managed to become a stable and lasting monastic community. Fr Denis had some success as a healer and exorcist, taking care of visitors from morning to evening, but there were not many parishioners. 'The Western Eucharistic Rite used by Père Denis ... was that of Fr Winnaert's devising, revised, corrected and "Orthodoxised" by a group of Orthodox scholars of whom Vladimir Lossky was one. It had in it elements of the Catholic rites, some echoes of the Anglican Communion service, but certainly strong echoes of Liberal Catholic practices. To observe it outwardly it was like a Catholic Mass in French and many Catholics came to the chapel for that reason.[12] The offices were those of the Benedictine breviary in French, adapted and arranged and officially approved by the Holy Synod at Moscow. To produce this work Père Jean [Peterfalvi, one of the original members of the community] visited several Benedictine Monasteries' (Burton 1985: 55). The chapel disappeared few years after Chambault's death.

Kovalevsky took a quite different route, engaging with other people in very active liturgical recreation work, and also setting up what would become an

---

12   At that time, Roman-rite Catholic Masses were said in Latin.

Orthodox diocese. There were initial experiments of celebration of the restored Western liturgy in Paris as early as 1944; improvements and adjustments were introduced over time. The work was not limited to the Mass: all the other liturgical services needed to be prepared, a labour that would take decades. A French theological institute was also inaugurated in 1944 (Institut Saint-Denis, of which Vladimir Lossky was the first dean). There was also the need to provide the nascent work with a stable place for celebrations. In 1946, such a place was found: the church belonging to the Old Catholic Church in Paris, which was no longer used. It was first rented, and later bought. The group started to use the name 'Orthodox Church of France', later 'Catholic Orthodox Church of France' (Église Catholique Orthodoxe de France – ECOF), before reverting to the original name.

Fr Evgraph had been looking quite early for an autonomous status for his Western Orthodox parishes, asking the Moscow Patriarchate as early as 1945, at a time the work was still nascent (Bourne 1978: 44). His supporters explain that this was meant to protect the Western Orthodox group from hostile reactions of some other Orthodox not willing to accept such developments. Indeed, Fr Evgraph and his work became quite controversial, although it is difficult to understand clearly what in this controversy was related to the issue of the Western rite itself and what pertained to other issues. Over the years, criticism followed more or less the same line, taking issue not only with the choice of a Western rite and the self-perception of the role of the work as the nucleus of the local Orthodox Church of France, but also accusing the French group of being too lax with church rules and porous to non-Orthodox teachings.

In 1953, the group broke with the Moscow Patriarchate. It briefly joined the Russian Exarchate under the Patriarchate of Constantinople (1953–1954) and then spent several years without any canonical anchoring. In 1959, the Orthodox Church of France was received by Archbishop John (Maximovitch) of Shanghai and San Francisco (1896–1966) – glorified in 1994 and now counted among the saints of the Orthodox Church – in the Russian Orthodox Church Outside of Russia. Fr Evgraph was consecrated as a bishop in 1964 and took the name of Jean-Nectaire de Saint-Denis. But there was again a break in 1966, followed by several years of isolation for the French Church. Bishop Jean passed away in 1970, leaving the group without a bishop. In 1972, it was accepted under the Patriarchate of Romania and a new bishop was consecrated, Germain de Saint-Denis (Gilles Bertrand-Hardy, b. 1930). Not without tensions,[13] this arrangement lasted until 1993, when Bishop Germain was deposed by the

---

[13]   In which the Western rite played a role: in 1987, the French Church accepted a demand of the Romanian Church that the Byzantine rite should be celebrated at least on one Sunday every month (see Kovalevsky 1990: 413–59).

Romanian Patriarchate. The Orthodox Church of France has been independent since that time.

While the figure of Evgraph Kovalevsky drew most attention, he was not the only one working at liturgical restoration of pre-schism rites. Alexis van der Mensbrugghe (1899–1980)[14] proposed his own restoration of the Western rite. Born in a Flemish family, he had become a Benedictine monk and ordained a Roman Catholic priest in 1925, but then had joined the Orthodox Church in 1929. From 1946, he taught patristics and liturgics at the newly founded French Orthodox Institute Saint-Denis in Paris. In 1948, he published a restoration of the Western rite in Latin and English (Mensbrugghe 1948). In 1960, Mensbrugghe was consecrated as a bishop in the Moscow Patriarchate. From 1968 to 1979, he served as bishop and archbishop in North America. During the 1960s, Bishop Alexis continued to show an active interest in the Western rite. He published in 1962 an 'Orthodox Missal' in French, containing both the Gallican and the 'Pre-Celestinian Italic' (early fifth century) rites (Mensbrugghe 1962). He celebrated the Western rite himself and had a few Western rite groups in Italy under his supervision. Thus, during a few years in the 1960s, both the Moscow Patriarchate and ROCOR had approved Western rite liturgies and Western rite parishes.

Both Kovalevsky (1956) and Mensbrugghe used a key witness for their restoration of a Gallican rite, beside other sources: the letters of St Germanus of Paris (496–576), in which there is a description of the liturgical celebration for the purpose of explaining its meaning. This is why the Orthodox Church of France calls its liturgy the 'Divine Liturgy *according* to St Germanus of Paris' (and not 'of'), since the saint had no part in establishing that liturgy, but only shared in his letters information that proved crucial for the work of restoration.

Those were years of intense liturgical work, with different paths explored. In the preface to his 1948 restored Western liturgy, Mensbrugghe explained the principles that guided him. The starting point should be the old Roman liturgy, since it was the one of the local Patriarchate: 'The fundamental principle in liturgical matters is that "the Liturgy follows the Patriarchate." Once established this Liturgy will continue to nourish the masses. If schisms or heresies happen, it will no doubt suffer from that; but its fundamental crystallisation, made of a nearly 1000-year old Orthodox capital, will remain throughout the following ages. Orthodoxy has the right – and the duty – to ask today's Westerner to "clean" its rite. But it is impossible, and useless anyway, to ask the masses to orientalise themselves' (Mensbrugghe 1948: vi–vii). Local uses should also be taken into consideration, for instance those of the Gauls and Spain, through which the Roman rite had come to integrate Byzantinisms. Thus Mensbrugghe

---

[14] A biographical notice was prepared by Fr Serge Model (2012).

Orthodoxy and Western Rites in Western Europe   277

had started from the Roman rite as it existed in the twentieth century, but going much further than Overbeck's corrections. He described his work as threefold:

a. Purify the liturgy from 'medieval deformations that have obscured the purity of the original line';
b. Reintroduce or put again in their proper place 'ancient Roman elements that are more authentic' but which were dismissed or misplaced during the Middle Ages;
c. Reintroduce those Gallican elements that underline essential values held in common by the entire Christian tradition (Mensbrugghe 1948: ix).

In 1954, some aspects of this restoration attempt came under criticism by Nicholas Uspensky (1900–1987), then professor of liturgy at the Leningrad Theological Academy, according to whom 'too much of the Archimandrite's personal tastes' were showing through (Abramtsov 1961a). Those criticisms were taken into consideration at the time of publishing the 1962 Missal.

In their own work, Kovalevsky and people who cooperated with him claimed that there was ample material available for a restoration of the Gallican rite (Tanazacq 1977), although the full text itself was no longer available. But the restored liturgy included borrowings from the Eastern rite, which members of the Orthodox Church of France prefer to describe as a legitimate 'compenetration' of rites as found throughout the history of the Church and as 'enrichments' (Saint-Denis 1977: 82–90). 'Local rites have always practised mutual "borrowings", as long as form and spirit would not be altered', wrote Fr Evgraph in his preface to the restoration of the Gallican Mass (Kovalevsky 1956: 32). The restorers disputed that what they did had anything in common with an 'archaeological reconstitution', but claimed that it rather was a 'resurrection', the 'resurgence of a latent tradition of the undivided Church', 'fecundated by the encounter with Orthodox tradition' (Kovalevsky 1984: 29). An English proponent of the Orthodox Western Rite commented in a more nuanced way on Kovalevsky's approach that 'one should speak of hybrid vigour. Although Fr Yevgraf was liturgically knowledgeable, when it came to determining the new "Gallican" liturgy he simply did pretty much as his sensibility suggested' (Coombs 1987: 48). In the preface to his own reconstruction of the Gallican rite, Roman Catholic liturgical scholar Klaus Gamber described Kovalevsky's version as 'a form adapted to the Byzantine use' (Gamber 1984: 5). The efforts went far beyond recreating a Gallican Mass. The considerable liturgical work of the Orthodox Church of France deserves more detailed examination, but this would go beyond the purpose of this chapter and the expertise of the author.

The fact that the (neo-)Gallican rite has been in continuous use for decades should also be kept in mind. The Liturgy according to St Germanus of Paris is not only served in that group. When the break with the Romanian Church took

278   *Orthodox Identities in Western Europe*

place, some parishes chose to remain under Bucharest; they are mostly using now the Byzantine rite, although the Gallican rite continues to be celebrated from time to time in some of them. Other parishes left in 2001; a few years later, those parishes were received in the Serbian Patriarchate (and one then came under Moscow); their celebrations are mostly in the Byzantine rite, but some of them also use the Gallican rite. In addition, some priests and parishes had left the Orthodox Church of France in 2000 and had come under the jurisdiction of the Coptic Orthodox Church, with the permission to keep the Gallican rite; after their bishop decided to restrict this rite in 2005, they broke with the Coptic Church in 2006 and formed the Orthodox Church of the Gauls, with one of their priests, Michel Mendez (b. 1941), being consecrated as Bishop Grégoire by hierarchs of independent, non-canonical Orthodox Churches. This group has glorified Bishop Jean de Saint-Denis as a saint in 2008; it too continues to use the Gallican rite.[15] Thus, besides the occasional celebrations from time to time in a few canonical Orthodox parishes in Europe, the liturgical legacy of the Orthodox Church of France is kept today mostly as the practice of just two groups, neither of them in communion with historical Orthodox Churches: the Orthodox Church of France (some 20 local parishes or groups in France, plus a few groups in other countries) and the Orthodox Church of the Gauls (about ten places of worship).[16] Unexpectedly, the only canonical Orthodox parishes where the Gallican rite is predominantly celebrated seem to be one in Iowa (USA) under the Russian Orthodox Church Outside of Russia since 2010 and another one in Argentina under the Ukrainian Orthodox Church of South America (Ecumenical Patriarchate). It seems that no Orthodox group today is using one of the two Western rites restored by Archbishop Alexis van der Mensbrugghe.

There is also another legacy of the Orthodox Church of France that should not be overlooked, which has proved at this point more significant for Orthodox life at large: a number of converts (including clergy) currently belonging to various Orthodox parishes in French-speaking countries originally came in touch with the Orthodox faith through the group born from Bishop Jean de Saint-Denis' vision.

---

[15]   Bishop Grégoire himself is the author of a book on the history and restoration of the Gallican rite (Mendez 2008).

[16]   Some other groups led by 'independent bishops' have also adopted the Gallican rite, but they are not in a direct filiation with the original group around Bishop Jean de Saint-Denis.

American Impulses and European Echoes

While our focus is on Western Europe, we need to allude briefly to developments in North America, since there has been some interaction. Lack of space will however prevent us from summarising some of the debates around the Western rite that have taken place there, reflected in theological journals.

In 1958, after having paid attention to the issue for years, Metropolitan Antony Bashir (1898–1966) received from the Patriarch of Antioch the blessing to authorise the Western rite in the Antiochian Orthodox Christian Archdiocese of North America. Metropolitan Antony had been in touch with the Society of Saint Basil, a group issued from an earlier attempt to start Western rite work in the United States (before the Second World War) and looking for a safe haven in a canonical Orthodox Church. Moreover, one of the priests in the Antiochian Archdiocese, Fr Paul Schneirla, who had converted to the Orthodox Church in the late 1930s and been ordained for the Byzantine rite in 1942, had kept a strong interest in Western liturgical traditions and had been encouraged by contacts with Fr Denis Chambault in France (Andersen, n.d.). In 1961, through Schneirla's mediation, the first group of Western rite converts was received in the Antiochian Archdiocese. The Western Rite Vicariate has developed since and counts more than 20 parishes across the United States. Beside the Rite of St Gregory (described on a website distributing it as the 'Antiochian Orthodox version of the traditional Roman Mass', approved in 1958), it has also allowed since 1977 an 'Antiochian Orthodox version of the traditional Anglo-Catholic Mass',[17] the 'Liturgy of St Tikhon',[18] after some groups uncomfortable with liberal trends in the Episcopal Church joined the Orthodox Church.

---

[17] 'As it stands, the core of the Liturgy of Saint Tikhon is taken from the classic Anglican Eucharistic Liturgy, with extensive borrowings from the Tridentine Missale Romanum and a modest contribution from the contemporary Byzantine Rite ... Before the Antiochian Archdiocese adopted the Liturgy of Saint Tikhon, this hybrid Romano-Anglican Liturgy was very commonly found in High Church, Anglo-Catholic parishes of the Protestant Episcopal Church in the United States' (Andersen 2005: 15). 'The Antiochian Western Rite Vicariate had but little to add ... Most of this work had already been accomplished in common Anglo-Catholic practice' (Andersen 2005: 13).

[18] The attribution to St Tikhon does not mean that Patriarch Tikhon (Bellavin, 1865–1925) was the author. However, at the time he was the head of the Orthodox Church in America, he had asked the Holy Synod if, in case an entire Anglican parish and its minister would join the Orthodox Church, they could be allowed to keep the Book of Common Prayer, and what changes should be made. A commission established by the Holy Synod answered in 1904 (Frere 1917); interestingly, one of the members of the commission was the future Patriarch Sergius, who later authorised the use of the Western rite in France. Since Episcopalians who had considered coming under the Russian Church then decided otherwise, the question remained a theoretical one in the early twentieth century. 'Tikhon

There have also been Western rite groups in ROCOR in North America. A 1953 decree had stated the acceptability of Western liturgical traditions for groups joining the Orthodox Church, while individual converts would have to observe the Eastern liturgical traditions (ROCOR 1953). In 1968, a Western rite deanery was even established under the supervision of Archpriest George Grabbe (1902–1995), but it lasted only for a few years; it used the Roman rite. In 1975, Fr Augustine (Whitfield) (1924–2010), Abbot of Mount-Royal congregation, a group of Old Catholic lineage that had been received in the Exarchate of the Moscow Patriarchate in 1962, joined ROCOR with the blessing of Archbishop Nikon (Rklitski, 1882–1976).[19] In 1978, the Council of Bishops of ROCOR decided that it was 'not ... possible to allow the Western Rite in the Russian Church'. But Fr Augustine had apparently been forgotten, and thus a barely noticed Western rite presence persisted in ROCOR (ROCOR 2013). In the 1990s, the future Metropolitan Hilarion (Kapral, b. 1948) accepted a handful of very small Western rite groups, first in the United States (including the monastic community of Christminster) and subsequently in Australia. In May 2011, the Council of Bishops of the Russian Orthodox Church Outside of Russia established a Western Rite Vicariate under the Metropolitan, with Bishop Jerome (John Shaw, b. 1946) as his assistant. Applicant groups were received at a rather rapid pace, reaching some 25 congregations (mostly small ones). Due to serious disagreements with the way Bishop Jerome was administering the Western rite parishes, he was retired in July 2013, without the right to perform ordinations. All the existing communities are directly under the oversight and omophorion of the Metropolitan. A commission was established to take care of the Western rite groups. In August 2013, the commission published a statement affirming that '[i]t is not the intention of the Commission nor the Synod of Bishops to dismantle the Western-Rite Community within ROCOR, nor is it the objective to perpetrate some sort of "forced Byzantination"'.[20]

Developments in the United States have also had an impact on the European continent. In the 1990s, a group of Anglican clergy gathered under the name Pilgrimage to Orthodoxy followed a path similar to some of their Episcopalian colleagues and turned to Orthodoxy: led by a priest of Charismatic orientation, Fr Michael Harper (1931–2010), they began to be received in the Antiochian

---

authored no Eucharistic Liturgy; but he did play the crucial role in raising the possibility of using corrected Anglican liturgical forms in the North American Orthodox missionary context' (Andersen 2005: 7).

[19]   Archbishop Nikon was a ROCOR bishop supportive of Western Rite Orthodoxy: he sent a long and warm message after the passing away of Bishop Jean de Saint-Denis (*Jean de Saint-Denis, Eugraph Kovalevsky, 1905–1970, In Memoriam*, Paris: Présence Orthodoxe, n.d., 93–4).

[20]   Published on the official website of ROCOR Western Rite Community (www.rwrv. org).

Archdiocese of Europe in 1995. Three priests used the Western rite at the start, but it was abandoned a year later: 'the communities concerned all abandoned the western rite voluntarily. There was no episcopal edict'.[21]

Regarding the Russian Orthodox Church Outside of Russia, there have been in the United Kingdom a handful of small mission groups for several years; Hieromonk Michael (Mansbridge-Wood) first used to take pastoral care of them, then another priest, Fr Thomas Cook, was ordained in 2012 for the Western rite mission. The liturgy 'is based on the English Missal (therefore broadly Tridentine), with a number of modifications. It is similar to the Antiochian Liturgy of St Gregory'.[22] The group is small, but most participants – including the priest – were already Orthodox before the Western rite was available to them; lay people attend Byzantine rite parishes when there is no Western rite being served in their area.

In Germany, a small Benedictine monastic community (three people) was received in ROCOR in February 2013. The group had been an independent Catholic congregation. The abbot, Fr Thomas (Komossa), had been ordained in the Orthodox Church of France at a time it was still in communion with the Romanian Church: thus his priesthood was recognised, but not the episcopal consecration he had received in 2003 from independent bishops. The two other members of the community were (re)ordained, since their orders were not Orthodox. The small community follows mostly an orthodoxised form of the Roman rite, but also celebrates once a week the Liturgy according to St Germanus of Paris.

Moreover, also in Western Europe, but outside of the Western Rite Vicariate, a few parishes located in Spain, calling themselves the Hispanic Orthodox Church, have been received into the Western European Archdiocese of ROCOR in 2012: while they use the Byzantine rite most of the time, the Mozarabic rite is used twice a year (on the feast of St Isidore of Seville and of St Helen) and occasionally on special feast days.[23]

While this overview covers most of the developments pertaining to the Western rite in (canonical) Orthodox Churches in Western Europe, it should also take into account efforts by various individual Orthodox faithful, although they have not resulted in the creation of parishes. One example was Raymond Winch (1921–2000), who converted to the Orthodox Church from Roman Catholicism, but kept a strong interest for the Western liturgical heritage. 'His interest in the idea of a Western Orthodox rite originated in his previous dissatisfaction with the reform of the Roman Catholic liturgy following the

---

[21] Fr Gregory Hallam, personal communication, 27 August 2013.
[22] Fr Thomas Cook, personal communication, 22 August 2013.
[23] Fr Pablo M. Alvarez, personal communication, 24 August 2013.

282   *Orthodox Identities in Western Europe*

Second Vatican council'.[24] He founded in Oxford a Gregorian Club 'for the restoration of Orthodoxy's Western heritage', for missionary reasons, but not only, according to its Statement of Principles: 'Hitherto the great heritage of Latin Christendom has in some measure been preserved by those who are not Orthodox. Now it is being rapidly abandoned. We believe our heritage to be of great intrinsic worth. If it is not to be lost altogether, we Western Orthodox must make it our own once again. We wish to worship and live according to our own traditions – those of our saints'. The Gregorian Club did not envision separate Western Orthodox dioceses, but hoped for unity of the Church, with one bishop in each place, over communities of different rites. The Gregorian Club did not last, but it had a few issues of a bulletin as well as some booklets printed, including what its founder envisioned as the 'Canonical Mass of the English Orthodox'.[25] A supporter of the Club published a study suggesting that the 'historical point of departure [for a restoration of a Western Orthodox rite] must be the period just before the schism, about 800–1000 – obvious, one would have said, yet none of the previous Western Orthodox restorers has taken this line' (Coombs 1987: 60).

Missing from our overview are non-canonical[26] Churches understanding themselves as Orthodox and their efforts of liturgical restoration: one example would be the so-called 'Celtic Orthodox Church' (Seraïdari and Leonard 2007) as well as attempts by other groups to recreate a Celtic liturgy;[27] other non-canonical groups have been involved in perseverant efforts to restore uses of 'Orthodox England' or other liturgical forms. However, those groups fall beyond the scope of this chapter.

Western Rite: Open Questions for Orthodox Churches

Due to the current status of the Orthodox Church of France, most of the Western rite communities are now found on the other side of the ocean. Between the Antiochian Archdiocese and ROCOR, there were 40 to 50

---

[24]   Stephen Coombs, personal communication, 2 September 2013.

[25]   Rev. Anthony Chadwick, a priest of the Anglican Catholic Church, has made this out-of-print text available online (Winch 2007).

[26]   This is used here in a purely technical, non-polemical way: the borders between what is 'canonical' and what is not can change rapidly in some of the cases discussed here (Seraïdari and Léonard 2007: 88).

[27]   Sometimes with echoes within canonical Orthodox Churches: in the early 2000s, an Orthodox monastery under the Moscow Patriarchate in Belgium translated and used during some time a Celtic liturgy (based on the 'Lorrha-Stowe Missal'): this was an adaptation of a Missal published in English by Bishop Maelruain (Kristopher Dowling, 1955–2013), founder of a 'Celtic Orthodox Christian Church' in Akron (Ohio).

Western rite communities in canonical Orthodox Churches in North America in summer 2013. A few more were found in other parts of the world, including a handful in Europe. There are also those parishes using occasionally one of the Western rites. Despite considerable work done by some groups or individuals, the numerical results thus remain modest. Not a few priests and faithful who started with a Western rite now serve with the Byzantine rite.

Looking through Orthodox lenses for recovering the fullness of Christianity or the 'true' Christian identity of the West can take several routes: either joining a Byzantine rite parish while cultivating the veneration of local saints, or looking for a way to create a space for Western Rite Orthodoxy. It is not surprising that most people willing to embrace the Orthodox faith follow the first option and find their way to the Byzantine rite: not only due to its more general availability, but also because the beauty and attraction of Orthodox liturgy itself is frequently a starting point.

Moreover, which Western rite? There is a surprising variety of liturgical forms compared to the small number of canonical Western rite communities.[28] If we look at the list of 'currently approved versions of the Divine Liturgy for use in the ROCOR Western Rite', we find two different versions of the Orthodox Roman rite (named 'Liturgy of St Gregory'), plus a restoration of the Use of Sarum,[29] and the Gallican liturgy; moreover, as mentioned, a few Spanish parishes sometimes use the Mozarabic liturgy. If we look at the Antiochian Western Rite Vicariate, there are two liturgies in use: the Liturgy of St Tikhon and the Liturgy of St Gregory.

Such diversity reveals the different backgrounds of people involved in Western rite efforts: tailor-made solutions have been devised for different Western rite aspirations. In contrast with the Orthodox Church of France and its work of restoration, in which there were interactions with impulses from the Liturgical Movement in Roman Catholic circles,[30] some of the Western rite parishes, mostly in the United States, are the products of reactions against changes (liturgical and otherwise) in the religious bodies they used to belong to. The Orthodox Church is seen as a refuge (Turner 2011: 334–5). It is praised for its steadfast attachment to tradition, and this is why it is seen as a possible way out of chaos, even for people eager to keep their own liturgical traditions, different from Byzantine

---

[28]   Coombs had distinguished three types of Western rites: 'historical' (Mensbrugghe), 'modern-pragmatic' (pre-Vatican II Roman rite with some adaptations) and 'personal-eclectic' (Coombs 1987: 59; see Turner 2012c).

[29]   A different restoration of Sarum had already been blessed by Metropolitan Hilarion and published in 2008.

[30]   For instance, Dom Lambert Beauduin (1873–1960), also well-known as the founder of Chevetogne Abbey in Belgium, was in touch with Fr Evgraph and gave lectures at the newly-founded Institute Saint-Denis in 1944–1945, before his superiors asked him in early 1946 to suspend his collaboration (Loonbeek and Mortiau 2001: 1257–9).

ones. It is not only for Western rite Orthodox that the Orthodox Church can look like a haven for souls aspiring to escape the turmoils of contemporary Western Christian religious bodies: such feelings are expressed by a number of converts who follow the Byzantine rite as well as by 'philo-Orthodox' in other Christian Churches, who are not willing to switch their religious affiliation for a variety of reasons (including the desire to keep their own liturgical tradition), but who admire the Orthodox Church for its alleged 'conservatism'. In the same way attention is paid to Orthodox perceptions of the West, much could be said about perceptions of Orthodoxy in Western imaginaries.

If Western Orthodox liturgies were more widely available, especially those close to still familiar old Western liturgical forms, some among those philo-Orthodox would certainly convert. But it is unlikely that it would become a mass movement, as experience has taught. Most tradition-minded Catholics or Anglicans can find settings other than Orthodox ones for a liturgical life as they want it: those having the desire to combine it with the confession of the Orthodox faith (and not merely an Orthodox jurisdictional option) are likely to remain a small minority. One of the arguments for using an existing form of Western rite continues to be a missionary one: converts to the Orthodox Church would thus be able to keep liturgical forms they were already familiar with. Except in the case of religiously conservative circles (e.g. 'continuing Anglicans'), this argument seems to have lost part of its relevance after liturgical reforms: unless they have been participants in traditional Roman Catholic masses, converts from Roman Catholicism would hardly be familiar today with ancient Catholic liturgical forms, and nobody has suggested that the *Novus Ordo Missae* (what is known today as the 'ordinary form of the Roman rite') currently used by most Catholics should be adjusted to Orthodox requirements.

The approach developed by Bishop Jean de Saint-Denis and the Orthodox Church of France as well as by other 'restorative' liturgical undertakings has been a different one, that cannot be found elsewhere: it offers both discontinuity with the Western liturgical tradition, since the rites used are different from those practising Western Christians have grown with and borrowings are made from Eastern liturgies, and continuity, due to retention of a number of Western traditions and to the call to a more ancient, pre-schism local legacy.

Ironically, even if the wish to keep or recover tradition leads people to the Western rite, the result cannot avoid being innovative, with different levels of intensity: first, because the existence of Western rite communities creates a new situation in Orthodox Churches and sometimes unease about the way to deal with such communities; second, because – even liturgically – all those groups need to accept at least some adjustments in order to meet Orthodox requirements, when not engaging into daring reconstructions.

But what should be done in order to make a liturgy 'Orthodox', not even speaking about the way to perform it? Removing the *filioque* and making sure a clear epiclesis is present are steps taken by every Western Orthodox project since Overbeck.[31] After that, how far to go with revisions? In a report to the Brotherhood of St Photios in 1937, Vladimir Lossky gave an example to illustrate issues raised by corrections of Winnaert's 'evangelical catholic' liturgy: the doxological formula referring to Jesus Christ who liveth and reigneth with the Father 'in unitate Spiritus Sancti' ('in the unity of the Holy Spirit') was, according to him, 'an obvious consequence of filioquism', that could not be justified dogmatically, since 'it makes from the Person of the Holy Spirit a mere function of unity of the Father and the Son, their common love, "nexus amoris"'. But as early as the eighth century, this formula was already found in missals. Finally, Lossky explained, looking at critical editions of the oldest sacramentaries, with their variations, the 'primitive Trinitarian formula of Western liturgies was found': 'qui vivit et regnat cum Deo Patre et Spiritu Sancto' (Lossky 1980, 11). Nevertheless, a number of Western rite advocates disagree with that opinion: several approved liturgies being used in Western Orthodox communities contain 'in unitate Spiritus Sancti'.

Similarly, there are a number of variations regarding acceptable devotions: for instance, there are Western rite Antiochian parishes that celebrate the feasts of the Sacred Heart or of Corpus Christi, something many Orthodox would object to. The veneration of post-schism saints in some Western rite communities can also become a contentious issue. Statues are another debated topic (especially when they do not follow some neo-Romanesque style, but rather nineteenth-century Sulpician models). Some Western rite communities, however, completely reject post-schism practices in principle and even follow the old (Julian) calendar (no doubt a consistent step for people eager to

---

[31]   Some bishops have been willing to consider a different approach, as illustrated by a document in Russian, discovered by Bernard Le Caro (whom we thank for sharing it and translating extracts) in the ROCOR archives in New York. The title of the unsigned and undated document is 'O dopustimosti zapadnago bogoslužebnago čina dlja pravoslavnyh zapadnyh obščin' ('On the permissibility of the Western liturgical rite for Orthodox of Western communities'). Internal evidence makes clear that this 15-page-long text was prepared by Bishop (later Archbishop) Nathaniel (Lvov, 1906–1986) and written around 1950. In the late 1930s, in Ceylon, he had accepted a group of former Roman Catholics in the Orthodox Church, and they had been allowed to use the Western rite. In the document, Bishop Nathaniel writes that the epiclesis was absent from several ancient liturgical formularies in the West, such as those of St Gelasius, St Gregory the Great or St Leo of Rome: 'either we must condemn the liturgical practice of such great saints ... or we must acknowledge that the Western liturgy is possible without the epiclesis' (p. 8). On the other hand, communion under both kinds was mandatory: according to Bishop Nathaniel, depriving the faithful of the Blood of Christ was anyway a later deviation in the Latin Church. Bishop Nathaniel's approach placed the emphasis on avoiding as much as possible the introduction of arbitrary changes in liturgical traditions.

cultivate tradition, since the Gregorian calendar was not accepted in England before 1752).

Thus, the question of hybridity unavoidably occurs when dealing with the Western rite. 'What is mostly striking is an intimate entanglement between Eastern and Western elements' in the Orthodox Church of France (Erny 1983: 231). Hybridity may seem at first sight to be less an issue in communities using the Roman rite, but it appears under other forms, as we have just seen. A priest explained to us how a fellow clergyman was ordained for the Western rite by an Orthodox bishop using the Byzantine rite of ordination, but in Latin. The same priest, resident in an area where Orthodox parishes are few, reported serving in the Byzantine rite for the pastoral care of migrants from Orthodox countries when needed. Without being aware of it, the Orthodox Western rite movement is also a child of a context of globalisation and individualisation. In French-speaking Europe, it is also an outcome of migration: it is unlikely that the modern Gallican liturgy would ever have seen the light of the day if it had not been for the vision of bright young Russians who felt that the personal tragedy of exile should be invested with a meaning and mission.

Despite all hurdles and problems encountered, the Western rite option remains an attractive idea for some Orthodox. The inclusion of the Western rite as a way of affirming 'the universalist character of Orthodoxy' was a main argument advanced by Fr Lev Gillet for supporting the reception of Winnaert's community into the Orthodox Church (Behr-Siegel 1993: 260). Such an affirmation is bound to give rise to debates beyond Orthodox circles: it has obvious implications for ecumenical relations (Turner 2012b). But it may first be a question for the self-understanding of Orthodox Churches in their encounter with 'the West'.

Bibliography

Abramtsov, D.F. 1961a. A Brief History of Western Orthodoxy in Modern Times. Available at: http://www.allmercifulsavior.com/Liturgy/Abramtsov.html [accessed 25 August 2013]. Previously published in three instalments in 1961 in the journal *One Church*, 15(7–8): 226–36; 15(9–10): 295–305; 15(11–12): 355–65.

Abramtsov, D.F. 1961b. *The Western Rite and the Eastern Church: Dr J.J. Overbeck and his Scheme for the Re-Establishment of the Orthodox Church in the West*. MA Thesis submitted to the Graduate Faculty in the Division of the Social Sciences, University of Pittsburgh, 1961. Available at: http://anglicanhistory.org/orthodoxy/abramtsov.pdf [accessed 23 August 2013].

Andersen, B.J. n.d. A Short History of the Western Rite Vicariate. Available at: http://www.antiochian.org/sites/default/files/wrv_history.pdf [accessed 25 August 2013].

Andersen, B.J. 2005. *An Anglican Liturgy in the Orthodox Church: The Origins and Development of the Antiochian Orthodox Liturgy of Saint Tikhon.* MDiv Thesis, St Vladimir's Orthodox Theological Seminary.

Bange, R. and Bange, C. 2013. La Confrérie de Saint-Photius et ses travaux sur la liturgie occidentale (1925–1945). *Présence Orthodoxe,* 173: 19–40.

Basil, J.D. 1991. Alexander Kireev: Turn-of-the-Century Slavophile and the Russian Orthodox Church, 1890–1910. *Cahiers du monde russe et soviétique,* 32(3): 337–47.

Behr-Siegel, E. 1993. *Une Moine de l'Église d'Orient: Le Père Lev Gillet.* Paris: Éditions du Cerf.

Besse, J.-P. 1992. *Un précurseur: Wladimir Guettée, du Gallicanisme à l'Orthodoxie.* Lavardac: Monastère Orthodoxe Saint-Michel.

Bourne, V. 1966. *La Queste de Vérité d'Irénée Winnaert.* Geneva: Labor et Fides.

Bourne, V. 1975. *La Divine Contradiction: L'avenir catholique orthodoxe de la France.* Paris: Librairie des Cinq Continents.

Bourne, V. 1978. *La Divine Contradiction: Le chant et la lutte de l'Orthodoxie.* Paris: Éditions Présence Orthodoxe.

Burton, B. [Archimandrite Barnabas]. 1985. *Strange Pilgrimage.* Welshpool: Stylite Publishing.

Coombs, S. 1987. *The Eucharistic Prayer in the Orthodox West.* Oxford: Gregorian Club.

Dederen, R. 1963. *Un Réformateur catholique au XIXe siècle: Eugène Michaud (1839–1917). Vieux-catholicisme – Œcuménisme.* Genève: Droz.

Erny, P. 1983. Une nouvelle arrivée dans le paysage religieux de la France de l'Est: L'Église Catholique Orthodoxe de France. *Revue des Sciences Sociales de la France de l'Est,* 12–12 bis: 225–33.

Florovsky, G. 1989. Russian Orthodox Ecumenism in the Nineteenth Century, in *Ecumenism II: A Historical Approach. The Collected Works of Georges Florovsky, Vol. XIV,* edited by Richard S. Haugh. Vaduz: Büchervertriebsanstalt, 110–63.

Frere, W.H. 1917. *Russian Observations upon the American Prayer Book.* London: A.R. Mowbray.

Gamber, K. 1984. *Die Messfeier nach altgallikanischem Ritus.* Regensburg: Kommissionsverlag F. Pustet.

Guettée, W. 1866. *Exposition de la Doctrine de l'Église catholique orthodoxe, accompagnée des différences qui se rencontrent dans les autres Églises chrétiennes.* Paris: Librairie de l'Union Chrétienne.

Guettée, W. 1889. *Souvenirs d'un prêtre romain devenu prêtre orthodoxe.* Paris: Fischbacher.

288   *Orthodox Identities in Western Europe*

Kahle, W. 1968. *Westliche Orthodoxie: Leben und Ziele Julian Joseph Overbecks.* Leiden and Cologne: Brill.

Kovalevsky, E. 1956. *La Sainte Messe selon l'Ancien Rite des Gaules ou Liturgie selon S. Germain de Paris.* Paris: Éditions Orthodoxes Saint-Irénée.

Kovalevsky, M. 1984. *Retrouver la Source oubliée: Paroles sur la Liturgie d'un Homme qui chante Dieu.* Paris: Éditions Présence Orthodoxe.

Kovalevsky, M. 1990. *Orthodoxie et Occident: Renaissance d'une Église locale.* Paris: Carbonnel.

Loonbeek, R. and Mortiau, J. 2001. *Un Pionnier, Dom Lambert Beauduin (1873–1960): Liturgie et Unité des Chrétiens.* Vol. II. Louvain-la-Neuve: Collège Erasme.

Lossky, V. 1980. Pour une Orthodoxie occidentale: Arguments historiques. *Présence Orthodoxe,* 44: 5–12.

Mayer, J.-F. 1997. L'Orthodoxie doit-elle être byzantine? Les tentatives de création d'un rite orthodoxe occidental, in *Regards sur l'Orthodoxie: Mélanges offerts à Jacques Goudet,* edited by G. Ivanoff-Trinadtzaty. Lausanne: L'Âge d'Homme, 191–213.

Mendez, M. 2008. *La Messe de l'Ancien Rite des Gaules: Origine et Restauration.* Paris: L'Harmattan.

Mensbrugghe, A. van der. 1948. *La Liturgie orthodoxe de Rite occidental: Essai de restauration.* Paris: Éditions Œcuméniques Setor.

Mensbrugghe, A. van der. 1962. *Missel ou Livre de la Synaxe liturgique approuvé et autorisé pour les Églises Orthodoxes de Rit occidental relevant du Patriarcat de Moscou.* Paris: Contacts.

Model, S. 2012. Mgr Alexis van der Mensbrugghe: Évêque orthodoxe en France, Amérique et Allemagne; Théologien, spécialiste reconnu des liturgies anciennes!. Available at: http://www.egliserusse.eu/blogdiscussion/Mgr-Alexis-van-der-Mensbrugghe-eveque-orthodoxe-en-France-Amerique-et-Allemagne-theologien-specialiste-reconnu-des_a2366.html [accessed 24 August 2013].

Novikoff, O. 1914. *Le Général Alexandre Kiréeff et l'ancien-catholicisme* (new augmented edition). Bern: Librairie Staempfli.

Overbeck, J.J. 1869. *Die providentielle Stellung des Orthodoxen Russland und sein Beruf zur Wiederherstellung der rechtgläubigen katholischen Kirche des Abendlands.* Halle: W. Schmidt.

Overbeck, J.J. n.d. [c. 1871a]. *Liturgia Missæ Orthodoxo-catholicæ occidentalis* [*The Liturgy of the Western Orthodox-Catholic Mass*]. London: Taylor.

Overbeck, J.J. 1871b. *Libellus Invitatorius ad Clerum Laicosque Romano-Catholicos, qui antiquam Occidentis Ecclesiam Catholicam ad pristinam puritatem et gloriam restauratam videre cupiunt.* Halle: W. Schmidt.

Overbeck, J.J. 1876. *Die Bonner Unions-Conferenzen, oder Altkatholicismus und Anglikanismus in ihrem Verhältnis zur Orthodoxie. Eine Appellation an die*

Patriarchen und Heiligen Synoden der orthodox-katholischen Kirche. Halle: W. Schmidt.

Pnevmatikakis, V. 2012. L'émigration russe et la naissance d'une orthodoxie française 1925–1953. *Slavica bruxellensia*, 8. Available at: http://slavica. revues.org/1068 [accessed 24 August 2013].

ROCOR. 1953. Decree of the Council of Bishops of the Russian Orthodox Church Outside Russia. Available at: http://www.rocorstudies.org/ documents/2013/06/16/on-the-western-liturgical-tradition [accessed 26 August 2013].

ROCOR. 2013. His Grace Bishop Jerome of Manhattan on the Western Rite in ROCOR. Available at: http://www.rocorstudies.org/ interviews/2013/06/17/bishop-jerome-of-manhatan-on-western-rite-in-the-rocor/ [accessed 25 August 2013].

Saint-Denis, G. de. 1977. Sur l'histoire de l'étude et de la restauration dans l'Orthodoxie de la Liturgie de l'ancien Rite des Gaules dite 'Liturgie selon Saint Germain de Paris'. *Présence Orthodoxe*, 36: 5–91.

Seraïdari, K. and Léonard, A. 2007. Quand les Celtes deviennent Orthodoxes: De l'exaltation du passé à la modernité religieuse. *Archives de Sciences Sociales des Religions*, 139: 79–99.

Tanazacq, N. 1977. Bibliographie de l'ancien rite des Gaules et de sa restauration. *Présence Orthodoxe*, 36(3): 4–49.

Thomann, G.H. 1995. *The Western Rite in Orthodoxy: Union and Reunion Schemes of Western and Eastern Churches with Eastern Orthodoxy. A Brief Historical Outline*, 2nd edition. Nuremberg: G.H. Thomann.

Turner, J. 2009. The Journey Thus Far: A Review of the Literature on Western-Rite Orthodoxy. *St Vladimir's Theological Quarterly*, 53(4): 477–505.

Turner, J. 2011.Western Rite Orthodoxy as a Liturgical Problem. *Journal of Eastern Christian Studies*, 63(3–4): 333–52.

Turner, J. 2012a. *O Salutaris Hostia*: The Challenge of Eucharistic Adoration in Western Rite Orthodoxy. *Religious Studies and Theology*, 31(1): 41–54.

Turner, J. 2012b. Western Rite Orthodoxy as an Ecumenical Problem. *Journal of Ecumenical Studies*, 47(4): 541–54.

Turner, J. 2012c. Journeying Onwards: An Overview of the Liturgical Books in Western-Rite Orthodoxy. *St Vladimir's Theological Quarterly*, 56(1): 93–112.

Winch, R. 2007. *The Canonical Mass of the English Orthodox*, 3rd edition. Available at: http://civitas-dei.eu/winch.pdf [accessed 26 August 2013].

Chapter 15

Innovation in the Russian Orthodox Church: The Crisis in the Diocese of Sourozh in Britain

Maria Hämmerli and Edmund Mucha

In line with the theme of the present volume, this chapter intends to illustrate the diversity of Orthodox identities in Western Europe. We will not dwell here on aspects such as ethnicity, language, liturgical style, or migration patterns, as these have already been addressed by other authors; instead, we will focus on diversity of representations of Orthodox identity and the vocation of the Orthodox Church in the context of deterritorialised Orthodoxy, which occasions experimentation and innovation. Though innovation is apparently incompatible with the Orthodox Church, which is bound to tradition and devoted to continuity with early Christianity (the Church Fathers and the seven Ecumenical Councils), in fact innovation of a kind has been an 'inherent modality of this religious tradition' (Willert and Molokotos-Liederman 2012: 3).

We will discuss the early twenty-first century crisis that arose in the Moscow Patriarchate Diocese of Sourozh in Great Britain and Ireland. Originally a small Russian community, this diocese had steadily assimilated into British culture and life and had grown numerically with British converts up through the 1990s, when it received a massive new influx of Russian-speaking immigrants. The 'old-timers' and the 'newly-arrived', however, upheld dissimilar and conflicting visions of the Church and its vocation, with no final agreement or reconciliation. We chose to examine this specific episode in the history of the Orthodox presence in Great Britain because we consider it to be symptomatic of the issues raised by various Orthodox actors, individuals and institutions alike, in the process of construction and negotiation of an Orthodox identity in the West, which supposes adaptations and innovation.

After a brief summary of the history of the diocese and of the circumstances that caused turmoil and ultimately a split in 2006, we will expose the rationale referred to by each side involved in the conflict and provide an analysis of their representations about the vocation of the Orthodox Church in the West and about the Orthodox identity. We base our argument on discourse analysis of documents (e.g. letters, testimonials and reports) both sides produced on the internet (mainly the diocese's website) during the crisis in order to justify and explain their respective positions.[1]

Much has been written about this crisis, but generally in terms of reporting the course of events that led to the division of the diocese; the respective authors do not claim objectivity, as most of them are Orthodox observers who take a stand about one or the other aspect of the crisis. The aim of this paper is not to reproduce the sequence of incidents, but to reflect on the content of the innovation steered by the Sourozh diocese, on the conditions that made it possible and the circumstances that challenged it, to the point that it became a point of contention and of division. Our argument is structured by what lies at the heart of both the innovations and the resistance to innovation – namely, the differing representations regarding the Orthodox Church and Orthodox identity.

Brief Historical Overview of the Sourozh Diocese

The Russian Orthodox presence in the British Isles dates back to the eighteenth century, when the London parish of the Dormition of the Mother of God was created as an embassy church in 1716. The parish location changed several times in the course of its history, before finally settling into the cathedral at Ennismore Gardens. In terms of jurisdictional allegiance, the parish experienced a complicated journey in the years following the Russian Revolution, passing from the Moscow Patriarchate to the Russian Orthodox Church Outside of Russia (ROCOR), then to the Patriarchate of Constantinople (1931), and finally back to the Moscow Patriarchate (1945) – without, however, canonical release from Constantinople.[2]

By the 1950s, other Russian parishes had been created in Great Britain. An ecumenical dialogue had also been established with the Anglican Church, through the Fellowship of Saint Alban and Saint Sergius. Hieromonk Anthony Bloom, appointed chaplain of this fellowship, became the rector of the London parish and later, in 1957, was appointed bishop of the newly formed Russian vicariate of Sergievo. In very short time, new parishes were created and converts started joining under the guidance and inspiration of Bishop Anthony. His work and vision did not leave Moscow indifferent, and in 1962 the Patriarchate decided to turn the vicariate into an independent diocese. Initially, it was to be designated 'of London and Great Britain', but after a personal discussion with

---

[1]   Many of these documents were collected during the crisis, but have since been removed from the internet. Therefore, some of the links we provide do not exist anymore. We have them in our personal archives, which interested readers can access upon request.

[2]   For a more detailed history of the Sourozh diocese, see 'Russian Orthodox Diocese of Sourozh' [online], available at: http://en.wikipedia.org/wiki/Russian_Orthodox_Diocese_of_Sourozh.

the Archbishop of Canterbury, Bishop Anthony understood that taking an English geographical title might offend the Anglican Church. In order to avoid spoiling good relations with the local established church, it was decided that the diocese would receive a Russian name, from a defunct diocese in the Crimea, Sourozh (Crow 2005). Bishop Anthony became archbishop of the diocese of Sourozh and remained its head until his death in 2003.

The diocese continued to grow and expanded also to Wales, Scotland and Northern Ireland, but remained predominantly located in Southern England and centred on the Cathedral in London and the parish in Oxford. It added to its numbers local converts, especially of Anglican background and Oxford-educated intellectuals. Conversions were not the result of active proselytising, because the Orthodox refrained from it in order to maintain good relations with local Christian denominations. It was mainly internal developments in the Catholic and Anglican Churches that drew away some of their members, who subsequently requested acceptance and spiritual shelter in the Orthodox Church.

Metropolitan Anthony's close and lifelong collaborator Gillian Crow (2005) talks about how he became very quickly a well-known figure in the British religious landscape through his lectures and conferences, his attendance of intellectual religious forums, his presence in the media, particularly on the radio, and his publications; in this way he gained high visibility as a representative of the Orthodox Church in Great Britain. Metropolitan Anthony's spiritual charisma and his energetic style of leadership were key to the progress of the diocese.

Other achievements of Sourozh included the translation of Orthodox services into English and the adaptation of traditional liturgical music to the local language, the opening of chaplaincy services in prisons, hospitals and at London University, the creation of youth summer camps and two charitable organisations, and the publication of a respected diocesan journal, *Sourozh*, with international distribution. The diocese maintained one feature of its émigré origins, namely financial independence from Moscow, relying instead on its members' human and financial resources. These developments spanned over a period of 40 years, gradually leading to assimilation in British life and culture.

A new page in the history of the Sourozh diocese was to be written after the fall of Communism in the former Soviet Union, which occasioned a considerable influx of new Russian-speaking members. The profile of the diocese (and especially of the Cathedral in London) did not meet the expectations of the new wave of migrants, who expected a Russian parish to be a piece of home in a linguistically and culturally alien context. Instead of 'an outpost of Russia', they found 'a living offspring of the Russian church which does encompass the Russian experience familiar to them, but ... at the same time offers a worship

294 *Orthodox Identities in Western Europe*

and way of life in Orthodoxy coloured by British ways'[3] – a parish of Russian tradition, but one in which the Russian culture had shrunk in favour of a multicultural ethos with British tints. Subsequent attempts to make the parish life look more like what the church immigrants were used to in the homeland amounted for some to 'normalisation', whereas others saw it as 'Russification' and a step back to an Orthodoxy limited to an ethnic ghetto.

The cultural misunderstandings between 'old-timers' and the 'newly-arrived' developed into tensions that took the form of protests and petitions to the Moscow Patriarchate and ultimately grew into frictions among clergy. The main conflict occurred between the Sourozh diocese administrator Bishop Basil Osbourne and his supporters versus Moscow-sent clergy at the service of the Russian-speaking immigrants, priest Andrey Teterin, Archbishop Anatoly of Kerch and Bishop Hilarion Alfeyev.

The crisis came to a climax after Metropolitan Anthony's death, which opened the thorny question of his succession and, for the 'old-timers', of the preservation and continuation of his work. Fearing potential seizure of property by the Moscow Patriarchate and the latter's interference in the diocesan administrative matters and pastoral line, Bishop Basil approached the Ecumenical Patriarchate of Constantinople and asked to be received, together with the clergy and believers who would wish to follow him, in the Exarchate of Orthodox Parishes of Russian Tradition in Western Europe. He considered this move to be the only solution to avoid 'Russification' and to preserve the 'distinctive ethos' the Sourozh diocese developed under Metropolitan Anthony. Despite the Moscow Patriarchate's attempts to reconcile both 'camps' and its disapproval of this transfer of jurisdiction, in 2006 the Sourozh diocese split into those who followed Bishop Basil and those who wished to stay loyal to their original canonical allegiance. Moscow appointed Bishop Elisey as head of the remaining flock and the conflict ended, though it was only in 2007 that Moscow officially released Bishop Basil and regularised his canonical situation.

Innovation and the 'Distinctive Ethos' of the Sourozh Diocese

First, by 'innovation' we do not mean radical change or break with the past, but rather a creative response to a specific situation at a particular moment in time, starting from existing models and examples provided by tradition. As noted by Willert and Molokotos-Liederman, in the Orthodox Church 'changes are often presented not as introducing something new or modern, but as reintroducing

---

[3] 'Some purely personal thoughts by a Sourozh parishioner on the nature of our Diocese and its relationship to the Russian Orthodox Church', document in the personal archive of Maria Hämmerli.

Innovation in the Russian Orthodox Church 295

what is perceived as a traditional and authentic religious framework because the existing one is considered to have deteriorated or removed itself from its intended origin and mission' (Willert and Molokotos-Liederman 2012: 6). Therefore, what we designate as 'change' or 'novelty' in the Sourozh diocese does not describe 'unheard-of' practices.

Second, in order to grasp the nature of innovation, we have to understand how, by comparison with past practice, it constitutes an innovation: i.e., we have to make a brief account of the state of the Russian Orthodox Church and the Diocese before Metropolitan Anthony took over its leadership.

Back in Russia, the Church was subject to state hostility, to political denigration and persecution. The Church survived more or less as an underground institution, reduced to liturgical activities, cut off from and unable to serve society according to its own principle of *diakonia*. Few churches and monasteries were still functioning. Theological training for clergy was hardly available. Lay believers maintained a diluted contact with Orthodoxy through their socialisation in Russian culture (which was itself being 'purified' of religious influence) or through oral transmission by grandparents and older generations. Religion served also as a form of resistance to the political regime, especially among intelligentsia; as such, it was taken very seriously by believers with regard to dogma, ascetic practices and religious authority (clergy).

In Britain, Russians were free from all this pressure and free to organise their religious life. Until the 1950s, the Russian Orthodox presence more or less coalesced around the London parish, with services attended mainly by elderly Russian émigrés and the younger generations driven away from the Church because of their inability to understand Slavonic. While continuing to pledge canonical allegiance to the Moscow Patriarchate, Metropolitan Anthony did not lead his diocese according to the pattern set by the Soviet state-repressed Moscow Patriarchate.[4] Instead, he had the vision to take inspiration from the provisions of the 1917 All-Russian Council, which brought a stream of renewal and theological freshness. In its hostility to religion and its interference with the functioning, scope and action of the Orthodox Church, the Bolshevik regime prevented this council from being implemented in Russia. Yet Metropolitan Anthony took the liberty of putting into effect some of the provisions of the 1917 Council, mainly those with respect to church hierarchy: first, bishops were to be elected by the people in the diocese and not to be imposed by the Synod back in Russia; and second, the clergy were to give more space for lay involvement in the running of the parish life.

This novelty, grounded in Church decrees, but nourished by the Western ideal of democracy, led Metropolitan Anthony to innovate about the church

---

[4]   On this precise point, Metropolitan Anthony was in the same line with ROCOR parishes in Western Europe.

hierarchy as 'a hierarchy of service, not of dominion', which can exercise 'authority, but not power' (Crow 2005: 160). By relativising the strong sense of hierarchy that characterised the Russian Orthodox Church, Metropolitan Anthony meant to open the way for lay people, men and women alike, to take a more mature engagement in the life of the Church. The laity were encouraged to transcend a passive type of membership in the Church and to become active and responsible for their parish. Inspired by Fr Nikolai Afanasiev's theology of laity, Metropolitan Anthony often invoked the aspect of royal priesthood of all members of the Church and encouraged his flock to take that role seriously and not to be intimidated by the priesthood of the clergy, which was a special form of service and not a privilege. His theological innovation went further, stating that there was 'no ontological difference' between laity and clergy, 'but merely a functional one' (Filonenko 1999: 67). This relativisation of clerical authority had practical consequences not only for the existing members of the Diocese; it also made Orthodoxy more acceptable and attractive to the non-Orthodox British people interested in Eastern Christianity.

Another point of innovation characteristic of Sourozh was the strategy of enculturating Orthodoxy in Great Britain by shifting the focus from Russian traditions and Russianness to the local culture and its 'Orthodox' aspects. Metropolitan Anthony often underlined the universal vocation of Orthodoxy, which was not only the religion of Russians or of other Eastern European peoples, but which had to be available and comprehensible also to the British people. To this effect services were translated into English, liturgical music was adapted to the Western style, and the veneration of pre-1054 schism British saints was introduced into the religious calendar. This led to a gradual loosening of the bond between religion and ethnicity and prepared the way for Orthodoxy to enter into dialogue with the host culture, which had not been historically and organically connected to it (Filonenko 1999; Crow 2005). Since Orthodoxy no longer appeared so much a Russian speciality, but as a religion with a universal message, it attracted many converts during the 1970s, many of them highly educated 'high church' Anglicans.[5]

The strategy of outreach to the receiving society and the relation to other Christian denominations represents an area in which Sourozh brought novelty. Traditionally, the Orthodox tend to describe non-Orthodox Christians as heretics, and therefore relate to them on the conversion mode. Sourozh preferred to approach local Christians, mainly Roman Catholics and Anglicans, in terms of 'brotherhood' and promised to engage in no active proselytism. They

---

[5]   Details about the social composition of parishes and their activities are available in the letters and other documents produced during the crisis by priests and key lay figures in the diocese; these are often narratives about the history of the diocese, of their parish problems and of their conversion after meeting Metropolitan Anthony.

did receive converts, but after a long preparation and not based on the mere rejection of their former creed (Filonenko 1999; Crow 2005). During the 1980s and 1990s, the diocese counted more English-speaking priests and parishioners than native Russians (Crow 2005). Moreover, the success of the outreach to British society amounted not only to recruitment of new members among the local Christians. It also included an intensive ecumenical dialogue and visibility in the British media (Metropolitan Anthony's sermons were broadcast by BBC radio and television), religious circles and even high society (Metropolitan Anthony was given compliments by the Queen on the fortieth anniversary of his ordination to the episcopate).

The Church's outreach to the larger society was further substantiated by the Orthodox principle of *diakonia*, service to society. This was understood not as social activism, but as 'a duty to be everywhere, to participate in human activity with a feeling of responsibility' (Metropolitan Anthony, cited in Filonenko 1999) and to witness to the Orthodox faith to those who needed it or were interested in it. Therefore Sourozh provided spiritual assistance in hospitals, prisons and universities, organised youth activities and ran charities. This appeared as innovation not only compared to the situation in Russia, where the Church was reduced to a ritual-performing role and was prevented from being a social actor, but also among other Russian Orthodox in the West (especially ROCOR), who were reluctant to engage in social service for fear it would divert the Church from its liturgical and spiritual mission.

Other changes with respect to conduct, lifestyle or dress-code were introduced in the Diocese of Sourozh, which were perceived by some as innovation, by others as normalisation. Women were dispensed from wearing headscarves in church and permitted to wear trousers; weddings were allowed to be celebrated on Saturdays; fasting rules were eased; people did not need to confess each time before receiving communion, etc.

All these changes were introduced under the guise not of innovation but a 'deepening' of tradition, wrapped in a discourse of a 'living tradition' that is not a mere fossil of the past, but is able to take different cultural forms, respectful of the spirit of tradition. However, this Sourozh ethos, supposed to be in line with tradition, was also contested and criticised by advocates of 'authentic Russian Orthodoxy' as disrespectful of tradition and an attempt to 'modernise' the Church.

The question that arises after the enumeration of all these novelties introduced by Sourozh is this: what made such innovation plausible? First, there is the charismatic figure of the diocese's leader, Metropolitan Anthony, who instilled enthusiasm in his spiritual children, especially the British converts, and who was surrounded and assisted by highly talented and multi-skilled people. His personal charisma and his rich social capital were one of the key factors for the successful implementation of his innovative vision. If we try to apply Weber's sociology of charisma to the Sourozh case and Metropolitan Anthony's leadership, we could assume that the latter corresponds to Weber's description of charismatic authority as 'a specifically revolutionary force' (Weber 1964: 361–2) that repudiates the past and steers innovation. Yet, in his sermons and writings, Metropolitan Anthony never speaks of repudiating the past or introducing something new for the sake of novelty and change, but rather of the need to reinterpret tradition and canon law in light of a particular historical, ecclesiastical and political context. Being part of a 'chain of memory' (Hervieu-Léger 2000) is a specificity of Orthodoxy, and spiritual charisma derives its legitimacy from faithful continuation of the forerunners' legacy (Hämmerli 2014; Denizeau 2012). Thus Metropolitan Anthony always invoked the Church Fathers and tradition in order to substantiate his vision for the Russian Orthodox Church in Britain. In this sense, his discourse was not disruptive with the past, as described with Weber, while nonetheless in practice significant changes were implemented.

The second factor that enabled innovation in Sourozh was the geographical distance from Russia and its political situation. This distance prevented the Moscow Patriarchate from controlling the diocese and from interfering with its organisation and pastoral issues. Decades of geographical and ecclesial isolation allowed Sourozh to foster its own style of worship and its own theological stands (for example, Metropolitan Anthony was reportedly in favour of women's ordination[6]).

Third, innovation was possible because of the stable social composition of the parishes: there were no, or very few, new Russian migrants, the émigrés were steadily assimilating into British life and culture and the diocese grew numerically with British converts. Orthodoxy looked less exotic and the cultural difference and distance with the local society was attenuated. In this way, the novelties introduced, which were inspired by local religious and social ethos, were no more perceived as innovation, but as normalisation. Moreover, as Metropolitan Anthony's energetic leadership spanned over four decades, his work on adjusting Orthodoxy to its new setting became the ethos of the diocese, its everyday life and character.

What circumstances then challenged the course of this innovation? First, it was the very change of the sociology of parishes: after the fall of Communism, a massive influx of Russian-speaking Orthodox arrived in Britain and needed special pastoral care in their mother tongue. Their experience with the Orthodox Church and their representations of it were shaped by the social and political context of origin, back in the former Soviet Union. The cultural, theological

---

[6] 'Nevertheless, while he was eager to put the subject of the place of women in the Church, and even their ordination, on the agenda for discussion, he knew that he could not go beyond that' (Crow, 2005: 167).

and ideological clash between, roughly speaking, the Russian-speaking newly-arrived and the English-speaking old-timers was the first factor that destabilised the Sourozh Diocese's perceived steady stream of renewal.

Second, Metropolitan Anthony's old age and declining health prevented him from dealing with this challenge and defending his work. When the presence of the charismatic figure that had united the life of the diocese diminished, the revolutionary force of his authority came under the pressure of those searching to reassert and reinstate tradition. Weber showed that charismatic authority cannot survive in a pure form, but gets 'routinised' (Weber 1964). One of the crucial moments of routinisation is the succession of the initial charismatic figure. Metropolitan Anthony reportedly had not prepared the filling of his position and his failed attempts to designate a successor resulted in a series of conflicts among clergy and hierarchs. Innovation appears thus strongly related to the charisma that effected it initially, and to the successful routinisation of charisma.

Third, innovation was challenged by church politics, with the Moscow Patriarchate, following the fall of the Soviet Union, wanting to get closer to its 'diaspora' and to reintegrate the diocese not just formally, but through concrete participation in its life and compliance with its ecclesiological line. The Moscow Patriarchate appointed bishops for each 'camp' in conflict, later dismissing the bishop in charge of the 'progressive' part of the diocese and strongly supporting the pro-Russian bishop's stand. This caused accusations of an intended seizure of power over the Russian ethnic diaspora through church networks. On the other hand, the Ecumenical Patriarchate, which received the parishes that left the Sourozh diocese, was suspected of disloyal intentions in gaining parishes and asserting itself as 'ecumenical', i.e. universal in its jurisdiction. Though arguments of both patriarchates drew their legitimacy from Orthodox ecclesiology and defended their position as canonically correct, this type of clash reflects a tacit rivalry and competition between different Orthodox jurisdictions in the West, in terms of number of parishes or of territorial representation.

The subsequent division and split in the Sourozh Diocese was described in terms of being between English-speaking 'old-timers' versus Russian-speaking 'newly-arrived'. This might have been the case in an initial stage of the crisis, when disputes occurred around practical issues, such as language, liturgical style and specific pastoral needs of the newly-arrived. Other testimonies, however, paint the conflict as a class-conflict, opposing middle class (both English and Russian-speaking) to higher and upper class members of the diocese (Kensington and Oxford educated elites and highly skilled Russians with transnational experience). The more the crisis deepened, the more it revealed an ideological conflict between conservative and progressive values, between those who were bound to an 'authentic' tradition, as inherited from the past, and those who were openly in favour of innovation understood as a 'reinterpretation' of tradition and a cultural 'adaptation' of Orthodoxy in Britain. These lines of division are underpinned by different representations of the Orthodox Church, its mission and identity. The next section will look at these representations and their rationales.

Orthodox Identity According to the Progressive Factions in Sourozh

Sourozh members that held progressive views defined themselves as 'continuators of the work and spirit of Metropolitan Anthony' and of his endeavour to enculturate Orthodoxy in British life. They militated for an Orthodox identity free from national folklore or from the ethnic colours of a remote culture, which they considered to lead to the isolation and ghettoisation of the Orthodox Church in the long term. They were also advocates of gender equality in the Church (the debate about women's ordination) and of anticlericalism (diminishing the social distance between priests and laymen).

Though they tend to depict themselves as free of ethnic concerns, converts or born-and-raised British Orthodox of Russian descent do emphasise cultural references, such as the introduction of English language in services, the veneration of local saints, ordination of British-origin clergy, close cooperation with local Christian denominations, etc. It is about a double process: on the one hand *de*-culturation of Orthodoxy from Russianness, perceived as liberation from obsolete, nostalgic folklore alien to religion; on the other hand, *en*-culturation of Orthodoxy in Britishness, paradoxically perceived as culturally or ethnically neutral.

Yet the progressive factions in Sourozh are not unaffected by their cultural background. Their representations of Orthodox identity as a universal faith that incarnates locally and is ready to embrace everyone are not only pure Orthodox theology, but imbued also with their own cultural background, marked by a few decades of multiculturalism and multi-faith cohabitation. Moreover, the very criticism of the bond between religion and ethnicity, or a particular national culture, stems from a cultural specificity of the West, which has experienced a long-lasting process of separation of religion and the public sphere. This explains partly why the progressive fractions of the Sourozh Diocese strongly asserted the universality of Orthodoxy and the need for cultural diversity. Converts describe this as the condition for Orthodoxy to expand in the world and not to remain confined to traditionally Orthodox countries. And it was also what made possible their own conversion and religious identity. Unlike many newly-arrived Russian-speaking members, British converts in Sourozh had the necessary intellectual-analytical skills and theological knowledge to make the distinction between what belongs to the religious sphere and what is cultural. They felt that their theological literacy legitimated their intervention in the Church's life and organisation and that the newly-arrived 'neophytes' were to comply with this.

The greater openness to women's service in the Church, the involvement of laity in parish management and the less strict division of gender roles are not only a result of applying the Orthodox principle of *oikonomia*, but also an influence from the local British culture. One can read between the lines the influence of two trends that have shaped the last century's Western cultures: the feminist movement and secularisation, with its weakening of religious authority and of religious leaders' influence on people's private life and in public affairs.

Orthodox Identity According to the Conservative Factions in the Sourozh Diocese

The conservative factions involved in the crisis that affected the Sourozh Diocese can be divided into two categories: first, those English-speaking who also militated for Orthodoxy to incarnate in its new social setting, but without letting itself influenced by what they interpreted as liberal values of the West (namely feminism, secularisation, anticlericalism, liberalism regarding sexual conduct, etc.). The second category is constituted by newly-arrived Russian-speakers, who had their own representations about and expectations from the Orthodox Church in their receiving country: the Russian Orthodox Church's mission in Western locations was to serve the Russian migrants, offer them the spiritual environment they need in a migration situation and a feeling of home in an alien culture. In the early stages of the migration process, the parish often appears as a source of community where one can socialise within familiar cultural patterns. First-generation or newly-arrived immigrants often describe their parish as a 'home away from home', where they search for identity markers that help alleviate the initial difficulties of adjusting to a new culture. This representation of the Church roused suspicions of transforming the Church into a vehicle for preserving national identity and for the Moscow Patriarchate to expand its influence on the Russian ethnic diaspora.

Conclusion

The Sourozh case, with its history and its crisis, indicates that migration occasions adjustment, not only from individuals and their personal religious views, but also from their religious institutions. When deterritorialised, the Orthodox Church is faced with the need to innovate in order to adapt to a new social and cultural setting. This generates tension between, on the one hand, continuity and tradition, which is the foundation stone of Orthodoxy, and renewal and change on the other hand.

Innovation occurs under the cover of a traditionalist discourse and in the name of staying faithful to the spirit of a living tradition. It can be achieved under specific circumstances: first, the long-term leadership of a charismatic figure with a vision; second, a stable internal social composition with people holding similar and compatible representations about the Orthodox Church's mission in society; third, a certain independence from the mother church, its influence and its politics. If these factors undergo changes, then innovation fails to incarnate in a sustainable model.

As long as the Orthodox Churches in the West keep growing because of new migratory fluxes, introducing and ratifying innovation will continue to be a challenging endeavour, owing to the fact that different migration waves uphold different approaches to their religious identity, different expectations from the Church and from their parish life and relate differently to tradition.

Bibliography

Crow, G. 2005. *This Holy Man: Impressions of Metropolitan Anthony*. New York: St Vladimir's Seminary Press.

Denizeau, L. 2012. Abba, donne-nous une parole: La tradition à la lumière de la filiation spirituelle dans le monachisme orthodoxe, in *Maître et disciple: La transmission dans les religions*, edited by M. Younès. Lyon: Profac, 103–120.

Filonenko, A. 1999. The Russian Orthodox Church in Twentieth-Century Britain: Laity and Openness to the World. *Religion, State & Society*, 27(1): 59–71.

Hervieu-Léger, D. 2000. *Religion as a Chain of Memory*. New Brunswick, NJ: Rutgers University Press.

Hämmerli, M. 2014. On Obedience in the Orthodox Monastic Tradition, in *Sociology and Monasticism: Annual Review of the Sociology of Religion* (forthcoming).

Weber, M. 1964. *The Theory of Social and Economic Organization*. New York: The Free Press.

Willert, T.S. and Molokotos-Liederman, L. 2012. *Innovation in the Orthodox Christian Tradition? The Question of Change in Greek Orthodox Thought and Practice*. Farnham: Ashgate.

Index

Alexy II, Patriarch 95, 185
Alfeyev, Metropolitan Hilarion 102, 138,
    193, 294
Anglican and Eastern Churches Association
    144–5
Antiochian Orthodox Church
    Ireland 142, 237–8, 240–1, 245–6
    United Kingdom 142, 280–1
    Western Rite Vicariate 279–280, 283
Arndt, Archbishop Mark 105
Assyrian Church of the East, *see* Church of
    the East
Assyrian identity 5, 62-3, 67, 70
Assyrians
    leadership 51–65
    Sweden 67–86
        church attendance 83
        civic engagement 73–5
        norms 78–82
        social networks 82–4
Athos, influence of Mount 93, 137, 147,
    238, 245, 251–265
Austria 12
autochthonism 20, 229–230, 232, 242–7
Osbourne, Bishop Basil 138, 139, 147, 294

Belgium 6, 12
Bertrand-Hardy, Gilles 275–6
Bloom, Metropolitan Anthony 138–9,
    292–300
BOR, *see* Romanian Orthodox Church
British Council of Churches 147
Bulgarian Orthodox Church 93, 110,
    142–3, 182, 196–7

calendar, ecclesiastical 158–159, 173,
    204–6, 257, 285–6

Celtic Christianity and Orthodox Church
    240, 242–6
Celtic Orthodox Church 282
Chaldean Church 67, 70
Chambault, Fr Denis (Lucien) 274, 279
children
    religious education of 38, 123–4, 203,
        123–4, 185, 220
    mother tongue language classes for 71,
        136, 149, 220–1
Church of the East 2, 67, 95
Churches Together in the United Kingdom
    147
clergy 11, 191, 193–4
    authority 197, 200, 202–3, 206, 208,
        218
    Norway 191–209
    part-time 10, 184–5
    roles, changing 39–41, 53, 55, 57,
        60–64, 296
Conference of Orthodox Bishops (in
    various countries) 91–2, 101,
    143–4, 183
Confrérie de Saint Photius 272–3, 285
converts 3, 15, 21, 94, 107–8, 126, 135,
    136, 138–9, 142, 149, 164, 187–8,
    195–6, 205, 218–225, 229–230,
    232, 236–247, 253–4, 260–1,
    267–272, 278–281, 284, 191–293,
    296–298, 300

Denmark 214–225
Deseille, Fr Placide 252–4, 262–4
diaspora
    concept 8, 13–14
    Orthodox 14–17, 31, 33, 51, 192, 201,
        205–6, 216, 218, 225, 231

304 *Orthodox Identities in Western Europe*

Eastern Orthodox and Oriental Orthodox 2–3, 9, 12, 14

ECOF, *see* Église catholique orthodoxe de France

ecumenical relations 45, 91, 95–6, 99–112, 119, 124, 144–9, 186, 225, 232, 240–2, 271, 286, 292, 297

Église catholique orthodoxe de France 94, 182–3, 187, 264, 275–8, 281–4, 286

epiclesis 112, 270, 285

Ethiopian and Eritrean 94–95, 110, 166, 170

ethnicity and religion 3, 5, 7, 10, 58, 139, 170, 201, 218, 296, 300

Exarchate of Orthodox Parishes of Russian Tradition in Western Europe 19, 93, 134, 137, 139, 180, 219, 221, 252, 275, 294

Fellowship of St Alban and St Sergius 138, 145, 292

female priests 222

Finland 12, 151–173

Food 39, 205

France 19
  Alsace 179–189
  monasteries 251–265
  Western rite 267, 271–8

Friedeberg, Ilse 91

Gallican rite 94, 264, 271–8, 283–6

Georgian Orthodox Church
  France 19, 182
  Ireland 241
  United Kingdom 134, 143

Germain de Saint-Denis, *see* Bertrand-Hardy, Gilles

Germany 89–96, 99–112, 181
  Dresden 102–105
  Erfurt 106–107
  Frankfurt (Oder) 107–108
  Hamburg 108–110
  Jena 106–107
  Weimar 105–107

Gillet, Fr Lev 273, 286

glocalization 20-21

Great Britain, *see* United Kingdom

Greek Orthodox
  Denmark 120
  France 181, 183, 185–6, 253–4
  Germany 90
  Ireland 233–6, 241–2, 247
  Norway 196
  Switzerland 116–118, 120, 122, 127
  United Kingdom 135–7

Gregorian Club 282

Guettée, Wladimir 271–3

Heitz, Archpriest Sergius 91–92

Hispanic Orthodox Church 281

identity issues among Orthodox migrants 4–10, 12, 14–18, 20, 22, 32, 35–39, 45–46, 51–52, 56–58, 63–65, 67, 70, 91–92, 118–123, 127–8, 142, 149, 162, 170–2, 230–2, 251, 261, 284, 291–2, 300–302

innovation, Orthodox Church and 21–22, 291–302,

International Commission for Anglican–Orthodox Theological Dialogue 136, 146

Ireland 138–9, 142–3, 229–247

Italy 29–46, 276

Jean de Saint-Denis, *see* Kovalevsky, Evgraf

jurisdiction, changes of 18, 19, 104, 106, 137–9, 188, 195, 199–202, 206–208, 217–219, 233, 292, 294

Karelian Orthodox161–4, 171–3

KOKiD, *see* Kommission der Orthodoxen Kirchen in Deutschland

Kommission der Orthodoxen Kirchen in Deutschland 89–92

Kovalevsky, Evgraf 273–7

language
  preservation of 38–39, 46, 71, 118, 123, 136, 141, 149, 181, 185, 217

Index 305

liturgical 15, 111, 117, 136–7, 158, 165, 171, 179–181, 189, 193, 206, 220–221, 254, 269, 273, 293, 300
lay elites, Syriac Orthodox 54, 57–58, 63–64
legal status 11–12
    Alsace 179–180, 183–4, 186
    Belgium 12
    Denmark 213, 215, 217
    Italy 34
    Norway 198
    Switzerland 125–6
    Orthodox monasteries in France 257–260
Lossky, Vladimir 273–5, 285
Luxembourg 11

marriages, mixed 37, 118, 162–4, 220, 229
Mensbrugghe, Archbishop Alexis van der 92, 276–8
migration and religion, theory of 1, 5–23
millet system 12, 52–53, 55
Moldovan Orthodox 41, 232, 235–7
Moscow Patriarchate, *see* Russian Orthodox Church
Mozarabic rite 271, 281, 283

Nestorian Church, *see* Church of the East
non-canonical groups 19, 94, 278, 282
Norway 191-209

oikonomia, principle of 33, 112, 128, 194, 206–208, 301
Orthodox Church of the Gauls 182, 278
Orthodoxy as a category of analysis 2–4
Overbeck, Julian Joseph 269–272

parish councils, role of 33, 42, 198–200, 217–8
parish styles, different types of 126–7
priests, *see* clergy

ROC, *see* Russian Orthodox Church
ROCOR, *see* Russian Orthodox Church Outside of Russia

Roman rite 264, 273–4, 276–7, 281, 283–4, 286
Romanian Orthodox Church 18, 275–6
    Alsace 180–182, 185–6
    Denmark 213
    Germany 90, 93–4
    Ireland 232, 235–7, 241–2, 245
    Italy 29–46
    Norway 196
    Switzerland 117–120, 123–4, 126–7
    United Kingdom 134, 141–2
Russian Orthodox Church 18, 144
    Alsace 182–3, 185, 188
    Denmark 213–223
    Finland 151, 165–173
    Germany 90, 93, 99–112
    Ireland 236–7
    Switzerland 117
    United Kingdom 137–140, 291–302
Russian Orthodox Church Outside of Russia
    Alsace 180, 188
    Denmark 213, 217–221
    Germany 100–110
    Ireland 234, 236–7
    Switzerland 121, 126
    United Kingdom 134, 292, 295, 297

Sarum, Use of 283
Serbian Orthodox Church
    Alsace 182
    Norway 203–204
    Switzerland 118–119, 121–4, 126
    United Kingdom 134, 140–141,
Shaw, Bishop Jerome 280
social capital 6, 20, 67–72, 74, 76, 78–80, 82–86, 118, 198, 297
Sourozh, Diocese of 22, 138–9, 142, 236, 291–302
St Germanus of Paris, Liturgy according to 94, 276–8, 281
St Gregory, Liturgy of 279, 281, 283
St Tikhon, Liturgy of 279, 283
Suryoye 52, 54–67
Switzerland 115–130

Syriac Orthodox Church 51–56, 67, 70, 72, 74, 83

theological schools in Western Europe, Orthodox 19, 119, 144, 252, 275,
tradition in the Orthodox Church, importance of 2, 21–22, 193, 202, 205, 223, 251–2, 254–7, 260–265, 283, 294–302
transnationalism 8, 13, 17–20, 45
transnational Orthodox space 7-8, 17–18, 43–46, 247
Tur 'Abdin 52, 55–56, 71

Ukrainian Orthodox Church 19, 94, 134, 137, 278

United Kingdom 15, 133–150, 281

Ware, Metropolitan Kallistos 19, 134, 136, 144, 150, 224
Western rites in the Orthodox Church 267–286
Western saints, veneration of 44, 124–5, 148, 244–6, 264, 268, 283, 285, 296, 300
Winch, Raymond 281–2
Winnaert, Louis-Charles (Irénée) 273–4, 285–6

Zernov, Nicholas and Militsa 138, 245

CPSIA information can be obtained
at www.ICGtesting.com
Printed in the USA
BVHW042003100519
547987BV00010B/45/P